Methods of Group Psychotherapy and Encounter

A Tradition of Innovation

Jerrold Lee Shapiro

University of Hawaii &
King Kalakaua Clinic

F. E. PEACOCK PUBLISHERS, INC.
ITASCA, ILLINOIS 60143

Dedication

To my parents, sister, relatives, friends, and others who have loved me, and to all my teachers, students, and fellow strugglers in groups, I give my thanks and my love. I offer you this book as yours and mine.

mahalo and aloha

Contents

UNIT I   **Development**

Chapter 1	**3**	Introduction
Chapter 2	**14**	Historical Developments
Chapter 3	**40**	Major Theoretical Orientations

UNIT II   **Method and Practice**

Chapter 4	**67**	The Process of a Typical Group: Part 1
Chapter 5	**97**	The Process of a Typical Group: Part 2
Chapter 6	**114**	The Group Therapist
Chapter 7	**139**	Professional Issues in Group Leadership
Chapter 8	**187**	Group Techniques and Exercises

UNIT III   **Scope**

| Chapter 9 | **233** | Applications of Group Psychotherapy |
| Chapter 10 | **275** | Evaluating Group Psychotherapy |

Preface

This text is designed to present the several faces of group psychotherapy and encounter. This is no easy task. There are literally hundreds of different, apparently contrasting group methods. The group
literature is replete with reactions (both strongly positive and fiercely
negative), clinical judgments, and wide-ranging research data. The
methods included under the rubric are so diverse that even a definition
of what comprises group therapy is difficult.

Three major perspectives of this phenomenon are described in this
text: history and development; practice and methods; scope and research. Unit I examines the history and development of the group
phenomenon. Chapter 1 of this unit provides a working definition;
Chapter 2, a modest account of the history; and Chapter 3, a brief survey of major theoretical orientations. In Unit II, a guide to the practice
of group therapy is offered. Group process is described in Chapters 4
and 5. Group leadership techniques, training, ethics, and methods are
detailed in Chapters 6, 7, and 8. Unit III includes an extensive view of
the uses to which groups have been put (Chapter 9) and an account of
the state of research in this field (Chapter 10). In addition, a model
experimental paradigm is presented in Chapter 10.

This text grew out of a project designed to update the excellent
Methods of Group Psychotherapy text written by my colleague Dr. Raymond J. Corsini in 1957. Portions of this text, particularly in the chapters on history, evaluation, and applications, have been reprinted here
in slightly modified form, with the permission of Dr. Corsini. These
portions are examples of superior scholarship and are as valuable today

as they were 20 years ago. In the remainder of the text the current state of the field is updated, and an innovative approach to group leadership methods is suggested.

I wish to thank Dr. Corsini for his assistance during this project. Special acknowledgment is also extended to Ailene Lichter, Pamela Matsuda, and Drs. Linda and Rene Tillich for their support and valuable editorial assistance, and to Gail Tamashiro for her research support. Dr. Michael Jay Diamond, my close friend and colleague, provided an appreciated critical assessment of each stage of the manuscript and is responsible for many of the theoretical and research innovations described in the text. He also provided continual support for the project. I especially wish to thank Dr. Diamond.

All artwork in the text was done by Pamela Matsuda of Honolulu.

I have learned about groups from many professors, students, and colleagues. The names of the group leaders depicted in the text often are similar to the real names of these people. In each case, however, actual events and names have been altered for professional or ethical reasons. The names of the group leaders in the text are emphasized in each example for the reader's benefit.

The following people have been most influential in my learning about groups: Dita Altman, Gwen Arakaki, John Avella, Cliff Bailey, Minnie Boggs, Bruce Buckbee, Gary Carlson, Linda Ekroth, Mary Farrow, Caroline Garrett, Fred Gilbert, Olaf Gitter, Tom Glass, Judith Gregory, Jim Hardin, Laurette Harvey, Sidney Heilveil, Bonnie Henkels, Fahy Holwill, Bob Hunt, Linda Hurley, Mardy Ireland, Peter Jackson, Roger Katsutani, Harriet Kirihara, Sharolyn Lee, Ailene Lichter, Ed Maeda, Kevin Maloney, Paul Marano, Mavis Mizumoto, Sharon Moyer, Marcia Murphy, Judy Nakashima, Yoko Okumura, Larry Pearson, Larry Peltz, Norman Piianaia, Charlene Porter, Doris Read, Pat Reen, Beppie Shapiro, Bruce Shimomoto, Bob Sigall, Caroline Stephenson, Roger Swier, Jim Talone, Gail Tamashiro, Linda Tillich, Rene Tillich, Natalie Vanderburg, Linda Vogt, Kathleen Wells, Joann Whittington, Rick Whittington, Ken Willinger, Wanita Willinger, Janet Wright, Michael Wong, Wendie Yumori, Dana Zichittella, and Michael Jay Diamond.

I thank you all for sharing this era of my life.

Kailua, Hawaii   JERROLD LEE SHAPIRO

Development

Chapter 1

Introduction

In the not too distant past, traditional psychotherapists were reluctant to acknowledge group therapy methods, even as minor adjuncts to individual psychotherapy. In the not too distant future, it is likely that group psychotherapists will be employing individual psychotherapy as an occasionally valuable adjunct to group psychotherapy, which will be the major change agent.

The methods of group psychotherapy are known variously as group psychoanalysis, psychodrama, the class method, activity group therapy, guided group interaction, group guidance, group counseling, encounter, laboratory training, sensitivity, T groups, human relations training, and so on, or generically as *group psychotherapy* or group therapy. These methods represent a major revolution in mental health and seem to be providing answers for previously unsolved problems in the field of psychotherapy.

The initial, and perhaps most compelling, argument for employing group approaches is an economic one. If a highly specialized professional can see six to eight patients in the same amount of time previously required for only one patient, time and money are saved. While this economic criterion is sufficient reason for the use of group therapy, there are several other characteristics of group therapies which favor their use over the more traditional individual approaches. Primary among these are opportunities for socialization, a notion of shared experience and problems, opportunities to learn and practice new behaviors in a setting which more closely resembles the interpersonal nature of the "real world," and reduction of transference toward "om-

3

niscient" individual therapists. Group methods also provide for mutual support, vicarious learning, opportunities to try out new behaviors in a nurturant environment, a chance to obtain multiple reactions and peer-level feedback, development of a postgroup support system, and a chance to demonstrate altruism. Indeed, many former group members' primary memories of their group experience concern the closeness of other members and the instances when they helped other members. They remember it as an ego-building, self-satisfying, and emotionally colored growth experience.

In short, the unique characteristics of groups allow for certain types of learning and therapeutic change that are less likely to occur in individual psychotherapies. These characteristics, and the explosion in the use of group techniques in the past 25 years, make it imperative for anyone concerned with psychotherapy to examine the range of possibilities of group therapy and to study them independently and systematically.

The purposes of this introductory chapter are to provide a definition of the subject of the book, to review reasons for the emergence and existence of group therapy, and to summarize its current status.

DEFINITION

As Corsini (1957) notes, "several writers have felt that the term *group psychotherapy* is ambiguous and not capable of being defined simply and inclusively." Renouvier (1948), for example, states that "Group therapy is a collective name for various methods which often contradict each other." N. W. Ackerman (1943) argues that group therapy has been inadequately defined, "encompassing a variety of material almost as different in concepts as the men who practice them." Hulse (1948) combines both ideas in stating, "Group therapy is a not too well defined method of treatment embracing a number of different procedures that often have little in common." Similarly, Yalom (1970) notes that "From the group therapists we obtain a variegated and internally inconsistent inventory of curative factors." Group encounter has also been described variously as a universal panacea, a communist conspiracy, the antidote to alienation and dehumanization in our culture, and a new form of entertainment (Shapiro, 1973).

These difficulties in deriving a common definition of group psychotherapy may be dispelled by the view that there are a number of specific group procedures based on a variety of theories and philosophies and having varied objectives. Contributing to the confusion is the fact that the term *group psychotherapy* may be used in two specific ways. It may be thought of as a generic term, encompassing a variety of procedures. It may also be thought of as a name for a single procedure. If by group psychotherapy therapist A means method X, and therapist B understands group psychotherapy to mean method Y, it is obvious that the two are not communicating. As evidence of the complexity of this problem, consider that by 1957, Corsini had delineated 25 specific, separate methods. Today, that figure could be *multiplied tenfold,* and the wide range of group methods would still not be completely encompassed. One goal of this text is to delineate certain core process dimensions which are common to all successful group methods.

The term *group psychotherapy* was introduced in 1932 by J. L. Moreno (1932). Moreno used the term to define a method of relocating people in a community into new groups based on sociometric evaluations. He believed that social and personal problems would be ameliorated spontaneously as a function of the interpersonal interactions of the group members. Moreno said, "group therapy . . . is a method of psychotherapy which combines the technique of assignments with the technique of spontaneous treatments" (1932). Later definitions have been offered by Abrahams and Slavson. Abrahams (1950) states that group therapy is "a group process led by someone significantly less involved in the pathology, to ameliorate the problems of group members in relations to themselves and society." Slavson (1951) approaches the subject in quite a different way: "a special application of the principles of individual therapy to two or more persons simultaneously which also brings into the situation the phenomena and problems of interpersonal relations." More recently, Yalom (1970) notes that "the term 'group therapy' is an oversimplification" and recommends that we think instead of group therapies.

An Approach to a General Definition

According to a War Department bulletin, "in a broad sense any procedure which tends to improve the mental health of more than one individual is group psychotherapy." This broad definition does not differentiate between ameliorative group situations that are therapy and those that are not therapy. For example, the superintendent of an institution once said, "We have a great deal of group therapy in this school. The boys march together; they attend movies; they listen to music; they go to school. As a matter of fact, everything they do is in groups."

Definitions also can be too narrow. Cotton (1948), for example, defines group therapy as "an attempt to reinforce and strengthen the individual's defenses against anxiety by identification with, analysis by, and support from the group." A colleague once said about a particular method, "This is not group psychotherapy, because the members do not sit in a circle and talk." It seems clear, from the plethora of current methodologies, that any definition imposing such structural limitations will not encompass the range of therapeutic groups.

In general, all psychotherapy involves the application of specific techniques and procedures designed to modify an individual's personality, world view, attitudes, thoughts, psychophysiological functioning, or behavior. This characteristic distinguishes therapy from such endeavors as medicine, entertainment, religion, or exercise. There are five basic formats for psychotherapy: autonomous, pair, small group, large group, and community. *Autonomous therapy,* or "self-therapy," occurs whenever an individual establishes a planned system of self-treatment. By means of such techniques as meditation, prayer, chanting, reading, work, exercise, or martial arts, the individual may consciously attempt to attain certain goals, such as better self-understanding, greater comfort with self, or improved social adjustment. Reik (1948) and Horney (1942) have discussed autonomous therapy at length and have a great regard for its possibilities. The description of "Kaikan" therapy by Murase (1970) is a recent example of an innovative autonomous therapy which brings together Western therapies and Eastern philosophy.

Pair psychotherapy, the kind which is best known and which also goes under the name of *individual therapy,* consists of interviews between two people, one of whom is called the patient, counselee, or client and the other, the therapist, counselor, or facilitator. The most familiar examples are psychoanalysis, psychoanalytically oriented psychotherapy, Rogerian psychotherapy, Gestalt therapy, transactional analysis, and behavior modification. There are many varieties of individual therapy, such as hypnotherapy, conditioned-reflex therapy, Gestalt therapy, cognitive therapy, nondirective therapy, direct analysis. There also are innumerable variations of Freud's psychoanalysis, as propounded by Ferenczi, Horney, Sullivan, Fromm, Rank, Weiss, Levy, Steckel, and others.

The third kind of psychotherapy, *group psychotherapy,* is the concern of this book. It is confined mostly to groups ranging from 5 to 20.

The fourth type of therapy is the *large-group method.* These groups employ a speaker or leader and audience participation. Alcoholics Anonymous, Weight Watchers, a number of "pop psych" seminars, and several religious approaches fit in this category.

The fifth general kind of psychotherapy is community or *milieu therapy,* in which an entire community is established as a beneficial organism. Jones (1948), Bierer (1944), Freeman and Schwartz (1953), and Polansky, Miller, and White (1955) have discussed this variety of psychotherapy. Examples include Synanon, Daytop Village, Halfway houses, and so on.

The third kind of psychotherapy, the subject of this book, must be defined in such a way that only groups that are truly psychotherapeutic will be included. The following definition will be used in this book:

> Group psychotherapy consists of processes occurring in formally organized, protected groups, conducted by a trained leader. The group is designed to produce rapid amelioration in attitudes and behavior of individual members and the leaders. Such changes occur as a function of specified and controlled group interactions.

These changes occur between members, and between members and the leader. Furthermore, changes which occur as a function of these therapeutic interactions are intrinsic to each member and are not designed for external group action as a unit. The significant elements in this definition are examined below.

Psychotherapy is a *formal,* not an incidental, process. It is not the result of other more primary activities. Psychotherapy is *the* primary activity. Although it may do one "good" to read, play gin rummy, or go to ball games, these activities are not examples of autonomous, individual, or group therapy—unless these processes are entered into with the explicit prior understanding that they are undertaken for the purpose of therapy. Nothing can be called psychotherapy unless there has been a formal prior commitment to engage in the particular process for the amelioration of personal-social conditions or relations.

An essential concept in psychotherapy is that of *protection.* In psychotherapy there is always an understanding, whether implicit or explicit, that the individual members are freed from some of the usual responsibilities for their behavior. In a therapeutic situation a person can say and do things that a group would not permit under other circumstances. The member of a therapeutic group understands that, as a part of the process of self-exploration, he may safely operate in certain ways not generally acceptable in society. He expects that his communications will be regarded as privileged (i.e., confidential), and he understands that he is to respect the secrets of other members. Typically, the group leader contracts with the members at the outset of the group to assure this confidentiality.

Group psychotherapy is a complex endeavor which requires a highly skilled, well-*trained* professional leader. Of all the variables operating in a group therapy setting, leadership effectiveness is most directly related to the success of the group. A skillful leader can facilitate the group process and help to make group benefits available to each individual member. An untrained or unethical leader could interfere with the group process and produce casualties among the members by inappropriate activity or poor timing.

Psychotherapy is designed to bring about desired results. No results can be assured, and no absolute standards of success can be applied. Instead, each member determines what success is for him or her in conjunction with social pressures from significant others and through discussion with the therapist. This mutual setting of goals is frequently called a *contract*. In a typical contract, the patient agrees to follow group procedures and to work on the problem in specific ways. The therapist fulfills his part of the contract by operating in ways that he believes may assist the client in the attainment of these goals. The type and amount of change desired are *mutually determined,* and they can be altered by consent of both parties as the group progresses. The relative success of any procedure is not a criterion in determining whether or not the activity is to be called group psychotherapy. No ultimate guarantee of success can be honestly proferred.

To deserve the name of psychotherapy, a process must aim at *rapidity* of results. Amelioration of personality or behavior disorders may occur in many ways—through accidental environmental happenings, self-analysis, and so on—but formal psychotherapy has the inherent concept that through the procedure a hastening of change processes will occur. For example, a procedure that will cure enuresis but takes 20 years to complete must be considered poor, solely because it takes too long. Therapy is a formal process which is believed to produce more rapid results than life in general could. Several studies (to be cited in Chapter 10) have indicated significant observable changes as a function of 10-30 hours of group membership.

It is difficult to state with exactitude what the final purpose of therapy is. It may be called *amelioration* or *improvement,* but of what? A patient may seek understanding or want to be comfortable with himself or to find a way to stop some undesired habit such as smoking or drinking. A therapist may desire insight, specific behavior change, or improved social capacity. Significant others in the patient's environment may want him to exhibit better social behavior. In all these cases, amelioration refers to changes of particular kinds within one of two contexts: *subjective* (i.e., within the patient's own phenomenological system) and *objective* (i.e., in terms of evident behavior). Different observers may work toward different changes, but usually there is agreement on the part of all concerned as to what "good" changes are.

Whatever the changes desired, it is agreed that they will occur as a function of *specified and controlled group interactions.* Members and leaders alike agree to achieve their goals via certain types of verbal and nonverbal interactions. Violent and dangerous methods will not be employed, nor will patients ever relinquish their right to decide not to participate in the group or any part of it.

The above definition and explanation will serve as the criteria for deciding what is and what is not group therapy. For heuristic reasons, however, the definition will not be stringently interpreted.

REASONS FOR THE EMERGENCE OF GROUP PSYCHOTHERAPY

Forty years ago the concept of group therapy was rarely known. Today every person in the field of applied social relations attempts to understand it. Three kinds of explanations of why this particular procedure came about have been offered.

The first reason, the economic one, has been advanced by many persons. Statements such as the following indicate this line of thinking: "There is a lamentable lack of adequately trained psychotherapists now available to handle the large number of patients who seek treatment" (Alexander & French, 1946); "the dearth of psychiatrists and the disproportionate number of psychotic subjects in large institutions has created a need for a group method" (Bettis, 1947). Put in terms of therapists, the argument goes somewhat as follows. Some individual therapists were faced with case loads that were impossibly large. Having heard about the group method, they tried it out, sometimes in desperation, though they had little belief in it or understanding of it. Thus the method was developed out of necessity. The following quotations tell this story: "Group therapy was . . . introduced at the V.A. because of a scarcity of psychiatrists" (Kline, 1947); "Group psychotherapy grew out of social intuition and was fostered by expediency" (Cotton, 1948); "The group approach was adopted because of its expediency" (Wender, 1946).

Another argument for the rise of group psychotherapy which is compatible with the economic one has been advanced. This point of view is fostered by the observation that at least 20 different people, entirely independent of one another, have been credited with discovering group psychotherapy. This theory is based on the idea of a cultural demand or zeitgeist. Riesman (1950) has suggested the idea of the "lonely crowd." There is no question that the development of society has isolated people from one another. Paradoxically, advances in communication and transportation appear to have split the primary family unit apart and to have decreased the intimacy in personal relationships. It may be that group therapy represents a correction against the social isolation engendered by technological improvements. A strong need has developed for people to get close together and this need is met to some extent by group psychotherapy.

A third argument for the rise of group therapy is its record of successes. Group therapy is more effective than individual therapies for a wide range of patients. It allows for sharing and helping behaviors, vicarious learning, peer pressure and assistance, faster incorporation of group norms and values, cooperation, and altruism, none of which can be accomplished as expediently by individual psychotherapy.

Group therapy is not without its detractors, however. Several mental health professionals (with and without group experience) are convinced that groups are not as effective as individual therapy for a variety of reasons. A summary of these reasons includes:

1. Members of groups will not divulge important or sensitive material, since they will not trust the judgment or sincerity of the other members. For this reason, group psychotherapy is more superficial than individual psychotherapy.
2. Patients may take advantage of other patients by discussing their affairs with others or may try to seduce them.
3. A patient may be harmed in a group through hearing upsetting or shocking material.
4. Some aggressive patients may overwhelm the therapist and gain control of the group.
5. Shy patients will not get much attention.
6. Group progress may be limited by the most severely disturbed patient.
7. Transference relationships cannot be adequately formed and worked through.
8. Group settings foster sexual congress and produce acting-out behavior in this area.

Supporters of group therapy deny that these events occur in groups and suggest instead that group therapy has some uniquely positive characteristics. The following arguments are typically advanced:

1. Psychotherapy need not be considered a private confessional. It can be carried out in the open community—it should be a part of life.
2. Life is primarily social, and psychotherapy should be a social experience.

3. There is less chance that the therapist will make consistent errors in groups, since he must bring out his ideas in a public forum.
4. Group psychotherapy is inherently democratic and consistent with the current values of society.
5. The group provides an individual with valuable interpersonal experiences with peers.
6. Because the group provides a community setting, transfer of training is more readily accomplished.
7. There are possibilities for multiple transferences.
8. Self-confidence can be substantially enhanced by altruism and success experiences in interpersonal relationships.

My own opinion is that group therapies represent important and powerful environments for attitude and behavior change. While group therapy cannot replace individual therapy in all instances, it is generally more economical and rapid, and it is the treatment of choice for a great number of patients.

Group Therapy vs. Group Encounter

This text examines a host of group methods, several of which have been employed effectively by encounter group leaders as well as by group therapists. Methods are not the only commonality between encounter and therapy groups; frequently the same people lead both types of groups. There is a similar emphasis on feelings, the here-and-now orientation is practiced, and a focus on the positive potential of the individual is common to both types of groups. Despite the existence of these similarities, there are major differences between these two group methods. The primary dissimilarities are group population and group goals.

Group Population.   Members of therapy groups are generally seen as having some emotional, attitudinal, or behavioral deficit that regularly impedes their day-to-day functioning in the world. Such people have low thresholds for anxiety or depression, normally find their interpersonal interactions unsatisfying and unhappy, or consistently fail to reach their goals. Sometimes a single life event or trauma or problem (death of loved one, illness, alcoholism, divorce) interferes with their overall functioning. They may feel overwhelmed by their problems or by life itself. They are typically patients at clinics, in private practices, or in total institutions such as hospitals or prisons.

Members of encounter groups could well be staff members (therapists) at such facilities. Generally, people in encounter groups are considered to be functioning well. They do not exhibit consistent anxiety, depression, or interpersonal failure. This should not suggest that such group members do not have any problems, however. Rather, the problems they do have are less debilitating, often more a function of unfulfilled potential, moderate inhibition, or mild self-defeatism. Furthermore, the focus in encounter groups is generally much more interpersonal, whereas the focus in a therapy group is generally more intrapsychic. Yalom (1975) suggests that encounter group members have relatively high levels of self-esteem and "a reservoir of professional and interpersonal success" which is atypical for therapy group members.

Group Goals. Closely related to group population are group goals. People with levels of ego strength characteristic of encounter group members generally have goals like enhanced interpersonal functioning, fuller realization of one's intrinsic (creative) potential, more humanness, self-actualization, termination of uncomfortable habits, a better outlook on life. By contrast, therapy group members typically set goals like learning how to talk to people, stopping drinking (smoking, promiscuity, etc.), getting (holding) a job, getting over a relationship, being able to get out of bed in the morning, building up strength to talk to mother (father, brother, spouse, etc.), getting back on keel, or starting a new life. In short, a therapy group holds out interpersonal and intrapsychic *adequacy* as its goal. In an encounter group, adequacy is presumed, and *growth* is the reward for success.

In addition to the differences in population and goals between therapy and encounter groups, there are some other differences. Generally, therapy groups are smaller (5-10 members) than encounter groups (8-15). They are also of longer duration. Encounter groups more frequently employ marathon (massed practice) time formats. They also may be only one component of a laboratory experience, whereas therapy groups are often used in conjunction with individual psychotherapy. The leader in an encounter group is much more likely to play the role of member than is the group therapist.

It is important to keep these differences in mind. In the literature and in this text, the generic term *group* or *group therapy* is used to describe events common to all groups. Furthermore, all authors and researchers have not made distinctions between these two methods, and it is difficult to include their work except in the most universal sense. There are good reasons to view both types of groups together. While the content and achievements of the encounter and therapy groups are markedly different, the *process* of all groups is essentially the same. Group process is extensively considered in Chapters 4 and 5. For purposes of this text the generic term is used except where a differentiation of the two methods will enhance understanding.

PRESENT STATUS OF GROUP PSYCHOTHERAPY

There are no accurate statistics available in the field of group psychotherapy. However, by means of a variety of approaches and some
speculation, a picture of the field is emerging. One indicator of how
group psychotherapy has developed and how it stands at present may
be obtained from the statistics of publications.

Between 1906 and 1930, 34 books, articles, and dissertations on
group experiences were recorded in the literature. In the next 10 years,
there were another 89 works; and in the 10 years between 1941 and
1950, 739 books, articles, and dissertations. Between 1951 and 1955,
879 group therapy works alone were surveyed. This geometric growth
has continued. Between 1971 and 1975, over 2,500 books, articles, and
dissertations appeared.

It is not known how many therapists or how many patients are
taking part in group therapy. The two associations of group therapists
have a total of well over 1,000 members, and more than 1,000 people
have contributed to the literature. Groups have become big business,
and each major city boasts group centers or institutes. A recent survey
of graduate students in mental health fields indicated that over 50
percent of them had been members of some type of therapy or encounter
group (Shapiro, 1975). It is a rare (and ill-equipped) graduate of
programs in clinical and counseling psychology, psychiatry, social work,
psychiatric nursing, and related fields who has not been trained in the
use of group methods and has not participated in groups as part of
the training. From surveys such as those made by Geller (1950),
McCorkle (1953), and Corsini and Lundin (1955), it appears that in
at least one-half of all mental hospitals and one-quarter of correctional
institutions, group psychotherapy is employed. One recent survey in
Hawaii (Shapiro, 1975) indicated that between 1970 and 1975 over
700 people had conducted therapy or encounter groups on the island
of Oahu, which has a population under 700,000.

The group method has been used in schools, in outpatient clinics, in
somatic and mental hospitals, in the military, in prisons and reformatories, in social agencies, in institutions for defectives and for the
handicapped, in industry, and in guidance clinics. It has been used with
a wide variety of individuals and for diverse problems. Every month new
and ingenious applications of group psychotherapy in specific institutions or to specific problems are reported in the literature.

The consistent enthusiasm of those who report their group experiences, frequently people who also have had experience in individual
therapy, is striking, and independent research supports many of these
subjective reports. There is no doubt that group psychotherapy has
emerged as a significant factor in our cultural pattern. It is here to stay.

Chapter 2

Historical
Developments

Psychotherapy and encounter groups as we know them today did not spring up as full blown-sophisticated entities. Modern-day groups are the result of a variety of developmental trends. The plethora of group methods existing today accurately reflects the myriad approaches and techniques which have been employed in groups over the years. The major sources of existing and emergent groups can be seen as the results of four major trends: clinical practice, experimental research, pragmatic social needs, and philosophical orientation.

The prototype for the clinical-practice type of group is the group session conducted by psychologists, psychiatrists, and other mental health professionals in hospitals, clinics, and community mental health centers. These groups have typically emerged from personal experimentation by clinical practitioners who were seeking alternatives to classical one-to-one individual therapies. Representative of the experimental research trend is the "laboratory" group, which grew out of the work of social psychology and had as a primary goal the understanding of the group behavior of individuals. The trend concerned with pragmatic social needs is best demonstrated by self-help groups such as Alcoholics Anonymous. In these groups persons with similar problems meet to discuss their mutual afflictions and to support one another's corrective actions. The prototype group of the philosophical trend is the humanistically oriented encounter group. This movement, which has mystical religion as its basis, encourages mutual "I-thou" contact between individuals. Its basic tenet is that if each individual shares openly, honestly, and caringly with others, all will grow through a process called self-actualization.

No one person can be credited with having "discovered" group methods. Rather, there have been multiple discoverers. Hulse (1948) calls Anton Mesmer the father of group psychotherapy; Klapman (1946) and H. I. Ruitenbeek (1969) assign primary credit to Joseph H. Pratt; Bierer (1940) feels the honors should be divided by Pratt and Alfred Adler; and Meiers (1945) states that the earliest founders of true group therapy were Pratt and Moreno. Dreikurs, one of the earliest proponents of group techniques, gives primary credit to Mesmer in his 1952 article and to Adler in his 1959 historical review.

While all are correct in giving these individuals credit for their contributions (which differ considerably), none is correct in trying to establish primacy. Group psychotherapy is not a unidimensional entity or an organic whole; it is, instead, a conglomerate of methods and theories with diverse multiple origins in the past, resulting inevitably from social demands, and developed in various forms by many persons. Each contributor has borrowed from the past and has made advances, but group psychotherapy is the product of many minds.

APPROACH TO THE HISTORY OF GROUP PSYCHOTHERAPY

In the survey of the history of group psychotherapy to be presented in this chapter, four major divisions will be made: *origins,* beginning with the historic past and extending up to the turn of the 20th century; the *pioneer period,* from about 1905 to 1930; the *developmental period,* beginning in 1931, and the *modern period,* which began with the explosion of numbers and kinds of groups in the middle 1960s.

There are two ways to study history: idiographically and nomothetically. In the former approach, individuals are examined for their unique contributions. In the latter, trends are examined. While each approach has its unique benefits, I have chosen the idiographic approach because major four trends overlap considerably, and the explication of trends and people over time is more complicated than the examination of individual contributions.

ORIGINS

Mankind has probably always lived, worked, worshipped and played in groups. Not only does the group provide greater facility in task performance, but people obtain other benefits from group association. Such consequences as feelings of good fellowship, belonging, and identification with the group have substantial impact on the psychological well-being of the individual.

The human is a social creature who needs to belong, to be accepted, to be valued, to be wanted. If these social feelings are not experienced, the individual suffers and may behave maladaptively. Indeed infants deprived of social stimulation are said to develop depressions accompanied by physical and mental deterioration which can be treated only through emotional interchanges described as mothering (Spitz & Wolf, 1946).

While people have worked and played in groups throughout history, until recently there has been no explicit understanding of the importance of group association for the psychological health of the individual. In a manner of speaking, every group into which one enters freely, in which one feels compatible, and from which one gets pleasure, is therapeutic.

Natural groups that serve the same purposes as artificial (therapy) groups are certainly more desirable. In a sense, formal groups merely provide a substitute for whatever cannot be obtained from natural groups. It is when the latter do not exist that formal, artificial, or contrived groups have a place.

Historically, there are many examples of groups which apparently gave their members intangible benefits which were quite similar to those obtained from modern, formal group psychotherapy. An outstanding example is the healing temple that existed at Epidaurus in Greece from 600 B.C. to 200 A.D. (Janet, 1925). People afflicted with mental and physical ailments went to this temple to obtain relief from their symptoms. The procedures involved talks, lectures, rest, baths, and what appears to have been a kind of general suggestion therapy. (A current analogue, Esalen in California, has been a center for the group movement in the 1960s and 1970s.) The effects philosophers and religious leaders produced in their audiences and congregations were no doubt quite like those obtained in group therapy.

Although the intentions of early divine law were quite different from those of group therapists, the feelings generated in those who listened to the *Apology* or the Sermon on the Mount must have been basically similar to those engendered in a therapeutic group. E. N. Jackson, a minister, has in fact observed that "The sermon is the oldest form of group psychotherapy" (1950). Tillich (1976) and Frank (1974) suggest that witch's covens and the primitive shaman provided the same functions in ancient times, albeit with different intent. It was not until the 18th century that a group was purported to be intentionally therapeutic. Anton Mesmer's group may be considered the first example of formal group therapy.

Mesmer

Anton Mesmer, an Austrian physician, began to practice mental healing in Paris about 1776. He believed that he could cure physical ailments through certain emanations from his own body. Groups of afflicted persons sat around a wooden tub from which iron bars protruded and held the affected parts of their bodies against these bars. Mesmer believed that a "magnetism" was thus sent into the bodies of his patients (Allport, 1937).

Mesmer obtained what appeared to be genuine cures. He was investigated by a number of scientific commissions, including one which had Benjamin Franklin as a member. The reports of these commissions stated in effect that the cures were real, but the maladies were imaginary.

We have in this case a curious situation, not unusual in the history of science, wherein an individual successfully used certain methods but ascribed incorrect reasons to the results. Today more is known about hysteria, suggestion, hypnotism, and psychosomatic medicine. Nevertheless, those who have given Mesmer the title of father of group psychotherapy do appear to have good reason.

De Sade

It will surprise those who think of the Marquis de Sade solely as a sexual degenerate to learn that in one respect he has been maligned. While there is no doubt that he was sexually perverse and deserved his many long imprisonments, at one time he was confined in a mental asylum as a political prisoner by Napoleon. While a patient in the asylum of Charenton, De Sade wrote and directed plays which were acted by other patients before the general public (Gorer, 1934). There was some opposition to De Sade's activities by the doctors of the asylum, but the institution superintendent supported the theatricals because of the good effects they had on the patients. So De Sade, even though he probably engaged in this activity to relieve his own boredom, deserves mention in the history of group psychotherapy. A modern play and film, *The Persecution and Assassination of John Paul Marat as Played by the Inmates of the Asylum at Charenton and Directed by the Marquis de Sade* (also called *Marat/Sade*) depicts these events.

Camus and Pagniez

Jean Camus and Paul Pagniez, two French psychiatrists, were pupils of Jules Dejerine who applied the S. Weir Mitchell rest-cure treatment for neurotics. They observed that patients treated in wards improved more rapidly than those treated in solitude (Camus & Pagniez, 1904). This information was neither understood nor followed up by anyone. It is an example, familiar in science, of the observation of an important fact without realization of its significance.

Freud

No method of psychotherapy can be considered apart from the influence of Sigmund Freud, even if the theory and method are not in consonance with those of the great Viennese doctor. Although Freud never used the group method and there seems to be no evidence that he even knew about it, he did discuss group psychology in his 1922 treatise, *Group Psychology and the Analysis of the Ego*. He distinguished between transient and permanent groups, homogeneous and heterogeneous groups, natural and artificial groups, and so on; as Anthony (1971) points out, his 'major differentiation was undoubtedly between leadered and leaderless groups" (page 8). Anthony also notes Freud's work on identification and empathy as mechanisms of group effects on the individual.

Mark Kanzer (1971), using the *Minutes of the Vienna Psychoanalytic Society,* culled from Freud's posthumous papers which were unpublished until 1960, argues that a great deal of group psychoanalysis was concomitant with the educational process of the Wednesday Evening Society. In these meetings, held from 1901 through 1907, Freud was both group leader and a discussant. Later, when discontent and rebellion caused him to reconsider his role in the group, his contentions that the group symbolically represented the primal horde or mass and his concern that such groups could become a mob were supported. Nevertheless, this evidence, along with Freud's influence on Stekel, Eitington, Rank, Wittels, and Adler, led Kanzer to describe Freud as the first psychoanalytic group leader.

Whatever his understanding of group process and group method, Freud's insights into individual processes, particularly as regards the importance of the unconscious and mental dynamics, make his contribution to the training and development of group leaders one of major impact. Freud's concern that groups were symbolically reenacting the primal horde's killing and eating of the leader and could become disorganized were not unique to him. Le Bon noted that when a person joins a group he "sacrifices something of his precious individuality" (Anthony, 1971, p. 6), and McDougall likened the unorganized group to a wild beast (Ruitenbeek, 1970). Such notions of contagion and mob psychology (perhaps an outgrowth of the French Revolution), persist and have severely limited the growth of group psychotherapy in France and other parts of Western Europe, even today. In the United States in the 1960s, groups were described as Communist brainwashing plots and the site of orgies and murders (Tillich, 1976).

THE PIONEER PERIOD

The pioneer period of group psychotherapy extends from about 1906 through 1931, from Joseph H. Pratt's first description of his class method through J. L. Moreno's naming of the field. This crucial period has not been completely clarified because, although there was considerable early use of groups for therapeutic purposes, there have been relatively few published accounts of these experiences. This is especially true of early European efforts. Teirich (1951a) and Dreikurs (1952), summarizing some of the early developments, mention in passing such practitioners and observers as Ozertzovsky, Rosenstein, Stransky, Metzel, Kauders, Spiel, Schultz, Hoff, Urban, Betz, Hirschfield, and Guilarowsky, but little is known of their specific theories or procedures.

Consequently, it is necessary to concentrate on the relatively few persons about whose efforts something is known. The importance of a person's position in any field depends not only on his insights and operations but also on whether he communicated his ideas. Six men who did major work from 1906 to 1931 deserve to be called the pioneers of group psychotherapy: Pratt, Lazell, Marsh, Adler, Moreno, and Burrow.

Pratt

In 1906, Joseph H. Pratt, an internist in the city of Boston, presented a lecture at the Johns Hopkins Medical School on the topic, "The Home Sanitarium Treatment of Consumption." In this paper, Dr. Pratt stated that he believed it possible to treat indigent tuberculosis patients in their homes. He believed that if those afflicted with this dread disease would follow his rigid regimen, which included rest, fresh air, and good food, they might survive the white plague. He obtained funds and assistance from the ministers of the Emmanuel Church of Boston. To save time he gathered tuberculosis patients into groups for instruction in his strict hygienic rules. These groups, which were gathered solely to save Pratt's time by making it unnecessary for him to explain and exhort over and over again, are often considered the beginning of scientific group psychotherapy (Klapman, 1946).

Pratt's early efforts were followed with great interest. Drs. David Riesman of Philadelphia, F. J. Ripley of Brockton, P. Denker of Boston, and F. T. Fulton of Providence were among the physicians who employed the class method for the treatment of a variety of physical ailments. In addition, Elwood Worcester and Samuel McComb, ministers of the Emmanuel Church, established the Emmanuel Church Health Class and published a series of pamphlets and a book (Worcester, McComb, & Coriat, 1908) in which they examined the place of religion in medicine. The marriage between group treatment and religion has continued to the present day, and the mutual germination of ideas has fertilized both areas. For example, one religious writer, Martin Buber (1947), is given credit as one of the fathers of the existential-humanistic approach to group therapy and encounter.

However, medical societies of Pratt's day (as today) did not take kindly to the intrusion of the clergy into medicine. Kiernan's "Limitations of the Emmanuel Movement" (1909) is a good example of the resistance of established medical thinking at the time. As a result of the criticism and lack of acceptance, the class method and the group movement initiated by Pratt in 1906 appear to have died by the beginning of World War I.

Buckley (1910) said of Worcester and McComb, "Their efforts are ostensibly to aid legitimate medicine, as they proclaim, but in reality are to usurp the doctor's function in all disease." It is interesting that modern critics of groups are as concerned as Buckley was with status, roles, and images of group leaders, despite the success of groups which minimize such differences as a basic tool.

Pratt's 1906 lecture was published that year in two journals (1906a, 1906b). In 1907 two more articles (Pratt, 1907a, 1907b) on the class method appeared. In 1908 he reported further on results (Pratt, 1908), and in 1911, probably affected by some of the criticisms, in an article describing what the class method had accomplished, he said, "In this class . . . it seems to me that too much importance is attached to the class itself—the weekly meetings, the record books and the home visitations of the nurse—and too little importance to the three essentials of rest, fresh air, and good food" (Pratt, 1911). In 1917 another article describing the tuberculosis class (Pratt, 1917) appeared. In 1922 Pratt published a discussion of the application of the principles of class methods to various chronic diseases (Pratt, 1922). Twelve years later an article on the emotions and their effects on psychoneurosis (Pratt, 1934) was published, and 11 years after that he summarized the group method in the treatment of psychosomatic disorders (Pratt, 1945). In 1950, Pratt and P. E. Johnson edited a booklet summarizing Pratt's 20 years of work since 1930 (Pratt & Johnson, 1950), and later Pratt published another article concerning the use of Dejerine's methods in the treatment of the neuroses (Pratt, 1953). Pratt's long, intimate association with the therapeutic group procedure accords him primary consideration in any account of its history.

Pratt's career has two distinct phases. In 1906 he was interested in curing a purely somatic disease, tuberculosis, by the application of hygienic principles, and he called groups together to instruct members in a therapeutic regimen. In 1930, when he established a clinic at the Boston Dispensary, his concern was no longer with disease but, on the contrary, with persons who had nothing organically wrong with them but who nevertheless complained of physical symptoms. Now, instead of deprecating the class method, he made it the central therapeutic focus. In 1906 Pratt was an internist; in 1930 he had become a psychiatrist. What may have led to this change? We know that he had been in contact with the ministers Worcester and McComb, who were well versed in psychology and who preached psychosomatic medicine. We know that he read Ross's (1924) book on the common neurosis, and that from this he apparently became interested in the theories of Dejerine, who had been translated into English by Dr. Smith Ely Jelliffe (Dejerine & Gauchler, 1913). Having achieved a psychological frame of reference, he changed both his approach and his purpose. It is of interest to note that up to 1953 Pratt was apparently not influenced to any extent by the dynamic psychotherapists who followed in the wake of Freud, despite the fact that most medical people involved in group work at this time were psychoanalytically oriented.

Marsh and Lazell

The proper place of L. C. Marsh and E. W. Lazell, both psychiatrists, in the history of psychotherapy is not easy to assess. The first to publish his views was Lazell, whose earliest paper (Lazell, 1921) appeared in 1921, but the more important was Marsh, whose writings did not begin to appear until ten years later (Marsh, 1931). Marsh stated that he began to do group work as early as 1909 and that Lazell antedated him. Neither gives any indication whether they were influenced by Pratt; the presumption is that both of them started their work independently of each other as well as of Pratt.

Marsh and Lazell used a procedure, quite similar to that employed by Pratt, which came to be known as the *repressive-inspirational* technique and is still used in mental hospitals. Marsh had the idea of the therapeutic community, or *milieu therapy,* in which all the personnel of an institution would be involved in a common effort to develop themselves to the fullest extent (Marsh, 1933). He was a man well ahead of his time. His credo of group therapy, "By the crowd have they been broken; by the crowd they shall be healed," explains succinctly one essential message of group psychotherapy. However, neither Marsh nor Lazell appears to have had any great effect on other therapists; the statistics of the literature indicate that they did not fan the spark of group therapy into life.

Adler

Seidler (1936) notes that as early as 1921, Alfred Adler began to counsel children in front of groups. His first purpose, it appears, was instructional. He was not then interested in affecting the group; he wanted to treat his patient and to demonstrate his procedures. However, as had previously happened in the Wednesday Evening Society and would subsequently occur with the T-group movement, Adler's group procedure was having personal effects on the doctors, the social workers, the teachers, and the psychologists who attended his demonstrations. More important, it appeared that the group, instead of damaging the intimate doctor-patient relationship, as was expected, actually improved it.

Nevertheless, it is not quite accurate to say that Adler actually carried out group psychotherapy; in reality he engaged in individual counseling in front of a group. If the group members participated, they did so as quasi therapists rather than as patients. The method Adler developed has continued in use, with variation, to this day. With the above reservation in mind, it may be said to be one of the oldest forms of group psychotherapy in existence (Dreikurs, 1959).

Moreno

Probably the most important individual in the history of group psychotherapy is J. L. Moreno, who like Freud, Mesmer, and Adler, was a Viennese physician. Moreno reported some diverting accounts of his early work; even in his childhood, he said, he acted out elaborate improvised dramas. He took part in psychodramatic acting with children in the playgrounds of Vienna. He became interested in the Spontaneity Theatre and tried, without success, to establish a new religion. While a medical student, he attempted to help prostitutes rehabilitate themselves through group procedures (Moreno, 1952b). At this time he became aware of the importance of "one individual becoming the therapeutic agent of the other." He experimented with a variety of action methods employing spontaneity and improvisations and became interested in psychotherapy but strongly rejected psychoanalysis.

Moreno (1932) claimed that he used formal group therapy as early as 1910. In 1931, he suggested a new method of prison classification, arguing that if prisoners were grouped sociometrically, the resulting interactions would be beneficial. In his monograph on this thesis, he used the words *group therapy*. It must be noted that Moreno's meaning of the term and current usage are quite different. Indeed, for the prison group, the group therapist did not even have to come into contact with the group members, since groups were to be constituted on paper in terms of analysis of members' strengths and weaknesses. H. M. Ruitenbeek (1970) also gives credit to Moreno for coining the word *encounter* in 1912. Quoting from P. E. Johnson (1959), Moreno's term *encounter,* a central theme in the existential movement, is "two persons exchanging eyes to comprehend and know each other: A meeting of two: eye to eye, face to face. And when you are near I will tear your eyes out, and place them instead of mine, and you will tear my eyes out and place them instead of yours, then I will look at you with your eyes and you will look at me with mine." Similarly, in 1918 Moreno first used the phrase *interpersonal communication* with regard to such encounter (Ruitenbeek, 1970).

In 1931, Moreno began to publish *Impromptu*, a journal concerned for the most part with dramatics, not psychotherapy. In 1937, his journal *Sociometry* appeared, and in 1947 *Sociatry* (later called *Group Psychotherapy*). He organized the first society of group therapists in 1942 and became its first president. His writings in the field of group therapy, especially in sociometry, a method of measuring social interactions, are voluminous. In addition, Moreno greatly proselytized his highly original doctrines both in the United States and Europe.

For our perspective, Moreno's impact is fourfold: first, he introduced sociometric theory to account for group structure and operations; second, he introduced a new method of therapy in groups (psychodrama); third, he was the indefatigable exponent of the group therapeutic movement; fourth, he provided certain additions to our language which have assuredly had great heuristic value in the development of the burgeoning group literature he stimulated.

Burrow

Trigant Burrow was another of Freud's pupils who dissented from his teaching. He developed an elaborate social theory of behavior known as Phyloanalysis, which, probably because of the obscurity of his writing style, never became popular. Burrow's basic notion (like that of Horney, Sullivan, and Adler) was that Freud's emphasis on the individual was wrong, and the individual had to be studied as a member of various groups in society. Burrow abandoned classical analysis and for several years practiced "group analysis." In 1928, he wrote, "For several years I have, in association with others, been daily occupied with the practical observation of these interactions as they were found to occur in the experimental condition of actual group setting" (Burrow, 1928).

Burrow's groups encouraged spontaneity, immediacy and a bridging of the gap between words and feelings. He focused on nonverbal communication as a buffer against the tendency of group members to make socially desirable responses in a group setting, that is, to present their most favorable aspects. If his frame of reference were not based so strongly in psychoanalysis and later in Phyloanalysis, his work could easily be seen as a basis for the later T-group movement.

For whatever reasons, Burrow's direct influence was on later therapeutic group work. He gave up his clinical groups later in his career and devoted himself almost exclusively to the development of Phyloanalysis.

Group Psychotherapy up to 1931

Pratt had his class method, Marsh and Lazell their repressive-inspirational technique, Adler his group guidance, Moreno his psychodrama, and Burrow his group analysis. In Europe, group workers called their procedures by a variety of names, including *kollective Therapie*. In 1931 these methods had little in common. In the way words have of establishing concepts, it seems that Moreno's term, *group therapy,* which he used to indicate a sociometric method of reclassifying prisoners, actually helped establish the concept of psychotherapy of individuals in groups. This term became the generic name for all methods of therapeutic group work. The developmental period of group psychotherapy began with the introduction of the new term, which established a common conceptual frame of reference.

THE DEVELOPMENTAL PERIOD

In surveying historical developments from 1932 to the mid-1960s, it is difficult to understand and be objective about work that has not yet met the full test of time and hard experimentation. In order to get a grasp on what the field looked like before the modern period, I will summarize some of the major accomplishments of the more significant workers. Some 70 individuals are named below, essentially in alphabetical order, to indicate some of the contributions of major workers in the field of group psychotherapy.

Major Workers in the Field

Joseph Abrahams has been concerned with the use of group methods in the rehabilitation of military prisoners (1946) and, with Lloyd McCorkle (1946), has analyzed the use of guided group interaction. Abrahams has also written on the use of group methods in the treatment of schizophrenics (1948). Nathan W. Ackerman has dealt with a wide variety of topics, including evaluations of psychoanalytic group procedures (1954b), military uses of group methods (1946), and family therapy (1966). I. M. Altshuler (1940, 1945) has emphasized the importance of music and rhythm in the group treatment of psychotics. Chris Argyris (1962, 1967) has provided important insights into organization development (O.D.) and the early laboratory group movement in the National Training Laboratory (NTL).

George R. Bach has made a major contribution in a full-scale description of his intensive group procedure (1954), which is noteworthy for its theoretical rationale, its complexity, and its length. Bach's presentation gives evidence that the group method can parallel individual procedures in terms of depth of treatment. Kurt Back, whose later work chronicles much of the T-group movement (1972), wrote about the interpersonal dynamics in groups as early as the late forties (Back, 1948). R. F. Bales (1944, 1945) brought sociological perspectives and decision making under the purview of groups. Dorothy Baruch and Hyman Miller, working together, have used group procedures, including analyses of projective drawings (Baruch & Miller, 1946) psychodrama, and nondirective discussions in the treatment of allergic patients (Miller & Baruch, 1948). Lauretta Bender has experimented with group methods of treating institutionalized children in hospital wards (1937) and, with A. G. Woltman, has discussed the use of puppets as a therapeutic medium (Bender & Woltman, 1936). Kenneth Benne (1964) and his colleagues, Jack Gibb (1952, 1960, 1964; Gibb & Gorman, 1954), Leland Bradford (1953, 1961, 1964), and Matthew Miles (1957, 1958, 1959, 1960) have all done yeoman work in researching and describing the NTL movement and small-group human relations training. Joshua Bierer introduced a group psychotherapy to Great Britain and has developed the concept of therapeutic social clubs in mental hospitals (1940, 1948). W. R. Bion, a member of the Tavistock Clinic in Great Britain (1946, 1961), has been concerned with an analysis of processes that occur in groups. Nathan Blackman (1950) has used group methods with aphasics and has experimented with bibliotherapy with schizophrenics (1940). Blake and Mouton (1961, 1962, 1964, 1965) have reported on the introduction of group methods into management.

Edgar F. Borgatta edited two journals, *Sociometry* and *Group Psychotherapy,* and investigated various aspects of the group process arguing for the importance of scientific research in this field (1955). Robert W. Buck (1937), an early follower of J. H. Pratt, used the class method in the treatment of essential hypertension.

M. H. Chappell, together with J. J. Stefano, J. S. Rogerson, and H. S. Pike, worked with matched groups of stomach ulcer patients and published the first experimental study of the use of group psychotherapy in the treatment of a somatic condition (Chappell, Stefano, Rogerson, & Pike, 1937). Hubert Coffey, together with various collaborators, instituted a group therapy program in a church and has been engaged in the construction of a complex system for describing group dynamics (1954). Robert R. Cohen was one of the first workers in this field to use visual aids (1945). He has written chiefly about military applications of group therapeutic methods (1944, 1947). Raymond Corsini's text (1957) provides a classification system and a comprehensive review of group psychotherapy in the 1950s.

Rudolph Dreikurs, a pupil of Alfred Adler, brought the method of Adlerian family counseling to America and is the author of numerous articles in the field, stressing primarily the democratic implications of the therapeutic group (e.g., Dreikurs, 1948, 1951a). He was instrumental in the establishment of training centers for group therapists. As early as 1928 Dreikurs conducted groups with alcoholics. With Burrow, he was one of the first to employ therapy in private practice. He also developed multiple therapy (1950). H. Ezkiel, a psychoanalyst, focused on insight in group therapy and brought the Jungian notion of collective fantasy in the group to attention as a central process issue (1950). G. W. Fairweather (Fairweather & Simon, 1963) developed mental hospital therapeutic communities and did early research on groups. S. H. Foulkes (1946, 1948, 1965; Foulkes & Anthony, 1957) is an outstanding exponent of the use of the psychoanalytic technique in group psychotherapy. Foulkes has written a most complete account of psychoanalytic group therapy and brought the social network into group therapy. J. D. Frank has investigated a number of areas of interest in this field and has been concerned with research developments. With Florence Powdermaker, Frank has published a detailed study of the group process (Powdermaker & Frank, 1953). R. W. Gans (1957, 1962) has written about the use of co-therapy and its effects on transference.

Joseph J. Geller, an early statistician of the group therapy movement, made periodic surveys of its growth (1950). He has written one of the most satisfactory accounts of the introduction and use of group psychotherapy in a mental hospital (1949). Thomas Gordon, a client-centered counselor who is better known for his later work on Parent Effectiveness Training (Gordon, 1970) interpreted the group process in terms of Rogers' psychotherapeutic theory (Gordon, 1951). Leon Gorlow and his collaborators, E. L. Hoch and Earl Telschow, also working in the client-centered frame of reference, have produced a scholarly research study of processes and evaluations of group therapy with college students (1952). S. B. Hadden (1943, 1944, 1951a) has employed Pratt's class method, has been a student of the therapeutic process in groups (1951b) and is one of the historians of the movement (1955). Roger Harrison (1962, 1967) has provided insights into the nature of human relations training and problems of research in this area.

Gertrude Harrow (1952) conducted a detailed study of psychodrama in the treatment of schizophrenics. Nicholas Hobbs (1948, 1949, 1951, 1955), a client-centered group therapist, has discussed the theory and method of therapeutic group work in several publications. Thomas Hora (1962) brought Ludwig Binswanger's existential notions of openness, receptivity, and responsiveness to the group setting.

Wilfred Hulse (1951, 1952), who appears to be one of the early international representatives of this field, has employed group therapy in military situations (1948) and has been interested in various aspects of the group process (1950a, 1950b). Walter Joel and David Shapiro have conducted one of the most careful investigations of group mechanisms in therapy (1950). F. D. Jones and H. N. Peters have made some precise studies of processes and gains in group psychotherapy (Jones & Peters, 1952).

One of the most prolific writers in this field and the author of the first general text in group psychotherapy is J. W. Klapman (1946), who has developed a bibliotherapeutic method which stresses the role of reason and logic in therapy (e.g., Klapman, 1950a, 1950b, 1951, 1953). He has been a strong defender of didactic and directive procedures and is at one pole of a continuum with Rogers at the opposite end. He founded Resurgo, an organization of ex-mental hospital patients, using group activities for further development. Nathan S. Kline, a student of Paul Schilder, has investigated various aspects of group psychotherapy, including psychodrama, and has written about ethical issues in this field (1952). Investigations of the use of the Rorschach test for the evaluation of group psychotherapy have been made by Walter Klopfer (1945). Gisela Konopka used the group method with children (1949) and with delinquents (1954). She has also employed group therapy to combat prejudice (1947). Benjamin Kotkov has compiled a bibliography of group therapy (1950), investigated group methods in obesity control (1953a), and with Burchard and Michaels, has attempted a conceptual structuring of the field (Burchard, Michaels & Kotkov, 1948).

Martin Lakin, whose later work on ethics has distinguished him in the encounter group area, has been writing of process and outcome in sensitivity groups and therapy groups (Dickoff & Lakin, 1964; Ganung, Lakin, & Thompson, 1966; Lakin, 1960; Lakin & Carson, 1963, 1964).

Rudolf Lassner experimented with dramatic methods in correctional institutions, employing theatricals with delinquent children (1947) and psychodrama with adult prisoners (1950). A. A. Lazarus (1961) has written of systematic desensitization in group settings.

One of the most important authors in the development of growth groups is Kurt Lewin (1948, 1951), a social psychologist and theorist. Lewin left an indelible mark on the NTL movement even though he died before the end of the first year of its operation. Lewin's notions of conflict and conflict resolution, as well as the situational demands of a group and the effects on the individual, are important considerations today. His student, Ronald Lippitt (1949), has written persuasively of the value of democratic groups.

Stanley Lipkin (1948), a client-centered psychotherapist, used group methods in the treatment of military prisoners. Abraham A. Low developed a unique procedure using community social clubs for ex-inmates of mental hospitals (1941, 1952). Abraham Luchins used group methods in mental hospitals and has been concerned with evaluation of results (1946, 1947, 1950). The increasingly popular method of co-therapy has been studied by William H. Lundin and Bernard Aronov (1952). Willis McCann and Albert Almada (1950) originated the round-table method and have made some highly original contributions to the theory and practice of group psychotherapy in mental hospitals; their method is an extension of the idea of milieu therapy. McCann (1953) introduced a long-range investigation of this procedure.

In the penal field, Lloyd McCorkle (1949, 1952, 1953, 1954) was an outstanding exponent of the use of group methods. He employed a technique known as guided group interaction. He has written several accounts of this method with others, including Joseph Abrahams (Abrahams & McCorkle, 1946, 1947) and F. L. Bixby (Bixby & McCorkle, 1951). In addition, McCorkle has surveyed the use of group methods in penal-correctional work (1953). J. L. Moreno (1956, 1970), whose contributions have already been discussed, continued to influence the field during this period.

Fritz Perls (Perls, Hefferline, & Goodman, 1951, 1965), a major force in the modern period, brought Gestalt therapy to groups during these developmental years. Miguel Prados has centered his attention on the use of visual methods in group psychotherapy (1951b). He has produced a series of motion pictures widely used in mental hygiene work (1951a). Fritz Redl has employed group procedures in the treatment of disturbed children. His work approaches milieu therapy in concept. He has investigated a number of basic problems, including leadership and resistance (1942, 1948), and has been concerned with the diagnostic possibilities of the group (1944).

Carl Rogers (1951, 1961) and client-centered therapy had a major impact on the development of group therapy and practice. His ideas served as a contrasting approach to the Freudian, behavioral, directive, and Gestalt approaches. Harold P. Rome has used the cinema for group therapy (1945a) and has employed group methods in military psychiatry (1943, 1945b).

Paul Schilder (1937, 1940) was important in group psychotherapy for several reasons. His penetrating observations and his enthusiasm for the potentials of groups helped establish the group method in this country, since his prestige in the field was great. He directly in-fluenced such persons as Lauretta Bender, Frank Curran, Karl Bowman, Nathan Kline, S. H. Foulkes, and many others who later made contributions to this field. Donald A. Shaskan (1947, 1948) has demonstrated a wide diversity of interests in this area. Shaskan, with H. Lindt (1948), with Miriam Jolesch (1944), with Robert Plank and Helen Blum (1949), and with Dorothy Conrad and J. D. Grant (1951), has investigated military uses of group therapy and the functioning and prediction of behavior in groups. Joel Shor (1948) was one of the first to modify Moreno's psychodrama in the form called psychodramatic group therapy, in which the auxiliary egos come out of the group itself. This less complex procedure has also been used by Lassner (1950) and by R. O. Boring and Herdis Deabler (1951).

A most important person in group psychotherapy is S. R. Slavson. About 1934 he began to experiment with a permissive group method of dealing with disturbed youth in their latency period. This method, known as activity group therapy, has been described in detail in some of Slavson's many articles and books (1943, 1946, 1947a, 1947b, 1948, 1951). He has contributed greatly to the literature with articles, reviews, textbook chapters, collections of articles, and so on. He was the prime mover in establishing the American Group Therapy Association and publishing *The International Journal of Group Psychotherapy*. Slavson has influenced a number of persons in the field, including Mortimer Schiffler, Betty Gabriel, and Saul Scheidlinger.

Hyman Spotnitz (1961, 1965) has discussed such topical group problems as failures in group therapy and resistance phenomena. Dorothy Stock has reviewed the NTL and T-group research and investigated various process issues within the group (Stock, 1952, 1964; Stock & Ben-Zeev, 1958; Stock & Luft, 1960). Under her married name (Whitaker), she worked with Morton Lieberman (Whitaker & Lieberman, 1964) in applying French's focal conflict theory to the group setting. J. D. Sutherland (1952), a British psychiatrist, has used the group method in military situations and has been concerned with the question of training group therapists.

R. Tannenbaum and his colleagues, Irving Weschler and Fred Massarik (Tannenbaum, Weschler, & Massarik, 1961; Weschler, Massarik, & Tannenbaum, 1962) have provided insights into leadership and sensitivity groups in human relations training.

H. R. Teirich (1951a, 1955) has written on a variety of issues in group psychotherapy; his major contribution may be his discussions of the status of this field in Europe. Zerka Toeman Moreno, originally writing under her maiden name, has made a number of contributions to the literature of psychodrama and the therapeutic film (Toeman, 1945; Z. T. Moreno, 1954).

Louis Wender, an early worker in this field, has written on a variety of topics, including group dynamics (1936), history of group therapy, and various applications of therapeutic groups (1940, 1945, 1946, 1951a, 1951b, 1951c). Carl A. Whitaker, with his collaborators John Warkentin and Nan Johnson, has discussed philosophic issues in group therapy and the use of supermultiple groups, in which one patient is treated by a number of therapists (Whitaker, Warkentin, & Johnson, 1949a).

Alexander Wolf has been concerned with definitions and applications of psychoanalytic group psychotherapy (1949; Wolf, Locke, Rosenbaum, Hillpern, Goldfarb, Kadis, Obers, Milberg, & Abell, 1952). He established a group workshop for investigation of the potentialities of groups operating under psychoanalytic principles. With E. K. Schwartz, he argued the group's superiority to individual psychotherapy because of the ego support it offers (Wolf & Schwartz, 1962). Schwartz and Wolf (1963a, 1963b, 1968), and Schwartz (1965a, 1965b) have written extensively on various components of group psychotherapy from the psychoanalytic framework. Katherine Wright and J. R. Jacobson (Jacobson & Wright, 1942; Wright, 1946) have developed a unique procedure for use with deteriorated mental patients.

Emergent Trends

Before looking at the modern period of group psychotherapy, it is important to label the two emergent trends of the developmental period:

1. Application of the group method to a great variety of clinical populations.
2. The use of the group for growth and preservation.

The first trend is attested to in the examples given above. The second has an identifiable start in 1946 in New Britain, Connecticut.

The National Training Laboratory (NTL). Kenneth Benne, a training leader in the laboratory education method since its beginning, notes that "the genesis of the principles underlying the T-group may be traced to a workshop held on the campus of the State Teachers College in New Britain, Connecticut, during the summer of 1946" (Bradford, Gibb, & Benne, 1964, p. 81). This workshop was a program of group discussion and role playing, designed to develop more effective local leaders to facilitate understanding of interracial problems.

During this conference, Kurt Lewin, a conference director, arranged for evening meetings of staff members to pool and analyze tapes and information from the daily sessions. Workshop participants as well as staff attended these meetings, and when the participants were confronted with more or less objective data on their own behavior, they responded in personally meaningful ways. It was through this "accident" that the early T-group notions were formulated. When participants received objective feedback about their behavior and could accept and acknowledge these data, they could understand themselves as well as others' reactions to them better. In this way, they could attain some personal notions about group behavior and group development in general. The following summer (1947), the first attempt to create a group designed especially to work with these variables was instituted at the Gould Academy in Bethel, Maine.

Benne (1964) lists a number of expectations of early basic skills training groups (BST), the first of which was that members would internalize systematic sets of concepts regarding change, change agents, and group development. A second expectation was that members would get practice in applying the diagnostic and action skills of a change agent. Skill practice through role playing took a healthy part of the BST group's time in 1947 and 1948. A third expectation was that the content of group discussion would run the gamut from here and now to there and then. A fourth expectation was that the group experience would allow members to plan applications of learnings to their back-home situations. In addition, the group was viewed as a vehicle wherein members could attain more objective and accurate self-percepts and gain an increased understanding of democratic values. Finally, the training directors expected that members would not only acquire skills and understanding to help them function more adequately as change agents and as group members, but that they would also acquire trainer skills and could communicate them to others.

Since these initial BST groups, there have been two periods of development. From 1948 to 1955 there were a variety of attempts to segregate T-group processes from other extraneous processes. During this time, several of the learning and skill-practicing techniques were segregated from the T groups and downgraded in importance. There was a reduced emphasis on back-home situations and an increased focus on interpersonal events. Analytic and Rogerian terms replaced Lewinian ones as the official language of the groups, and the trainers' role likewise changed. To Lewin's traditional trainer, group operation was perceived as a process of cooperative inquiry, after the model of action research. This trainer was member oriented, especially with regard to the amount and timing of interventions and in the openness with which the trainer's own feelings were disclosed. With the influx of analytically oriented trainers in 1949, the trainer became more of a "projection screen" within the group. The trainer's role as an authority figure became ambiguous and far less open to self-expression, since it was assumed self-disclosure would reduce ambiguity and hence limit projection. This separation of T-group and theory sessions lasted until 1955.

The second phase of development, 1955 to 1964, was marked by the reintegration of the T group into the laboratory design. By 1964 different laboratories were offering different types of learning experiences, with the T group as the central common experience in all laboratories. At the first, and largest, laboratory, the National Training Laboratory (NTL) at Bethel, Maine, the following procedures were involved:

1. Early presentations of individual and small-group dynamics, while T groups met several times daily.
2. Presentations of organization and role dynamics. T groups used part of their time in developing and analyzing various organizational experiences.
3. Discussion of change, change agents, and applications of learning to community situations.

By 1965, in addition to the Bethel laboratory, three other major laboratories were offering alternative programs. The Graduate School of Business Administration at the University of California, Los Angeles, had as its primary focus the sensitivity training itself (K. F. Taylor, 1967). Weschler, Massarik, and Tannenbaum (1962) have suggested that the differences between sensitivity training and group therapy are mostly nonexistent, and thus learning not related to sensitivity groups was minimized.

The Western Behavioral Sciences Institute utilized large numbers of non-verbal training procedures and began experimenting with leaderless groups. A fourth major laboratory, the South West Human Relations Laboratory, began extensive use of instruments such as rating scales, wall charts, and other overt feedback procedures in conjunction with its training.

Thus the training group was well established by 1965. Its similarities to and differences from therapy groups were already being argued, and the time was right for the emergence of the modern period.

THE MODERN PERIOD

If it is difficult to weigh the contributions made during the developmental period, it is presumptuous to attempt to analyze current phenomena. In discussing historical developments from 1965 to 1978 we are dealing with the work of contemporaries, which is always difficult to assess objectively. In doing this, I am likely to overemphasize the contributions of some, underemphasize the work of others, and possibly even let some work go unmentioned. Major trends within the group therapy field will be discussed in this section. Empirical research is presented in much greater detail in Chapter 10, and major theories are outlined in Chapter 3 of the text.

The Explosion in Numbers and Kinds of Groups

If there is a single truism about group psychotherapy during the modern period, it is that there has been a great movement toward specificity. In every major city in America the consumer has a plethora of groups from which to choose. An example can be found in the offerings of a typical university counseling center. For the spring semester in 1977, the San Diego State University Counseling Center made 24 groups available to members of the university community, including assertive training, assertiveness training for women, male-female assertiveness, behavioral self-control, female sexuality, life and death, parents without children, sexuality, time, stress reduction and relaxation, sex-role awareness, women in transition, black women, Chicanos, two different couples groups, and two men's groups. There were also workshops on time, radical therapy, life and career exploration, life planning and "letting your child go." This list does not seem unusual in scope. Indeed, there are groups available for a wide variety of populations (couples, overweight people, drug addicts, Jewish men, Catholic women, Unitarians, vegetarians, Canadians, etc.). There is also a wide range of available approaches. Individuals can join psychoanalytic groups, gestalt groups, T groups, transactional analysis groups, sensitivity groups, rational-emotive groups, Sullivanian groups, Adlerian groups, encounter groups, leaderless groups, D groups, behavioral therapy groups, bioenergetics groups, Rogerian groups, and so on.

The explosion of numbers and kinds of groups which began in the 1960s has continued. Most people seem to be in a group or to have an opinion about groups. There is some kind of group for everyone. This makes it easy for individuals to find a group but very difficult to know which one to choose. In addition to this increased specificity with regard to groups, there has been a second major trend within the group movement, away from strictly therapeutic goals and toward growth and prevention.

Cultural Setting of the Encounter Movement

In order to understand the explosive increase in group methods and applications during the late 1960s, it is important to view the location and time of this explosion in larger perspective. The detonation occurred in the United States, and it occurred, for the most part, in college-educated, suburban, mobile parts of American society. While generalizations about whole segments of culture are always necessarily incomplete, it seems acceptable to describe the America of the late 1960s as a disrupted, torn culture in the throes of major changes in awareness and action. Assassinations, a divisive and unpopular war, an emergent drug culture, a generation gap of huge proportions, massive mobility, open rejection of parental values by vast numbers of youth, motorcycle gangs, increases in poverty, racial violence, disruption of the family system, disrespect and misuse of authority, flower children, future shock (Toffler, 1970), and general mistrust in all contributed to feelings of alienation, loneliness, rootlessness, and loss of purpose.

In analyzing the development of the sensitivity group movement, Back (1972) notes three trends in the changing society of the 1960s and 1970s: mobility, affluence, and secularism. It seems clear that the time-honored institutions of community, family, and religion have lost their impact for large segments of the population. In an age of jet travel, instantaneous communication, glamorization of experimental lifestyles, communal living, open sexual freedom, and the enhancement of pleasure as a goal in and of itself, it is no wonder that traditional values have lost their potency. One of the most notable changes in this time period has been an alteration in the locus of reinforcement. Whereas traditional rewards came from the strength of the institution to which one belonged, the new focus is on the rewards that could come from the strength of the individual. Millions of people began experimenting with introspective methods such as meditation, Eastern religions, and drugs. Self-growth became a major educational issue. While traditional educational and religious systems, as well as the traditional family, had high levels of competence in traditional types of learning, they had practically no competence in these emergent areas of enhancement of self-growth.

The encounter group offered an antidote to loneliness, alienation, rootlessness, anxiety, and existential despair. The group offered an opportunity for members to discover or rediscover a sense of belonging, an acknowledgment of and responsiveness to feelings, intimacy with others, and self-actualization (variously defined). The group is not the only path for the modern pilgrim seeking contemporary salvation, but it is one of a few methods that have flourished, endured, and been scientifically researched. It is no accident that the encounter group became prominent in an environment supporting all forms of the human potential movement. The T group had already made an impact in the areas of here-and-now thinking, focus on feelings, and use of feedback. It only remained for these techniques to be popularized. This popularization occurred in California, and its shrine was Esalen.

The Esalen Institute

The Esalen Institute, located in Big Sur, California, was founded in 1962 by Michael Murphy and Richard Price. It was named after an Indian tribe which once lived in the area and the physical setting mirrors the changes expected. The geography is dramatic, offering sudden changes in terrain, natural hot springs, and truly breathtaking perspectives. It is a growth center. If it is the concern of psychotherapy to help people function adequately and to adjust to their environment, it is the function of the Esalen Institute to help people who have succeeded in functioning and adjusting to the extent that they have lost the division between their self and their environment. As Fritz Perls, a dominant individual in the Esalen movement, was so fond of saying, "I offer them the opportunity to lose their mind and come to their senses."

Perls was the resident guru of Esalen, but others also had an impact. William Schutz introduced the massive use of nonverbal techniques into groups, and Bernard Gunther brought an emphasis on the body and sensory parts of the human experience. Both were heavily influenced by Perls. Other influences were also strongly felt during the early years of Esalen. Alan Watts applied Zen thinking to Western applications, Paul Tillich introduced the avant-garde of Protestant theology, Rollo May combined a psychotherapeutic approach with a spiritual one. Abraham Maslow provided a hierarchical base and theoretical path to self-actualization, and Carl Rogers, a dominant force in both education and psychology, lent his integrity and his strong belief in the human potential movement. These men were not residents of Esalen like Perls, Schutz, and Gunther, but their influence gave respectability and popularity to the Esalen phenomenon. At present, the Esalen program brochures are mailed to almost 25,000 subscribers annually, and similar centers modeled after the Esalen prototype now number over 300. In the state of Hawaii alone, six such centers have been operated within the past five years.

Contributors in the Modern Period

The Esalen encounter movement has been the glamor trend in the modern period. Group therapy per se has not stood still either. Many encounter techniques have influenced group therapy methods and theory, but group therapy has also influenced these techniques. Groups have been brought into an almost limitless number of settings. In most settings where a group program has been instituted professionally, cautiously, and flexibly, with the needs of the setting and participants in mind, the effects have been positive. Adaptations of groups are almost as numerous as the rolls of leaders: estimable only in the thousands. The following summary of contributors, again in alphabetical order, is not intended to be comprehensive but only to provide a sampling of the modern period.

E. James Anthony (1968, 1971) has discussed historical perspectives in group therapy, comparisons of individual and group therapies, and family therapies. George Bach (1967, 1968) has been influential in the encounter group movement and in the development and popularization of marathon groups. Kurt Back has written an excellent chronicle on the NTL movement in *Beyond Words* (1972). Kenneth Benne (1967) and Warren Bennis (1970) have continued to write about the NTL movement, but their efforts seem more related to educational applications than to groups per se. A. E. Bergin (1967) has written of psychotherapy research and helped set a model of group research. Betty Berzon and Larry Solomon (1966) and their associates have written extensively on the value of leaderless groups and have developed the *Encountertapes*. Murray Bowen (1965, 1966, 1970) has continued his family therapy work with schizophrenics, and Arthur Burton (1969) has pulled together much of the work in the encounter literature.

One of the most important pieces of literature during the period has been a classic article by Joseph Campbell and Marvin Dunnette (1968). Their summary of T-group research and recommendations for future research have inspired innumerable research efforts. Dunnette has also contributed descriptive studies of encounter groups. J. J. Christmas (1966) has done yeoman work in bringing group therapy to disadvantaged populations. A. M. Cohen and R. D. Smith (1972, 1976) have introduced the *critical incident* approach to group leadership. Cary Cooper (1969), with I. L. Mangham (Cooper & Mangham, 1971), and S. A. Culbert (1965, 1968) have investigated trainer effects on T-group outcomes.

Max Day (1967; Day & Semrad, 1971) has discussed the group process and groups for neurotics and psychotics. Michael Jay Diamond (1972, 1974, 1974a) has added substantially to the group literature of the 1970s in theory and practice. (Diamond's contributions are discussed in Chapter 10.) Chuck Dederich has had a major influence on group methods through his development of Synanon. Richard Diedrich and H. Allen Dye have produced an excellent compilation of group-related articles (1972). L. E. Durham, J. R. Gibb, and E. S. Knowles have had several research bibliographies (1967, 1969, 1970) published.

John Dusay has been a major proponent of Eric Berne's ideas and transactional analysis (1966, 1970, 1971). Gerard Egan (1970) has elucidated and expanded the notion of contract in groups. Albert Ellis has continued his prolific writing during this period, espousing "rational encounter" (1969). Martin Fiebert (1968) has elucidated leadership roles and intervention procedures. F. F. Flach (1971) has brought group programs to medical education. Jerome Frank (1974) has remained an important figure in the psychotherapy literature and has continued to apply his work to group therapy approaches.

George Gazda (1968) has edited and written several texts on innovations in group psychotherapy and applications of groups to school systems and classrooms. Jack and Lorraine Gibb have presented papers on training groups, TORI, and leaderless groups (1968a, 1968b). Lewis Gottschalk (1966, 1968; Gottschalk & Pattison, 1969) has written on psychoanalysis in groups, and the use of drugs, research, and general psychiatric viewpoints in both therapy and encounter groups. H. Greenbaum (1966) and H. Grunebaum and J. Christ (1968) have brought group therapy for couples to the fore. Martin Grotjahn (1951, 1969, 1971) has written extensively of the use of groups in training and the qualities of group therapies. Bernard Gunther's work on sensory relaxation (1968, 1969, 1971a) has helped popularize the Esalen movement. Rasa Gustaitis's *Turning On* (1969) has provided a popular personal account of the human potential movement, as has Jane Howard's *Please Touch* (1970).

S. B. Hadden, a prolific writer since the 1940s, has brought groups to sexually maladjusted patients (1966). Jay Haley (1963a, 1963b, 1972) has brought communications theory to psychotherapy and family therapy and has influenced large numbers of clinicians. R. J. House (1967) has produced an excellent critical review of the literature on leadership effectiveness, and P. S. Houts and M. Serber (1972) have introduced some notes of caution to the encounter movement.

Don Jackson's work with family therapy and communication patterns (1966, 1968) is also notable. Asya Kadis has worked with couples and co-therapy in groups (Kadis & Markowitz, 1966, 1968). Mark Kanzer (1971) has maintained psychoanalytic perspectives on groups and has related Freud's early work to the group literature. Harold Kaplan and Benjamin Sadock (1972) have written of training programs, structured interactional group therapy, and encounter groups and have edited a major text, *Comprehensive Group Psychotherapy* (1971). Irving Kraft (1966, 1968) has conducted groups with adolescents.

Martin Lakin (1968, 1972) has been an outspoken advocate of ethical considerations in groups and a theoretician for encounter group processes. Arnold Lazarus has applied behavior therapy in groups (1968, 1971). Morton Lieberman and his colleagues, Irvin Yalom and Matt Miles, have produced several articles (1972, 1973) and a major research project comparing 10 encounter group methodologies. Alexander Lowen has contributed several theoretical notes on the interplay between the psychological and physical components of growth (e.g., 1967, 1971). Alice and Bernard Lubin and their colleagues (Lubin & Eddy, 1970; Lubin & Lubin, 1966, 1973; Lubin & Zuckerman, 1969) have produced a comprehensive bibliography, yearly summaries of group research, and process studies.

Beryce MacLennan has written of co-therapy (1965) and has reviewed the group psychotherapy literature with Naomi Levy (1971). George Meyer has summarized the group psychotherapy literature for several years, along with Morton Lieberman, Jerry Perlmutter, and others (e.g., Meyer, Lieberman, & Perlmutter, 1967). Elizabeth Mintz has continued her work on co-therapists and has written extensively on marathons (1963, 1965, 1969).

Herbert Otto (1968) and John Mann (Otto & Mann, 1968) have listed several techniques and approaches in growth groups. Helene Papanek (1965) has written of community mental health program groups (1970a), groups with wives of alcoholics (1970b), and evaluative reviews (1965, 1969). Fritz Perls (1969, 1970; Perls, Hefferline, & Goodman, 1965) was a dominant voice in Gestalt therapy, group encounter, and Esalen and has influenced current theory substantially. J. W. Pfeiffer and J. E. Jones have produced yearly handbooks of exercises for human relations training (1969, 1970, 1971, 1972).

W. Brendon Reddy has written on almost all aspects of encounter groups, summarized the literature (Reddy & Lansky, 1974; Reddy, Colson, & Keys, 1976), done independent outcome research, and suggested screening procedures (1972). Carl Rogers, like Perls, has been a major theoretical voice in the development of encounter groups, providing both a philosophy and a method in books, articles, demonstrations, and films (1967, 1968b, 1969a, 1969c). Max Rosenbaum has discussed group psychotherapy and psychodrama (1965) and co-therapy (1971).

Saul Scheidlinger has stressed the uses of groups in community mental health (1968, 1969) and has served as editor of the *International Journal of Group Psychotherapy*. William Schutz has helped popularize Esalen and the human potential movement (1967, 1972, 1973) and has been a critic of the Lieberman, Yalom, and Miles studies (Schutz, 1975). Emanuel Schwartz and Alexander Wolf have written of psychoanalytic notions in groups, conflict resolution, and group leadership (1968). Jerrold Shapiro has written articles with Michael Diamond and Robert Ross on outcome and process variables in encounter groups, has developed a group leader training program, and has produced the first behavioral measure of group induced change (Shapiro, 1970,

1971, 1972a, 1972b, 1972c, 1973, 1975; Shapiro & Diamond, 1972; Diamond & Shapiro, 1973a). Diamond and Shapiro (1975b) have also developed a method and paradigm for group research (see Chapter 10). E. Steiner has brought transactional analysis to groups (1971, 1976). Frederick Stoller (1967, 1968a, 1968b, 1972) has regularly experimented with marathon groups and extolled their values.

Charles Truax and his associates have written extensively of core dimensions in individual and group therapy (1966a, 1966b; Truax & Carkhuff, 1967). Alexander Wolf (1967) continued to be influential in psychoanalytic approaches to group therapy. Irvin Yalom and his associates have been prolific in the research, development, and theory of group therapy and encounter. They have developed a major training perspective (Yalom, 1970, 1975; Yalom, Houts, Newell, & Rand, 1967; Yalom, Houts, Zimberg, & Rand, 1967; Yalom & Lieberman, 1971; Yalom & Rand, 1971).

The history of group therapy and encounter is varied and multidimensional. No one person or single force can claim a primary influence. Thousands have contributed to research, theory, and practice. Thousands more will determine the future of group therapy.

Chapter 3

Major Theoretical
Orientations

As the historical survey in Chapter 2 demonstrates, numerous diverse approaches have been successfully applied in group therapy and encounter. Many of these approaches seem to be in essence mutually exclusive. There are three possible reasons for this apparent paradox.

1. In group therapy there is a global Hawthorne effect; that is, it does not matter which approach is used as long as sufficient attention is paid to the group members.
2. There is a variety of paths to the desired goal of mental health or adequacy, and each type of therapy arrives at the goal via a different access route.
3. There is no real objective success in group therapy. Each school is simply advancing one belief system over another.

The state of the art is such that none of the alternative methods can be rejected outright. However, research evidence (see Chapter 10) and the test of endurance indicate that some approaches are more effective than others, at least for certain populations.

The familiar Hawthorne effect is considered an integral component of all modern therapies. In general, patients do get better when therapists pay attention to them. However, since some therapies work more efficiently than others, it seems likely that the effect of attention may be more of a necessary than a sufficient condition for growth and behavior change. If we view mental health (self-actualization, behavioral adequacy) as a static goal, it is possible that a variety of very different paths may be seen as leading to that goal. Some of these paths may be longer and more complicated or approach the goal from a different direction than others, but ultimately they all lead to the same place.

Such an explanation would allow us to accept the vast number of approaches with some comfort. Unfortunately, there is no such universal consensus of the construct *mental health*. While mental health professionals agree generally as to the nature of normal and abnormal behavior, they often disagree markedly when it comes to specifics. In this way, what is "compulsivity" for one therapist is "stick-to-itiveness" for another, and what is "paranoia" to one is "creativity" to another.

This being the case, readers are cautioned that not only are there many paths to the same goal (mental health), but different theorists use the same words to describe different goals. Each theorist is viewing a somewhat different set of attitudes, feelings, and behaviors when he or she uses the terms *adequate, well-functioning, self-actualizing,* or *healthy* person. For each theorist, the concept of mental health is a function of his own self-perceptions, feelings, values, beliefs, thoughts, and projections.

The evidence of experimental research and logic indicates that no one particular group theory or method is uniformly better or worse than any other in terms of treatment effectiveness. Rather, certain approaches work better than others for one therapist with one type of patient. Some therapists are inclined toward certain types of therapeutic approaches because of their own personalities, values, training, and lifestyles. Similarly, certain patients seek out therapists whose approaches, or values or personalities, fit their own, as well as their expectations regarding the nature of therapy.

While no one theory can be seen as most likely to lead to greater therapeutic success than any other, each therapist must operate within the structure of a consistent personality theory. A consistent personality theory allows the therapist to locate, evaluate, and understand the data presented in his interactions with patients and to provide directions for altering such behavior.

FUNCTIONS OF THEORY

Rychlak (1968) describes four major functions of a scientific theory: *descriptive, delimiting, generative,* and *integrative.* The *descriptive* function allows an individual to explain the phenomenon. In psychological theories this descriptive function typically consists of operational definitions: full descriptions of the relevant variables and the conditions under which they vary. The *delimiting* function provides a point of view, a way of organizing the data. In a sense, this component of theory is like a pair of glasses which operates like filters, blocking out all but certain types of information and organizing the input so that meaning can be ascribed within the purview of the theory. The *generative* function of the theory refers to its heuristic, metaphorical, and analogical value. In short, does the theory allow for a steady stream of new hypotheses? Is it fruitful? This function of theories also has to do with whether or not it is fertile and can be tested. A theory that does not allow for the generation of a multiplicity of testable hypotheses must wither away and die. The *integrative* function refers to the value of the theory in allowing for the systematic bringing together of theoretical constructs and observable data into a consistent, meaningful and unified whole. This subsequently allows for explanations of observable behavior and generalization to new situations.

A personality theory is only useful to a psychotherapist to the extent that it serves these four functions. The function that most differentiates theories is the delimiting function.

The Delimiting Function

By providing a set of filters, or a point of view, this component of theory provides not only a way of thinking about the input received, it also actually restricts the stimuli that the therapist has available.

Human behavior is extremely complex and heterogeneous, and the instruments with which psychologists measure it are also manifold and dissimilar. A single objective event will be seen in different ways by a number of independent observers. People viewing an event do not simply perceive what has occurred. Rather, they perceive the phenomenon as filtered thru their past experiences, hopes, dreams, wishes, expectations, and the media of presentation. The phenomenon of a number of observers reporting contrasting views of the same event is known as the eyewitness fallacy. This is beautifully depicted in the classic Japanese film *Rashomon*. In like fashion, a therapist's theory will determine not only how he will understand and assist his clients, it will also determine what client behaviors he sees at all!

The following example of a monologue should clarify this point. This is a group member's statement of the nature of his problem. The reader is encouraged to decide what components of the statement are important for therapeutic intervention and to devise a tentative approach to therapy. The entire monologue was spoken in a fast-paced, jocular manner and presented to the therapist almost challengingly. The patient is a 26-year-old male college graduate.

. . I don't know, Doc, maybe it's just bad Karma or something, or maybe I'm just a classic loser. Everything I do turns to shit. No

not to shit . . . to perfectly round, juicy, smelly shit. When I lose
I really go all the way. . . . It's all tied up to my schmucky behavior
around women. I just can't make it. It's been like that since I was
a little kid. Maybe I'm secretly gay and my whole anger trip
with women is to cover up my homosexual desires . . . whenever I
get near one though I just fall apart. Get sweaty palms, sweaty
armpits, keep shifting my weight from leg to leg and say some of
the most amazingly stupid things you ever heard. I wish I could
be like you, Doc, you're so cool, calm, collected, bet you have
the broads just hanging all over you. . . . Actually I hear a rumor
that you . . . no . . . I guess you wouldn't want to talk about that.
I mean, this is my session . . . resistant aren't I? You probably
even have a decent relationship with your mother. Now before you
start analyzing *that,* drop it, it was just a joke . . . my analyst . . .
the last one . . . was always wanting to know about me and my
mother . . . so we didn't get along . . . as far as I understand it
nobody gets along with mothers these days. I don't think it's such a
big thing for me. I don't get along with any women. I have fantasies
about them and I always am one super stud, but whenever I get
close to them in the flesh . . . ha, ha, . . . everything deflates and I'm
left holding the bag. Not bad, sexual double entendre. At least I'm
verbally sexual. Anyhow, let me tell you what happened with this
woman I met last weekend at the Blue Nun. Things were really
going good until she suggested we leave and go someplace quieter.
Right away I fantasized that she was a hooker or a tramp. . . .

There is a vast amount of information available in this three-minute
monologue. A psychotherapist wishing to help this individual would be
lost without a theory to organize and delimit the data and to indicate
a point of entry. The nature of the organization and direction, as well
as the content of discussion, would be dependent on the theory employed.

For clarification, we can look at the response that would be made by
representatives of several psychotherapeutic schools. Note how the
theoretical orientation of each of these therapists determines what
component of the data is considered to be signal (figure) and what is
considered as noise (background).

A *psychoanalytically oriented psychotherapist* might respond:
    You say your relationship with your mother is somehow
    representative of your relationships with all other women.

A *client-centered therapist* might deal with a very different content:
    You feel like a failure in each of these relationships, and you
    wonder about your abilities to develop and maintain a closeness
    with anyone.

A *rational emotive therapist* could use another point of entry:
> I hear that you failed with a woman this weekend, and that's sad, but from there you make an irrational leap to being a shit or being gay. It's indeed unfortunate or inconvenient that you couldn't establish a satisfactory relationship, but do you hear that you're catastrophizing this incident by saying "Isn't it horrible, terrible that I don't get the love I need?" It is such inner statements that you're telling yourself that are causing your depression.

A *Gestalt therapist* might take yet another approach:
> I hear you talking about very sad things, and yet I notice that you joke and laugh about these.

A *behavior therapist* might reply:
> Well, a starting point would be for us to examine the specifics of your failures with women. Let's go through a recent example in detail. Describe it for me.

An *existential therapist* could respond:
> You talk about being rejected and messing up in relationships, and I find myself feeling distant also even after only a few minutes. I feel like I've been pushed away.

An *eclectic therapist* could deal with him this way:
> So even when you are being successful with a woman, you ruin it by thinking "she's easy" or a professional.

Each of these therapists would begin work with the same client in a distinctly different way. The differences are a function of their theories of personality and psychotherapy. It is impossible to predict which of these therapists would be most successful with this patient. Perhaps they would all have equivalent results. Perhaps the reader would suggest yet another approach. There seems to be an almost unlimited number possible.

SOME REPRESENTATIVE THEORIES OF GROUP THERAPY

There is an apparent paradox in the notion of group psychotherapy. The locus of therapy is the group, and yet the group is not in need of treatment. Unless the group in question is a natural group (family, management, etc.), group therapists are using a group format to treat individuals. The goal of the leader is not to alter the group per se but to provide treatment and growth for the members of the group. This problem is reflected in the development of therapeutic approaches to groups. Most of the extant group therapies are in fact individual therapies which subsequently were applied in group settings for reasons of economy. This is one reason many of the therapies discussed below fail to utilize all the benefits inherent in the group setting.

The presentation of group therapies in this chapter is intended to be representative rather than comprehensive. More complete reviews can be found in R. A. Harper (1959, 1975), Ruitenbeek (1969), and Shaffer and Galinsky (1974).

To provide some perspective on the theoretical orientations to group psychotherapy, the following major types of theories are considered:

1. Psychoanalytic group therapy.
2. Gestalt group therapy.
3. Behavioral group therapy.
4. Existential group therapy.
5. Client-centered therapy.
6. Transactional analysis.
7. Dynamic group therapy.

PSYCHOANALYTIC GROUP THERAPY

Psychoanalytic group psychotherapy is an extension of classical Freudian psychoanalysis to the group setting. Three authors who have written extensively on these procedures are Schwartz (1965b, 1972a, 1972b; Schwartz & Wolf, 1963a, 1963b), Slavson (1943, 1946, 1964), and Wolf (1949, 1965, 1967).

In psychoanalytic group psychotherapy an intrapsychic orientation is practiced. In a sense, patients are treated just as in individual therapy, except that the treatment is done in the presence of others. Normally these groups have a heterogeneous membership.

Theoretical Concepts

For individual psychoanalysis, the constructs of free association, transference, resistance, working through, acting out, interpretation, and countertransference are considered central to therapeutic progress. The same is true in psychoanalytical group therapy.

Free Association. In individual psychoanalysis the patient is told, "Say whatever comes into your mind." The process is enhanced by having the patient lie down, facing away from the therapist. In a group setting this procedure is of course impossible, and a modified technique is employed. In the group, all members are encouraged, "Speak what's on your minds openly and as it occurs." The group leader attempts to enhance this process by being tolerant, receptive, and nondirective. The goal is to produce an atmosphere of permissiveness in which the patients' unconscious dynamics can be revealed.

Transference. The process whereby unresolved conflicts from patients' past lives cause distortions in their present perception is called transference. This mechanism adds an emotional valence to the therapeutic process, in terms of increasing the level of affect experienced and in the projection of these affects onto the therapist. The nature of the transferences also gives the therapist useful diagnostic information.

Resistance. Everything that prevents patients from bringing forth the contents of their unconscious is termed resistance. This concept encompasses the ego defenses as well as characterological attitudes which tend to disguise unconscious motivation. Often resistance is expressed in inappropriate or asocial behaviors; this is called *acting out*. Furthermore, resistances will not dissolve as a function of a single interpretation; they must be *worked through*.

Countertransference. In response to the transference projections and fantasies generated in the patients' unconscious and expressed in their behavior toward the therapist, other feelings are produced in the therapist. This is called countertransference.

Interpretation. The therapist's most formidable intervention technique is interpretation. In this technique the therapist verbally applies theoretical constructs to the patients' behavior. Interpretations must be timed and sequenced properly for maximum effectiveness. For example, a defense must be interpreted before the conflict or emotion generating the defense is acknowledged.

Leadership

The analytic group therapist is fairly passive and nondirective. He or she essentially sets limits for the group and facilitates member interaction by helping to establish an open, accepting environment. The therapist offers support for members' free associations, seeks out manifestations of resistance and transference, and verbally indicates these to the members by interpreting some of their meanings.

Advantages of Groups in Therapy

In a group, patients can reexperience early family relationships in a safer setting, experience universality and altruism, and demonstrate their interaction patterns to the therapist instead of simply discussing them. Often members of the group, as well as the therapist, can serve as transference screens. In addition, they can understand the indiscriminateness of such transference distortions, since the same image will be projected onto several group members. Members also become able to see resistance in others and hence in themselves more quickly. They learn to express emotion verbally, via modeling, and they spend less time in therapy (this is an economy).

Furthermore, the group setting and group pressure enable the therapist to discern his own traits and emotional conflicts more easily from the transference distortions of patients.

Adjuncts

Often psychoanalytic group therapy is combined with individual therapy. Therapists may employ alternate sessions in which they are absent from the groups and the patients are encouraged to explore their peer relationships without the presence of an authority figure.

GESTALT GROUP THERAPY

Like psychoanalytic group therapy, gestalt group therapy represents an extension of an individual therapy into a group setting. The predominant theorist of the gestalt method was Fritz Perls (1969, 1970; Levitsky & Perls, 1971; Perls, Hefferline, & Goodman, 1965). Gestalt group therapy represents an example of individual therapy done in a group setting. In classical gestalt therapy, as performed by Perls, individual patients would take the "hot seat" when they were ready to "work" on their concerns. Some (less traditional) gestalt therapists allow for more spontaneous interactions between patients and employ gestalt techniques only for selected pieces of business.

Gestalt therapy is intrapsychic in orientation, and the focus is on the individual's moment-to-moment, here-and-now experience. Therapy is seen as a means whereby patients become increasingly aware of their immediate experience. They do this by experiencing it rather than discussing it.

Theoretical Concepts

Figure-ground. The perceptual psychology of the early gestaltists plays an important role in the evolution of gestalt psychotherapy. The notion of the interplay between what is perceived as figure (in conscious awareness), and what as ground (preconscious) underlies a major construct of gestalt therapy. Whereas psychoanalysis has resolution of conflicts as a goal, gestalt therapy has integration. The patient's awareness that both figure and ground are temporary and part of the same whole is an important step in successful therapy.

The awareness continuum. This is the *how* of experience for gestalt therapists. The focus on the senses (i.e., "How are you experiencing your fear?") is considered essential in getting patients to distinguish between objective reality and fantasy projections. The awareness continuum involves the patients' attention to the stream of life events as experienced by their senses.

Now. The central focus of gestalt therapy is a here-and-now aware-ness. It is assumed that only present events and feelings can be worked on. Hence the gestalt therapist encourages the patients to experience emotion in the here and now rather than to simply talk about it.

Unfinished Business. Emotions, events, and feelings which linger unexpressed in the individual are called unfinished business. They in-terfere with daily functioning by reducing the patients' present centered-ness which is necessary for their awareness. The individual tries to escape from such feelings by *avoidance.* The therapist who does not pay careful attention to the patients' continuum of awareness and does not thus discover these avoidances cannot be successful. The therapist usually is able to do this through close observation of the minutiae of the patients' *body language.*

Projection. Perls believed that individuals *project* disowned aspects of themselves onto others, particularly in dreams. Since integration and acceptance are core constructs for gestalt therapy, individuals are encouraged to role play (center their awareness, or figure) each aspect of the dream or behavior. Thus they are encouraged to "be" or "act as if they were" each person and image in the dream. It is through this process that patients discover the inherent meaning in the dream, or the behavior for themselves.

Leadership

The gestalt therapist is active and directive, at least in the sense that he or she instructs the patients what to do. However, the contents of any part of the therapy is unique to, and directed by, the patients. The leader's contribution lies in his or her skill in suggesting techniques (games) that will help patients exaggerate and intensify some portion of their awareness.

There is a major focus on the examination of nonverbal actions and having patients discover their meaning. The leader does not interpret these actions or get personally involved in the group process. Rather he tries to create an environment in which the patients can focus on their own moment-to-moment experience and in which meaning will emerge in the spontaneous action of the gestalt dialogue.

Thus the leader is essentially a catalyst and environment manipulator whose goal is getting patients to live the experience of their senses in the here-and-now group setting so that they can subsequently be in-tegrated.

Advantages of Groups in Therapy

Economy, vicarious learning, and what Cohn (1970) calls the "Greek chorus" which "forecasts, underlines, and cements strivings and achievements of the working patient in a way that combines conditioning with a very limited but effective form of group interaction" are some of the advantages of gestalt therapy in group setting. Some gestalt therapists have recently employed less classic models with more group interaction. Perls essentially limited therapy to a series of one-to-one interactions.

Adjuncts

Occasionally encounter groups are used along with Gestalt group therapy.

BEHAVIORAL GROUP THERAPY

Behavioral group therapy grew out of the individual psychotherapy of Wolpe (1958) and ultimately was based on theories and experiments developed in the animal learning laboratory. The principal spokesmen for behavioral group therapy are Fensterheim (1972), Lazarus (1961, 1968), and Wolpe (Wolpe & Lazarus, 1966).

In behavioral group therapy the primary focus is on overt, specific behaviors. It is essentially a treatment of individuals in a group setting. Normally these groups have a homogeneous population.

Theoretical Concepts

There are actually several varieties of behavioral therapy in groups, and each is somewhat different. However, a set of core concepts does apply to all such groups.

Reinforcement and Extinction. A basic construct in all learning-based theories is that behaviors that are followed by a positive response from the environment increase in potency or frequency, and those that are not followed by a positive response decrease in potency or frequency and are eliminated. Behaviors that are desired can be increased by judicious use of reinforcement, and behaviors that are not desired can likewise be eliminated.

Overt Behaviors. In order to determine which behaviors are to be strengthened, maintained, or eliminated, it is essential that the therapist determine the optimal timing for reinforcements. He or she is able to do this by focusing on the measurable *overt behavior* of the patients. Often, extremely close observation is necessary as a prelude to determining the contingencies of reinforcement.

Specificity. Treatment plans in behavior therapy are always specific with regard to measurement of outcome. These outcome measures are *objectively* evaluated, and a follow-up is frequently done.

Reciprocal Inhibition. At least for the systematic desensitization treatment, the principle of reciprocal inhibition is central to behavior change. Simply put, this principle states that anxiety (the central component of all neurotic states) cannot coexist temporally with certain other behaviors, including relaxation. Systematic desensitization thus involves the imposition of a relaxation response in the presence of stimuli which previously have elicited anxiety in the individual.

Anxiety Hierarchy. Systematic desensitization involves development of specific anxiety-provoking stimuli, ordered with regard to intensity. This anxiety hierarchy is then presented in fantasy form, in order from lowest to highest intensity, by the therapist to relaxed individuals. As they experience anxiety, they are again relaxed. This procedure continues until the stimulus which formerly elicited an anxiety response elicits a relaxation response.

Leadership

The behavior therapist in groups is essentially an expert. He or she instigates and carries through a *preset treatment sequence.* Between-member interactions are limited, and the therapist keeps the group moving through the predetermined tasks as readily as possible. He is active, directive, and assumes overall responsibility for the proceedings, which are normally structurally identical across groups. Each session is preplanned and follows a systematic organization.

Advantages of Groups in Therapy

Economy of the therapist's time is one advantage of using groups in behavioral therapy. Some support for patients is provided by seeing the success of others. The setting also permits universality of experience in a homogeneous group.

Adjuncts

Specific homework may be given for patients to do between sessions of behavioral therapy groups.

EXISTENTIAL GROUP THERAPY

Existential group therapy is an extension of existential individual therapy and grew out of existential philosophy. It is keyed by an individual, conscious acknowledgement of the inevitability of death and a concomitant understanding that meaning in life can be confirmed only subjectively. Two authors who have written of existential group therapy are Hora (1959) and Mullan (1955). The client-centered group therapy of Carl Rogers (1951) is considered as a special type of existential group therapy and will be discussed separately.

Existential group therapy deals with the materials of conscious behavior. Like the psychoanalytic, behavioral, and gestalt therapies, existential group therapy is, in effect, individual therapy done in a group setting rather than a group therapy per se.

Theoretical Concepts

The essential concept in the existential approaches is man's understanding of the finiteness of his existence, his subjective adaptation to this knowledge, and his behavioral reactions to it.

Subjective Experience. The basis for this therapy is the patients' descriptions of their subjective experiences in their worlds. Since people presumably construct their worlds in the act of perceiving them, subjective data are the only form that has meaning.

Being in the World. Each interaction between an individual and her or his environment redefines his reality. In a sense each person is in a continuous state of *becoming.* Being fully with another person involves a mutual encounter called the I–thou relationship. This relationship of mutual sharing and allowing each other complete freedom to change or not to change is characteristic of the optimal therapist–patient relationship.

Anxiety. The desire to alter one's subjective experience and behavior is generated by anxiety. There are two types of anxiety: existential and neurotic. *Existential anxiety* is considered a normal reaction to the need to make *choices* in ambiguous situations. It can also arise as a function of *individuation,* the ambiguity of never being fully able to know what it is like to be someone else. *Neurotic anxiety* arises as a function of evading existential anxiety.

Self as Subject. The goal of existential psychotherapy is the experience of *authentic existence*: of confronting existential anxiety and making choices despite it. The process of making choices, of having an internal rather than external locus of control, is the experience of one's *self as subject,* not an object controlled by other forces.

Leadership

The therapist acts as a group member, constantly trying to engage members in I–thou interactions. He or she is seen as the most experienced patient and attempts to be open, accepting, spontaneous, and mutually involved. He frequently shares his immediate experience and own past. In this environment, it is claimed, the patients become free to express all aspects of their being.

The therapist's overall goal is enlargement of the patients' awareness. Thus the therapist feels free to express any selective aspects of his own being, however realistic or fantasied they are. This is based on the notion of cognitive unfoldment by which the leader lives therapy instead of trying to do it. This should help the patients achieve truthfulness of expression, develop mutual regard and respect for the dignity and freedom of one another, and become more perceptive and creative.

Advantages of Groups in Therapy

Group therapy offers a much wider range of possible I–thou relationships for the existentialist. The individual therapist is only one person in the group, but he does need to focus on the task of therapy and to be *selectively* authentic. While he is being a therapist, he is somewhat less than totally open.

The group also provides a laboratory setting for the development of authentic relationships. Furthermore, the group setting, being ambiguous, can push individuals to relate in their characteristic inauthentic ways. Hence their ways are made visible and thus subject to change.

Adjuncts

Occasionally bibliotherapy is used with existential group therapy.

CLIENT-CENTERED THERAPY

A special form of existential group therapy is represented by Rogers's client-centered method. It is a short-term type of therapy which is predominantly used with neurotic and situationally disturbed patients. The key to this nondirective treatment is the development of an open, honest, caring, nonjudgmental environment in which clients can begin to value and integrate all aspects of their selves. The therapeutic goal is a reconstruction of the clients' self-concepts. This is accomplished through paraphrasing and feeding back to them the contents of their own communications. Special emphasis is placed on the affective component of these communications.

The therapist is less active than the existential therapist and rarely shares his own feelings and percepts. He plays more of an orchestrating than a participant role.

TRANSACTIONAL ANALYSIS

Transactional analysis (TA) is primarily a group form of therapy which was developed by Eric Berne. In addition to Berne (1966), Dusay and Steiner (1972), among others, have written about the group applications.

In transactional analysis, an interpersonal orientation is practiced. The basic assumption of TA is that human personality consists of three separate ego states (Child, Adult, and Parent). The therapy consists of a structured analysis of the three ego states, and a transactional analysis of interpersonal interactions. Normally these groups have a heterogeneous membership.

Theoretical Concepts

Transactional analysis employs a vernacular, simple language system and a relatively small number of constructs. Much of TA represents Berne's rejection of the more complex psychoanalytic constructs.

Ego States. Each individual has three distinct, coherent systems of feelings and related behavior patterns. An individual reacts out of any one of these ego states at any given time. They include:

Child. Characterized by little control. Behavior associated with this ego state is generally impulsive, irrational, unrealistic, self-defeating, and stimulus bound. A person dominated by the Child ego state encounters difficulty with Adult responsibilities.

Parent. Characterized by internalized impressions of social demands. A person's Parent is seen as a subjective misrepresentation of how his or her actual parents seemed to be. A person dominated by the Parent is usually rule oriented and attempts to produce suitable behavior. Such a person often does what he "ought to" or "should," and moralizes to others.

Adult. Characterized by logic, clear thinking, and so on. Unlike the Child and Parent states, the Adult ego state develops gradually and has no emotions in and of itself. Rather, it acts to appraise the Child and Parent emotions. A person dominated by this ego state is normally impassive, like a computer, and makes logical decisions readily without affect.

Structural Analysis. The process of identifying and clarifying the ego states in a given individual is called *structural analysis* and is basic to therapy.

Stabilization. One goal of TA is to assist the individual in developing the ability to change from one ego state to another easily and volitionally. This ability is called stabilization.

Theory of Social Intercourse. Berne postulated that each human being has both biological needs and stimulus needs. These stimulus needs include stimulus hunger, excitement hunger, leadership hunger, and recognition hunger. These hungers are satisfied through transactions with other people. Recognition of another person's presence is seen as a *stroke*.

Games and Scripts. According to TA, there are six types of social

behavior: withdrawal, rituals (characterized by highly stylized interchanges), activities (work behavior programmed by the intrinsic nature
of the materials), pastimes (repetitive, socially acceptable behaviors),
games, and intimacy (candid, nonexploitative, game-free, mutual giving
and taking).

Games are sets of ulterior transactions that are characterized by a
well-defined psychological payoff. They involve transactions between
two ego states simultaneously. On the surface it is an Adult–Adult
interaction, but it is simultaneously a Child and/or Parent hooking
another Child or Parent. Games are like cons.

The *script* is a preconscious life plan which an individual uses to
structure longer periods of time. Games, as well as the other types
of social behavior, can be understood as furthering the larger blueprint
of the script.

Contract. Each patient in the group makes a contract with the
therapist with regard to what he or she is seeking in the group. The
contract is normally in simple, direct language and provides a base
line from which effectiveness can be evaluated.

Leadership

The TA therapist is direct and active. He or she engages in structural analysis early in the group, differentiating for the patients when
each of them is feeling (thinking, behaving) as Parent, Adult or Child.
Each behavior a patient emits is classified as part of one of three ego
states. Awareness of which ego states function in response to each
stimulus situation is necessary for patients to understand their transactional analyses.

The therapist manipulates the situation and provides information so
that the patient can assume greater control over her or his mental life.
Once the patient understands the games he plays and the payoffs he
receives with regard to his scripts, he can choose to drop the games in
favor of intimacy. There are normally eight patients and one therapist
(hence 27 ego states) in each group.

Advantages of Groups in Therapy

Transactions occur in group settings and can be dealt with as they
occur. In groups it is claimed there is a natural drive toward health.
Patients are also mutually recognized as human beings in groups and
can obtain strokes from a number of others. Vicarious learning takes
place, and it is also easier to see others' ego states as a first step to
seeing one's own. There is a multitude of Parents, Adults, and Children
with whom social interactions can occur in each group.

Adjuncts

Bibliotherapy is often used with transactional analysis. Many gestalt and psychodrama techniques are employed in dealing with games, and homework is sometimes given.

DYNAMIC GROUP THERAPY

Dynamic group therapy is truly a group form of psychotherapy. Several authors have discussed variations of this approach (Bach, 1954; Bion, 1961; Ezkiel, 1950; Whitaker & Lieberman, 1964). Whereas the theories discussed above have grown out of individual psychotherapies, group dynamic therapy emerged from social-psychological experimentation in small-group behavior and was greatly influenced by the theoretical work of Kurt Lewin and the practical work of Jerome Frank. The particular model described below is *Focal Conflict Group Therapy*, which represents the application of French's (1952) theories of social behavior to the therapy group. The most complete description of Focal Conflict Group Therapy is by Dorothy Stock Whitaker and Morton A. Lieberman (1964).

In focal-conflict therapy, the group processes are central to the therapeutic process. The goal of this therapy is to promote the growth of patients via corrective emotional experiences. Individuals' conflicts are dealt with as they are manifested in the group conflict. Normally groups are homogeneous with regard to ability to handle anxiety, but heterogeneous with regard to the contents of these conflicts.

Theoretical Concepts

Focal Conflict. All group therapy is viewed in terms of a single overriding focus or concern. This *focal conflict* is a conflict between two competing motives: disturbing and reactive. The *disturbing* motive represents a wish, and the *reactive* motive, a fear. Thus the disturbing motive might be a resentment toward the therapist and the reactive motive a fear of the therapist's retaliatory angry reaction and abandonment. The focal conflict changes throughout the group but always exists in some form. This conflict produces anxiety in the members.

Group Solution. The group's need to reduce the anxiety generated by the focal conflict leads the group members to effect a compromise between the two conflicting motives. This mutually accepted compromise serves to reduce the level of group anxiety and is called the group solution. These solutions generally consist of determinations of acceptable and unacceptable behaviors for the group members. The solutions to successive focal conflicts determine the *group culture*.

Types of Solutions. The quality of the group culture is seen as a function of the extent to which the solutions are enabling and not restrictive. *Enabling solutions* are characterized by behaviors which not only reduce anxiety but also allow for partial satisfaction of the disturbing motive. *Restrictive solutions,* on the other hand, do not allow for satisfaction of the unacceptable wish. Restrictive solutions, while inevitable in the group process, are generally short-lived. Since restrictive solutions do not allow for satisfaction of the disturbing motive, anxiety is increased and new solutions need to be found. Enabling solutions always allow for greater amounts of self-expression, but as self-expression increases, anxiety also increases, and restrictive solutions are instigated to reduce some of this anxiety temporarily. Thus a dynamic equilibrium is generated. A series of focal conflicts linked by similarity in their disturbing motives is called the *group theme* and is unique to each group.

Leadership

The primary function of the group therapist is to control the group climate. He or she is relatively inactive and nondirective, employing and encouraging the use of feedback. He makes group-level interpretations about aspects of group process. The therapist encourages consensually reached decisions, even about standards such as confidentiality, and uses the group to provide a safe environment in which natural consequences to members' actions occur. The group leader also manipulates the environment such that members experience moderate levels of anxiety. Thus the patients experience personal focal conflicts related to the group focal conflict and discover new enabling solutions.

Advantages of Groups in Therapy

For the dynamic group therapies, the group is a sine qua non. It is a group-based therapy in which intervention is made at the group level. The group focal conflicts are seen as inextricably interwoven with the patients' personal focal conflicts. This group-level intervention leads to personal solutions and vice versa. The group is also often seen as representing the individual's social world more directly than individual therapy can.

AN EMERGING ECLECTICISM

The characteristics of seven major group therapies have been outlined above. Each of these therapies views human behavior from a singular perspective and has a corresponding technology. In each approach different data are comprehended in a different way, and different methods are instigated to alter patients' behaviors and attitudes. A patient entering a psychoanalytic group, for example, will talk about different things in different ways than if he or she had entered a gestalt group. Furthermore, the problems that are solved or resolved in these groups are also different.

These therapies, however, represent only a small portion of the hundreds of available group methods. A slightly more comprehensive outline is presented in Table 3-1, but a more complete presentation of all the various group therapies is beyond the scope of this text.

In view of the vast number of schools of group therapies, and the fact that intraschool differences are often as great or greater than between-school differences, it is clear that direct evaluative comparisons of therapies are fruitful only heuristically. Instead of trying to determine which is the best theory, readers are encouraged to sample from many and to develop their own consistent models. From a practical viewpoint, personal utility might well be the most important variable to consider. The techniques, theories, or methods that one reader finds most valuable in this text may be of little consequence to others.

In line with these recommendations, Unit II presents my own emering eclectic model of group psychotherapy. Methods of each of the theories discussed above, and several others, are combined into a single comprehensive group therapy. This model is based on my clinical and research experience with over 200 groups and the input of colleagues. Readers should apply the same test of utility to this model as they do to the others that have been developed.

TABLE 3–1: Comparative Group Approaches

Type of Group Theory	Duration (in months)	Frequency and Format	Contents	Therapist Behavior
Psychoanalytic	12–24	1–3 sessions/week 1½–3 hours/session	Symptoms, extra therapy events, free association	Passive, nondirective, interprets, supports free association, speaks infrequently
Gestalt	4–24	1–2 sessions/week 1½–3 hours/session Occasional marathons	Symptoms, here-and-now events and feelings, moment-to-moment awareness, nonverbal behavior	Active, directive, confrontive, challenging, manipulates environment, catalyst
Experiential	6–24	1 session/week 1½–3 hours/session Marathons	Subjective experience, symptoms, beliefs, intrapsychic awareness	Approaches member role, model-participant, catalyzes thru involvement
Behavior modification	3–9	1–3 sessions/week 1–2 hours/session	Symptoms, anxieties, problems, overt behaviors, rehearsal for new behaviors	Expert, programmer, controls movement thru preset sequence

TABLE 3–1 (Continued)

Type of Group Theory	Therapist-Patient Relationship	Therapeutic Focus	Type of Patients	Dreams	Adjuncts
Psychoanalytic	Vague, changeable, spontaneous, doctor–patient	Intrapsychic events	Neurotic, situational disturbances	Commonly used, interpreted as symbols and wish fulfillment	Individual therapy
Gestalt	Challenging, doctor–patient	Awareness, intrapsychic	Neurotic, situational disturbances	Frequently used, patient plays out each role in dream	Individual therapy, encounter groups
Experiential	Positive, warm, equality stressed	Subjective experiences, intrapsychic, interpersonal	Neurotic, situational disturbances, existential crises	Occasionally discussed for subjective reactions	Bibliotherapy
Behavior modification	Businesslike, expert-learner	Specific behaviors	Phobias, some specific behavior disorders, psychoses and character disorders	Used for guided fantasy and desensitization only	Specific homework between sessions

TABLE 3-1 (Continued)

Type of Group Theory	Duration (in months)	Frequency and Format	Contents	Therapist Behavior
Transactional analysis	6–12	1 session/week 1–3 hours/session	Interactions between members and between members and significant others, description of behaviors and ego states	Direct, active, analyzes structures and interactions within group
Focal conflict	6–12	1–2 sessions/week 1½–3 hours/session	Anxiety, symptoms, conflicts of change and fear of change, members' interactions with one another	Controls environment via manipulation of ambiguity-anxiety, active, nondirective
Rational-emotive	4–18	1–3 sessions/week 1–3 hours/session	Current problems and symptoms, cognitive systems	Active, directive, interpretive, argues cognitive framework
Adlerian	3–15	1 session/week 1–4 hours/session	Symptoms, problems, practical solutions, natural consequences of behavior	Active, directive, seeks solutions

TABLE 3–1 (Continued)

Type of Group Theory	Therapist-Patient Relationship	Therapeutic Focus	Type of Patients	Dreams	Adjuncts
Transactional analysis	Contractual, expert-learner	Interpersonal interactions, intrapsychic	Neurotic, situational disturbances	Not used	Bibliotherapy, homework
Focal conflict	Doctor-patient	Interpersonal interactions	Neurotic, situational disturbances	Occasionally discussed for manifest content and reaction	None
Rational-emotive	Expert-learner, challenging	Cognitive mediators, irrational thoughts	Neurotic, situational disturbances	Not used	Specific homework between sessions
Adlerian	Teacher-student, warm, positive	Behaviors, subjective states	Situational disturbances, some neurosis	Not used	Specific homework between sessions

TABLE 3–1 (Continued)

Type of Group Theory	Duration (in months)	Frequency and Format	Contents	Therapist Behavior
Client centered	4–18	1 session/week 1½–3 hours/session	Symptoms, anxieties, feelings, relationships	Nondirective, somewhat active as listener, empathic, paraphrases, supportive
Emerging eclectic	3–12	1 session/week 1½–3 hours/session Occasional marathons	Feelings, symptoms, interpersonal interactions, practice new behaviors	Active, nondirective, catalyzes, manipulates environment via control of level of anxiety, orchestrates, model-participant

TABLE 3–1 (Continued)

Type of Group Theory	Therapist-Patient Relationship	Therapeutic Focus	Type of Patients	Dreams	Adjuncts
Client centered	Warm, positive, open, doctor–patient	Subjective experiences, somewhat intrapsychic	Situational disturbances, self-concept difficulties, some neurosis	Rarely used, except for subjective reactions	Individual therapy
Emerging eclectic	Varies, leader–member, changeable	Interpersonal and intrapsychic	Situational disturbances, neurosis, some specific psychotic and character disorders	Often interpreted and/or role played, discussed for subjective and shared	Specific homework, individual therapy, encounter groups

Method and Practice

Chapter 4

The Process of
a Typical Group:
Part 1

Each therapeutic group is distinctly different. The problems discussed, the therapeutic approaches employed, and the conflicts resolved in a group are specific to that particular group. Since each group is made up of several uniquely different personalities and thus is not duplicative, singularity of expression within a group is to be expected.

Despite this dissimilarity, however, there are commonalities across groups. While the specific *content* of group discussion will vary from group to group, the *process* of different groups is remarkably similar. In an effective and successful group, certain stages must occur in a reliable sequence. Several authors (Fiebert, 1968; Schutz, 1967; Stoute, 1950; Wender, 1936) have discussed the stages of group process development. Wender, for example, describes four stages: (1) intellectualization, (2) transference between patients, (3) catharsis, and (4) group interest. Dreikurs (1951b), working from an Adlerian perspective, also indicated four stages: (1) establishment of relations, (2) interpretation of dynamics, (3) patients gaining understanding, and (4) reorientation. Schutz (1973) describes only three stages and sees these as an inevitable sequence. He indicates that each group deals with the development of inclusion, control, and affection as members work through their conflicts in belonging to the group, their role in the group pecking order, and their closeness to other members.

Yalom (1970) sees the early stages of groups as follows:

Initial stage—orientation, hesitant participation, search for similarities, search for meaning.

Second stage—conflict, dominance, rebellion.

Third stage—development of cohesiveness.

These are markedly similar to Schutz's formulations. However, Yalom describes several qualifying factors which can dramatically affect this sequence: leadership qualities, patient qualities, additions to and deletions from membership, attendance, and so on. Yalom also suggests that discrete stages can be described reliably only early in a group's development. Many other authors also describe similar global developmental stages. Such formulations do have some descriptive value, but they are of little benefit in portraying the specifics of group process.

The chronological process analysis presented in this chapter and the following was developed by means of my own experience in clinical practice over a number of years and through a series of careful experiments in our laboratories. It represents an attempt to achieve greater descriptive specificity than has been realized elsewhere. I am especially thankful to Dr. Michael Diamond for his aid in constructing this descriptive look at group process. There are four phases in our formulation, and 37 stages within these phases. They are descriptive of an *optimally functioning, closed* group led by an accomplished leader with therapeutically viable clients in either an encounter or therapy format. In some ways, this is seen as an *ideal* model; it is acknowledged that all groups do not complete all the stages successfully. It is my contention that the success of any group can be measured by the extent to which it moves through these phases and stages. Successful completion of each previous stage is prerequisite to dealing with subsequent stages.

The four phases are *preparation, learning the group rules, therapeutic intervention,* and *termination.* Phases I and II will be presented in this chapter, and Phases III and IV in Chapter 5. To provide an overview of the group process, an outline of all four phases and 37 stages follows:

Phase I. Preparation
    Stage   1: Leader announces group and logistics
    Stage   2: Members apply for the group
    Stage   3: Screening

Phase II: Learning the Group Rules
    Stage   4: Leader specifies ground rules
    Stage   5: Introductions
    Stage   6: The short silence
    Stage   7: Short silence is broken
    Stage   8: Discussion of there-and-then topic
    Stage   9: Natural death of discussion

Stage 10: The long silence
Stage 11: Members' first sortie
Stage 12: The negative response
Stage 13: Group leader focuses on here-and-now process
Stage 14: The major there-and-then problem
Stage 15: Leader focuses on feeling
Stage 16: A real personal problem
Stage 17: Attempts are made to solve the problem
Stage 18: All suggestions fail to resolve problem
Stage 19: Leader refers to group process
Stage 20: Expression of feelings about this process and the group in general
Stage 21: Leader encourages the expression of emotion

Phase III: Therapeutic Intervention
Stage 22: Norms are solidified
Stage 23: Multiple roles of leadership
Stage 24: Intensity increases
Stage 25: Leader employs therapeutic skills
Stage 26: Minority members identified
Stage 27: Discussion of inclusion/exclusion
Stage 28: Minority members make their decision
Stage 29: The group reacts
Stage 30: Problem-solving orientation practiced

Phase IV: Termination
Stage 31: Leader announces imminent end of group time
Stage 32: Invitation to work
Stage 33: Trust boost
Stage 34: Transfer of training
Stage 35: Good and welfare
Stage 36: Leader's closing
Stage 37: Aloha

PHASE I: Preparation

Stage 1: Leader Announces Group and Logistics

With the announcement and statement of critical logistics for the group, much of what is to occur within it will be determined. Such factors as where and in what way the group is publicized, cost, meeting place, number of sessions, time of sessions, group goals and leader's reputation, theoretical background, and age, will all substantially affect the subsequent group membership. Figures 4–1 through 4–3 are examples of several recent group announcements. Names and identities or other distinguishing characteristics have been changed for professional reasons.

FIGURE 4–1: Sample Group Announcement

A Weekend Workshop
Awareness and Movement
led by Jean Smith, M.A., and Bill Jones, Ph.D.

Jean is an advanced practitioner in Rolfing and a dance and yoga instructor. She teaches creative movement and has done substantial work in integrating movement techniques.

Bill is a certified clinical psychologist and a Gestalt therapist. He has been practicing psychotherapy for over 10 years in this community. He is also on the Ethics Committee of the State Mental Health Board and works as a program developer for the state's mental health services.

We will work with the group to help members integrate the different components of their beings. Through a series of movement exercises and individual and group work, members will have an opportunity to come to a better understanding of self and of the body as a source of energy and expression.

Dates:	February 6 & 7, 1976
Schedule:	February 6: 8–11 p.m., Friday
	February 7: 10–6 p.m., Saturday
Fee:	$45.00; students $35.00
Location:	Central Church
	6245 Hoebrown Lane
	Honolulu, Hawaii 96823

The awareness and movement group described in Figure 4–1 was advertised via flyers to members of a selected mailing list. Such an advertisement is likely to draw such participants as students in mental health-related professions, mental health professionals, dancers, and college-educated, somewhat sophisticated, middle-class working people. It is unlikely to draw severely disturbed or poverty-level participants. Members of such a group (in the encounter format) would typically be functioning adequately and wanting to experiment with growth activities.

For comparison, examine the effects of a different location and fee on a similar advertisement to a similar mailing list (Figure 4–2). It is

FIGURE 4–2: Sample Group Announcement

Dr. Elizabeth Van Wheeler, B.A., M.Sc., M.D., Ed.D., is happy to announce the occurrence of an awareness workshop. Dr. Van Wheeler was educated at Oxford and Paris and is a lifetime member of the American Psychoanalytic Association. This workshop will use a variety of techniques, especially movement and body awareness, to reintroduce and help reintegrate body energy and self. Members will become in touch with and learn new ways to express themselves. Membership is very limited.

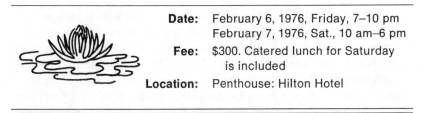

Date:	February 6, 1976, Friday, 7–10 pm
	February 7, 1976, Sat., 10 am–6 pm
Fee:	$300. Catered lunch for Saturday
	is included
Location:	Penthouse: Hilton Hotel

clear that Dr. Van Wheeler is working hard to attract "the wealthy." Cost, location, and presentation all are geared to eliminate patients and students in the middle and lower socioeconomic levels. While she offers virtually the same services as Smith and Jones, a very different participant is likely to apply.

Another flyer type of advertisement for group members has recently appeared on university campus bulletin boards (Figure 4–3). It is unlikely that Guru Rakar will compete for the same populations as Dr. Van Wheeler. Another means of inviting members is with memoranda such as those reproduced in Figure 4–4.

A major factor in the announcement of groups is the extent to which they are voluntary. In the advertisements shown in Figures 4–1 through 4–4, group membership is by application and selection. Such is not

FIGURE 4–3: Sample Group Announcement

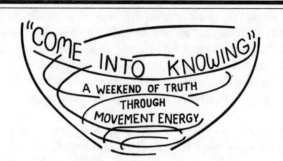

"COME INTO KNOWING"
A WEEKEND OF TRUTH
THROUGH
MOVEMENT ENERGY

The Dynamic Spiritual Learning Center of Honolulu presents a weekend group experience with the renowned Guru Rakar, recently returned from India, and his assistants Sandy and Elaine, B.A. The guru will work with individuals in attaining knowledge in a group setting designed to enhance knowledge of self and of one's own inner strengths.

Cost:	$50.00—one person/$80.00—couple
Time:	Sunrise to sunset, Saturday, Feb. 7, 1976
Place:	Behind Green Chapel

always the case, however. The membership of institutional groups, such as those for hospitalized patients, the military, prisoners, school students, business or management representatives, or court-directed participants is frequently by assignment, not choice. In these cases, a primary consideration is dealing with the resentment and resistance members may have in an attempt to make the group at least nominally voluntary. It is highly unlikely that any positive results will occur unless members are in the group through their own choice.

Two examples of a nonvoluntary group assignment are presented in Figure 4–5. Such introductions to group membership carry with them inevitable destructive elements. Members must want to be in the group at least occasionally, and people will exhibit very different behaviors in a voluntary group than in a mandatory one.

In short, a great deal of control of the group membership is exercised through such practical considerations as fees, locations, type and plan of advertisement, time format, or time of day, and so on.

Stage 2: Members Apply for the Group

Application for group membership can take several forms also. It can be made directly by the members themselves, by completing a form

FIGURE 4–4: Representative Memorandums to Advertise Groups

MEMORANDUM   March 19, 1976

To: Selected Psychotherapists in Private Practice
Selected Psychotherapists in State Mental Health Centers
From: Kuhio Mental Health Clinic
Re: Referrals of Nonpsychotic Patients

This is to inform you that Drs. Joe Smith and Elaine Brown will be
conducting weekly group therapy sessions on Tuesday evenings,
7–10 p.m., commencing May 1, 1976, for 12 consecutive Tuesday
evenings. The group membership will consist of 8–10 patients who are
diagnosed as neurotic or situational adjustment problems. The focus of
this group is interpersonal, and it is seen as an excellent adjunct to
ongoing individual therapy. If you have any nonpsychotic patients that
you feel would benefit from this group, referrals will be accepted
and appreciated. Sessions will cost $20.00 per participant per session.

We will screen all members carefully for "goodness of fit" in the
groups. Please contact Joe and Elaine at KMHC 941–9590.

                                              June 1, 1976
INTRADEPARTMENTAL MEMO

To: All Therapists
From: Director, State Mental Health Clinic

This fall two of our psychology interns and two psychiatric residents
will be leading couples groups in the evenings. There will be one
resident and one intern co-leading groups on Tuesday and Wednesday
evenings. The groups are designed to help couples in conflict learn
more effective communication patterns and to help reduce our waiting
list rolls. Please make referrals directly to Dr. Matsuda, intern training
coordinator. We will need at least 8 couples to fill both groups. All costs
will be covered by my office, and services to patients are free. I trust
you will consider *need* as one factor in selection.

---

and mailing or bringing it to the growth center, mental health clinic,
or appropriate leader. It also can be by referral from appropriate
sources, such as other therapists, physicians, clergy, parents, or spouses.
The most important aspect of this phase is that it is an application, not
a guarantee of participation.

FIGURE 4–5: Notice of Mandatory Attendance Groups

Letter sent to parents of school children:

Dear Mr. & Mrs. White:

Your son/daughter has been reported to the school principal repeatedly for smoking in the school lavatories. In lieu of punishment, he/she has been assigned to a group therapy session with Miss Young, the school counselor. The sessions will occur every Monday, Wednesday, and Friday from 10–11 am. Attendance is mandatory for one month.

Sincerely,

John Edwards

John Edwards, Principal

MEMO

To: Inmates, Black, White, Brown, Green, Redd.
       Alcatraz Penitentiary
From: J. E. M. Cauliflower, Warden *JEMC*

You have been assigned to group therapy with psychology students S. Marlowe and L. Linn. The group commences 0900 Wednesday, May 1 and will terminate at 1030. The group will last for 15 weeks or until your release. It is expected that you will learn social skills necessary upon your upcoming release from this center. On-time attendance is mandatory.

Stage 3: Screening

Screening is one of the most critical components of the entire group process. This stage is frequently minimized by therapists and leaders who want to fill their groups. Indeed, if the group gets bogged down or if casualties occur, they are most frequently a direct result of inadequate screening rather than any other variable.

There are two major screening questions in a group setting:

1. Is this group appropriate for the client?
2. Is the client appropriate for this group?

While homogeneous membership within a group can have deleterious effects on interest and the ability of group members to give a variety of feedback responses to one another, certain types of heterogeneous membership can bog down a group even more effectively. One of my clients, a 17-year-old high school senior, came to me after two years in a particularly trying group therapy experience. This group, led by a locally well known psychiatrist, consisted of nine members—the teen-ager and four couples aged 29–45 who were having marital problems. Suzanne (my client) simply did not belong in this married couples group. Not only did she misunderstand many of the conflicts between the couples, but she emerged with an especially pessimistic view of marriage and heterosexual relationships. Subsequent discussions with the group therapist confirmed that not only did Suzanne not "get much out of the group," but several of the other members were reticent to discuss some of their sexual problems "in front of a 16-year-old child." This was a clear case of poor or absent screening based on the simplistic notion that since all nine of these people needed a group, they could function well as a single group:

In a similar case, I was recently asked to help clear up a "block" in an ongoing women's awareness group. As a male I was surprised to receive this request and hesitant about accepting it. This surprise was minor by comparison to the shock I experienced on entering the group room. In addition to four single women (Mary, Kathy, Ann, Peggy) and three married women (Martha, Linda, Sandy), there was another group member by the name of Edward. Ed was a social worker, the former husband of Linda and the current lover of Peggy. The block in this women's awareness group was that, dynamically, the group process centered around a *MAN*. Screening Ed out "solved the problem."

Such differences based on demographic variables are easier to spot and screen out than differences based on symbiotic pathological systems, level or type of problem to be discussed, or readiness and motivation for the group experience.

As discussed in Chapter 1, there are differences in populations and goals for encounter-type and therapy-type groups. Members thus must be screened accordingly. Mixing psychotherapy patients and growth-oriented clients will limit the learning of both types of group members. A major component of group learning revolves around a series of agreements or compromises as to what type of materials, in what language system and to what end, the group will discuss. The sooner these agreements can be made, the further the group can progress in the allotted time. A group with widely divergent goals cannot make these agreements readily and hence suffers diminished capacity.

Some No-No's and Deadly Combinations for Groups

In groups with nonhomogeneous memberships held in a setting other than a total institution, several types of members can be extremely counterproductive for group progress. Brain-damaged, mentally defective, and severely psychotic (especially withdrawn and paranoid) patients, psychopathic individuals, drug or alcohol addicts, suicidal clients, and very assaultive patients are all bad risks in an outpatient group and have no business at all in encounter groups. Not only will these types of members get minimal benefits or even regress as a function of group membership, they will also severely limit the benefits accrued by other members of the group. These clinical observations have been confirmed in the group therapy literature by Slavson (e.g., 1951), Yalom (1970), Rosenbaum and Hartley (1962), and Corsini and Lundin (1955).

Certain combinations of group members also can cause grief for the group leader and destroy the group process. One such combination is a person who uses hysteric defenses and an authoritarian personality type who tends to avoid intimacy by "protecting" (fathering, mothering) others. One such combination occurred in a student-led group at the very beginning of an encounter group during members' introduction (Phase 2, Stage 5 below). Three members of the group had already given their names and expectations when a fourth said,

> My name is Christine, but I don't like to be called that, I hate that
> name . . . so call me Moana. . . . I don't know if I should be
> here. . . . I get scared easy and I'm afraid of you two especially (she
> indicated two of the men in the group). When people start getting
> upset and emotional I freak out. I even tried suicide three times.

As quickly as an "Amen" to a particularly moving prayer, Dan, one of the men in the group, responded in a crisp, booming voice, "Well, you don't have to worry here, sweets, anyone who tries to get you upset will have to answer to me first."

This symbiotic relationship was a group process interruptor for several sessions. The partners allowed one another to express the feelings that they were unable to express directly. Whenever other group members began to discuss anything that involved high levels of affect, Christine-Moana would begin to shake and cower and express the need to run from the room, and Dan would then attack the person who was expressing the high levels of emotion. In this way Christine-Moana never had to deal with her "unacceptable" anger, and Dan never had to deal with his unacceptable fear. By using these types of interactions, they could effectively keep the group from getting to deeper (more frightening) levels of interaction. The student co-leaders had their hands very full with this relationship, and the group only began to progress when Christine-Moana tried to threaten the group by being absent after having been seen in the hall outside the group room minutes earlier. Once they were separated, the group was able to confront feelings of being threatened by her fragility, and by Dan's as well.

Another combination of members that makes for great difficulties is two people in a group who have had a serious previous relationship but are no longer involved. This is especially powerful when the group is made up of others who do not know one another well. The case of Denise and Larry is a classic example of this. This was a group designed to help people learn to relate more comfortably and effectively with members of the opposite sex. Since this group was designed to help members learn new ways of dealing with members of the opposite sex, there was a prerequisite that members did not know each other beforehand. As the group progressed, it became clear that each time Larry spoke, Denise made the next statement and put him down as a "typical" male. Similarly, whenever Denise spoke, Larry accused her of "coming on sexually nonverbally, but denying it verbally" (a perception which subsequently turned out to be accurate). The other group members and leaders confronted them several times with this pattern, with no apparent behavior change. This interaction became so dominant that the group leader finally confronted them with the following statement: "You two sound like a married couple deciding to get a divorce and wanting to gain some measure of revenge." This was followed by a pregnant silence during which both Denise and Larry got very pale. Finally, they admitted that they had been married for four years and were competing to see who could seduce more of the opposite sex group members in the group. The group continued only after they decided to drop out and seek individual psychotherapy.

One other type of person that makes group work especially complex is the person who has "something to sell." These individuals come to groups essentially to convince others to join with them in some belief system or value. They are either insecure enough, or convinced of their righteousness enough, to be unaccepting of other members' values or beliefs or language systems. Recent converts to religious, spiritual, or pop psychology sects can frequently spend much of the group's time attempting to induce the group to accept verbatim their own elitist and myopic approach to understanding their experience and their own singular language system (jargon). In the process, they reject all others as not sophisticated enough or not understanding. Such members often seduce other members and unsuspecting leaders into expending vast amounts of time attempting to "work with them and be fair."

The screening stage of group process is thus a critically important one. Errors of omission and of commission come back to haunt group leaders in a variety of ways. Poor screening can seriously limit the group outcome. A leader who attempts to do bargain basement screening will pay for it several times over during the remainder of the group.

One personal example of incomplete screening will make this point clear. A one-day marathon group I was to co-lead several years ago had nine members signed up. On the last day before the group was to meet, I was talking casually to a colleague about the group and my desire for a tenth member when the colleague said that he had a gal on his waiting list and suggested that I call her. Since it was so late a very brief and inadequate telephone screening was done, and the woman was invited to come to the group the following day. I rationalized: There's not enough time to call her in and screen in person; she's been on a waiting list for a group, so she couldn't be in urgent need of help; she's a professional person in a mental health profession—a psychiatric nurse. Such rationalizations were used in the absence of the typical screening.

The client who was not screened was the fourth member to introduce herself the next day. Her speech was exceptionally fast and pressured, and her eyes seemed to focus and unfocus repeatedly each few seconds. A short excerpt of her eight-minute self-introduction follows:

> Well, my name is Tina, but it isn't really Tina that's only since it happened, before that it was different but really the same—Sally or Rudy but that was before the man-husband-father rolled over the kids with the steam roller-crusher-flat but not really only but they were dead but I didn't so now they cry but it seems no he didn't exist—they are are. God punishes them but I save-savior-saved . . .

During this the other group members seemed terrified and appeared to be increasing the size of the group circle, almost as if they wanted to push the walls of the room out and increase the space. The group co-leader had a look of shock, surprise, and what could best be described as "How could you do this to me?" on his face.

Once Tina was through with her introduction, the remaining members introduced themselves. Then the group wrestled with Tina's pathology for approximately two hours, when the leaders were able to call a break and contact a colleague. They arranged for emergency treatment and reconvened the rather shaken group once she had departed.

We have focused on screening as an exclusion method. It is also used for inclusion. Thus screening for the group necessitates finding a good mix of people—similar enough to understand one another, yet different enough to be able to learn new viewpoints, behaviors, and solutions to problems from one another. One or two good members can bridge a gap between two otherwise discrete groups of people within a single group. Similarly, the group membership needs to coincide with the ability and level of functioning of the leaders. No group can proceed beyond the level of functioning of the leader. This will be discussed in detail in Chapters 6 and 7.

Once the group members are screened and the logistics are set, Phase I of the group process is over.

PHASE II: Learning the Group Rules

The early stages of group process have some therapeutic value, but their greatest impact is in teaching the members the language, focuses, ethics, and process of the group. These stages can be quite lengthy, taking several sessions, or quite short, as with a group consisting of graduate students enrolled in a class focusing on group process.

A perceptive group leader can glean a great deal of interesting data from the members' pregroup behavior. Do members linger outside the group room or come directly in? Do they speak to others socially or keep to themselves? Are they early, on time, or late? How have they dressed for the group? Where do they sit? While no group leader will make final or absolute judgments about group members based on such nonverbal behavior, he or she can develop hypotheses which can be subsequently tested in the group. For example, the leader may make tentative assumptions about group members based on where they sit in the group. Typically, members tend to sit next to people they feel support them, across from people who attract them, and at right angles to people who threaten them. Such information can help a group leader make early estimates of interpersonal reactivity among members.

Stage 4: Leader Specifies Ground Rules

Each group and each group leader will have certain idiosyncratic rules and regulations regarding participation in the group. The specifics of such instructions seem less important than the level of structure they convey. Therapy groups, children's groups, and classroom groups generally have more restrictive and structured ground rules than do encounter, T-, and growth-oriented groups.

Frequently the entire tone for the group is set by the leader's introductory remarks. The manner in which the group leader presents himself and the ground rules will be the first cue members have for learning how to behave and talk in the group. One of the most critical factors to be determined is the level of anxiety which will be employed in the group. It seems clear that as the level of ambiguity (or the lack of structure) increases, anxiety increases, and this affects the level of performance. Figure 4–6 illustrates the relationship of performance and anxiety.

Figure 4–6: Pictorial Representation of the Relationship of Performance and Anxiety

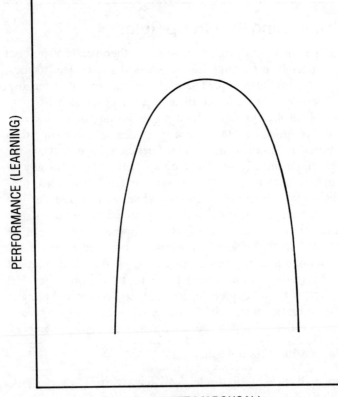

PERFORMANCE (LEARNING)

ANXIETY (AROUSAL)

The group leader can effectively control the level of anxiety in the group setting by maintaining control over the amount of structure present in the group at any one time. We know that optimal learning in any setting occurs when the learner's anxiety (motivation) is at moderate levels. Therefore a group leader can enhance the effectiveness of the group process by maintaining levels of structure that engender moderate levels of anxiety.

Some representative ground rules are included in the *sample* introduction given below:

RENE (LEADER 1): Hello, my name is Rene. I'll be co-leading this group with Jerry (indicates co-leader). Our goal in this group is for open, honest communication between members. We will stress getting in touch with and expressing feelings because that's something we all share and understand. We will be focusing a great deal on the here and now, or what's going on within this group in the present, because we can all look at that much more effectively than we can a there and then memory.

Needless to say *here and now feelings* about there and then events are very much grist for our group mill. Jerry, would you like to add anything?

JERRY (LEADER 2): Thanks, Rene. I'd like to begin by underscoring what Rene has already said. I'd also like to bring up a few other ground rules. First and foremost is *confidentiality*—what is said in this group must remain within the group. That is to say, if something really important happens to you in the group we encourage you to bring that back home to important people—spouses, family, friends—but we ask you not to share anyone else's words or experience or to identify anyone else. Is that OK?

A second form of confidentiality involves the question of whether or not members of the group can meet outside of the group, say over coffee, and discuss group events. How do you feel about that?

Discussion follows until a group decision is reached.

JERRY: Another ground rule for this group has to do with the expectancies that people often bring into the group with them. Unlike *Time* magazine articles or other sensationalized accounts, there will be no nudity, sexual touching, or violence within this group. Also, since this is an enclosed room and the air is recirculated, we ask you to refrain from smoking for the two-hour session.* We also ask that you not eat or drink during the session.* Please also do not come to future sessions either drunk, high, or stoned.

---

* These rules are optional and clearly depend on leader's preferences.

One last point is that if you do not wish to do something or talk about something, all you need say is "I don't want to do (talk about) that," and we won't push you, nor will we allow the group to push you. However, if you say "I can't"—generally a defensive reaction—we'll bug you.

Are there any questions?

RENE: Two additional points; this is a place for us to bring up and discuss things that are bothering us. It's a safe place to take risks and talk about our real problems. Finally, you've probably noticed the videotaping (audiotaping) equipment in the room. These sessions will all be taped. These tapes will only be available to members and leaders in the group. Their purpose is to help us better understand and remember what went on in the session. The tape of each session is only kept until the next session.* Any questions, comments, issues, and so on?

Even in this short opening, several ground rules are established, and yet the level of ambiguity is still high. Briefly, these rules were followed:

> First names used; leaders identified; open, honest communication stated as goal; focus on feelings stated; expression of feelings stressed; here and now defined; taking one's experience home suggested; confidentiality identified as foremost group rule; no nudity, sexual touching, or violence; no smoking; no eating; no one to attend while drunk, high, or stoned.

In addition, members were cautioned to say they won't talk about something, not can't talk about it. They were told the group could discuss issues and make group decisions, and that they should bring up their own problems.

A much less structured, not uncommon opening for encounter groups leads to a very different level of anxiety: "Hello, my name is George and this is my co-leader, Sue. The only rules for this group are that there'll be no homicide or screwing."

No matter what the introduction, as the rules are given by the group leader(s), the level of ambiguity and hence the level of anxiety are set. In this way, a basic tone for the group is determined.

Stage 5: Introductions

Each member of the group is asked to introduce himself or herself. The three most important components of this process are *entry, getting used to sharing information about oneself,* and *open communication of expectancies.* Leaders frequently ask members to give their names, describe what they hope to gain from their group participation, and state what they fear most about the group. Such an introduction allows members to enter the group by participating. Giving this information is typically nonthreatening, since members have already rehearsed it during the screening procedure and in their heads while thinking about the group. Talking, on instruction, about fears and expectancies is also excellent basic training for later group participation. Hence right from the outset, the leader's expectancy that members will discuss such things in the group are already being made clear.

One interesting phenomenon that occurs in many groups is that members are so busy rehearsing what they'll say when their own turn comes that they do not "hear" the names or introductions of other members who precede them. In pointing this out, the leader begins to establish the notion that the topic for discussion is members' behavior within the group.

It is important to finish the whole round of introductions before any major issues are allowed to develop. Often a group member has been thinking about a problem for so long and waiting to share it for so long that simply giving her or his name is a cue for a rush of affect and a plea for assistance. It is the leader's task to help everyone become a member of the group before any issues occur that could shut members out. One example of this already cited was that of Tina, the improperly screened member.

Another less bizarre example occurred in an encounter group led by two supervised student group leaders. One of the leaders introduced himself (the fifth person to do so), and a member who had also introduced himself began engaging the leader in a fairly intense manner, asking for help, advice, and so on. The leader mistakenly began to do therapy, and this piece of process lasted almost an hour of the two-hour session. During this time the group members who had not yet been introduced and the other co-leader maintained a watchful, anxious silence. Only after this "therapy" ended were they able to join the group. Not only did they report feeling like outsiders, but they also said they felt like latecomers to the group. Furthermore, the co-leader who was left out felt that her effectiveness as an *equal* co-leader had been permanently diminished. Her status as a leader was in fact lower than his for several sessions, despite the fact that she was the more experienced of the two.

Stage 6: The Short Silence

After introductions have been completed, members typically turn to the leader with expectancies that he or she provide some structure.

When the leader does not do this, a short silence ensues. This silence lasts typically less than two minutes.

Stage 7: Short Silence Is Broken

The short silence is ended by one or more members in one of the following ways:

1. Request for information.
2. Demand for leader structure.
3. Expression of frustration or discomfort.
4. Nonverbal signs of anxiety.

In our culture, silence in a group setting that is not precipitated by a special request for it (e.g., "Let us pray") or by particular situational demands (e.g., library, funeral parlor) seems to be anxiety provoking. The ending of this short silence (often seemingly only microseconds) appears to be a function of this increasing anxiety.

Because the silence is ended as a way of reducing the anxiety provoked by its existence, the manner of its termination often appears less than rational. Requests for information can run the gamut from "Tell me what to do now" to "What do you think of Patty Hearst?" to "Can the Dodgers catch the Reds this year?" One fascinating instance occurred in a group led by a woman therapist whose husband is a locally famous therapist and whose father-in-law is an internationally known author. The request for information proceeded as follows:

Member 1: You said your last name was _____? Was your husband in the paper last week?

Therapist: Uh, huh.

Member 2: Are you related to _____ (father-in-law)? Oh, wow. I've read a lot of his stuff.

Member 3: Me too, he's brilliant.

Member 4: Well, his philosophies are intriguing from a Western point of view, but hardly complete when considering Eastern approaches.

This request for information served the function of reducing the anxiety and distracting the group from its primary *here-and-now* focus. Fortunately, the leader was able to focus members back onto their anxiety, and the remainder of the group was less involved in such cognitive, *there-and-then* philosophical discussions. While such discussions are frowned on and need to be terminated, the therapist was able to garner a tremendous amount of information about members' styles of responding even from this brief, early episode.

Demands for leader structure can also be apparently discrepant from the situation. Frequently they consist of such comments as

OK, you're the leader, what do we do now?
Do you have any starting (ice-breaking) exercises? I hear that's a good way to start a group.
What are you going to do now?

One impressive example of this occurred during a human relations training workshop with administrators from a community college. This short silence lasted a total of *90* seconds and was broken with:

Member 1: Look, I just can't stay here all day, I've got work to do.
Member 2: Time is money.
Member 3: What's the matter with you?
Member 4: Look if you don't want to teach this class, one of us can.

Each of these statements, directed at the leader, was uttered with increased intensity. Incredible as it may seem, four years after this 90-second silence, group members still remember the "agony of nobody never saying nothing."
Expressions of nervousness and discomfort are such as:

I just can't stand it when it's so quiet.
Somebody say something!
I'm starting to sweat and my heart is thumping and I feel really shaky and hot.

Nonverbal expressions include tremulous shaking, constant shifting of position, leg jiggling, crying, giggling, dropping or spilling something, whispering something to another member, and whistling.

Stage 8: Discussion of There-and-Then Topic

Once the silence is broken, members of the group will frequently pick up any topic for discussion with a there-and-then rather than here-and-now focus. This discussion of some external communality is both an effort to get things going in the group and a hedge against another (painful) silence. The topic is frequently interesting and most often safe, objective, and something the majority of members can share. This is especially true for groups who have out-of-group activities in common and, of course, natural groups.
This there-and-then discussion of seemingly irrelevant topics is a

time that is difficult and rich for therapists. During these conversations it is imperative that the group leader does *not* get involved in the *content* of the discussion. No matter how interesting the topic, the leaders' task here is primarily diagnostic. While the therapist may make a few process comments during Stage 8, by far the most important task for the group leader is to observe the group members developing their "pecking order" and establishing their various roles in the group.

If the leader does not get involved in the discussion of the there-and-then topic and hence does not keep it alive, this conversation will die a natural death.

Stage 9: Natural Death of Discussion

After a time, members begin to drop out of the there-and-then discussion. Perhaps boredom, perhaps by hearing the process comments of the leader, or perhaps the anxiety is lowered enough to facilitate movement to less safe topics. In any case, the discussion pales and finally terminates. In some groups of highly anxious, highly verbal people, the group therapist may have to be more directive in terminating this discussion, especially if group time is limited. Normally, leader references to group process will be sufficient to encourage the demise of this discussion.

Stage 10: The Long Silence

With the death of the there-and-then discussion, a longer period of silence commences. This silence, which can last from a few minutes to over an hour, is characterized by nervous fidgeting, lack of eye contact, avoidance of physical contact, maintenance of social distance, and increasing anxiety.

Some group leaders will break this silence as certain optimal levels of anxiety are attained and focus on an individual member or piece of process. Others will rely on group members to end the long silence. For the most part, the latter (a greater number) argue that if the therapist ends the silence, group members will learn to rely on him or her to continue to do this in the future. This is a responsibility they prefer to leave with group members. Except in special circumstances, (such as completely inexperienced group members or groups with severe time limitations) it is best for leaders not to terminate the silence. Rather, they may take the time of the silence to observe the members' nonverbal behaviors for later use in the therapy phase of the group process.

Since silence in a group setting is anxiety producing, it is imperative for group therapists to discover their own tolerance for such anxiety and to work to increase their own thresholds for silence. Lengthy silences can be very difficult for leaders to withstand and can have dramatic effects on members. I have described the longest silence I have ever dealt with:

> I was co-leading a one-day 15-hour marathon group with
> _____. Since most of the group members knew me already,
> it was agreed that my co-leader would take the lead during the
> early phases of the group. . . . The silence lasted for 46 minutes and
> 22 seconds (but who was counting), punctuated only once by one
> member of the group remarking after 21 minutes, "I bought a
> Toyota yesterday." . . . The laughter release was immense for most
> of the members and myself. . . . After the entire silence, one
> women began to discuss a very heavy problem and the group really
> took off from there. . . . There couldn't have been another 20-
> second silence for the duration of the 15 hours. . . . It seemed
> almost as if nobody was going to risk another massive silence like
> the last one. . . . In retrospect it was one of the most powerful
> groups I've ever been involved in. Most members used the
> experience to make decisions they wanted to make, and the transfer
> of training was immense. . . . Sometimes I think a large part of
> the power of that group was the members' working on real
> problems out of fear of another silence occurring as painful
> as the first. (Shapiro, 1975)

Stage 11: Members' First Sortie

Whether the leader encourages a member to speak or a member volunteers, one member will express himself in an attempt to define his role in the group. The member can do this by:

1. Asking for group help in problem-solving.
2. Asking for group attention.
3. Winning the affection of the group or of a particular member.
4. Meeting some perceived group expectancies.
5. Obtaining leadership of the group.

Haley (1963b) argues that each time a member of the group speaks, he or she is both conveying information and defining the relationships of members in the particular setting. This concept seems especially applicable to the silence breaker in a group. Frequently the person who speaks first and thus terminates the long silence predisposes the other group members and leaders to perceive him in a particular way. For example, this person may define himself as the identified patient: "Well, I've got this heavy problem I need help with," or may nonverbally indicate that he needs group attention by crying, flirting, fainting, getting up and moving around, and so on. Of course, verbal expressions of almost any type will also call group attention to the speaker. In addition to requesting group help in solving a problem, a member might ask the group to share in other feelings he or she may be experiencing. For example, a group member may express comfort or discomfort with the silence and look to other members for confirmation or support:

> I really get uptight when it's so quiet.
> I wish someone would say something.
> Wow, this is the first relaxing moment I've had all day.
> Is that what's supposed to happen?

Such interactions can help determine a member's role in the group, gain attention, meet perceived expectancies, or win affection from the group or a particular member. Indeed, a moderate amount of problem sharing at this stage often wins a member the role of star patient and exempts him or her from subsequent pressures.

One common pattern following the silence breaking is commonly called *leadership challenge*. This event, which occurs almost universally in encounter groups and frequently in therapy groups, often occurs at this point in the group process. It is characterized by questions regarding the leader's competence, training, or background or as a series of recommendations as to how the group may proceed:

> Well, if nothing is going to happen, why don't you (directed to
> the leader) suggest technique or exercise? If you don't know any,
> I could suggest a few. . . . I hate wasting time like this, why don't
> we try _____?

Another example, spoken angrily and forcefully, might be:

> OK, let's get this show on the road, obviously they (addressed to
> leaders) aren't going to do anything. Why don't we elect a
> chairman to bring up topics or something?

In addition to being delivered at high volume, it has become fashionable to punctuate such statements by the words *fuck* or *fucking* interspersed not only between the other words but also within them, such as *any-fuckingthing,* or *somefuckingthing.* Unless the leader is prepared for this, the group can remain rooted at Stage 11 for an excessive time.

If the leader does not succumb to the pressure to institute an exercise or to take the lead in dealing with whatever the individual has brought up, other members will begin to respond to the silence-breaking member. Then the group is on its way to greater growth.

Stage 12: The Negative Response

As soon as the first member breaks the speaking barrier, other members also let their thoughts and reactions be heard. While a few members may support the statements of the first speaker, the most outspoken or majority opinion will be critical of the first one. Sometimes members will defend the leader. At other times criticism for breaking the silence is leveled. In yet other groups, the attempt to win attention is rejected or the problem brought up is viewed as inappropriate. For whatever the stated reason, the reaction to the silence breaker is generally negative, and under no circumstances is group leadership handed over to him or her.

During all this discussion, the leader must not join in or take sides. It is the leader's task to use this interaction to train the group in the process of group therapy.

Stage 13: Group Leader Focuses on Here-and-Now Process

While the entire interchange regarding the first speaker's communication unfolds, the leader must continually focus the group's attention on the on-going process. Instead of joining in on either side of the issue, the leader-therapist must make statements which answer the unasked question: "What's going on between us, at this time, in this room?"

Sample leaders' interactions at this point might be:

> What I saw happening was George was saying he was dissatisfied with what was happening and requesting that the leaders put in an exercise. Then Joan and Marie expressed their anger with him for doing that and pointed out that they didn't want to do an exercise.
>
> I saw George asking for help with his problem of making positive sounding statements and somehow getting people angry with him, and now it seems like Joan and Marie are angry with him. Seems like whatever you do on the outside to get people angry is happening right here. I wonder what's going on?

Similar leader interactions, all focusing on the *here-and-now,* continue throughout this period of the group. In essence, the group members are being trained to look at their behavior *as it occurs*. Then they can see the impact and consequences of this behavior via observation and feedback from their fellow members and the leader, and ultimately they can make changes based on the information.

As the leader continues to make here-and-now process comments, members begin to open up or "unfreeze" some of their less threatening, but still important, concerns.

Stage 14: The Major There-and-Then Problem

As members talk about problems, one member will bring up a serious-sounding, major problem. This problem, which seems serious, is presented in a detached, summarized, analytical fashion. In a recent group, one member talked about his rejection by his parents and twin sister following his public announcement that he was a homosexual. While this event would seem noteworthy, most of his presentation involved his analysis of how they were victims of social pressures and prejudice. He said he felt it was an understandably defensive reaction on the part of his twin, since, he psychologized, if he were really emotionally female, then she must be afraid of her own masculine tendencies. Similarly, in another group, a woman spoke of the recent sudden death of her husband as if he were going to the corner to buy a loaf of bread.

Such detached discussions of issues that would seem traumatic are cues for the therapist to single out the *affective* components of the here-and-now process.

Stage 15: Leader Focuses on Feeling

As the members discuss this there-and-then problem, and as it develops long enough for most members to have some feelings about the presenter and the problem, the leader focuses on the presenting individual and requests feelings. Typically this is a long-drawn-out, difficult procedure, but the leader's interventions are designed to assist members in identifying, clarifying, and understanding their emotions as primary motivators of behavior. Thus the leader will ask members to describe and pay attention to the affective component of their statements as a way to keep a here-and-now focus in the group. To follow up on one of the previous examples, here is an excerpt from such a sequence.

Herb: . . . anyways I think my sister is truly afraid of her own homosexuality.
Will: What are you afraid of?

Herb: Nothing. I've already come out. . . . She's just headed for trouble unless she comes to grips with her inner psyche.

Martha: Maybe she doesn't have any homosexual feelings. I don't, and I don't think that makes me screwed up.

Sallie: I've never had attraction, sexually, for other women, but I sure get off on men (directed at the male co-leader . . . an issue that was to become dominant a short time later).

Herb: Well, I think if she looked deeper she'd see that she's repressed all those feelings.

Martha: So you think I've repressed mine also.

Herb was silent at this point, but he had an expression on his face that could have been translated, "If the shoe fits, wear it."

AILENE (LEADER 1): Martha, what are you feeling now?

Martha: Well, he just called me a queer in some ways.

AILENE: So you're feeling. . . .

Martha: I'm pissed at Herb, shit, he as much as said that everyone's either a *homo* and knows it or they're *homo* and repressed it.

ROGER (LEADER 2): Herb, what do you hear Martha saying?

Herb: Oh, she's just uptight.

ROGER: What do you hear in her anger at you?

Herb: She's threatened and feeling scared of her inner tendencies.

ROGER: What are *you* feeling?

Herb: Oh, I know where she's at, I was there once too.

ROGER: What are you *feeling*?

Herb: Oh, well, what she's rea. . . .

ROGER: WHAT ARE YOU FEELING?

Herb: I don't know, I'm pissed at you for jumping me like this.

ROGER: Good. I am pressuring you and I'd be angry too if I was on the receiving end. What are you feeling towards Martha?

Herb: Mad, I hate words like *homo* and *queer*.

ROGER: They put you down.

Herb: Yeah.

ROGER: What's happening now?

Herb: I don't know.

ROGER: Focus on your body, what feelings come up?

Herb: Funny feeling in my stomach. . . .

ROGER: What emotion usually comes from your stomach?

Herb: When I'm afraid.

ROGER: Afraid of?

Herb: The group won't accept me, because I'm gay.

ROGER: Anyone in particular?

Herb: Joe . . . (indicating a young male in group).

Joe: Wow, that really scares me.

AILENE: That could mean. . . .

Joe: Yeah, I really don't know where I'm at with that.

AILENE: I can see you're shaking.

Joe: Well, I'd like to be close to Herb, but it really scares me to think of sexual. . . .

AILENE: Can you tell Herb what kind of feelings you're experiencing and what limits you have?

Joe: Yeah.

AILENE: Go ahead.

Notice how both leaders consistently focus on the here-and-now group process and on feelings. The group has come a long way—from discussing Herb's twin sister and her purported problems of repression, to the impact of a relationship between two males when one has described himself as a homosexual. Such pieces of process occur regularly during this time period. The leaders continue to respond in this way until these two major group norms are well established and the group members are comfortable in employing:

1:    *A focus on the here and now.*
2.   *A focus on feelings.*

Once these norms are adopted, the stage is set for the next major piece of process: the help-rejecting complainer.

Stage 16: A Real Personal Problem

At this stage, one member begins to talk about a personal problem (most frequently a marital or relationship problem) which occurs outside the group but which presumably affects his or her group behavior. The presentation of the problem and the feelings of indecision are lengthy, time-consuming, and frequently accompanied by sadness, crying, anger, frustration, or fearfulness. Often the problem area—marriage, separation, divorce, affairs, sexual inadequacies—is one that affects or interests many group members. A spirited discussion ensues, with the presenter discussing the problem and expressing feelings in more and more detail.

Stage 17: Attempts Are Made to Solve the Problem

As the problem emerges, other group members attempt to help by giving advice, recommending alternative solutions, and offering assistance. Frequently members will share their own similar experiences in this area, expressing how they handled or mishandled similar situations in their own lives. This advice is freely offered and presented with caring, concern, and support for the individual, but it falls on seemingly deaf ears.

Stage 18: All Suggestions Fail to Resolve Problem (or, in transactional analysis terms, "Why don't you . . . Yes, but.")

Despite the concern, support, and caring with which the advice is given, it is all rejected. The problem is maintained in full force despite a wealth of alternative suggestions. This is reflected by:

1. A failure to move on—the patient holds on to the problem and the discussion of it.
2. A lack of change in the expression of feelings. This member's affect remains the same, despite the input.
3. Active rejection of or disagreement with the advice.

The following vignette excerpted from a recent group illustrates this process:

Marty: I wonder if it'd be ok to talk about this problem I'm having with my wife.
LEADERS: (Nonverbal signal to go ahead.)
Marty: Well, I don't even know where to start—my marriage is really bad now. I don't know, it was, you know, good for a while, but now . . . it's like I don't know anymore . . . seems like she's angry at me all the time and I'm angry at her all the time . . . just dread going home even . . . really feel guilty about that (nonverbal signs of sadness, frustration).
Val: How long has it been like this?
Marty: Almost two years.
Val: Have you done anything about it?
Marty: I feel like I'm at my wits' end . . . like I've tried everything . . . nothing seems to work.
Susan: You know I went thru that for six years before I finally got a divorce. Have you thought about that?
Marty: I think about it all the time, but then I think I just haven't tried hard enough. You know, I always believed that if *I* really worked at it, I could be married to anyone. . . .
Mel: That sounds self-defeating to me.
Sue: Yeah, when do you know you've tried enough? I went back

and forth like that for years before I finally walked out one day
—never to return.

Marty: Well, you know I've thought about divorce, but I've just
been brought up to think divorce is wrong . . . failure.

Flo: You know, when George and I had problems like that, we
had a baby—that really changed our lives for the better.

Mel: Whoa, that seems it'd really compound the problem if things
didn't get better.

Marty: I always wanted kids, but now I'm afraid of being even
more entrapped. Maybe I just ought to drop it, nothing seems
to help.

Val: What about counseling?

Marty: She won't go . . . she says that since I'm a counselor
professionally . . . me and the counselor would just gang up
on her.

Peter: What about your minister, or a friend of the family that
she trusts?

Marty: That's a good idea, but she's really a loner, you know, I
don't think she'd trust anyone.

Sue: It just seems like nothing will work . . . really frustrating.

Marty: Yeah, I feel like that too, but I keep hoping and believing
there must be some way out of this mess.

Sue: Do you do anything together, maybe if you took up a hobby
or a class together.

Marty: You know, I thought that was it too. We took this ceramics
class together, and I really got into it even though it was her
suggestion. But then she began resenting my being better than her
and dropped the course, so I dropped it too. I was only doing it
to be with her.

Peter: I'm really frustrated.

GAIL (LEADER 1; addressing a member who appears bored):
Sandy, where are you?

Sandy: Bored and frustrated.

John: Me too, I just feel guilty saying it, but there's no way to help
him.

CLIFF (LEADER 2):   What I see happening here is Marty presenting a real problem, many people offering advice and the
advice being rejected, and several people becoming frustrated and
feeling helpless.

Stage 19: Leader Refers to Group Process

If the leader gets involved in giving advice or doing therapy with
the help-rejecting complainer, Stage 18 can be maintained indefinitely.

Consequently, it is important for the leader to wait until the group members become frustrated, bored, or angry before pointing out what the help-rejecting complainer is doing. Thus the leader's job at this stage is to be patient and then, at the optimal time, to describe the process: presentation of the problem, several offers of advice, a rejection of the advice, a lack of resolution, an emergent group sense of frustration.

Stage 20: Expression of Feelings about This Process and the Group in General

After the leader has focused on the here-and-now feelings and identified the feelings of helplessness, anger, and frustration, group members begin to express a variety of their own feelings. They may express frustration about the situation, anxiety about talking, fear that the group really cannot help anyone, anger at the leader for not being a good therapist (and helping the help-rejecting complainer), empathy with other members, boredom, pressure to bring up one's own problem. This expression must be supported.

Stage 21: Leader Encourages the Expression of Emotion

No matter how negative the verbally expressed emotion may be for the leader, he or she must support its expression. Members must learn that the group is a safe place to say even difficult things. The leader's encouragement of the discussion of affect is crucial for the development of group trust and cohesion, two central components of the therapeutic outcome of the group process.

At this point the final major group norm is established: the *open honest expression of feelings*. To review, the three major group norms which members must learn to incorporate are:

1. A focus on here and now.
2. A focus on feelings.
3. An open expression of feelings.

This marks the end of Phase II. Members now know what it takes to be a group member. They still need to practice these skills and to try them out for comfort and value, but by this stage in the group process all the information as to what's expected of members is available. Phase III, the therapeutic phase, and Phase IV, termination, are presented in the next chapter.

Readers should recognize that each of the stages is depicted as if it occurs distinctly in the actual group process. A text must present them this way for descriptive purposes. In the real-life group situation, however, the movement from stage to stage is less clear-cut. Often stages need to be repeated, and the fact that a group is working on Stage 11 during a given session is no guarantee that it will begin the next session at Stage 11 or 12. Indeed, it may "regress" to Stage 9 or 10. Furthermore, some members may persist in behaviors customary at earlier stages through subsequent stages. In short, the distinctions between stages are often more clear on paper than in the actual group.

Chapter 5

The Process of
a Typical Group:
Part 2

The leader's work during the therapeutic and termination phases will determine whether the group is to serve any function besides entertainment and time consumption. In a sense, the differentiation between the professional and the paraprofessional leader can be made on the basis of her or his activity within these time frames. The differences between *competent professional* group leaders and nonprofessional dabblers are spelled out in greater detail in Chapters 6 and 7. It is important to note, however, that the extent to which group leaders are effective is determined by their therapeutic abilities in producing insight and behavior change.

Much has been written about the "instant intimacy" of the here-and-now group. Such intimacy has certain therapeutic as well as entertainment values, but it is only the means to an end if the group is truly designed for relatively permanent behavior change. The professional therapist understands that group members must be ready to learn before they can learn. Thus many hours of the group sessions are spent in preparation of members for the therapy which is to follow. At the conclusion of Chapter 4 we noted the members' readiness for the *therapy* portions of group therapy once they have learned the group norms and have begun to operate within the purview of these norms. In short, once the group members are comfortable in sharing feelings in the here and now they are prepared to learn how to change those behaviors that they find maladaptive.

As will be clear in the following process analysis, learning in group therapy occurs just as it does in all other settings. It is essential for the group leader to provide an environment wherein members may safely *experiment* with new behavior and learn by trial and error through receiving *immediate reinforcement* for desired behaviors. It is similarly crucial that members have opportunities to learn vicariously through the behavior of others via *imitation* or *modeling*. Provision must also be made for members' *expectancies* to be explored and tested under conditions in which *honest feedback* is assured.

In the description of the group process to follow, notice how group members participate in each others' problem solving and in giving and receiving reinforcement. Under these circumstances, learning is enhanced both in amount and in speed of acquisition. The group's reputation as a "psychological pressure cooker"—a place where behavior change can occur more rapidly than in normal social situations, with less loss of energy—is well earned.

PHASE III: Therapeutic Intervention

Stage 22: Norms Are Solidified

In Stage 22 of the group, members become involved in the expression and interchange of feelings about themselves and one another. They use the theoretical language system of the leaders more consistently and focus on the here-and-now process of the group. They expose more of their deeper feelings and experiment with them, with one another, and with the leaders. Members abide by the group rules more and more, eventually incorporating items into a common language and becoming, for the most part, unaware of the uniqueness of these forms of communication. An example of this type of communication is:

Janice: Bill, I sense that something is bothering you.
Bill: What makes you say that?
Janice: Well, I guess I'm picking up on your nonverbals.
Andy: Yeah, I've noticed you kind of moving around a lot and looking uncomfortable, especially when Sally was talking.
LINDA (LEADER 1): What are you experiencing, Bill?
Bill: Well, it's like everyone is ganging up on me and trying to get me on the hot seat.
LINDA: And you're feeling?
Bill: I'm not ready to be on the spot.
Janice: You are uncomfortable about something, but you want to bring it up at your own speed.
Bill: Yeah. Is that OK? (directed to male co-leader who has not yet spoken).

KEVIN (LEADER 2):   It's OK with me for you to wait, but I do hope you'll feel free to share it when it's important to you.

Note the use of the group language in this example and the focus on the here-and-now group feelings. While these words may sound stiff and stilted, their use predisposes the group to discuss feelings as the content of subsequent discussion.

Stage 23: Multiple Roles of Leadership

While members are practicing these group norms, the leader has several roles. He or she must act as a catalyst, cajoling and igniting expressions of feelings. He must also be a major source of reinforcement and support for members as they express their here-and-now feelings. To some extent, the leader serves as a model of appropriate behaviors.

It is also the leader's job to orchestrate the group. In this role, the leader encourages and controls the relative give and take among members, attempting to bring the needs of one member into coordination with the resources of other members. The multiple roles of leadership are extensively examined in the next chapter.

Stage 24: Intensity Increases

As the group becomes more comfortable with the use of the specialized language and topics of group discussion, members expose more and more of the normally hidden parts of their personality. In return they receive acceptance and caring from the leader and fellow members. In this way group trust and cohesion are enhanced, and members feel safer in exposing progressively deeper components of themselves.

With the increase in the depth of the discussion comes a contiguous increase in the frequency and intensity of emotion expressed. Members begin describing a multitude of life events and their reactions to them. Often such descriptions are extremely affect laden. Under the encouragement of the leader, and to some extent the other members, individuals are urged to describe emotionally charged events in detail and to share their present affect regarding these events. As members express these feelings, intensity increases, and frequently they begin to display behavioral concomitants of these high levels of arousal. Anger is expressed in amplified tones of voice and yelling, hurt is accompanied with signs of sadness such as tears, and fear can be seen with trembling lips, shaking, and "frightened" glances.

For the most part, the leader and other group members will support the expressers in displaying their affect in this way. This support naturally engenders further expressions along these lines. It is during these emotional manifestations that the leader employs a multitude of therapeutic skills.

It is important to note that as levels of emotional expression intensify, other group members often become frightened. It is imperative that the group therapist support these members and give them permission to express this fear and, at the same time, support the continuing display of high levels of affect. Each group has limits of allowable levels of intensity. The group leader must be aware of these limits and keep the level of arousal within them. The leader wants to allow for enough anxiety for optimal learning, but not so much as to cause disruption of such learning. Thus in some groups dramatic displays of high levels of affect are acceptable, whereas in other groups, a more quiet, subdued acknowledgment of shared feelings is appropriate to foster the same amounts of learning.

So far, the discussion has concerned the typical group, where levels of affect must be *increased*. There are certain therapy groups wherein the group leader must operate in diametrically opposite ways. In such groups as "acting-out" patients, teenagers adjudged "delinquent," or inmates in prisons, learning frequently can occur only if the level of affect is substantially *decreased*. In a recent group of violent prison inmates, I spent several sessions teaching group members how to respond at lower levels of aggression. In this group, each time the intensity of emotional expression began to increase, a mediating response was interposed. Members were encouraged to discriminate between several levels of anger and to respond to them differently. In addition, they were instructed to attend to the consequences of their actions before expressing these feelings physically, as opposed to behaving spontaneously and living with the subsequent reactions. In this group of inmates, the level of affect displayed was controlled just as it is in most groups. The major difference was that encouragement was given for *lower* levels of expression.

The important point is for the group leader to manipulate the group to operate within meaningful levels of arousal. Levels of intensity which allow members to be uncomfortable with their own current functioning and open to learning new behaviors must be determined by the psychological characteristics of the membership, as well as leadership style and abilities. It is only within these limits that therapy occurs.

Stage 25: Leader Employs Therapeutic Skills

Each accomplished group therapist has a variety of skills, techniques, and manipulations designed to assist group members in changing behaviors and attitudes. Whatever their theoretical background, psychotherapists have two aligned goals: insight and behavior change. Most therapeutic endeavors involve (1) discussion of problems and feelings, (2) reconstruction of the problems in some viable theoretical framework, (3) exploration of possible solutions, (4) attempts at new solutions or conflict resolution, (5) feedback on the attempts, (6) incorporation of new behaviors into the entire repertoire of the individual, (7) refinement, and (8) adjustments to back-home solutions. The therapists' tools in accomplishing these are predominantly verbal. Therapists listen, summarize, analyze, provide feedback, make commitments and contracts, offer suggestions, and provide support.

During this stage of the group, many individual therapy skills are utilized. Role playing, role reversals, psychodrama, focusing, sensory awareness exercises, desensitization, guided fantasy, and a thousand and one related techniques are employed, dependent on the individual members' receptivity and the therapist's armanentarium of techniques. Individual, depth psychotherapy techniques are also employed, suggestions are made, information or analysis is provided, hypnosis or other one-to-one work is done in front of the group, and so on.

In all these therapeutic endeavors, perhaps the most important element is *timing*. As with every other professional skill, sequence and timing play a major role. Many of us have watched a baseball player with a "picturebook" swing—when he swings a bat it looks ideal. However, if he cannot apply this ideal swing at the precise moment the ball crosses the plate, he is destined to a minor league career—or having his picture taken. So it is for therapists; the best planned, most elaborate intervention can be valueless unless the members are ready to receive it. One of the most common mistakes made by novice therapists is to verbalize an analysis or understanding of the group process prematurely. Since group leaders are focusing on group process and most of the members are not, the leaders are likely to comprehend process much earlier than the members. If they go ahead and blurt out what they see, members will honestly not understand what the therapists are addressing and will reject it, or they will simply appear not to have heard it at all. It is imperative that the therapist wait with an interpretation until the group is emotionally and cognitively prepared to hear it. Those "off the wall" dramatic interpretations that seem to work so well in movies about therapy are much less likely to be effective in a real-life group.

The multiple roles and skills of group leadership and a model of requisite training for group leaders are discussed in detail in Chapters 6 and 7.

To discuss Stages 24 and 25 as we have the other stages may be somewhat misleading. While they represent only two points in the process, they typically last longer than all the others. In an effective long-term group, fully 40 percent of the entire group time will be consumed during this part of the therapeutic phase.

In the course of Stages 24 and 25 most members verbally participate in the group activity. These members will ask for and offer help, aid, and assistance. They will form close emotional ties with the other members and develop the levels of trust and cohesion that lead to a real sense of intimacy. Such intimacy enhances subsequent behavior change.

Stage 26: Minority Members Identified

As the members grow closer, it becomes clear that some members have not participated verbally in the group. They are identified by the other members or the leader and a request is made for their participation.

Most leaders allow the group members to recognize these minority members before offering them an opportunity to get verbally involved in the group. This is done because there is generally less threat in an invitation from fellow members than in a request from the leader. It is generally assumed that these heretofore nonparticipatory members have remained on the fringe of the group out of fears associated with being more involved. A request for participation on the part of the leader could aggravate the fear and make it *more difficult* for members to enter. An important exception to this suggestion is related to the time left in the group. If time remaining is short, the leader must recognize these minority members and request their feelings.

Stage 27: Discussion of Inclusion/Exclusion

The majority group members discuss and analyze the nonparticipation of these minority members and the effects of such nonparticipation on them. A typical discussion follows:

Fred: Hey, you know Rita, Gayle, and Herb haven't said anything in weeks. I wonder if you're bored or something.

Herb: I'm not bored.

Sheila: I think it's cultural, you know, I mean. . . . Rita and Gayle are Oriental and I think they tend to be more reserved (said smilingly and caringly at Rita and Gayle, who are sitting together).

Gayle: I think that's true, nobody in my family talks much. But Rita and I talk outside. I just don't have anything to say.

Fred: Well, I think it's unfair, I unloaded all my shit and you know me, but I just don't know you at all.

OLAF (LEADER 1): Sounds like it's important for *you* to have them talk more.

Fred: Yeah, damn right. I've talked about some pretty deep stuff and I don't know if I can trust them.

MAVIS (LEADER 2): Tell them.

Fred: I don't trust any of you (looking directly at Herb).

OLAF: What would you like from Herb?

Fred: I want him . . .

MAVIS: (interrupting): Tell him.

Fred: I want you (to Herb) to stop judging me and putting me down in your mind.

Herb: I'm not judging you.

Sandra: Well, I feel judged too, it's like I say something and you just look at me and I think it's disapproval.

MAVIS: Herb, what are you feeling now?

This dialogue will continue for some time now, but its course will be altered slightly. Not only must the feelings of Fred and Sandra be attended to, but it is also necessary to consider the feelings of Herb, Gayle, and Rita. Hence the group leaders must deal with:

1. Inclusion of the three members.
2. Fear of participation of the three.
3. Needs for approval of at least two of the previously participating members.
4. Acceptance of alternative styles of communication.
5. Feelings of anger at having been lumped into an "Orientals don't talk much" category, instead of having one's current silent behavior accepted.
6. Leaders' own feelings of inadequacy and need to have every member have a positive experience in the group.

During this stage an invitation is extended to the minority members to enter or withdraw.

Stage 28: Minority Members Make Their Decision

The minority members will enter the group as verbal participants; negotiate with the group for their inclusion, albeit as quiet members; attack the members; withdraw from the group altogether; or remain nonverbal.

A member may enter the group verbally in a variety of ways. In one classic example of this, a woman member was asked why she was so quiet. She replied, "Nobody asked me anything." Another member asked her, "Is there anything you'd like to share with us?" Her reply was (Example 1):

> Well, yes, I have so much to share. I don't know where to start . . .
> I guess the biggest thing is that I'm deathly afraid this group will
> end . . . It's the most important thing in my life . . . you're the only
> people I've allowed myself to care for since my husband died
> nine months ago.

At this point her eyes became moist and she found it difficult to continue talking. But, with group support, she was center stage in the group for almost two hours.

An example of negotiation occurred in the same group. Almost as soon as the previous piece of process was terminated, another "quiet" member said (Example 2):

> I also feel the group is important, but I feel very uncomfortable
> sharing things when they're happening . . . always been intro-
> spective. I'm not bored at all. I feel like I've been emotionally
> involved each minute . . . like when Joe talked about the operation
> and losing his arm, I just put myself in his place and imagined the
> pain and fear and felt incomplete and ugly, and when Marie
> talked about the mess with her husband, I just knew I had to go
> home and talk to my husband. We had a good talk, but I don't
> know what's gonna happen to us. Oh, when Joanie talked about
> having an affair, I felt all the excitement and all the guilt. It's just
> hard for me to just open up, but I really feel a part of this group.

If minority members choose to attack, several avenues are open: defensive protestations of how many things they did say; distraction techniques, such as "Well, I'd *really* like to know what's going on with Pete"; or confrontation. One extraordinary event occurred in a group of mental health professionals. A person who had a master's degree and ten years' experience with counseling and casework responded to a request for his participation like this (Example 3):

> Damn right, I haven't said anything. I thought this was a high-level
> group and you people have all been acting like freaks or patients.
> Jesus, you all have problems and share things like feelings that are
> best kept to oneself. You're a bunch of sickies. I don't want to
> associate with you and surely wouldn't tell you a thing about me.
> I mean, how could you help me, I'm much healthier than all of
> you.

Then addressing one of the leaders, he continued:

> I'm really surprised at you for letting this go on. A competent
> leader wouldn't allow a member to be attacked like I have been.
> I'd leave now if I didn't have to show on my time sheet that I'd
> been here.

Ultimately this individual withdrew from the group and from the mental
health field. The group experience allowed him to feel so different
from other therapists that he was able to get into a different and more
appropriate profession.

Members may also simply state that they feel that the request for
their verbal participation is too much to ask and that they wish to
withdraw, and may do so. Other members may not respond verbally to
the request and may simply remain silent.

Stage 29: The Group Reacts

If the minority group members become verbal and do join in, as in
the first example above, they are invariably accepted into full membership and receive a great deal of support from the other members. If,
however, they reject the group and want to withdraw, the group may
elect to allow them to withdraw or request that they stay. If the member
attacks (Example 3), the group may choose to fight, allow the person
entry into the group, or ostracize the attacker and not allow his inclusion. If the member negotiates (Example 2), the group will negotiate
also. It may allow the member to stay quiet but ask him to try to
express more for the sake of other members, or make a deal that he
need not talk unless asked a specific question, in which case he will
try to respond. In situations where the nonverbal member is *emotionally*
tuned into the group, as in Example 2, the likelihood is high that total
acceptance will ensue. However, if the nonverbal negotiating member
is emotionally as well as verbally out of touch with the other group
members, rejection has a higher probability.

In any case, no matter what decisions the group makes, the leaders
must deal with the plethora of emotions released at this time. Such
feelings as insecurity, belongingness, loneliness, communion, paranoia,
fear, and anger all emerge; members must recognize and work on these
feelings until they reach some understanding and resolution. The inclusion issue is the last major stumbling block to the therapeutic
group process. Once these conflicts are resolved, the group can turn
its attention freely to any personal or nonpersonal problem and work
toward solutions.

Stage 30: Problem-Solving Orientation Practiced

Once the issue of who is in the group and who is out is resolved, strong feelings of communality emerge and are shared. Members of the group have had to struggle together and face a great deal of adversity. As a result of this common struggle, they have become very close. They have shared more intimate parts of themselves than they normally do and hence have a deep sense of trust in the other members.

It is within this context that problem solving in both intrapsychic and interpersonal areas can be accomplished effectively. At this time, real, present, meaningful concerns are shared and dealt with by the group. Because the level of interpersonal trust is so high, help is not rejected, as it was earlier in the group, but is actively sought. Members frequently attempt to solve problems together and confront each other honestly and with caring. Interpersonal conflicts between members of the group are discussed with greater understanding of each person's position and concerns.

In short, this is the stage of the group that members hoped for when they entered. This is also the stage at which the leaders (in encounter-type groups only) can be participants to some extent and can share some of their own conflicts without concern for their leader role. Indeed, at this point in an effective encounter group, members can comfortably facilitate the learning of the leaders.

This is also the stage of the therapeutic group process that is so rudely cut off by termination.

PHASE IV: Termination

Unlike all of the preceding phases, *termination is an unnatural occurrence*. Whereas up to this time entry into each succeeding stage was determined by completion of the previous one, termination is determined by a separate criterion. The length of the group was set before the group ever began, and the group must end at the appointed time. Very often, this timing is intrusive and inconvenient and clearly insensitive to the stage of group process.

Termination of a group, however, is not simply acknowledgment of the end of allotted time. Termination of the group is certainly equal in importance to screening or therapeutic skill. It is during termination that the crucial process of *transfer of training* must occur.

Of all the skills group leaders must possess, none are more important than those that assist members to transfer the group learning to their back-home situation. It is my belief, based on years of clinical observation, that this is generally the part of group therapy that leaders do most poorly. There are several reasons for this, but the most important are:

1. The leaders' own resistance to terminating.
2. The leaders' own needs for reassurance.
3. A lack of training in closing.

The third point requires special attention. No one would respect a plumber who could clear a clogged drain but could not reconnect the pipes; a mechanic who could take an automobile engine apart but could not put it back together; or a surgeon who could open up a patient but could not close the wound: "The operation was a success but the patient died" is simply not acceptable. Each of these individuals performs at a level below our threshold for tolerance. Yet we tolerate the analogous situation in group therapists. In most graduate programs, such training stress is placed on opening skills that students finish their training before they learn how to engage in those most critical skills, closing or transfer of training.

Stage 31: Leader Announces Imminent End of Group Time

Termination officially begins when the leader verbally announces the number of hours left in the group. This announcement should be made when approximately 25 to 30 percent of the group time remains. The first announcement typically is made at the beginning of a session (or at an appropriate gap in a marathon) and goes essentially like this: "I think it's important for us to keep in mind that we only have three more sessions to go after tonight."

This first announcement rarely has a noticeable effect on the group members; indeed, it seems to pass by almost totally unheard. The second such announcement may have only a slightly greater impact. This second notice of the imminent termination is accompanied by a request for members to bring up any unfinished business.

While the immediate impact of the leader's announcement is not readily visible, members do respond to it after a short period of time. Normally, one member begins to talk about a concern with or fear of the group ending, and not having enough time to deal with all the problems he wishes to discuss. This allows the leader to encourage members to begin working on the termination process.

Stage 32: Invitation to Work

Once members discuss their feelings about the group ending, the leader invites them to bring up and share any unfinished business or problems. Members who have heretofore been reticent to discuss their own concerns and who have spent most of their group time "therapizing" others often take the leader up on this invitation. This is probably due to some pressure from the other members.

Two forms of unfinished business are frequently discussed at this time: problems which members have in their outside-of-group lives, and problems between members of the group which are still unresolved. One member in a recent group chose this time to talk about his homosexuality and his fears that other members would have treated him differently throughout the group had they known earlier. In the same group, two of the women worked on their seemingly interminable competition with one another.

Like many of the other stages, this one can be quite time-consuming.

Stage 33: A Trust Boost

At Stage 33 of the group, it would be expected that trust between members would be high, and it is. However, if members are to navigate through the straits of transfer of training and departure, the highest levels of trust and cohesion are required.

There are several ways to ensure this. Two of the most straightforward have worked best for me. The first is pointing out to the group that the last few hours will be hard on everyone, and each person will need a great deal of support. This is followed by a request that members be therapists for each other. This has the advantage that the role of therapist is substantially ego building.

The "world's greatest technique" is the second approach. This modestly named technique, discussed in Chapter 8 in detail, is a straightforward exercise in which members are asked to share something with the group that they have not yet shared: "Something that is important to you in your life, but which you've had no reason to bring up here as yet." Major advantages of this technique are that it allows members to present a fuller picture of themselves and helps them coordinate their lives outside of the group and their behavior inside the group.

No matter which trust- and cohesion-building methods are employed, the members need to be prepared to bring their group learning back home.

Stage 34: Transfer of Training

A competent group leader has consistently stressed that members make a connection between the group and their outside environments throughout the group sessions. Whenever members have dealt with any complex issue, the leaders have requested that members attempt the group-engendered recommendations in their back-home environment. Consistent inferences are made of how group learning can be tried out in real-life situations. It is during this late group stage, however, that the leaders must require each member to make direct connections between the group work and the home environment.

Each individual group member is requested to provide answers to these four questions:

1. What have you learned new in this group?
2. What else? (sometimes repeated several times)
3. What will you now do with this new knowledge?
4. How will you do it specifically?

Some typical answers have included the following content:

> Well, I guess what I've learned is how I control other people by my sickness . . . it's hard and . . . you know . . . scary . . . but I realize that I've been acting crazy for so long, I'm not sure I can act any other way. I guess I know that my wife likes it when I act this way—that also seems weird. What am I going to do?. Well, I want to try to make it not crazy . . . me and my wife need to go into the therapy. I also need to stop screwing up on the job. I know when I'm gonna act crazy . . . I can just keep off my job on those days. It's OK 'cause it only happens on full and new moons—so two days a month sick leave . . . ha, ha (group joins in this joke). I think I can make it especially if we see Dr. —————.

This familiar response came from a military officer:

> You know what I've learned here? It's easy . . . being right all the time isn't all it's cracked up to be. I've spent my whole life believing that if I was right everything would be so perfect, so I did it . . . top of my class, service academy, two master's degrees . . . beautiful wife. What I learned here is how lonely I am and what I'll do is be more damn human and less a fuckin' computer. Maybe my kids will even stop viewing me as a mountain or something. I've never felt as good as I have in here . . . it's like I've got a new lease on life. I plan to go home, get my wife, and take off to this place I know . . . no, wait . . . I'll just tell her I miss and love her and let her decide what we'll do (group applauds).

The therapist asks, "What else?"

> I've got to let the troops in my shop do more. They all rely on
> me, and that's fine for me, 'cause I do the job best. But it really
> doesn't do much for their initiative . . . they really are good. I
> don't need to be the golden boy all the time.

Not all such reports are so positive, and sometimes much therapeutic
work is necessary to help the members make the transfer. The following
example is presented verbatim from a tape of a group of middle
managers of a large engineering firm. The client, Patrick, is 42 years old
and has been with the firm for almost 15 years. He is a good-looking,
sturdy individual who could easily pass for a man in his middle thirties.
He has a friendly smile, but during the group many other members
said that often when he smiled he looked angry.

GARY (LEADER 1): Patrick, what have you learned new in the
group?

Pat: Well, I guess I finally learned how to deal with problems
openly and honestly.

GARY: How do you mean?

Pat: Well, when problems come up, I'm going to be careful to pay
attention to my feelings now.

GARY: How will you do that?

Pat: Well, like I really need to talk to my boss.

GARY: For example?

Pat: Well, I think the shop could really run better with a few
alterations.

Joe: Like what?

Pat: Well, lots of things, I don't know, just I want to talk to him,
get some things off my chest.

CAROLINE (LEADER 2): Pat, let's role play it. Who here could
play your boss?

Pat: Charley.

CAROLINE: OK, Charley, will you?

Charley: Sure.

GARY: Pat, set the stage. When? Where? How?

Pat: Oh, I don't know.

CAROLINE: Try!

Pat: OK, Monday morning as soon as he comes in, I'm going to go
up to his office and tell him I need to talk.

CAROLINE: Tell your boss (gesturing toward Charley).

Pat: Sam (that's his name), you know we've worked together for 12 years now and until this weekend I never admitted to myself how you've really fucked up this company. I mean I'm so pissed at you . . . you really were an asshole about that _____ matter.

This speech went on for almost four minutes. As soon as it terminated, Charley looked up and said, "Patrick, you're fired." Patrick looked as if he'd been punched in the stomach. He was speechless, hurt, and confused, but he admitted that Charley had played the boss's role accurately. He kept saying how different it was in the group.

The therapy that followed actually took almost two full hours. During this time Patrick and Charley did eleven "takes" of the role playing until Patrick had a problem solution that the members agreed would work. The final decision was for Patrick to see his boss over their regular coffee later in the week and talk about his ideas for changes, without criticizing or calling Sam's parentage into question. We can add that this solution worked so well that Patrick is now Sam's partner in their own spin-off business. Had the group leader not pressed Patrick to reveal and try out his plan, the result could have been substantially negative.

So it is with all groups. Unless transfer of training is carefully and seriously administered, much of the total effectiveness of the group will be mitigated. Transfer thus is of great import in augmenting the positive effects in the group and in preventing casualties.

Stage 35: Good and Welfare

After each member has worked on the issue of his or her own personal use of the group experience, members and leaders often share their overall impressions of the group. Frequently valuable positive feedback is shared and feelings about ending the group are explored. Often the leaders share many of their own feelings and observations. This stage is often tearful and sensitive; it prepares the group for the leaders' final speech.

Stage 36: Leader's Closing

During the closing speech, the leader needs to accomplish two major goals: to give each member adequate feedback from the leader's point of view, and to provide a referral source. While many leaders tend to keep their closing remarks short, I and my colleagues have devised a system of providing evaluative feedback to each member of the group regarding his or her relative strengths and weaknesses with reference to the issues discussed in the group. One part of such a statement could be:

> Jeanie, I see you as a remarkably competent young woman with a great deal of strengths to work yourself through this divorce decision you've made. I think also that there's a danger of your finding another man to replace Len as a way of not testing those strengths.

The leader also owes it to his members to deal with issues which are kicked up by the group but which hibernate and come into fruition only after members have left the group setting. This does not mean that the leader has to do follow-up therapy with each member. It is important, however, for the leader to be available for consultation and referral, at least for issues that are group engendered. After completing over 200 groups, I have found that such an offer is not abused by group members.

This offer of follow-up, however, usually is not made by encounter group leaders. Nevertheless, such an offer is not very time-consuming, and it is ethically essential. It can go a long way in helping to prevent group casualties.

When the consultation is offered, the group session officially terminates, frequently with some physical contact such as hugging or holding hands.

Stage 37: Aloha

After termination, members tend to linger and extend nostalgic alohas, often sharing phone numbers and making plans to get together. It is not unusual for members to get together without the leader after the group terminates. I recall a couples group I led in 1969–70.

> We met on Tuesday nights from 7 to 10. There were four couples in the group, three of whom really wanted to stay together. The group ended in April 1970, and to this day those three couples still get together every Tuesday night. They formed a mixed doubles bowling team in a local league . . . done well, too—last Christmas (1975), they sent me a picture of the four trophies they had won last year. They not only got their relationships together, but they developed a workable mutual support system that goes far beyond any therapy (Shapiro, 1976).

The entire group process is an arduous journey, but a group that makes it all the way can reap a bountiful harvest for its members (and leaders). Every group does not make the entire journey, however. Often a group will have progressed through only half of the stages before termination must begin. Such a group can be of value in and of itself, and members can accrue a number of benefits. The phases discussed above comprise a reachable goal, not a bare minimum. The goal pertains exclusively to *closed* groups, however. Groups with open membership rarely progress past Phases I and II unless the membership is stable over an extended time. This is because as each new member is added to the group, Phases I and II are reinstituted for their benefit.

Chapter 6

The Group Therapist

Of the multitude of variables operating in a group therapy situation, leadership effectiveness is probably the most crucial. An inept leader can be harmful, as well as ineffective. Competent leadership involves mastery of a wide variety of skills and functions. This chapter investigates three major areas related to leadership: types of leadership, multiple leader roles, and leader functions. Ethics, training, and leadership skills are discussed in the following chapter.

Group therapists vary widely along several dimensions, including training and background, personality, conceptions of their roles, and aims and intentions. Some are well trained in group techniques, but these are in a minority. Most individuals who practice group therapy have been trained in cognate areas, such as medicine, nursing, psychology, education, public health, drug abuse, or social work. Some may have had considerable relevant training but very little experience in dealing with groups. Some group therapists have retiring personalities and are mild and gentle, while others are forceful and aggressive. Some have well-defined philosophies which their group work supports and emphasizes, but others take a pragmatic, mechanistic approach and are concerned with "improvement of personality" or "relief from symptoms," or perhaps with "amelioration of behavior." Some see themselves primarily as teachers who have something to contribute to the group members but should be relatively passive auditors and spectators. Others see themselves as clarifiers or analyzers, and still others see themselves as enablers or catalysts who help other people to find themselves. Some group therapists take a very modest view of their efforts and hope only to assist people in limited ways, while others take the grander view that they can reconstruct the entire personality. It has been persuasively argued that there are as many types of group therapy as there are group therapists.

Who is a group therapist? Anyone who is doing therapeutic group work? Or can only people within certain professions be so labeled? From a legal point of view, most states restrict the use of the terms *psychotherapy* and *group psychotherapy* to people with M.D.s. Often Ph.D.s, and occasionally M.S.W. credentials, are required. However, none of the 50 United States or the Canadian provinces restricts the use of such terms as *training group, T group, encounter group, sensitivity group.* There is no regulation of "educators" engaging in "group education" or "encounter classes." This frequently leads to paradoxical and ridiculous situations. Three years ago, in the state of Hawaii, an individual with a Ph.D. in clinical psychology and specific training in group work was legally held back from engaging in any group work until he had passed a licensing exam (which contained no questions on group psychotherapy). During the same period, a local proctologist with no group training was *legally* conducting sensitivity therapy groups, several ministers were conducting encounter groups, and untold numbers of educators, nonprofessionals, and recent group participants were leading groups without fear of legal consequences.

No evidence exists to indicate that members of any particular profession are superior group therapists. There is no evidence that psychiatrists can do better than teachers, nurses better than public health experts, psychologists better than counselors, or social workers better than sociologists. Spotnitz (1952), a psychiatrist, says that "A gifted lay individual psychologist or social worker may do much better work with certain groups than a physician who may lack intuitive understanding of the individual in the group or of group dynamics."

In training group therapists in all of the helping professions, I have found that some individuals who are otherwise well trained do not have either the interest or the capacity to do this work, while others take to group therapy naturally and eagerly. Handling therapeutic groups requires not only interest and technical knowledge but also direct experience in dealing with common, difficult interpersonal situations. Such experience can best be acquired by supervised practice. Corsini (1957) recalls an elderly psychiatrist who took a position in an institution and who was pressed into doing group therapy. He was observed lecturing to his semi-illiterate audience on brain pathology in the belief that this was group psychotherapy.

To some practitioners, group psychotherapy, with its multiple interrelationships, transferences, and fast-paced action, may seem chaotic.

To others, its attributes—speed, lack of protracted periods of relative inactivity, opportunities to work with several people simultaneously, patients' access to vicarious learning and general stimulation—are far less demanding than the patience and persistence required in individual psychotherapy.

For the most part, professionals will select those endeavors in which they are likely to be successful. However, the tremendous increase in popularity of encounter methodologies in the 1960s encouraged the appearance of thousands of untrained, self-styled group leaders. Often these self-proclaimed "gurus" lead dramatic, exciting, high-casualty groups.

One of the most dangerous components of the encounter methodologies is that they provide any "leader" with a set of materials which can be used to open up a group member incisively, but no corresponding closing skills. It is becoming clear to most professionals that some regulation is necessary. As early as 1955, Hadden argued that too many unqualified people were entering the field of group therapy. Cooper and Mangham (1971), Dreyfus and Kremenliev (1970), Grotjahn (1971b), Lakin (1972), Lieberman, Yalom, and Miles (1973), and Shapiro (1973) have all cautioned that the vast numbers of group leaders may be harmful and have suggested characteristics that constitute competent leadership.

The following discussion of the roles, functions, skills, ethics, and training necessary for effective group leadership is designed to provide guidelines for readers in evaluating their own abilities and those of others.

TYPES OF LEADERSHIP

There seem to be as many methods of group therapy as there are leaders; each leader brings his or her unique skills, personality, beliefs, and values to the group. Similarly, each co-leader team is unique in its approach to each set of group members. For this reason, any classification system will do injustice to individual group therapists. However, in order to investigate and compare the types of leadership, it is necessary to cluster leaders in some way. We have chosen two dimensions: theory of group psychotherapy, and leadership focus.

The theories of group psychotherapy were presented in Chapter 3, "Major Theoretical Orientations," and will not be examined here. Most group leaders proclaim themselves to be representatives of one of the following psychotherapeutic approaches: psychoanalytic, nondirective-Rogerian, gestalt, Adlerian, rational-emotive, psychodrama, existential, behavioral, Sullivanian, eclectic, encounter, transactional analysis, or self-help. Each of these methods approaches the group process from a more or less different perspective. Each provides a means for data collection and interpretation, focuses the leaders' attention on specific issues, and provides guidelines for behavior change. Since each theory considers different behaviors to be critical, leaders' behavior will be substantially different depending on their particular allegiance.

Not only are there great differences in therapist behavior in the different theories, but individual variations within a given method can be substantial. Thus, simply knowing that someone is "a gestalt therapist" does not mean that person's approach is identical with that of the late Fritz Perls. Students in the process of developing their own preferences among theories should be warned that being a Rogerian does not make them the therapeutic equivalent of Carl Rogers. Individual differences are still the meat of psychological investigation, and ultimately each group member must be dealt with uniquely. The therapist's theory provides, in a sense, eyeglasses through which an apparently chaotic group process can be viewed systematically, understood, and acted on strategically.

LEADERSHIP FOCUS: A CONTINUUM FOR COMPARISON

One dimension we have found useful in examining differences between group therapists is that of leadership orientation. As shown in Figure 6-1, the two poles of this dimension are the interpersonal and the intrapersonal or intrapsychic orientations. As with any continuum, the two ends represent extreme, low-frequency values. Individual leaders can be viewed in regard to their positions on the continuum, and their therapeutic effectiveness can be explored with this orientation in mind.

An intrapersonal or intrapsychic leader is generally more inclined toward a classic psychotherapeutic use of groups and demonstrates several behaviors that are substantially different from the interpersonal leader. The *strict intrapersonal leader,* for example, deals with individual members of the group in a *one-to-one* fashion. His or her techniques are designed to *isolate the individual.* The group itself is seen as a stimulus situation within which *the individual* can be studied. Success in such a group is measured by the *relationship of a member to himself,* i.e., balance of cognitive, sensory and perceptual systems; id, ego, and superego coordination; Parent, Adult, and Child working interdependently, and so on. A major *focus* of the group is *on the barriers* or defenses of an individual which prevent full expression. Techniques are thus designed to eliminate personal barriers and allow full expression. The leader's role approaches that of a therapist. He is often active and directive and frequently studies *unconscious determinants*

FIGURE 6–1: Leadership Focus Continuum

Extreme
Intrapsychic

Moderate Use of Both

Extreme
Interpersonal

INTRAPSYCHIC INTRAPERSONAL

Leaders dealing with individual members.
Group as stimulus situation to investigate individual.
Techniques isolate individual.
Source of therapeutic goals is therapist.
Historical focus.
Within-individual focus.
Leader ⟶ Therapist.
Unconscious determinants of behavior.
Success = Individual's relationship with self.

INTERPERSONAL

Leaders deal with interactions between members.
Group as situation to investigate interactions.
Techniques isolate interactions.
Source of therapeutic goals is members.
Here-and-now focus.
Between-people focus.
Leader ⟶ Members.
Conscious determinants of behavior.
Success = Individual's relationship with other people.

of behavior. This leader regularly employs an historical orientation. Such terms as *catharsis* and *working through* a relationship with the leader apply to this style of leadership. Classic analytic, Adlerian, and gestalt-oriented leaders can most often be described by this side of the continuum.

The *strict interpersonal leader* deals with *relationships between members.* His techniques are designed to *isolate interactions* between members. Rather than studying the individual, the group is seen as an unique stimulus situation within which interactions between members can be investigated. Success in such a group is measured by the *relationship of members to one another.* A major focus in the group is on the *between-people* barriers which prevent full interpersonal interaction, and techniques are designed to bring group members together. The leader's role approaches that of an orchestrator. He is often active but generally nondirective. There is a *here-and-now* rather than historical focus, and, in general, between-member rather than within-member variables are customarily stressed. Success is often measured by the ability of the group to exist "without a leader." The center of attention is thus the *group,* not the individual.

Examination of the behavior of successful leaders makes it readily apparent that they typically perform *both* interpersonal and intrapersonal behaviors in their groups. In general, however, the research suggests that there are some definite advantages in a group conducted by a leader who falls on the interpersonal side of the continuum.

What People Learn in Groups

Before comparing the interpersonal and intrapersonal styles, however, we would do well to examine exactly what it is that people learn in groups. What behaviors do change? What are the expectations for "a successful" graduate of group training?

At first, members must learn a new language system, a new way of looking at themselves and others, and a new set of rules or group ethics. Behaviors that make for good group membership are frequently quite different from those that provide back-home success. In addition, members must learn how to deal effectively with stress situations such as ambiguity, elimination of status or role behaviors that typically govern interactions, the giving and receiving of honest feedback, and so on. The group in general and the leader specifically create an environment where all this learning can take place.

In the process, members experience anxiety, respond to it in typical ways, and get feedback from others about their anxiety-reducing behaviors. In this way they learn how not to be anxious of their anxiety. They also learn how to reduce anxiety by self-expression and in turn how not to be anxious about self-expression (a response inimical to anxiety).

Other behaviors that can be effectively learned in a group setting include the reduction of fear of loss of control or rejection. Assertiveness skills in dealing with authority figures and increased empathic responsiveness have also been reported (Shapiro, 1970). Members also learn how to be more trusting (Shapiro & Diamond, 1972), how to internalize the contingencies of reinforcement (Diamond & Shapiro, 1973a), and how to live more in the present (Shapiro, 1971). There are also experiences of communality with others, experiences of helping another (altruism) and of being helped, and some serious problem-solving efforts.

Comparing Leaders' Roles and Skills

In order to maximize these gains, each leader must employ a variety of roles and skills. Two of the most critical components in generating the various types of group learning are the therapist's capabilities as a model for appropriate group behavior, and his enhanced power as a dispenser of reinforcements.

Despite protestations to the contrary by many group facilitators, trainers, and leaders, the group leader *does* lead. He plays several roles during the course of a group: catalyst, orchestrator, information disseminator, a model for sharing and communicating, reinforcer and participant (sometimes). Because of the nature of groups, with their ambiguous situation, elimination of typical roles, anxiety, and so on, the therapist's behavior stands out as a beacon and a model of appropriateness in this unique situation. In addition, since the therapist is usually the only person in the room who knows what is expected in this ambiguous situation, his power as a model and reinforcer is greatly enhanced.

In examining leadership orientation with reference to these abilities, it is important to keep in mind that in describing these leadership styles we are describing therapists' orientations which are on the extremes of the continuum. The individual leader's orientation will fall somewhere between the extremes.

In the role of therapist, the intrapersonal leader models behaviors such as getting someone to deal with the divergent aspects of his or her personality, probing, questioning, and interpreting past events, dreams, or unconscious determinants of behavior. These roles are hardly appropriate ones for members to adopt. Even if it were acceptable for members to behave this way in a group, it would be very inappropriate in their back-home situations. In fact, members exhibiting these types of behaviors even *in group* are confronted with that most feared expletive—"playing therapist."

Furthermore, members in a group with a strict intrapersonal or guru-type leader can learn to maximize rather than minimize problems. This is because problem solving occurs for the individual only in conjunction with the presence of a very potent, almost omniscient professional group therapist. This tends to lead the member to believe, via reverse logic, that he really must have been messed up because he needed that level of professional assistance. Indeed, strict intrapersonal leaders tend to make no distinction between therapy and encounter groups; they may see the clientele of encounter groups as suffering from some relatively less severe level of neurotic conflicts. By contrast, help received from a fellow member in the group setting tends to minimize the scope of the problem and helps a person perceive himself as less sick and the problem as more workable.

In addition, when the intrapersonal leader works individually with members, there is a tendency for members to "wait for their turn" to expose "their problem," and this is often a difficult, nonspontaneous, unfruitful, and boring endeavor. When members are encouraged to interact with one another, however, issues emerge spontaneously, without dependence on the leader, and with the full ownership of feelings by members. They have not been pushed into anything they can subsequently dismiss as "the therapist's trip." An additional danger of a leader with a strict intrapersonal approach is the ability to project his own intrapsychic conflicts to the group members and (assuming similarity) help them resolve *their* conflicts.

Furthermore, if the leader is the sole therapeutic agent, he cheats the members out of the altruistic experience of serving as therapeutic agents themselves and denies them an ego-building, self-satisfying, and emotionally growing experience. This also reduces the total amount of sharing members can have within the group, and they will have very low values as reinforcers for one another.

Finally, studies on encounter group casualties (e.g., Lieberman, Yalom, & Miles, 1973) have demonstrated that the intrapersonally oriented, Guru-like, high charismatic leader is the most likely to produce casualties. The guru is impressive and develops many "groupies," proselytizers, and converts to his personal religion, but a more interpersonal approach is more successful and less dangerous for group members.

Like the extreme intrapersonal therapist, the strict interpersonal group therapist also has failings. A leader who functions entirely as an interpersonal process commentator and simply gets people together with one another and then fades totally into the background is a poor model for problem solving, interpersonal interaction, and spontaneity and has a low value as a dispenser of reinforcement.

Therefore, the accomplished, successful leader is able to be either interpersonal and intrapersonal to varying degrees at different times with different members and must be able to distinguish when these times occur. Leaders also serve a group better if they allow members real freedom and control and encourage their interaction and mutual help. The communication patterns of the three leadership styles on the continuum can be represented by the diagrams in Figure 6-2.

A leader who is an accomplished, effective therapist will have an orientation which fits his own personality, beliefs, and values, and whether it leans more toward the interpersonal or intrapsychic is of little import. When the group therapist is ineffective, however, an interpersonal orientation is less dangerous than an intrapsychic one, since the positive strengths of group members are more easily elicited by interpersonal group leaders.

Group therapists can be compared to one another by reference to their leadership orientation, but this is not an absolute scale by any means. Rather it is presented as a means of clustering therapists and making generalizations as to their "fit" with a particular patient group. With young children, severely disturbed individuals, and many institutionalized populations, a more intrapersonal orientation may be necessary. With graduate students, natural groups, and industrial and professional populations, a more interpersonal focus is often more relevant.

Depending on orientation, each leader will fulfill the variety of leadership roles to varying degrees. The intrapersonal leader may put more effort and group time into the catalyst function than into orchestration. An interpersonal leader in an encounter group may actually participate in the group, not unlike a member might, whereas a more intrapersonal leader would not approach membership behaviors except in the rarest circumstances.

THE MULTIPLE ROLES OF GROUP LEADERSHIP

Group leaders generally play five major roles in the course of the group process:

1. Information disseminator.
2. Catalyst.
3. Orchestrator.
4. Model for learning–participant.
5. Dispenser of reinforcement and environment manipulator.

FIGURE 6–2: Patterns of Communication in Groups with Different Leadership Orientations

Strict Intrapsychic Leader

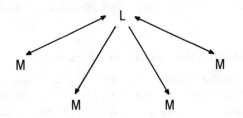

Mixed Interpersonal-intrapersonal Leader

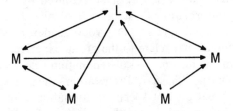

Strict Interpersonal Leader

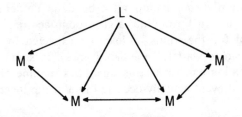

⟶ One-way Communication
⟷ Two-way Communication

L = Leader
M = Member

These roles continue throughout the process, but at certain times during the process the various roles have periods of primacy. The timing for heightened employment of a given role is often a major determinant of group outcomes. Figure 6–3 illustrates how the various leadership roles are coordinated temporally with the group process. The phases and stages of the process are defined and discussed in Chapters 4 and 5.

The Group Leader as a Disseminator of Information

In the most traditional role for leaders of groups, the leader provides information. The therapist is an expert who shares his or her expertise with group members. In a sense, the group can be considered an educational experience, much like a classroom situation, in which the leader is the teacher and the members are the students. The leader must present some curriculum which must be acquired by the members. To be effective, this information must be individualized to the recipients' needs and motivational levels. The group leader must be aware of resources and content that relate to the group experience.

The primacy of the information dissemination role occurs early in the group process. During Phase I, Preparation, the leader is presenting members with a great deal of specific information about the group. A second time for heightened use of this role is in the final phase of the group process, Phase IV. Thus information is most important during preparation of the group, the introductory stages, and termination.

The information dissemination must be done moderately. Overuse of this role can turn the group into a classroom lecture situation, which is hardly useful for the kinds of learning expected in a group, and underuse can lead to wasteful nondirectiveness. In some cases a single piece of information can save large quantities of time and effort. The following comical event actually occurred in a group meeting.

Bob: Lew, where's the bathroom?

LEW (LEADER):   You'd like to know where the bathroom is.

Bob: Yeah, that's what I asked.

LEW: You seem irritated.

Bob (patronizingly):   Lewis, where's the bathroom?

LEW: You're upset with me, because I haven't told you where the bathroom is.

Bob (angrily):   WHERE'S THE BATHROOM?

LEW: Now you sound angry.

Bob (with cold anger):   If you don't tell me where the bathroom is right now I'm going to use your pant leg as a urinal.

FIGURE 6–3: Coordination of Leadership Roles and Chronological Group Process

FREQUENCY OF ROLE RESPONSES

STAGE

PHASE I: PREPARATION
1. Leader announces group
2. Members apply
3. Screening

PHASE II: LEARNING THE RULES
4. Specification of ground rules
5. Introductions
6. Short silence
7. Short silence broken
8. There-and-then discussion
9. Natural death of discussion
10. Long silence
11. First sortie
12. Negative response
13. Leaders' here-and-now focus
14. Major there-and-then problem
15. Leaders' focus on feelings
16. A real personal problem
17. Solutions offered
18. Solutions fail
19. Leaders focus on process
20. Expression of emotion
21. Expression encouraged

PHASE III: THERAPY
22. Norms solidified
23. Multiple roles of leadership
24. Intensity increases
25. Leaders do therapy
26. Minority members identified
27. Discussion of inclusion
28. Minority members decide
29. Group reacts
30. Problem-solving practiced

PHASE IV: TERMINATION
31. Imminent end announced
32. Invitation to work
33. Trust boost
34. Transfer of training
35. Good and welfare
36. Leaders' closing
37. Aloha

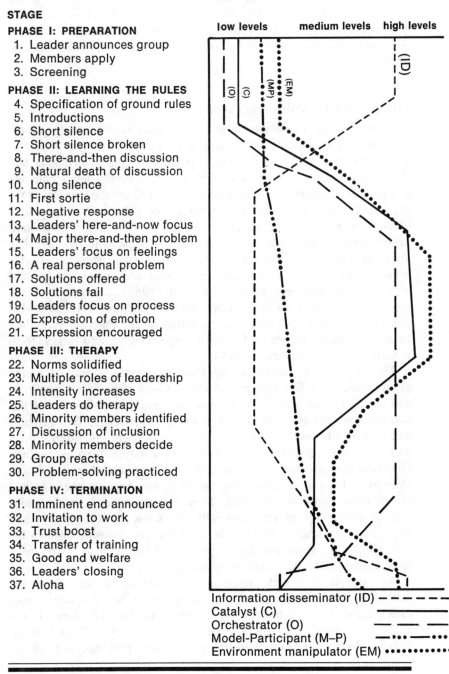

Information disseminator (ID) – – – – – –
Catalyst (C) ————————
Orchestrator (O) — — — —
Model-Participant (M–P) —•••—•••—
Environment manipulator (EM) •••••••••••••

At this point the "leader" produced a door key and instructions. Bob took the key and left. *He did not return for four sessions.*

While such evasive refusal to give information is atypical, many leaders do balk at providing facts for members. It seems important that a group therapist know when to give information, how much to give, and what the implications are of giving or withholding specific information.

THE GROUP LEADER AS CATALYST

In the role of a catalyst the group therapist serves two functions: As a generator of excitement and a spark plug for the group, and as a mover of the group to its critical point. He or she highlights and channels patterns of verbal and nonverbal communication within the group, acknowledges less obvious or nonverbal expressions of affect, requests feelings, and aims the group in the direction of a present, here-and-now focus. The leader uses a cooperative rather than competitive mode of communication and urges participants to risk revealing their personal beliefs and feelings rather than challenging others. He is most responsive to group levels of arousal and group feelings and tries to reflect members' concerns. Fiebert (1968), to whom credit is given for naming both the catalyst and orchestrator role, says that the catalyst "holds up a mirror to the group so that they can view their behavior, chides members for their superficiality, and urges them towards bonds of intimacy" (p. 935).

The catalyst role reaches its apex during Phases II and III of the group process, while members are learning how to be group members, and during the therapeutic intervention stages. Overemployment of this role can have the effect of creating a group dependency. The members will consistently look to the leader to entertain and "therapize" them and will not develop the ability to become catalysts for one another. Underuse can also have negative effects. In a group where the leader shies away from the catalyst role, members may become confused and directionless, bored and apathetic. They may also never learn the major foci of the group process and will not know what parts of their experience to discuss; they may therefore wander aimlessly through the time allotted for group meetings. The level of arousal may be so low as to be nonfacilitative as a motivating factor.

An example of a leader operating as a catalyst can be seen in the following vignette from a group experience during the therapeutic phase. One member had just finished talking about her lack of interest in sex with her husband as a result of her ongoing affair with one of his friends. As the group was working with this problem, one of the leaders noticed another woman member's face was pale and she was showing general signs of mild anxiety.

JERRY (LEADER 1): Betsy, could you verbalize that?

Betsy: Huh . . . what . . . well . . .

JERRY (supporting): What Joan was talking about seems to be affecting you a great deal.

Betsy: I feel scared.

JERRY: About what?

Betsy: My husband seems disinterested in me lately, and I'm really scared.

AILENE (LEADER 2): What Joan said makes you wonder whether or not he's having an affair and that's why he's not interested in sex with you.

Betsy (bursting into tears): Yes!

AILENE (after Betsy was somewhat consoled): Can you verbalize your feelings now?

Betsy: I'm really scared that he found someone better, and I've been ignoring his coming home late at night.

JERRY: You sound scared . . . and angry.

Betsy: Damn right I'm angry, I was a virgin when we got married and never had the chance to explore like Joan.

At this point the leaders orchestrated the process and had Joan and Betsy talk together.

The Group Leader as Orchestrator

The role of orchestrator takes precedence at the same time as the catalyst role in terms of group phases. The therapist serves as a conveyor of issues, feelings, and information. In a sense, she or he mediates the transmission of intercourse between members of the group. The job is to bring their problems and needs into contact with group resources.

As an orchestrator, the therapist encourages group members who have problems to explore them with other group members and the leaders. He works to get members with problems in touch with members who can assist in resolution. Rather than leading the discussion, the group leader assists it by asking questions, reflecting individuals' feelings, underlining considerations that are growth producing, and highlighting and interpreting communication patterns. The leader is particularly sensitive to nonverbal aspects of communication such as tone of voice, body language, kinetics, and discrepancies between verbal and nonverbal components of messages.

An effective orchestration requires an ongoing understanding of group process. Appropriately administered, it will maximize group learning as it increases members' participation in problem solving. It is thus a powerful mode of learning.

Perhaps the most crucial aspect of this role is that it is ultimately expendable. A major index of its success is obsolescence. When group members learn to communicate spontaneously, freely, and openly, they eliminate the need for the leader to practice the orchestration function.

An example of orchestration occurred in a couples group, at the onset of the therapeutic phase. Sherry and Michael are a young married couple.

John: (addressing the leaders): You know, I think Michael and Sherry really are in a bad way.

GAIL: (LEADER 1): Tell them that.

John: You guys seem angry at each other every single session.

PAUL: (LEADER 2): You're concerned about them?

John: Yeah, I'd like them to get it together more.

Sherry: I feel OK.

Michael: That's the problem: whenever I confront her she says, "Hey man, it's cool."

Peggy: Sherry, it doesn't look OK to me.

PAUL: Sherry, what do you hear John saying?

Sherry: That he's uptight.

PAUL: What was he saying . . .?

Sherry: Well, he says he's concerned, but it's more like a put down.

GAIL: So you feel . . .

Sherry: Angry and unwilling.

PAUL: John, is that what you wanted?

John: She just doesn't listen.

PAUL: What message did you want to give her?

John: That I do care and that I think she's denying and repressing.

PAUL: How could you say that so Sherry would hear it?

John: I could say, "Hey, I feel uptight when you look angry."

GAIL: Try that.

John: Sherry, I get scared to talk to you when you and Michael are fighting and you seem so angry.

GAIL: Sherry, what do you hear him saying?

Sherry: When I'm angry it scares him.

GAIL: But when you're angry you're also scared.

(Sherry: Nods and looks down.)

GAIL: Is there anyone in here that you'd like to know when you're scared, without having to tell them?

Sherry: Michael.
GAIL: How could you let him know?
Sherry: I don't know.
PAUL: Michael, what do you hear Sherry saying?

The orchestration done by both leaders was facilitative in allowing Michael and Sherry to become more empathic with each other and to improve their own communication. The leaders did not return to the other issue, John's role and motivation, until later. At this point the key issue was the couple.

Overutilization of the orchestration role at the expense of other roles can serve to eliminate the leader's special therapeutic expertise. In this case, the leader serves *only* as a conveyor/facilitator and not as a catalyst, information disseminator, model and so on. The highest level of functioning for the group then is determined by group members rather than the group leader. Since the group cannot surpass the functioning level of its highest individual, overuse of orchestration severely limits its effectiveness. Characteristically, this deficit occurs with an extreme interpersonal-style or novice leader.

Underemployment of the orchestration role also limits group effectiveness. Lack of orchestration reduces the amount of impact members can have on one another, ameliorates altruism on the part of the members, and limits between-member learning. A group with minimal orchestration will resemble individual psychotherapy in a group setting. This type of deficit is most likely to occur with a strict intrapersonal orientation or with an individual psychotherapist untrained in group dynamics.

The Group Leader as Model-Participant

A major component of most complex learning is imitation. In their role as models, leaders demonstrate abilities in sharing information and feelings and open, honest communication. The group leader needs to be flexible in his application of values, open to new learning about himself, and able to show, by example, the process of learning how to learn. Leaders can also model spontaneity, genuine caring for others, sincerity, assertiveness, and conflict resolution skills.

In an unstructured situation, participants will naturally attempt to reduce their anxiety by providing structure. A common tactic by which members accomplish this is to look to the authority figure for clues of appropriate (tension-reducing) behavior. It is here that most members begin to imitate leadership behaviors. Some obvious forms of this imitation are the adoption of the leader's language by members and the seemingly unconscious appropriation of the leader's nonverbal communication cues. One example of this occurred in a group led by a colleague who had a habit of rhythmically stroking her long hair during periods of silence and high tension. By the fourth week of the group all six of the female group members were stroking their own hair the same way. This was even true for one woman who had short hair and who in effect was stroking hair which would not be long enough for years!

These examples are an indication of external modeling. While interesting, they are relatively impermanent and not meaningful as changes; they simply illustrate how rapidly and insidiously modeling occurs. An example of a more important form of modeling occurred in a therapy group where a member was describing relatively dispassionately the recent death of his father.

Harvey:　So I had to go to the funeral . . . that was a bummer . . . missed all my friends here.

MICHAEL (LEADER 1):　You know, I hear a very sad-sounding message, but I don't see any emotion. (catalyst)

Marion:　Yeah, I can't even feel any sympathy for you.

Harvey (coldly):　I wasn't asking for any.

JERRY (LEADER 2):　Harvey, what was your dad like? (catalyst)

Harvey:　He was OK, pretty cold, never really paid much attention to any of us. I don't really miss him . . . but I feel like I should.

JERRY:　When someone is cold to me and I love them, it hurts a lot. (modeling-participating)

Marion:　I don't know, sometimes when someone is cold to me I just understand it's the way they are.

JERRY:　Like Harvey was to you just now. (orchestrating)

Marion:　Yeah. (Then smiling, almost embarrassed): I do care for you, Harv, and I don't like being shut out.

Harvey:　It's just hard to get into those feelings.

Sarah:　Do you want to?

Harvey:　Yes, but I'm not sure.

MICHAEL (with moist eyes):　Even the thought of losing someone I care about makes me very sad. (model-participant, catalyst)

Harvey (looking at Michael):　It's just so frustrating. There's so much I wanted to say and some of it is not nice at all . . . (Here he began crying and grieving.)

There is no question that the leader's empathy and willingness to share his own sadness played a huge role in helping this patient experience his necessary grief.

If the group leader can be accepting, spontaneous, self-disclosing, encouraging of others to examine themselves, cooperative, intimate, expressive of feelings in a here-and-now context, and nondefensive, group members can adopt these behaviors via imitation learning. Bandura and Walters (1963) have shown that imitation learning is maximized when the model has high status and receives positive reinforcement for behavior. The group leader fits these criteria for the model comfortably.

Overuse of the model-participant role can not only diminish its effectiveness but also reduce the value of all the other leadership roles. A leader who becomes, for all intents and purposes, a member of the group can cause it to follow his own personal agenda. In this way, the group members are used as therapists or sounding boards for the leader's own growth, instead of the reverse. In addition, the level of self-disclosure by the leader can be either more superficial or deeper than that of members. In this case members may hasten to conform to the leader's level of self-disclosure and in the process lose their own. When this happens, and one individual is more responsible than others for setting a level, a greater artificiality results.

An example of overuse of this role occurred in a 1976 group.

Bob (to leader):   You know, I'm not sure I feel comfortable enough here to really talk about some things.
BRIAN (LEADER):   That really pisses me off. You've just got to take more responsibility for you.
Bob: I'm trying to, I just feel put down and untrusting.
BRIAN: Bullshit, you're trying to suck me in to begging you to "tell us" and then (in a mocking voice), "I've got something to tell you but I won't tell you what it is, nyah, nyah."
Bob (angrily):   Sounds like you're laying your trip on me now.
BRIAN: *That* puts *me* down, like I'm not listening, or not following *your* expectation of me as a leader.
Pat: I think you're being a bit hard on Bob. Is this pushing one of your buttons?
BRIAN: You may be right. I guess it's my hangup with authority and being a good leader.

He then proceeded to analyze his own behavior in detail. This provided an excellent model of self-disclosure to the group, but very much at Bob's expense.

Underparticipation can also be detrimental to group process. When members see the leader engaging only in nonparticipatory roles, they are apt to imitate these behaviors. Such behavior on the part of members is inappropriate. Members are not encouraged to orchestrate and catalyze without self-disclosure. Indeed, they are often punished for doing so. If the leader does not model appropriate behaviors for members, his potency as a model will be diminished, and members will simply imitate the inappropriate behaviors.

The Group Leader as Dispenser of Reinforcement and Environment Manipulator

It has been noted that the group, as an ambiguous situation, is anxiety producing. It has also been suggested that certain moderate levels of anxiety must be present in order to produce optimal amounts of learning. Given these two postulates, the group leader is in a position to manipulate the group environment for maximal growth and learning by controlling the level of anxiety present. The most efficient way for the group leader to control the level of anxiety is to control the amount of ambiguity present. Since in our culture ambiguity and anxiety are related approximately linearly, the therapist can raise levels of anxiety by removing structure in the situation and can reduce anxiety by adding structure.

One manner of controlling structure is through judicious selective reinforcement. Reinforcement in a group setting can include such behaviors as head nodding, verbal acknowledgment, attention, or smiling. In providing such reinforcement, the leader lets members know that they are on the right track, that this is approved behavior, and that they should continue in this vein. Such reinforcement has double value. It makes members feel positively, and it helps reduce anxiety by structuring the situation. Conversely, the ambiguity anxiety can be increased by nonreinforcement from the leaders.

Leaders can cause group anxiety to fluctuate by other techniques. They can raise anxiety by calling attention to a specific group member's behavior or making expectant eye contact with one member. Conversely, by making group-level interpretations (e.g., "Seems like we're all feeling uncomfortable now, but it's hard for anyone to change the situation"), leaders can lower anxiety. In one sense, all learning in a group setting can be viewed as a function of motivation produced by the leaders' control of group anxiety.

In dispensing reinforcement, the group leader does more than simply provide structure. He or she is a powerful model and respected authority figure in the group, whose approval is valued tremendously. Members quickly learn how to please the therapist by acting in accordance with his desires. In the group setting, members are reinforced for openness, genuineness, honesty, hard work, self-disclosure, motivation to change, listening and responding to others, flexibility in application of values, acceptance of others, and so on. These abilities stand members in good stead outside the group setting also.

Overmanipulation by the group leader will cause group members to mistrust him. If they construe the group therapist as a somewhat inhuman dispenser of reinforcement, members will curry favor by producing reinforceable behaviors, without any commitment. This is similiar to students "psyching out" what a teacher wants to hear or see on an exam and producing those bits of information on paper, while forgetting their content and meaning almost simultaneously. Reinforcement in the form of high grades may ensue, but understanding of the material requires a much different type of incorporation.

By contrast, underutilization of this role produces a rather laissez-faire chaos. In this situation, the group can remain over- or under-structured, and hence over- or underaroused, for long periods of time. In such an environment, learning takes place only minimally and serendipitously.

There is more to group leadership than multiple roles. Stylistic and personality characteristics distinguish leaders. One long-unresolved question in the literature concerns specification of the characteristics mandatory for effective group leadership.

CHARACTERISTICS OF THE GROUP THERAPIST

Are there certain characteristics or personality traits mandatory for effective group leadership? Are the skills of group therapy learned, or do they require a certain "type" of individual? In this section, these questions are explored from the historical, practical, and training perspectives.

Relatively early in the history of group psychotherapy, a question arose regarding importance of the therapist's personality. In 1908, Pratt said that, "Success depends on gaining the friendship and confidence of the members." Pratt's (1934) theory was based on Dejerine's belief that, "Psychotherapy depends wholly and exclusively upon the beneficial influence of one person on another." A statement by Pfeffer, Friedland, and Wortis (1949) probably fairly represented opinion on this issue at that time: "As yet undefinable aspects of the therapist's personality may be more important for his results than the technique he says he uses."

More recently, research by Carkhuff and Berenson (1967), and Truax and his colleagues (Truax, 1966b; 1971; Truax & Carkhuff, 1967; Truax, Carkhuff, Wargo, & Kodman, 1966) has identified several variables which distinguish effective from ineffective therapists in each area of endeavor. High functioning levels of warmth, empathy, genuineness, and congruence are said to be necessary conditions for success in group therapy. Not only are these personality traits, but Truax et al. argue that they are trainable skills. Demonstration of this research with regard to individual therapy is impressive, but few direct applications to group therapy situations have been substantiated. If it can be demonstrated that these dimensions are in fact "core conditions," there still is the problem that they are in fact only necessary conditions for group therapists; they are not sufficient to guarantee success. Thus the question of the personality of the group therapist has as yet not been fully determined.

There are two ways of examining this issue—statically and dynamically. We can study the kind of person the therapist is or the behavior she or he demonstrates. The first way of looking at this issue is to consider the character structure of the therapist, his uniqueness as a person, perhaps using a series of adjectives for the purpose of description. We may feel that kind, considerate, sympathetic people may be better therapists than brusque, impatient, or insensitive people. The other way of thinking of personality is in terms of the role the therapist plays in the group. This distinction may seem somewhat artificial if we believe that one is what one does. But the issue is not simple, since a group therapist may be able to assume a particular role to conform to his conceptions of ideal therapist behavior, which may not resemble to any great extent his usual manner of social interaction. Indeed, the assumption that a person is what he does requires a total sampling of his behavior. To assume that a group leader's behavior in the group is representative of his total behavior is as spurious as to assume that his behavior in bed is equivalent to his total behavior.

Probably both issues need to be explored, and it may be that the latter is just as important as the former. It may be argued that while psychotherapists vary in much the same way as nonpsychotherapists with respect to essential personality, nevertheless all good therapists operate in more or less the same manner. If this were not true, there would be little point in professional selection and training.

THE IDEAL PERSONALITY FOR A GROUP THERAPIST

Is there a generalized ideal personality for group therapists? Do certain methods call for specific personalities? Probably both questions should have an affirmative answer. According to Slavson (1951), the therapist should be friendly, generous, tolerant, accepting, and quiet. Study of these requirements forces the conclusion that Slavson is defining an ideal personality in terms of our culture. Others may set up different personality criteria for the therapist who has to deal with groups. Grotjahn (1971b), a psychoanalyst like Slavson, argues that a group therapist "must be a man of all seasons. He must be reliable; he must invite trust and confidence." Other therapist qualities suggested by Grotjahn include honesty, sincerity, spontaneity, responsibility, courage, firmness, humor, fallibility, and the ability to perform skillfully.

My own formulation of the major essential characteristics of the effective group therapist is similar. I consider them to be honesty, integrity, patience, courage, flexibility, warmth, empathy, intelligence, timing, and self-knowledge.

Honesty. The first quality that comes to mind is truthfulness. The therapist must at all times respond to the members with honest feedback. This is not to say, however, that he or she needs always to be open. There are many situations in which he wisely keeps information to himself. If the group members are to change their negative patterns of communication, they need accurate information as to the consequences of their behavior. Similarly, since honest communication is one of the avowed goals of groups, the leader must be a model of this behavior. Honesty cannot be learned from an untruthful source.

Integrity. Integrity does not lag far behind honesty. Group members need to know that the leader will adhere to an agreed-upon code of ethics. The leader must interact with members with *their* interests in mind.

Patience. Another essential quality is patience. The therapist must have a high tolerance for boredom, frustration, and delay. He must have the ability to proceed doggedly in the face of disappointments and failure under conditions that induce anxiety, anger, and unrest. Patience should be the result of a deep conviction, amounting to faith in oneself, in the group, in the method, and in the theory. The patient therapist combines a feeling of assurance, security, determination, confidence, and hopefulness about himself and others. He must have an optimistic outlook on life.

Courage. Somewhat related to patience is courage. The therapist must have the capacity to act on his convictions and remain unswerved by immediate events. He needs faith to hold on to them with great tenacity, to follow with determination his line of attack, and to meet in an accepting manner the opposition, which at times can explode with some violence. Courage is needed to penetrate, sometimes blindly, into new areas or to meet crises with aplomb. The therapist must have inward qualities of fortitude.

Flexibility. Courage does not mean rigidity; while the therapist must hold on to basic principles with tenacity, he must nevertheless be able to modify tactics without changing goals. He needs extraordinary flexibility to go rapidly from topic to topic, emotion to emotion, person to person, while keeping a sense of the needs of the group as a whole. He must be sensitive to the needs of the group and of individuals, but he must also be alert to the demands of society and the desires of patients' families, and to ethical issues.

Warmth.   The ideal therapist is a warm person with a genuine liking for people, one who really wants to see others improve. While he may have preferences among patients, he must value them equally as striving individuals in trouble. He must be ready to give of himself fully. He must be open to them as they appear.

Empathy.   Closely related to warmth is empathy. An effective group therapist must be able to put himself into the shoes of his patients. He must experience their emotions as if they were his own, and he must be able to communicate this shared experience accurately and articulately to the members. He does not judge others; rather he shares in members' fears, pain, anger, and joy. At the same time, he must keep touch with other reality considerations. In a sense, the group therapist walks with one foot in the shoe of another and the other foot in his own shoe.

Intelligence.   It is not necessary for the therapist to be the most intelligent individual in the room, but he must be able to learn fairly rapidly, to be flexible enough to view the group from others' glasses, and to make some theoretical sense of the material of the group interactions. A leader who is limited in intelligence could effectively dampen higher level cognitive processing by the members.

Timing.   There is no human endeavor that does not require timing for maximum effectiveness. The best leadership observations are worthless if the group members are not prepared to listen. As the basketball player must fake his defender to leave his feet, then jump into the air, and then shoot at the apex of his own jump while his defender is coming down, in order to score regularly, so must the therapist help group members remove their defenses and become prepared to allow him to work on conflict resolution. With any variations in sequence, the effects will not be maximized. If the basketball shooter does not cause his defender to jump earlier than he does himself, the flight of the ball might be terminated in his face instead of the basket. Similarly, the group leader must time his interventions carefully for best results.

Self-knowledge.   Certainly not least important is the quality of self-knowledge. It is not essential that leaders be conflict free or completely self-actualizing; certainly this requirement would eliminate all current leaders. It is essential, however, that leaders be aware of their strong and weak areas. Unless the leader is self-aware, there is an ever-present danger that his own conflicts, inadequacies, and needs will guide his own group interactions instead of those of the members. It is far better for a leader to acknowledge that he is incapable or unwilling to venture into certain difficult areas than to unknowingly grope around in the dark with his patients, perhaps compounding their fears and conflicts. Shakespeare says this so well in *Hamlet* with Polonius's final advice to his son: "This above all, to thine own self be true; and it must follow as the night the day, thou canst not then be false to any man."

Who is this group therapist? Is he any more than the kind of friend or mate we all cherish? Can any person who has these qualities of honesty, integrity, patience, courage, flexibility, warmth, empathy, intelligence, timing, and self-awareness be a group leader? These are all necessary conditions for effective group leadership, but they are not sufficient. In the next chapter we will investigate the other characteristics—training and a code of ethics—and in effect take the reader inside the head of the group therapist during a session. Before doing so, there is one more important consideration for any therapist.

PERSONALITY AND METHOD

It was stated earlier that the method a group therapist uses is a function of his or her own personality. It is difficult to think of a really introverted therapist using psychodrama with any success, and it may be just as difficult for a really aggressive, outgoing person to contain himself within the limits of the nondirective procedure. If we accept the arguments that the best method for any person is one that accords with his own nature, and a person can do his best work with a procedure that is natural for him, we may be freed of the need to establish any hierarchy of values with respect to methods. Pratt makes his maximum contribution with the class method, Moreno with psychodrama, Rogers with nondirective therapy, and Dreikurs with family counseling. The thought of Freud attempting bioenergetics is enough to demonstrate how incongruous such a situation can be, especially when it is apparent that Freud's method—use of the couch, sitting behind the patient, and so on—was a function of Freud's own introvertive personality. We have direct evidence on this point from Freud himself, who said (1924), "I must, however, expressedly state that this technique (free association) has proved the only method suited to my individuality. I do not venture to deny that a physician quite differently constituted might feel impelled to adopt a different attitude to his patients and to the task before him."

Others have made similar remarks. Spotnitz (1952), for example, says "The personality of a therapist may determine whether the group has an active or passive type of therapy." Kline (1952) comments, "It is probable that the dynamics of different groups actually do differ radically with the personality of the therapist." Kline also gives a personal example: "I have always emphasized that within limits the organization of the group and the role of the therapist should be dependent largely on the personality of the therapist himself, rather than on rigid techniques. This conviction was derived from my initial unsuccessful attempts to emulate the procedures of Dr. Paul Schilder. . . ."

The therapist needs absolute freedom to follow his own judgment. No one can tell him how to do what he must do. For the purpose of research, Powdermaker and Frank (1953) tried to get therapists to operate in a uniform way. Even though the therapists wished to follow this established pattern, nevertheless they managed to make subtle changes, in each case making modifications suited to their own personalities.

It is in the spirit of freedom for the therapist to decide on his own methods that this book is written. It is hoped that explicit examples of a variety of attitudes and methods will help therapists make a better choice among them or will help provide the courage to strike out on their own. There was only one Sigmund Freud and one Fritz Perls, and there is only one Carl Rogers. When others learn from them and apply this learning in their own unique ways, it is a bonus. But, when other therapists try to be Freud, Perls, or Rogers, or Shapiro for that matter, they are not only doomed to failure, but they appear overstressed, phony, and foolish in the endeavor.

An effective group leader plays many roles and performs many functions concurrently and sequentially. Each of the five major roles complements the others. Tactfully and strategically employed, they help the group leader provide a fertile ground for group members' growth and learning. In addition, a number of personality characteristics enhance therapist effectiveness when they are present. Certainly, any individual who can play the major leadership roles and who also has the personality characteristics delineated above is a likely candidate for group leadership training. In the next chapter we will look at some additional variables and discuss some of the difficulties therapists face in the process of leading a group.

Chapter 7

Professional Issues in Group Leadership

The therapist should operate in a way natural for him, as noted in Chapter 6. Nevertheless, there may be a kind of etiquette of behavior for group therapists, and it is profitable to consider its outlines. In life there are many conventions that must be followed. For example, one does not eat in precisely the same way at a picnic, at home, in a restaurant, or at a banquet. The individual maintains his identity in these various places but adjusts to the situation.

We play different roles on the street, on the beach, at a party, or in the office. If we were to act in precisely the same manner, no matter what the occasion, we would demonstrate a lack of flexibility to adjust to different environments and circumstances. The same is true for the group therapist. Aspects of the role the group therapist plays are discussed in this chapter, not as a guide for action, but as a means of enhancing understanding of the functions.

ETHICS

Probably the major reason to require the group therapist to be a member of a responsible profession is to increase expectations that the proprieties will be observed. Many ethical issues can arise in therapeutic groups, and while a well-intentioned person of any background may deal with them adequately, it is more likely that a leader who has had professional training in proper behavior with patients will be able to meet them satisfactorily.

The therapist has a duty to help people. He can help them if they will cooperate with him, and therefore he must engender confidence in himself, but he must be scrupulously careful not to misinform or misrepresent. He should not present an exaggerated account of the benefits to be had from group therapy.

Patients may want to discuss matters that the therapist feels are unsuitable for group discussion; for example, they may wish to criticize the therapist's supervisor or other staff members. The therapist may decide that he does not wish to participate in such discussions. For him to put a stop to these discussions may be unwise, but it may be equally unwise to let the group proceed. Or, if one member makes sexual overtures to another, the therapist might feel that the problem no longer involved only the participants but that it also involved himself, the group, the other members, and the institution, as well as his profession. The therapist also may be asked questions about himself, other patients, or other people which he could answer but feels he ought not to. His refusal to answer may affect the group unfavorably, but there are limits to all human interactions, and it is the therapist's ethical responsibility to establish the limits in the therapy group. He must act in conformance to his conscience, the ethics of his profession, and the laws of society. Even with these limitations, there is usually plenty of latitude for expression.

In one sense, the strongest argument for requiring graduate school training for professionals is that it is in this setting that the ethics and mores of functioning professionals are learned. Untrained leaders often get into ethical double binds, or never see the ethical side of the issue at all. They may be very well meaning as leaders and still do grievous harm to group participants.

An untrained leader who does not understand the full scope of ethical responsibility can naively apply a few simplistic guidelines to all group situations. One common example of this is the issue of the locus of responsibility, on which many encounter group leaders place a primary emphasis. Schutz (1973), for example, argues that health and success for members are contingent on the extent to which they take responsibility for their actions. In this view, statements such as: "The devil made me do it," "I just can't do this," "You make me feel so sad," "If only my karma was better," or "I'm a Gemini, that's why that Pisces guy hates me," are all examples of unacceptable behaviors. The notion is that if individuals will own their feelings and actions, they will be able to be more assertive and more effective in their day-to-day interactions.

Ethical and responsible employment of this dictum within the structure of a delineated theory of personality can be extremely valuable. In this case responsibility-taking is defined clearly, modeled by the leader, and developed in concert with other skills. However, an unprofessional therapist can employ this dictum by itself, without placing it into a network of related constructs. Such misuse is characterized by many of the "pop psychology" movements and is typically manifested by the leader opening up an individual and then not engaging in the necessary closing behavior. An example of this follows. In this situation, the leader led the group on a guided fantasy and hypnotic regression. As this regression approached its end, he gave the following suggestions:

> ... Now you're feeling totally relaxed ... totally open to
> your experience ... and now as I count backwards from 10 to 1
> you'll get younger and younger. You'll actually be ten years
> old and you'll feel all the 10-year old feelings. 10 ... 9 ...
> 8 ... you're getting sleepy and open; 7 ... 6 ... 5 ...
> you know what it's like to be 10 years old; 4 ... 3 ...
> 2 ... 1 ... now be 10, act 10, feel 10. Now you see your parents.
> Look at them ... feel the helplessness you feel with them ...
> how much you need their love and how they never give you
> enough ...

At this point, one member burst into tears and began mournfully crying out, "Don't leave me, please don't leave me."

RAMA (LEADER): OK ... let's hold this exercise. (Turning to the crying member): What are you experiencing, Ben?

Ben: I don't want to lose her.

RAMA: Your mother?

Ben: She died when I was 10. She had no right to leave me alone like that.

RAMA: *You* didn't believe *she* had a right to die.

Ben: She made me so lonely.

RAMA: You mean you felt lonely when your mother died.

Ben: I can't help feeling so scared now and sad.

RAMA: You mean you're choosing to feel sad and scared.

Ben: I'm *not* choosing, you're setting me up to experience these things and I do.

RAMA: I'm not willing to take responsibility for your feelings.

Not only does this leader *not* deal with the issue, but he is a poor model. In instructing Ben to take responsibility, the leader was himself being irresponsible. Furthermore, instead of empathizing with Ben, he constantly restructured Ben's words to fit into his own theoretical language. In this case, a single dictum regarding the variable of responsibility is guiding the leader's total interaction. This is done to the detriment of all members. Charles Schulz sums this up in one of his "Peanuts" cartoon character's observations: "There's a difference between a bumper sticker and a philosophy of life."

A professional training program is a hedge against a "bumper sticker" approach. If students learn anything, they must learn the ethical guidelines of their profession.

The American Psychological Association has two sets of guidelines for group therapists and growth-group leaders. Relevant portions are summarized below. The American Psychiatric Association makes no distinction in responsibility for psychiatrists leading therapy or growth groups.

Group therapists are committed to acting objectively and with integrity, maintaining the highest standards in offered services. They must not violate accepted moral and legal codes of the community or misrepresent their qualifications.

With regard to client contacts, therapists are mandated to confidentiality and protection of the integrity and welfare of the individuals. In cases of conflicts between professionals, the psychologists' primary concern must be for the members' welfare. This includes the situation in which the psychologist believes that there is no reasonable expectancy of benefit to the client. In such a case, termination of this member from the group is required. In every case, psychologists must receive *informed* consent from clients and research subjects.

Administration of services, treatment diagnosis, or personalized advice can only occur within the context of a professional relationship. Professional standards are also maintained with regard to announcement of services. Direct solicitation for therapy, advertising, evaluative descriptions of services, and testimonials are all considered commercial rather than professional, and as such are inappropriate. Similarly, encouragement of exaggerated notions of success in clients are improper.

Financial and interprofessional matters must be in accord with community standards, and respect for other professionals and clients is expected. Regard for research subjects follows similar guidelines, and subjects' rights to privacy and nonparticipation are to be protected.

Several similar guidelines have been laid out for growth-group leaders. Growth-group participation should be voluntary. Explicit information regarding group purposes, procedures, goals, fees, availability of follow-up, training and education of the leaders, issues of confidentiality, and any restrictions on freedom of choice must be available. Screening is necessary for both inclusion and exclusion of members and for exploration of terms of the contract. Client welfare is considered more important than research or experimental concerns. Experimental procedures should be fully disclosed and evaluated publicly, and the relative responsibility of group leaders and members specified. It is expected that leaders will respond ethically both as therapists and educators.

Similar guidelines are observed by members of the medical, nursing, and social work professions and by the National Training Laboratories (NTL, 1970).

These ethical concerns are of primary import whether or not the leader is a psychologist. Members of groups must be informed of the group goals, procedures, purposes, and costs. They must give their consent to participate, and they have the right to refuse to participate in any specific group activity. They must be honestly assured that client welfare will be safeguarded. They must also be assured that the therapist will treat their activity within the group as privileged communication.

There are certain qualifications with regard to privileged communication. Where the patient is likely to be dangerous to himself or others and the therapist would violate other ethical responsibilities by maintaining such confidentiality, it is essential to reveal this information to the appropriate professional or public authorities. With respect to sensitive material, however, the therapist must consider the possibility that the information may harm the patient if it is transmitted by other persons. For this reason, the therapist will do well to warn group members that individual members may be fallible and can leak information to outsiders. To attempt to handle this problem by forcing a compact of silence is probably foolish. However, it is my experience that confidentiality is regularly maintained by group members. Corsini (1957), having done groups in prisons for over 10 years, reports that "Only one case of revealing of information came out—and it was reported by the guilty one himself!"

Without such guarantees of safety, group members are left unprotected and can be seriously hurt by the machinations of an unprofessional group leader. Martin Lakin of Duke University has been one of the strongest proponents of ethical standards in growth groups. In a series of articles and texts, Lakin (1969, 1972) elucidates critical concerns for leadership. He contrasts the psychotherapeutic intent in groups and the growth motive in groups: "The therapists' mandate is relatively clear—to provide a corrective experience for someone who presents himself as psychologically impaired" (1969, p. 924). On the other hand, in a training group, "There is no way for a participant to know in advance, much less to appraise intentions of trainers, processes of groups or their consequences for him" (p. 924).

Lakin also makes a distinction between participants of early and more recent groups. Early participants were mostly psychologically sophisticated, mainly professional, and in general had intellectual understanding as their goal. In contrast, the recent popularization of groups has resulted in an influx of vast segments of the general public as participants. In recent years, members of sensitivity groups have been generally less sophisticated, more psychologically disturbed, and seeking a cathartic rather than intellectual experience. Furthermore, today there are a great number of inadequately prepared group leaders.

In addition, Lakin decries the lack of adequate screening and group preparation for both members and leaders, and a corresponding lack of follow-up or posttraining. Coulson (1972), Beymer (1969), Shostrom (1969), and Dreyfus and Kremenliev (1970), as well as Lakin, have all warned against the ethic of drama in encounter groups. The tendency to view the value of an interaction as linearly related to the amount of affect expressed is a common one among encounter group leaders. Techniques and exercises designed to bring members to high levels of emotional arousal are easily obtainable and frequently used. Leader pressure and peer pressure in a group can push members to levels of emotion and affect-induced behaviors that are not easily reincorporated into their lives. Several group leaders rationalize such actions by arguing that members will not go beyond their own limits, that membership is voluntary, and that members who "flip out" are choosing to do so. These rationalizations are simply not defensible with unscreened, unsophisticated clients. Lakin (1969) and Shapiro (1975) point out that the *caveat emptor* principle is professionally undefensible. The "consumer" may in fact agree to a contract that he really does not understand. Lakin says, "It cannot be assumed that the participant really knows what he is letting himself in for" (1969, p. 926). At the request of a very powerful leader, or with group pressure, members may engage in affectional, aggressive, or sexual behavior in the group which will be regretted later and could have subsequent negative repercussions.

A leader who is unaware of the power he or she wields or of the nature of transferences formed in a group setting can tread on sensitive ground and create a vulnerability in members which the leader cannot or will not handle effectively. Even more dangerous is the leader who accepts this position of power as a means of self-enhancement. Instant gurus, people with a mission or point of view to sell, can comfortably bask in the facile glory of group leadership. Their self-aggrandizement can be at a high cost to members, however.

Such a guru was operating in Hawaii several years ago. He claimed to be a clinical psychologist, a claim that was later proven false. In the course of his group meetings, which consisted of approximately 10 to 12 regulars and 2 to 3 new members, each member was to take the "hot seat" and tell the thing that was most upsetting to them. In one case, a student of mine was accused of "not owning" his latent homosexual fears. The student in question seriously examined himself and after a time denied any homosexual leanings. The leader, with support from the group, then "worked" with this student *for six consecutive hours* to get him to accept his homosexual feelings. This student left the room when the leader suggested that he remove his clothes and let other men in the group touch him. The student called me to check out whether or not this procedure, which was very frightening to him, was acceptable. On my advice, he never returned to the group room, but the incident precipitated his entry into psychotherapy to work on feelings that had been instigated by the group. This particular student had a great deal of ego strength to sit through six hours of this kind of treatment and to leave the room to make a phone call. A group member with less strength could have suffered much more serious harm. The group leader was subsequently hospitalized after several similar incidents, and a credentials check came under the jurisdiction of the authorities.

SAFETY PRECAUTIONS ON ENTERING GROUPS

The public should be protected from excesses such as those described above and forewarned of the possible dangers of participation in certain types of groups. The set of guidelines to increase the probability of ethical, responsible application of group principles which is discussed below is intended as a bare minimum. There is, of course, no guarantee that any group will be effective. These criteria are intended to function as warning signals. To the extent that groups fail to conform to these indices, the probability of unethical, unresponsible, and dangerous leadership is increased.

Leaders' Credentials

While a degree from an accredited graduate training program in one of the mental health fields is no guarantee of ethical leadership, lack of such credentials is considered a negative index. There is a greater probability that a nonprofessional leader will fail to be aware of or to conform to ethical standards. If the leaders themselves are not professionals, they should be supervised by a recognized professional expert.

Advertising

Immodest claims of success, promises of dramatic life changes, erotic inducements, and open advertising in newspapers or public magazines are all examples of unacceptable ethical behavior for professionals. Professionals advertise groups via referrals, modest brochures to other professionals, members of a self-requested mailing list, and by word of mouth and reputation.

Screening

If a group does not provide screening, there can be no control over membership. Members can be placed in thoroughly inappropriate groups. The profit motive seems the only explainable justification for failure to screen out potential members. When dealing with one's personal beliefs, values, or behaviors, profit is a uniquely inappropriate decision criterion.

Group Size

Groups of less than 6 or more than 14 members are inappropriate except when dealing with certain specific patient populations. In a too-small group, cliques can form and scapegoating can occur. Each member also is required to produce a great deal of verbalization, often at a faster rate than is desirable. In a too-large group, process cannot be effectively monitored, trust is difficult to develop, cohesion is limited, and often the members who are shyest and most in need of attention can get lost in the shuffle.

Costs

The average rates for group work vary little in most settings, usually being set by professional consensus, insurance coverage, and population served. Groups that are offered for token low payments or excessively high costs should be investigated. Sometimes groups are offered at very low cost because they are subsidized by other funds, or competent professional leaders are trying to build practices and therefore offer services at a reduced rate. Sometimes professionals are doing their charity work. By contrast, other leaders charge low rates because that is all they are worth. That is not a true bargain. Group leadership is difficult work, and when professionals put in time and effort, they have a right to adequate remuneration.

Some group leaders charge excessively high rates for their work. They often rationalize by arguing that the more people pay, the more they will get out of the experience. This seems irresponsible to most professionals. Often, members pay for elaborate settings, resort costs, catered meals, and so on, which may be desirable but which are certainly unnecessary to successful group therapy. Sometimes these high-priced group leaders come into town for a session and leave promptly after with the money and no provisions for follow-up.

Follow-Up Services

If a group leader does not provide some level of follow-up services, group members can lose out on important group learning. Even worse, they can be left in a new wilderness, opened by the group, without adequate survival skills. If the leaders are not available for referral or therapy services after the group is over, a major safeguard against casualties is also neglected.

Group Goals and Procedures

Each group has methods and value systems that are tied to its goals. Members need to be made fully aware of the intent of the group before they can make an educated decision to join. Hidden agendas of group leaders often lead groups into directions they would not have chosen had they been better informed. An example of this occurred recently with a group leader who believed very strongly that members had to reject all aspects of their childhood, including their parents and relatives, before they could be totally functioning adults. However, he advertised his group as a place where members would "come to know themselves more fully, become freed of blocked energy, and gain a fuller connection with their past." Needless to say, his way of accomplishing this involved a series of procedures that many potential members would reject if they were informed in advance. Once in the situation, group pressure can be brought to bear on participants to force their compliance.

Confidentiality and Secrecy

In order to safeguard members' privacy, confidentiality must be a group norm. For members to open up their most secret parts without some sort of guarantee that these will not be reported to significant others is absolutely essential. Violators of this ethic, under a rationalization of total openness and honesty, severely limit positive group effects and can cause much damage to members' lives. Potential members need to be forewarned about any possibility of breach of confidentiality. If this issue is not specifically discussed in the group, the probability of such a violation is high.

While confidentiality is necessary, secrecy is severely discouraged. Group procedures and processes must be able to stand the test of scientific research. If a group leader does not wish to allow his methods to be open for public or professional scrutiny, the reasons for such secrecy should be seriously questioned. Secrecy in this case can enhance cohesion by increasing ingroup vs. outgroup distance. Such a maneuver makes transfer of training extremely difficult and produces elitism and jingoism among members. Hence it also increases subsequent alienation.

Groups as Parts of a Movement

Whenever the leader has a particular philosophy to sell or an axe to grind, group members can get lost in the process. Groups are designed for individual growth in directions determined by the individuals themselves. When individual needs become subjugated to more global designs, the individual must suffer. A member of a group led by a guru leader can find acceptance only within a certain framework. He must conform to role expectations of a larger body, and his development is limited to the lines sanctified by the movement. In such a situation, the individual frequently gets lost.

This is not to suggest that belonging to an organization larger than oneself cannot be a rewarding experience. However, group therapy or encounter is not the appropriate place for this. One man's mission can be another man's destruction.

Members' Rights

Entrance to a group is *not* a carte blanche acquiescence to anything that might follow. Members must be informed of their rights to participate or not and the ramifications of refusal to engage in any particular group activity. For example, if the group leader decides that nudity would enhance group communication, does a member have the right to decline? What pressures will be brought to bear? Does anyone have veto power over such a recommendation? Entering a group without having these issues specified is dangerous.

Jargon

Each group, of necessity, has its own language system to describe the group process. However, language systems can be used to mask differences as well as to highlight issues. Group jargon is often very imprecise language, and a variety of perceptions are lumped together under a single title. We have one word, *snow, t*o describe a naturalistic phenomenon; Eskimos have several words to delineate different types and qualities of snow. With all these words they can perceive much more in this weather condition than one who has only one such word.

So it is with group jargon. If a member finds people speaking in a manner he does not comprehend, he is in a high-risk situation. This situation is compounded when a group employs words a member understands, but the group places special meanings on the words; thus the member who is familiar with each word does not totally understand a single sentence. One example of this is the word *experience.* In some groups, this word describes the sum of all input for an individual. In another group, it refers only to emotion or feelings, and, in a third, experience means compliance. Thus if a leader is not easily understood, or if the group employs an unfamiliar or confusing language system, the group should be avoided.

Choosing Groups Carefully

A group experience can be very powerful, and entering into such a situation should not be done impulsively. A decision to enter a group should be weighed; each individual should be aware of what goals he or she has for participation. Several group approaches can be examined and a choice made in line with the individual's goals and abilities, if possible after consultation with trusted others.

To help the individual evaluate various groups, the ethics and standards of the group leaders must be clearly specified. These ethics are inextricably woven to the extent and quality of their training.

TRAINING

Two unqualified statements can be made at this point regarding the availability of qualified group leaders:

1. With the tremendous increase in the use of groups in a wide variety of settings, there is a great need for qualified group leaders.
2. Group leadership skills are complex and varied.

Given these two conditions, it is essential that training programs for group therapists provide for a wide variety of needs. Group leaders need to be able to understand and work with group process. They need to be aware of individual intrapsychic phenomena and interactions between people. They need to have a working theory of psychotherapy, normal and abnormal behavior, and respect for individual differences. They need to have a clear understanding of their own personal dynamics and their strengths and weaknesses.

Training programs for the most part have been fairly inadequate. In most programs, trainees have received excellent instruction in individual psychotherapy and only informal instruction in groups. It has generally been thought that expertise in individual therapy guaranteed corresponding expertise in group therapy. Kaplan and Sadock (1971) note, "The history of group psychotherapy is essentially the history of individual clinicians who experimented alone with a new and untried therapeutic approach" (p. 776). Because of this, the explosive growth of group approaches, and a negative prejudice regarding groups by the majority of the psychoanalytic establishment, there are many untrained or inadequately trained practitioners and few complete training programs.

In the group leader programs which do exist, certain core training seems to pertain. Thus, in the National Training Laboratories (NTL, T-group training) program; in the residency training programs at Stanford University Medical School, Mount Sinai Medical School, Columbus State Hospital; and in the University of Hawaii group leader training program, four universal, interrelated components can be found:

1. Supervised practice as a group leader, with extensive feedback.
2. Observation of professional group leaders.
3. Personal group experience as a member.
4. Theory and skill learning.

A fifth component, individual or group psychotherapy, is frequently recommended.

Supervised Practice

In any profession, the learning-by-doing approach seems central to mastery. The group therapy situation is so variable, the interactions between unique combinations of participants so manifold, that it is impossible to prepare a novice group leader adequately for all contingencies. The leader must learn in part through trial and error, but practice alone is insufficient. Without immediate and accurate feedback, a novice leader will continue to reproduce the same mistakes. It is *supervision* of the practice that makes the big difference. Supervisors must be able to observe the interactions between group members. They must also be able to offer suggestions and alternatives in such a way that trainees can listen undefensively and do not simply copy the supervisors' words in the next session. It is crucial that supervisory suggestions be incorporated into the leader's repertoire and applied as they fit the situation. I have found that feedback from several sources is of value. Co-leader feedback is essential, as is supervisor feedback, and feedback from less trained observers (videotape operators, students in training, group members, etc.) can be remarkably helpful.

In supervisory periods, the interactions which occur in the training sessions between the leaders and between leaders and supervisors are often the major topic of discussion. Frequently the blocks that inhibited interactions in the group sessions are reproduced in the supervisory hour. Competent supervision thus involves both knowledge sharing and a form of individual or group psychotherapy. The competent supervisor can use his or her own group leadership skills in the supervisory hour and hence almost simultaneously serve as a teacher, a therapist, and a model of effective therapy.

Observation of Professional Leaders

Imitation learning is exceptionally powerful when the model has attained a desired level of achievement. In most trades, the rewards of apprenticeship have consisted of the opportunity to practice developing skills under the supervision of a master craftsman and the opportunity to observe the craftsman in action. Watching a professional group leader is a golden opportunity for a trainee to get a realistic picture of the true nature of group leadership. Observing such a therapist, the trainee can view both successes and failures, can begin to discover weaknesses in his own developing skills, and can see the results of specific therapeutic interventions in specific situations. Hence he can save a lot of personal trial-and-error learning and can get some feeling for the scope of a therapist's duties.

Observation alone is valuable but insufficient for optimal effectiveness. Feedback sessions in which observers can discuss events of the group meeting with the professional leader are essential. It is during these sessions that questions can be asked, various solutions can be discussed and evaluated, and a great deal of mutual learning can take place. It is a rare professional who cannot benefit from such feedback. Yalom (1975), for example, states, "I have always found the reflections and feedback of observers, regardless of their level of experience, to be personally helpful to me and thus to the functioning of the group" (p. 504). Not every professional will be comfortable with observation, and it is important, for training purposes, to find group leaders who do not become overly defensive in discussing aspects of their groups and who are open to a variety of solutions to problems, not necessarily their own singular method.

Personal Group Experience as a Member

In order for trainees to learn about the effects of a group in non-academic, nonintellectual ways, they must experience a group as a member. The group experience is emotionally powerful. Unless a leader can empathize with the intense pressures and fears of membership, his or her understanding of members will be subsequently diminished. Group leaders must understand group phenomena affectively and sensorially as well as intellectually. They must fully comprehend what it is like to be vulnerable in a group. Before requesting self-disclosure by members, leaders must realize the level of fear this entails. They must know in a first-hand way what the fears of nonacceptance can be like. In this way, leaders learn how to make informed and timely requests for members' participation.

Empathy is only one component of this aspect of training. Trainees also have the opportunity of seeing an experienced leader in action, concurrent with their own high levels of affect. This is different from pure observation, in which trainees can view the group action more dispassionately. Trainee members in such a group can also observe the coordination between co-therapists and the maximum use of each co-leader's special strengths.

Finally, these training groups are therapeutic for members. Trainees can discover their personal strengths and weaknesses in such a group and take corrective steps. Typically, training groups are not designed for heavy therapeutic intervention, and members with deep-rooted or pervasive psychological problems are encouraged to resolve them in separate individual or group psychotherapy. Less severe problems can be effectively treated in training groups once competitive defensiveness is reduced.

In developing a training group, three cautions are mandatory. These involve (1) political, (2) personnel, and (3) competitive considerations.

Political. Even in this day of enlightenment, several faculty members are likely to be threatened by the use of groups. Often these individuals are very persuasive in developing support against any such nontraditional or popular innovations. In developing training programs in several locations, instigators of group training programs are regularly accused of "forcing psychotherapy onto students," "having his personal needs for sex met in group settings," "forcing students into nervous breakdowns," "playing with fire," "creating unemployable trainees," and "introducing students to communism." Despite a lack of information and the absence of truth in any of these statements, the harassment and threats to terminate group training programs continue. This sort of difficulty seems relatively universal and must be confronted in almost any setting in which a group training program is instituted.

Personnel. The best paper program or plan of action in the world cannot withstand the effects of inappropriate personnel. In this age of technical expertise, the critical component in virtually every equation is the human one. In a group leadership training program, proper staff is the *sine qua non.* Since the trainees will imitate the training group leaders, it is absolutely essential that these leaders have high levels of technical skills and integrity, follow the ethical standards of the profession, and be personally well adjusted and nondefensive. Despite their own professional orientation, these group leaders should also be eclectic with regard to their expectations of member behavior. Yalom (1975) believes "that the trainee's first group experience should not be one of a highly specialized format (for example TA or Gestalt)" (p. 511).

The particular profession of the leaders is less important than their skills in conducting these very difficult groups. In fact, I believe that it is often of value to have group leaders from a different profession than the one for which the students are training. This helps build necessary interdisciplinary respect.

Competitiveness. We have mentioned that training groups are difficult to lead. Members are generally highly competitive with one another and the leaders. After co-leading psychology intern training groups for a number of years, I feel that I shall never see a completely novel leadership challenge in the future. Because of the competitiveness and desire to practice the therapy role, training group members open up cautiously and slowly, by comparison to members in other groups. They take fewer personal risks, and a large part of the leaders' job is to enhance interpersonal trust, cohesion, and cooperation between members. The earlier in the training these groups are instituted, the easier it is to develop a cooperative, rather than competitive, mode. By the time trainees are clinical psychology interns, psychiatric residents, or last-semester masters of social work students, the task is massive. I maintain that the earlier in their training future group leaders are members of groups, the more effective training groups can be.

Theory and Skill Learning

The emphasis on the psychological needs of group leaders should not in any way lessen the importance of academic competencies. Several skills are mandatory. Group leaders must be able to perceive, understand, and articulate group process and content. They must have an active knowledge of normal and abnormal behavior patterns, including principles and theories of learning and motivation. They must also have a working theory of behavior and a solid understanding of the ethics of their profession. In addition to exemplary individual psychotherapy skills, group leaders must have an understanding of the effects of groups on individuals and the power of interaction matrices.

In the model group leaders training program presented in the next section, we note the relevancy of courses in personality and counseling theories, abnormal psychology, and psychopathology; individual training in counseling and psychotherapy; and a variety of listening and research skills.

A MODEL TRAINING PROGRAM

Appley and Winder (1973) have described a model NTL training program. They delineate five developmental stages in a T-group leader training program: *participant* (no experience necessary), *beginning trainer* (two labs of experience), *intermediate trainer* (20-25 labs required), *trainer of trainers* (lab experience, senior trainers, and current practice), and *consultant*. This program is essentially identical to the group leadership training program I designed which was formerly active at the University of Hawaii. It is a four-semester, two-year program during which group leader trainees experience a variety of roles associated with group leadership. The curriculum for the four semesters is described below.

Stage I: First Semester

In Stage I, potential group leaders are enrolled in a prepracticum course. As part of this course requirement each individual participates as a member of an interpersonally oriented encounter group led by two advanced trainees, who are in turn supervised by more advanced trainees and by the course instructor, who is a professional group leader. These groups are videotaped in their entirety, and members are encouraged to view the tapes after each session. In addition to their membership in the encounter group, trainees learn basic communication, listening, and counseling skills and engage in a great deal of supervised individual psychotherapy practice.

During this first semester, trainees are expected to consolidate their knowledge in two adjunct areas: abnormal psychology and theories of counseling and personality.

Stage II: Second Semester

Potential group leaders take an extensive course in the practice and procedures of group leadership in Stage II (this text could be the basis of such a course). In addition, trainees are required to be members in a second encounter group which is more intrapsychically oriented. They are also required to be apprentice co-leaders in a psychotherapy group of patients led by a professional group leader in the community.

In addition to these requirements, trainees also serve as videotape camera operators in the prepracticum course for the next group of first-semester trainees. In this role they have the opportunity of observing a group without being personally vulnerable. They are also included in the supervision sessions which follow each group session.

During this semester, trainees are expected to be engaged about one fourth of the time in an individual counseling or psychotherapy practicum class.

Stage III: Third Semester

Trainees co-lead in the prepracticum groups under direct supervision in Stage III. They meet the group for eight two-hour sessions and one

10-hour marathon (between the fifth and sixth sessions). Each session is videotaped and observed by a supervisor. During the session an audiotape is also made on a stereo cassette. Track 1 contains the conversation in the group meeting, and track 2 contains simultaneous process comments made by the trainees' supervisor. As soon as the session is over, trainee leaders meet with the supervisor and the videotapers for feedback and analysis of the session. Leaders are required to view the videotapes and to present the parts they found most difficult to handle to a class consisting of all the group leaders and supervisors, as well as the professor in charge. During these weekly class meetings, issues and problems in leadership and specific incidents in the groups are discussed. Trainees are expected to review the supervised audiotapes at least once during the week. They also review and supervise the individual psychotherapy interviews of first-semester trainees.

During this semester, trainees are also expected to do practicum or intern-level work under supervision at a mental health or counseling center and to co-lead a community group with a mental health population.

Stage IV: Fourth Semester

During Stage IV, trainees who have previously led groups serve as supervisors for succeeding-semester group leaders. They observe all sessions of the groups, provide simultaneous feedback via the audiotape cassette, and supervise group leaders immediately following each group session. They work closely with the supervising professor in learning the intricacies of the dual roles of supervision. They are trained to be both therapists and information givers in this capacity. They are also expected to be intimately involved as interns in a supervised professional setting offering individual and group psychotherapy.

The Group Training Sequence

During the entire four semesters of this model group leadership training program, appropriate reading is assigned, and adjunct courses to fill in related deficiencies are completed. Trainees are also encouraged to undertake individual and group therapy as clients, for both training and personal concerns.

Table 7–1 illustrates how trainees move through this group training sequence from membership to leadership to supervisory functioning. Each succeeding stage is built upon successful completion of the previous one, and each represents a building block for the next. Success in each stage requires a major effort and increasing responsibility. By the conclusion of the sequence, trainees must demonstrate competence in the identification and use of the group process. They must be effective

TABLE 7–1: Succeeding Stages of Model Group Leadership Training Program

Stage I	Stage II
Group Work Membership in interpersonally oriented encounter group, led by advanced students in program.	Membership in second encounter group. This group is more specialized, more intrapsychically oriented. Serve as apprentice co-leader in psychotherapy group with real patients and a professional co-leader. Videotape and observe Stage I groups and sit in on supervision.
Adjunct Work Training in basic communication skills. Supervised individual psychotherapy practice.	Course work in theories, practices, procedures of group leadership. Individual practicum counseling or psychotherapy work in community.
Remedial Work Consolidation of knowledge in theories of personality and counseling and abnormal psychology and psychopathology.	Individual or group psychotherapy as needed.

group leaders capable of using and transmitting the ethical values of professional leaders, and they must be aware of their own personal dynamics and limitations. Each trainee must also be able to work independently as well as a part of a co-therapist team.

I feel that a two-year intensive program is necessary to accomplish all these goals. While individuals with a broad background in mental health may not need to go through as extensive a group therapist traineeship, the total amount of training in this program is not excessive.

Stage III	Stage IV
Co-lead Stage I groups under direct supervision of former group leaders.	Supervise Stage III co-leaders of Stage I group.
Attend class sessions with other group leaders, supervisors, and training director.	Attend class sessions with other group leaders, supervisors, and training director.
Co-lead a mental health group in community setting.	Provide running audiotape supervision while group is in session.
Supervise individual therapy interviews of Stage I trainees.	Internship or equivalent in supervised professional setting, including consultation, individual and group psychotherapy, and in-service staff training.
Videotape replays.	
Audiotape replay with supervisors' comments.	
Class sessions with other leaders, supervisors, and training director.	
Review videotapes and problem areas.	
Practicum or internship work at community mental health center.	
Individual or group psychotherapy as needed.	Individual or group psychotherapy as needed.

CO-THERAPY

In most examples given above and in the model training program, the groups are led by two leaders. It is my firm belief that every group can be conducted best by more than one therapist. For the most part, clinical practice and some recent research also support the use of co-therapists for both training and therapy functions. Rosenbaum (1971) suggests that the presence of a co-therapist increases the validity and intensity of specific interpretations, helps root out and break through therapeutic impasses, helps neutralize or clarify neurotic problems of the therapist, increases the depth and movement in therapy, allows for simultaneous probing and support, and aids transference.

Such thinking is relatively new. For many years, the notion of using more than one therapist was directly discouraged. Psychoanalytic thinkers were particularly averse to the addition of a co-therapist on the grounds that it would severely and negatively affect the transference relationship. It also was considered uneconomical to consume the time of two therapists in a single group session.

Early proponents of co-therapy were Hadden (1947) and Whitaker (1949), who used co-therapy as a training device; Dreikurs (1950), Grotjahn (1951) and Hulse (1950b, Hulse, Ludlow, Rindsberg, & Epstein, 1956), who investigated the use and implications of multiple therapists in a group setting; and Lundin and Aranov (1952), who have provided a lengthy description of their use of two therapists in groups of schizophrenics receiving insulin treatment at Chicago State Hospital. Later work (e.g., Diamond & Shapiro, 1973b; Harari & Harari, 1971; Rosenbaum, 1971; Shapiro & Diamond, 1972; Shapiro, Marano, & Diamond, 1973; Yalom, 1975) all supports the use of co-therapists in a variety of group settings.

Two predominant reasons were given to support the use of co-therapists in the early work. Dreikurs (1950) and Hulse (1950b) and his associates (Hulse et al., 1956) favored co-therapists for their value in reproducing a "family setting" within the group therapy context. Hulse et al. also recommended the use of male and female co-therapists to simulate this "family" reaction. Several articles have reported investigating special considerations of the transference phenomena in such a setting for husband-and-wife co-therapy teams (Harari & Harari, 1971; Low & Low, 1975), father-and-son teams (Solomon & Solomon, 1963), and interracial leader teams (Shapiro, 1976). General cautions about co-therapy have consistently been issued by Slavson (1964).

In addition to the family simulation, the early use of co-therapists for training was frequently reported. Whitaker's (1949) early work training physicians and Hadden's (1947) training with interns and residents are excellent examples. Anderson, Pine, and Mee-Lee (1972), Gans (1957), Rosenbaum (1971), and Yalom (1975) have also indicated the value of a co-therapy model. Two forms of co-therapy can be used in training: an egalitarian model (Getty & Shannon, 1969; McGhee & Schuman, 1970), and an apprentice model. Most authors seem to feel that for greatest development, group co-leaders need to be equal. Yalom, for example, states that "a co-therapy arrangement of anything other than two therapists of completely equal status is, in my experience, inadvisable" (1975, p. 420).

In our training model, we attempt to keep co-leaders of equal ability together. However, I also feel that there is a place for the junior co-leader in training. There certainly has to be some consideration of status problems and role confusion, but if these are patiently worked out, this form of training experience can be especially valuable. Working out co-leadership with any two people is a difficult task which requires tremendous patience and flexibility. Since we are dealing with group leaders, however, we expect such patience and flexibility, and we have been successful in working out problems of co-leadership.

Advantages of Co-Therapy

While training and transference–family simulation issues were the early reasons for co-therapy, several other excellent *raisons d'être* have been advanced as co-therapists have worked together. Among these are better coverage for the group, mutual support, feedback mechanisms, opportunities for better interactional fit, self-therapy, on-the-job learning, greater opportunities for role flexibility, modeling, and greater effectiveness.

Better Group Coverage and Greater Effectiveness. Even the seemingly omniscient group therapist is not infallible. In every group, an individual leader's attention will be focused on some members and not on others. Whether because of theory, personality, or the interaction between leader and members, each leader will tune in to some members and some processes in a group and totally miss others. Every individual therapist has blind spots. The addition of a second leader with unique perceptions, theoretical orientation, and personal reactivity to members helps reduce the number and size of these blind spots. Where one leader cannot empathize with a particular member, the second leader can, and vice versa. In this way, co-leaders provide greater coverage.

Similarly, each therapist has preferences in terms of which members he or she works with effectively. With two leaders, the negative effects of such a preference can be minimized. Thus more voluntary and effective treatment can be offered to each individual.

Mutual Support and Self-Therapy. In addition to being able to fill in for each other, co-therapists also work together. When co-leaders support the same perception, it is more difficult for members to resist. Rosenbaum notes that, "Patients are more prone to accept two interpretations that are consonant than one solitary interpretation" (1971, p. 501). Similarly, when one leader makes a tentative response and finds support from the co-leader, he or she can then follow up with less fear of being totally off the track. If co-leaders disagree, they can negotiate and find an adequate alternate path, with less tentativeness by either. In this way, co-leaders check and balance one another.

There is also tremendous personal value in a co-therapy situation. It is highly unlikely that people can consistently be in a highly charged emotional climate like that of group therapy and not be in need of someone to talk to about their own feelings and reactions to group members and process. Group members regularly deal with their conflicts in the human condition. Group leaders share this condition and are not immune to personal response. The perfect partner for discussing these problems is another person who was subject to identical stimuli: in the leader's case, the co-therapist. Each co-therapist serves as a reality-based sounding board and therapist for the other partner.

This is one of the reasons why the choice of a co-leader is a major decision, not to be taken lightly. It is crucial for co-leaders to have a close enough personal relationship that they can be mutually therapeutic. This is especially important immediately following the group session. The co-leaders also serve as diagnosticians for each other. Often a co-leader's responses in the group meetings will be an indication of certain psychological blocks or problems. It is the other leader's job to observe and relay such information back to his or her partner.

Interactional Fit, On-the-Job Learning, Role Flexibility, and Modeling. Frequently in a group setting a member will need to have his defenses lowered and to feel support at the same time. Co-therapists are ideally set up to do this. Instead of having a single therapist engaging in both attacking and supporting behaviors, a very difficult and confusing task, each of the therapists can choose a single role. One of the therapists can provide enough support so that the patients feel safe enough to drop some of their defenses and hence be more receptive to previously frightening feedback. In this way, patients can attempt new behaviors without panic regarding the consequences.

Often these co-therapist roles switch, depending on the nature of the interactional matrix of the group. Thus it is easy for one leader to be the supportive "good guy" with some members and the confronting "bad guy" with others.

When groups are co-led by a male and a female therapist, members often see the female as warm and loving and the male as authoritarian. It is in the breaking down of such stereotyped projections that many members experience major therapeutic breakthroughs.

In the course of a group, co-leaders will of necessity disagree. If they can express this disagreement openly in the group and negotiate a settlement, they serve as powerful role models in effective conflict resolution. Harari and Harari (1971) discuss the value of a husband

and wife co-therapist team fighting fairly to resolution as a valuable component of the co-therapy approach. Naturally, co-therapist problem sharing should be kept to a minimum and dealt with only once the group has evolved far enough to deal with such conflicts. In terms of our group process model, Phase III should be well underway before such leadership problems are exposed. If too many co-therapy conflicts are publicly resolved in the group, members can get frightened off, lose their faith in the leadership, and develop feelings that the group is not equipped to deal with their own problems.

Other Values of Co-Therapy. In addition, co-therapy provides for personal growth (Benjamin, 1972) of the leaders. It is also convenient when one therapist is sick or on vacation (Rosenbaum, 1971), and economical in terms of better coverage, more therapeutic resources per hour, and so on.

Dangers of Co-Therapy

All the dangers in a co-therapy situation seem a function of inappropriate selection and/or competitiveness. Heilfron (1969), MacLennan (1965), and Yalom (1975) have all addressed the problems inherent in a co-therapy relationship.

Competitiveness in the co-therapist situation is devastating. In no case can one co-leader work to further himself at the expense of the other co-leader and still have an effective group. A crucial test of their cooperativeness comes in each group where a challenge is issued to one of the leaders. If the co-leader comes to the support of the challenging member(s) at the expense of the co-leader, an almost unclosable gap can ensue. Actually, the nonchallenged leader's role in this situation is to support both and focus on process. In any case, vying for the members' affection can be as destructive in a group as it is in a family when parents fight for children's affection.

Competitiveness seems especially prevalent in groups of advanced students where the status dissimilarity between the leaders and members is not apparently great, such as groups of clinical psychology interns or psychiatric residents. Having the co-leaders simultaneously be members of another training group usually reduces such competition.

Selection of a co-leader is an important decision; one leader should never feel like he or she is "stuck" with his or her partner. Co-therapists should like and respect each other and trust their partner's judgment. They should have complementary skills and styles rather than identical ones. Most authors agree that a male-female team is good, but physical characteristics are outweighed by skill and mutual sensitivity. It is also important that co-therapists be clear about their own relationship. If co-leaders have a dual relationship (professional and personal), it is essential for them to be explicit with regard to these roles and in agreement as to the relative place of each. Co-leaders must also be able to work at relatively equivalent speeds in order to keep the group process moving consistently.

To complete our examination of the group therapist's characteristics, roles, ethics, and problems in Chapters 6 and 7, we will take a look at the perceptual and information-processing components of these leaders and co-leaders.

INFORMATION SYSTEMS OF GROUP LEADERS

In order to conduct a group successfully, leaders must play the several roles described in Chapter 6: information disseminator, catalyst, orchestrator, model-participant, and dispenser of reinforcement and environment manipulator. To do this they rely on basic skills which govern the intake of information they need in order to intervene effectively. Above all, the leader must be perceptive and open to the data available in a group setting.

Five major sets of data must be simultaneously incorporated and evaluated by leaders in order to function in the multiple leadership roles. In a sense, the leader must operate as a five-track tape recorder, receiving messages from five overlapping yet distinct sources, mixing these inputs, and then producing a single response. The leader must be sensitive to:

1. The verbal content of members' messages.
2. Nonverbal messages of members.
3. Interactions between members.
4. His or her own feelings.
5. His or her theoretical understanding or interpretation of the group process.

Figure 7–1 depicts the interrelationships of these systems.

In order to respond to the group members effectively, the leader must be able to incorporate all five inputs and decode them. With all these data, however, the leader can respond to only a fraction of the information received. One of the distinguishing criteria between effective and ineffective leaders is related to which fraction the leader responds to and the timing of the response. This is a complex task involving each of the five data sources.

FIGURE 7–1: Multiple Informational Input Systems of Group Leaders for Various Members

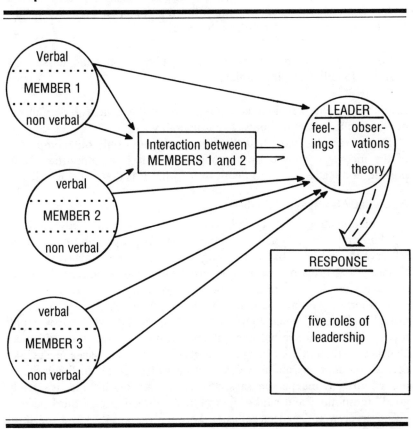

Content of Members' Messages

The most obvious source of data is what is being said by the members at a given time. The content of a message is simply the verbal component—the words—as they would appear in written form. The content of a message is the precise statement made by the sender.

Two examples help clarify this data source. One is:

Jim: I really feel happy today.

The content of this message, "I really feel happy today," can be less believable if, for example, it is said in a loud tone of voice, through clenched teeth, or as the person is banging on the door of the room trying to exit. Even though it is less believable, the *content* remains the same.

The content is the same in the following example, even though the total message may be interpreted otherwise:

Sam: Jim, you'd better sit down; I've got some really bad news.
Jim: I really feel happy today.

Here the content "I really feel happy today" is the same as it was above, but the context alters the message considerably.

These examples show that the verbal content is only one component of the message received by a group leader. It is an important component, and leaders need to be aware of what it is that is being said.

Nonverbal Messages of Members

Communication is not entirely verbal. Tones of voice, body positioning, body movement, relative distance between people, and eye contact all serve to qualify verbal and messages, and they communicate in and of themselves. Normally, verbal nonverbal components convey the same message, and the nonverbal components go relatively unnoticed. However, when the verbal and nonverbal messages are discrepant, as in the example above in which the verbal message was "I really feel happy today" and the nonverbal components included a loud tone of voice, clenched teeth, and door banging, the receiver of the message must make several assumptions about which part he will respond to. Similarly, in our culture, if one person says, "Have a taste of this pie, it's really good" to another, and winks one eye in the direction of a third person, an observer would expect collusion between the speaker and the third person and a surprise for the pie taster. The verbal message is qualified by the nonverbal wink.

Most people in mental health fields, trained in nonverbal communication, have a tendency to give primacy to nonverbal meanings. Such cues as eye contact or lack of eye contact are taken to reflect emotional states or veracity. Movement toward an individual while conversing is interpreted as a desire to communicate, and movement away, the reverse. Arms folded across the chest or sitting behind a barrier is generally interpreted as defensiveness. Nonverbal data are collected and analyzed even with reference to a person's location in the group; members tend to sit close to people they feel support them, across from people who attract them, and at right angles to people with whom they are not comfortable.

In receiving such nonverbal data, leaders must be cautious in their interpretations. If two distinctly different messages are received, it is generally a mistake to assume that one is correct and the other incorrect. Rather, the very fact that here were two conflicting messages is the critical piece of process in and of itself. This information may be presented as feedback to the member or filed away by the leader for later use. An example of feedback follows.

> *Kathy:* This group has helped me so much I feel like a new person.
> NORMAN (LEADER 1): You're saying something which would seem so happy, yet you look sad while you're saying it.
> *Kathy:* Well, the group *has* helped me.
> NORMAN: But there's more that you need.
> *Kathy:* Yes.
> NORMAN: Would you like to share that?
> *Kathy* (smiling at Norman and leaning forward): I'm not sure.
> HARRIET (LEADER 2): You'd like to share, but you want Norman to ask you.
> *Kathy* (angrily): Why do you always have to psychologize us?
> HARRIET: This is between you and Norm and you resent my joining in.
> *Kathy* (to Norman): When I saw you on the bus yesterday, you didn't even notice me. I felt put down.
> NORMAN: I never saw you. Did you say hello?
> *Kathy:* I was embarrassed.

Both leaders in this example confronted Kathy with her "double messages" in the context of several other leadership interventions. This type of feedback, properly timed, can be remarkably effective. For the most part, however, leaders will confront like this only after they have seen similar behaviors or have developed enough understanding of the individual that their confrontation occurs *with a particular goal in mind.* In this case, both leaders were willing to work with Kathy on her transference feelings with them.

Nonverbal behaviors are an important source of input with reference to other aspects of group process, especially when they contradict verbal content.

Interactions between Members

No communication is delivered in a void. As Haley (1963a) so effectively points out, each message contains two components: information, and a redefinition of the current relationship between the communicators. In a two-way communication, each message given by either party either confirms the current definition of the relationship as symmetrical or complementary, or it is an attempt to redefine the relationship.

Understanding the nature of such communication in a two-person situation is difficult; understanding such communication in a multi-person (group) setting is a mammoth undertaking. If we follow this assumption, each time a group member communicates with any other member or leader he or she is, in effect, simultaneously defining his or her relationships with each other member and leader as well. Whenever a person instigates a communication, the context in which this message is sent plays an important function. It may be appropriate to say something at a ball game that would be very inappropriate in a church. Whenever a member sends a message in a group, it is with some awareness of the total context, and frequently strategically emitted.

Thus a member may say something to the leader as a way of presenting himself to another member. In the following example, the member was talking directly to the leader but was much more interested in communicating to another member.

> *Peter:* I just think that if people dig each other, whatever they do is cool.
> *Betty* (looking at Doris, a leader):   You know, I think my husband's really uptight. He's old fashioned . . . it's like he thinks that if I ever get it on with another guy I'd be ruined forever.
> *Harold:* Does he feel that he can screw around?
> *Betty:* You mean double standard? No . . . he's not interested. (Then, turning to leader): Doris, what should I do if I feel turned on to someone and want to go with those feelings, but Herb (husband) would really flip out?
> DORIS (LEADER 1):   Is there someone here you're turned onto now?
> *Betty* (embarrassed):   That's not the issue. The issue is that he set the rule and he doesn't want to break it, but what if I do . . .?
> DORIS: Are you concerned about who makes the rules, or the consequences of violating them?
> *Len:* Why don't you do it and not tell him?
> *Betty:* But then if he found out. . . .
> RICHIE (LEADER 2):   Which is your concern?
> *Betty:* I don't think it's fair.
> RICHIE: Is there someone here you'd like to explore this with?
> *Betty* (looking down, and in a soft voice):   Claude.

At this point Peter looked very disappointed.

> *Claude:* Uh, oh, . . . um . . . I mean.
> RICHIE: That surprises you?

Claude: Yes.
DORIS: What about Peter?

Here both Betty and Peter blushed and proceeded to share some elaborate fantasies they harbored for one another. Peter's general comment to the group was accurately perceived by Betty as an invitation, and Betty's comments to Doris were as much an acknowledgment of Peter's invitation as they were a comment about her husband.

The leaders were cognizant of this, and they acted as catalysts and orchestrators to bring the issue to the fore and deal with it. It is interesting to note that in this situation Betty and Peter both felt tremendous relief in sharing their fantasies, and they did not act them out. Once the feelings were exposed the excitement was experienced, and the need for action was reduced.

In this case, the content and nonverbal messages were secondary to the implied relationship between members. The leaders' understanding and acknowledgment of the interactions between members made it possible to deal effectively with the issue.

Leaders' Own Feelings

Of all the sources of input, the most predominant spur to direct action is the leaders' emotions. Most individuals generally act out of what they feel rather than what they think. Group leaders are no exception. If a group leader feels angry or happy or sad in a group setting, his or her interactions with members will reflect this. For this reason, it is essential for leaders to know themselves well. If emotions are generated from group process, leaders can use their own emotions as a highly tuned pickup system. If, during the group, a leader suddenly starts feeling anxious, he must search around the group to discover the source of this anxiety. Is it something a member is saying? Is it a feeling state in the room due to what members are not saying? Is it that the topic has much unresolved conflict for the leader?

Two Crazy Yet Utilitarian Assumptions

Each leader makes two assumptions in a group setting that reflect otherwise indefensible beliefs.

1. *My feelings are an accurate and in-depth index of the group process.*
2. *Whatever I feel is due to something that is going on in the group.*

In order for these assumptions to serve leaders, they must be aware of their own needs, expectancies, weaknesses, and reactions, and they must have a clear understanding of any nongroup-related pressures. If the leader had a fight with his or her spouse before coming to the group session, his or her reactions to members may be more a reflection of these feelings than of anything actually occurring in the group.

One example of this occurred in a group where one of the co-leaders had painfully ended an important romantic relationship at 3 A.M. prior to a 9 A.M. marathon group. By the time the group began, he was feeling hurt, sad, lonely, and frightened. In this position, his sense receptors for such feelings in others were hypersensitive. As is so frequently the case in such situations, a member of the group had similar problems, and the leader was extra perceptive and effective in helping her through a five-year-old block. Since the situations were so similar—rejection, feelings of loss and helplessness—he was almost brilliant in his intervention and helped the member substantially. When the co-leader, who was aware of the entire situation, requested that the troubled leader share his own grief, the latter was unable to continue in a leadership role for several hours. Fortunately, the group could treat him as a member, and the co-leader could take charge. Had the co-leader not been fully aware of the situation, and had the outside problem not been the clear generator of all these feelings, misunderstanding and chaos could have resulted.

Leaders frequently rely on their feelings. They assume that if they are responding in a certain way to an individual, significant others may be responding similarly, and this may be a clue or manifestation of an individual client's problems. In order to keep this sensory channel clear, leaders must be self-aware and understand their own sensitivities.

Theoretical Understanding

From our perspective, a theory provides a leader with several essential qualities necessary to make sense out of the apparent chaos of group interactions. Theories operate as filters, letting in relevant (understandable) data and blocking out irrelevant stimuli. They increase the amplitude of the primary signal and reduce others as noise. In addition to pointing out where the leader should look, theories provide sets of constructs which explain what the data mean when the leader finds it. They also provide a manner of response so that the therapist, having discovered and interpreted the data, has clear options as to reactions to the data.

Thus leaders use their theories to tell them what is important, why it is important, and what to do about it. Without a theoretical or interpretive understanding of group behavior, a leader is confronted with a wide variety of uncoordinated data, no consistent means to understand it, and no step-by-step plan of action. In short, without a theory, a group leader will respond spontaneously, inconsistently, and ineffectively.

It does not seem to matter which theory group therapists hold. They must only apply it consistently and be aware of its limitations for identifying, classifying, and acting on diverse data.

One Piece of Group Process

In order to illustrate the way a group therapist uses these five systems and applies them to the leadership roles, the following example and process analysis are given. The 10 group members are briefly described as follows:

Agnes. 39 years old, divorcee. Very angry outwardly, seems to direct the anger at men in general. When not speaking, seems depressed.

Barbara. 30 years old, married, two children. Describes herself as happy but unfulfilled. Husband apparently treats her as an object of his own gratification rather than understanding her needs.

Betty. 29 years old, military wife, husband away for nine months. Working on BA at university, regularly has affairs while husband is away.

Charles. 48 years old, psychiatrist. Has been an effective private practitioner for several years. Divorced and living alone. Tends to be more "therapeutic" than involved in relationships with others.

Karl. 41 years old, minister, married, 5 children. Has been sexually involved with several women in congregation. Very concerned that wife or church authorities will find out.

Ray. 26 years old, married. Very athletic, engages in various sports at least three nights a week. Presents a strong machismo image but appears very sensitive underneath it. Currently his wife is very angry with him, threatening to leave him; he is confused about this.

Sandy. 28 years old, nurse, living with 49-year-old lover for five years. Not happy with the relationship but frightened of moving.

Susan. 29 years old, successful, high-paid model. Unsure of life goals, very unsure of relationships with men. Aware that she presents herself sexually but resents it when men relate "only to my body." Looking for permanent relationship. Divorced twice.

Toshio.   34 years old, immigrated to U.S. when five years old. Very quiet and polite, seems very accepting of others. Painfully unable to request anything for himself.

Willie.   32 years old, single. Describes himself as a swinger and has been in untold numbers of relationships. During early part of group, proudly announced that he had slept with 100 women in one year. Groupwise, he says all the right-sounding things, but they seem somehow disconnected from him. Has been in every "growth" experience to hit town in the past five years.

This event occurs during the early stages of the therapeutic phase of the group. The scenario is first presented in entirety, and then a process analysis is given in Table 7–2. Note that the entire sequence is described as if we were inside the leaders' heads.

Susan: There's something that is bothering me that I'd like to talk about.

FAY (LEADER 1):   Go ahead.

Susan: I just ended another relationship this weekend. He's a good guy, too.

FAY (expectantly):   But . . .

Susan: It's like all he's ever interested in is sex. I like sex too, but it's like my body is all he wants.

Ray: Well, you do have a really nice bod.

Susan: Ya, I know, and I feel good about that, but I'm more than just big boobs and a piece of ass.

FAY: You'd like him or anyone to appreciate your body, but also to appreciate the inner parts of yourself.

Susan (weeping):   Yeah, I need to know if he loves me.

Agnes: Your body won't last forever and as soon as you start to sag, he'll take off and find some other honey who's younger. You know, honey, most men are bastards like that.

Karl: I don't think that's fair. There's so much more important than a woman's figure.

Sandy: Sue, I know what you're talking about. I think a guy like that is better off gone.

Susan: Yeah, but what if they're all like that?

Willie (smiling and looking at Susan):   You just need to find another kind of man.

Sandy: Easier said than done.

Ray: Like Willie?

Charles: I wonder, Susan, if you attract only those kinds of men.

Agnes (sarcastically): Right, it's always the woman's fault—She didn't get raped, she led him on.

Charles: Your anger is really getting in the way. I feel that perhaps Susan is attracting these kinds of guys either because of where she looks, because of what she does with them, or possibly even as a way of proving that all men are no good.

Betty: Do you think that's possible?

Susan: Yeah, I've screwed up two marriages, and sometimes think I married bastards as a defense against letting myself go fully.

LARRY (LEADER 2): Sandy, can you verbalize that?

Sandy (tearfully): That just hits home.

LARRY: You're in a similar situation?

Sandy: (Nods.)

LARRY: Can you tell Susan?

Sandy: You know Bob, the guy I live with . . . well, he's a good man, but he's just insensitive to my needs. Maybe I won't let him try, but it's just that he won't listen to any really deep feelings.

FAY: That really hurts.

Sandy: God, it's like there's a part of me that's too ugly for anyone to live with.

Both women are crying now, and Larry moves over to where Barbara is sitting and puts his around her shoulders. She also begins to cry.

Ray (with trembling lips): That's not only true for women.

LARRY: You've felt that also.

Ray: (Nods.)

LARRY: I've experienced a feeling of not being understood also. It really hurts when you pay attention to it.

Charles: You've got to pay attention to it. If you understand it, you can come to grips with your humanity.

Willie: That's the asshole way. You just experience it as that's the way it is, and it's OK.

Karl: What does that mean?

Willie (condescendingly): It's all the same. It's what *is*. You can't take responsibility for anyone else.

FAY: Susan, where are you now?

Susan: Feeling hurt and scared.

FAY: Talk about the fear.

Susan: I'm scared I just drive all the men away because I'm not open. But if I open up I get clobbered. It's like if you're a model, only one kind of man approaches.

LARRY: Barbara, can you share your feelings with Susan?

TABLE 7–2: Process Analysis

Content	Nonverbal Message	Interactions between Members
Susan: There's something that is bothering me.	Susan's lips trembling. No large affect in others.	
FAY: Go ahead.	Eye contact between Fay and Susan.	Everyone tuned in to Susan.
Susan: I just ended another relationship this weekend. He's a good guy, too.	Looking down, sad. Sandy avoids eye contact.	Sandy leans towards Susan. Willie tries to make eye contact.
FAY: But . . .	Fay leans forward.	Everyone looks expectantly to Susan.
Susan: It's like all he's ever interested in is sex. I like sex too, but it's like my body is all he wants.	Susan close to tears. Fay/Larry very tuned in. Sandy looking down.	Agnes seems to be sitting above Susan. Ray, Karl, Charles all seem close and open to her.
Ray: Well, you do have a really nice bod.	Ray looking at Susan's breasts. Susan turns red, smiles.	Willie, Ray, Karl, looking at Susan's body. Agnes glares at the men.
Susan: Ya, I know, and I feel good about that, but I'm more than just big boobs and a piece of ass.	Susan looks embarrassed, also sticks out breasts while she talks about them.	Seduction, competition.
FAY: You'd like him or anyone to appreciate your body, but also to appreciate the inner parts of yourself.	Fay looks empathic. Susan about to cry. Agnes looks angry.	High anxiety. Each member seems to be focusing inward.

Leaders' Feelings	Theory/Leaders' Thoughts	Leaders' Role
Comfortable, anticipatory.		
Anticipatory.	Probably something to do with men.	Catalyst
Sadness about end of relationships in personal life. Caring for Susan.	Wonder what she does to pull men close and then push them away.	Participant-model (listening)
Caring for Susan.	I'd like to get her to share this openly.	Catalyst
Caring for Susan. Fear that she will stop half-way. Confidence that they can deal with problem.	Want to keep her talking and avoid interruptions of other members.	
Fear this will sidetrack. Slight initial anger at Ray for his lack of sensitivity.	Ray broke the tension, he probably tried to do something nice. It should backfire. Susan is embarrassed. Wonder if she'll be angry or seductive.	Model-participant
Attraction to Susan's body; competition.	She's being seductive. Could be an example of what she's describing—men treat her as sex object because she presents that part when she's emotional.	
Tenderness toward Susan. Understanding of both needs.	See the fear reaction— seduction. See how she needs both caring for inner self and attractiveness to physical self. Wonder about confronting. Want to see group reaction.	Catalyst Reinforcer

TABLE 7–2 (Continued)

Content	Nonverbal Message	Interactions between Members
Susan: Yeah, I need to know if he loves me.	Susan crying. Sandy near tears. Barbara pale. Agnes moving around a great deal.	Most members focusing inward, little contact. Willie seems to be looking at Susan.
Agnes: Your body won't last forever and as soon as you start to sag, he'll take off and find some other honey who's younger. You know, honey, most men are bastards like that.	Agnes talking thru clenched teeth, pressured speech, loud tone. Others pull back.	Attention moves away from Susan to Agnes.
30-second silence	Agnes glaring. Karl staring at Agnes. Susan weeping.	Karl staring at Agnes.
Karl: I don't think that's fair. There's so much more important than a woman's figure.	Karl looks like he's holding back anger by being calm. Barbara looks scared.	Lot of head nodding, Barbara looking at Susan with caring.
Sandy: Sue, I know what you're talking about. I think a guy like that is better off gone.	Turned toward Susan —back toward Karl. Karl staring at Sandy. Agnes lying down now.	Sandy obviously not reacting to Karl.
Susan: Yeah, but what if they're all like that?	Agnes sits up. Sandy shakes head.	

Leaders' Feelings	Theory/Leaders' Thoughts	Leaders' Role
Tenderness toward Susan. Remembered feelings of own hurt.	Susan is at point of crying and feeling better temporarily vs. going fully into the pattern. Decision to push her into greater awareness. Still waiting for group reaction.	Model-participant (listening, nonverbal encouragement to continue)
Anger, disappointment, anxiety at this turn of events.	Agnes is anxious, expressing it as anger. Really pulls the process away. She's doing her own form of seductiveness. Wonder if anyone will fall for it and get into a women's lib number. Wonder if I/my co-leader should intervene, or let group do it.	Model-participant (nonverbally looking at Susan, ignoring Agnes) Environment manipulator
Tense.		
Disappointment that Karl went to Agnes.	Resolve to get back to Susan, avoid Agnes's anger until more appropriate time.	Environment manipulator
Confused, a bit uncomfortable. Interest in process.	Wonder about Sandy's cutting off Karl—is it just desire to get back to Susan, or is she uptight about what Karl said. Could she have been involved with Karl?	
	Sounds a bit facile. Will wait it out—too easy a response.	

TABLE 7–2 (Continued)

Content	Nonverbal Message	Interactions between Members
Willie: You just need to find another kind of man.	Willie is smiling and looking directly at Susan. Agnes turning red.	Seductive move by Willie. Charles, Sandy, Karl, Agnes pull back.
Sandy: Easier said than done. *Ray:* Like Willie?	Ray grinning. Susan showing little affect.	General negative reaction to Willie.
Charles: I wonder, Susan, if you attract only those kinds of men.	Speaking quietly.	Group attention turning to Charles.
Agnes: Right, it's always the woman's fault—"she didn't get raped, she led him on."	Sarcastic tone.	Group almost audibly groans.
Charles: Your anger is really getting in the way. I feel that perhaps Susan is attracting these kinds of guys either because of where she looks, because of what she does with them, or possibly even as a way of proving that all men are no good.	Charles leaning forward. Seems confident.	Group looking at Charles and Susan.
Betty: Do you think that's possible?	Looking at Susan. Sandy looks sad.	Many members focusing inward.
Susan: Yeah, I've screwed up two marriages, and some-times I think I married bastards as a defense against letting myself go fully.	Susan has tears in eyes. Sandy looks very pale.	Group moving towards Sandy.
LARRY: Sandy, can you verbalize that?	Sandy apparently in great pain.	

Leaders' Feelings	Theory/Leaders' Thoughts	Leaders' Role
Initially angry at level of Willie's intervention. Jealousy.	Damn Willie—always seductive. OK, this is a chance for Susan to deal with the problem right here.	Participant
	Waiting to see how this comes out.	
	Charles is doing his therapist number— wonder if he'll do it well, wonder if he should be confronted.	
Sad that she maintains that stance.	Have to get back to her anger later. Got to keep it out now—bad time to deal with it.	
Glad he's doing it. Anxious about leadership challenge.	Well, he sounds right on. Hope it's concern for her and not defensiveness on his part.	
Concern for Susan and Sandy.	See if Susan can cop to this or pass it off.	
Concern for Susan and Sandy.	Want to get Susan and Sandy to support one another.	
Concern for Sandy.		Catalyst

TABLE 7–2 (Continued)

Content	Nonverbal Message	Interactions between Members
Sandy: That just hits home.	Begins to cry. Susan looks at Sandy.	Group moves towards Sandy.
LARRY: You're in a similar situation.	Sandy nods. Susan gets teary.	Group looks at Susan and Sandy.
LARRY: Can you tell Susan?	Sandy nods. Susan looks expectantly.	
Sandy: You know Bob, the guy I live with . . . well, he's a good man but he's just insensitive to my needs. Maybe I won't let him try, but it's just that he won't listen to any deep feelings.	Sandy's eyes are clear. Susan crying. Barbara looks sad. Ray avoiding eye contact.	Cohesiveness developing. Focus on Sandy.
FAY: That really hurts.	Said with caring and understanding:	
Sandy: God, it's like there's a part of me that's too ugly for anyone to live with.	Looks very hurt and angry. Susan crying. Barbara looking very sad.	Barbara, Charles, Ray, Susan all moving close.
Silence	Susan and Sandy crying in each others' arms. Larry puts arm around Barbara's shoulders and she cries. Ray's lips tremble.	Susan and Sandy holding each other. Larry holding Barbara.
Ray: That's not only true for women.	Lips trembling.	Women look to Ray with support.
LARRY: You've felt that also.	Ray nods.	

178

Leaders' Feelings	Theory/Leaders' Thoughts	Leaders' Role
Comfort in the process.	Want to connect Susan and Sandy and work on fear of intimacy for them and in the group.	
	Now need to connect them.	Catalyst
Comfortable now.	Need to get her to explain content now.	Orchestrator
Bit anxious about bringing feelings out more, but feel it's necessary.	Want to bring feelings to a head now—make it possible for them both to bring out all the feelings.	
Relief for saying it. Caring for them.	Bring arousal to optimal levels, will have to support them.	Catalyst Model/Participant
Empathy, hurt.	Desire to make physical contact. Better if Susan does it. Barbara needs help also.	
Sadness, concern, anxiety.	Have to check out reactions to this.	Participant Reinforcer Catalyst Orchestrator
Concern for Ray. Own feelings of sadness.	Ray's sensitivity really coming through.	
Sad feelings regarding rejection.	Want to support Ray.	Reinforcer Catalyst Participant

TABLE 7–2 (Continued)

Content	Nonverbal Message	Interactions between Members
LARRY: I've experienced a feeling of not being understood also. It really hurts when you pay attention to it.	Larry's eyes are moist. Susan, Sandy, Barbara weeping.	
Charles: You've got to pay attention to it. If you understand it, you can come to grips with your humanity.	Crying stops.	Members pull back— look to Charles skeptically.
Willie: That's the ass-hole way. You just experience it as that's the way it is, and it's OK.	Willie is smiling but looks pressured. Interpersonal group distance increases.	Members pull back further. Willie is somewhat isolated.
Karl: What does that mean?	Question posed in challenging way. Susan pulling back.	Most of sadness has changed to detach-ment, little closeness.
Willie: It's all the same. It's what is. You can't take responsibility for anyone else.	Pressured speech, almost detached. Susan staring at ground.	Group becoming more distanced.
FAY: Susan, where are you now?	Relief from group to focus on Susan. Agnes looks hurt.	Focus on Susan. Charles looks approvingly at Fay.
Susan: Feeling hurt and scared.	Group focusing on Susan. All look calm and involved except Agnes—still appears angry—and Willie, smiling almost conde-scendingly.	Barb and Sandy very tuned in to Susan.

Leaders' Feelings	Theory/Leaders' Thoughts	Leaders' Role
Sadness Concern Anxiety	Reaching out to Ray— good contact.	Participant-Model
Negative feelings about Charles's interruption.	Assume Charles is uncomfortable with the intimacy being expressed. Changed tone to be safe in his expert role.	
Fear of loss of control.	Charles reduced the anxiety enough for Willie to challenge him. Should get a strong reaction from group.	Participant
Glad for Karl's challenge, sad that Susan, Sandy, Barb lost.	Karl is challenging Willie. Need to get back to Susan, who seems to be withdrawing.	
Anger at Willie. Impatience with his theorizing and language.	Need to get away from this and back to main process.	
Comfort, anxious to get Susan back to her feelings.	Susan could pull out now. Important to get her to focus back on her feelings of hurt and fear, or it's another failure experience for her.	Catalyst Participant-Model Environment manipulator
Comfortable; anxious to get Susan back to her feelings.	Pressing in on Susan, this is the time for her to open—Sandy, Barbara seem likely sources of support.	

TABLE 7–2 (Continued)

Content	Nonverbal Message	Interactions between Members
FAY: Talk about the fear.	Susan fidgeting.	Attention focused on Susan.
Susan: I'm scared I just drive all the men away because I'm not open. But if I open up I get clobbered. It's like if you're a model only one kind of man approaches.	Susan fidgeting. Barbara shaking her head negatively.	
LARRY: Barbara, can you share your feelings with Susan?	Susan looking to Barbara. Barbara tearful.	Attention shifts to Barbara.
Barbara: It's not being a model. Bill and I have been married eight years and I really love the guy, but I use sex to avoid sharing really intimate parts of me. I started to get involved with Charley, just to have someone I could tell those things to, but it started to get sexual and I pulled out.	Barbara and Susan talking and looking to one another. Others looking at Barbara. Willie still smiling.	Barbara talking directly to Susan.
FAY: If you got involved that way with Bill, you'd be vulnerable to hurt, but if you don't open up with your husband, you need a relationship on the side, which has even greater problems.	Barbara looks scared. Susan is nodding her head. Karl looks pale.	

Barbara: Really!

Leaders' Feelings	Theory/Leaders' Thoughts	Leaders' Role
	Encourage Susan, be aware of effects on other group members.	Catalyst
Glad she's beginning.	Keep her focused on this—key is fear of involvement-commit-ment and possibility that this fear manifests itself in behaviors which are contrary to her desires.	
	Trying to get Barbara to share obvious feelings with Susan—get support for Susan and Barbara.	Orchestrator
	Interesting. Barbara is sharing her own identical fear—covered other fears of intimacy by in-creasing sexual closeness.	
Anxiety that they could lose Susan, but want-ing to support Barbara.	Try to tie together Barb's problem with husband to Susan's problem with men. Concern for Sandy and Karl.	Catalyst
	Keep Susan and Barb supporting each other.	

TABLE 7–2 (Continued)

Content	Nonverbal Message	Interactions between Members
FAY: That hooks into Susan's feelings of frustration also.	Barbara and Susan looking at each other. Karl more pale.	Barbara and Susan seem mutually supporting.
15-seconds silence	Willie smiling. Karl very pale.	Leaders making eye contact for support.
LARRY: Karl, you look like someone kicked you in the stomach. What are you feeling?	Karl exhales loudly.	Focus is on Karl.
Karl: It's like something really important is being said and I have to face it too.	Karl pale. Others look at Karl.	Focus is on Karl.
LARRY: You've gone the route of an affair also.	Karl exhales.	Others look nervously at Karl and admiringly at Larry.
Karl: Several.	Karl exhibiting several emotions: fear, pride, etc.	Focus on Karl.

Barbara (very tearfully): It's not being a model. Bill and I have been married eight years and I really love the guy, but I use sex to avoid sharing really intimate parts of me. I started to get involved with Charley, just to have someone I could tell those things to, but it started to get sexual and I pulled out.

FAY: If you got involved that way with Bill you'd be vulnerable to hurt, but if you don't open up with your husband, you need a relationship on the side, which has even greater problems.

Barbara: Really!

FAY: That hooks into Susan's feelings of frustration also.

LARRY: Karl, you look like someone kicked you in the stomach. What are you feeling?

Karl: It's like something really important is being said and I've got to face some stuff too.

Leaders' Feelings	Theory/Leaders' Thoughts	Leaders' Role
A bit confused but comfortable.	A lot of things going on simultaneously. Need to pick up most critical. Worried about Karl.	Orchestrator
Anxious about introducing Karl.	Decide to include Karl.	
	Hope Karl is in with Susan and Barbara. Want to keep this together and on topic of fear of intimacy.	Catalyst
Anxiety about Karl's secret.	He's probably had an affair also—related to Barbara's statement.	Catalyst Participant (nonverbally listening)
Fear of being wrong.	What if he didn't? Hope I didn't blow it. Important to keep it on fear of intimacy.	Catalyst
Interest.	Want to be careful about curiosity—is he being seductive? What's his affect?	

LARRY: You've gone the route of an affair also.
Karl: Several.

As the process analysis in Table 7–2 shows, the leaders respond verbally to only a fraction of the data they take in. For each comment they make, they must process their observations and feelings and incorporate them within their theoretical framework and with proper timing. These skills take training and extensive supervised practice. Groups do not always move smoothly. The process ebbs and flows, and leaders must be prepared for untold variability. This is another way in which the task of leadership is a complex one.

The analysis also shows that the leaders frequently respond verbally to nonverbal messages, interactions between members, and their own feelings. Both leaders choose carefully the content, function (role),

185

and timing of their interventions, helping the group members to move consistently to deeper levels of interactional involvement and to be more nourishing for each other. They participate, model, reinforce, catalyze and orchestrate in such a way that the group becomes a more therapeutic environment. It is important to realize, however, that not every intervention by the group leader has an immediate therapeutic impact. Often apparently well-timed, accurate, and meaning-laden leader statements have little to no noticeable corresponding response by the group members. Learning and behavior change in group therapy occurs as it does in other settings; it requires time, practice, and repetition.

Chapter 8

Group Techniques
and Exercises

Among the multitude of skills in a qualified leader's repertoire is a set of structured techniques and exercises. Often such techniques produce dramatic results and are remembered by group members long after the group has terminated.

Like most powerful tools in a craftsman's kit, structured techniques can produce a wide range of positive and negative results. Improperly used or poorly timed, these techniques can inhibit and seriously damage the group process. When they are carefully and moderately employed, however, they can spur an entire group to action, eliminate defenses, provide the group leader with valuable information for subsequent action, and reduce the total time necessary for the group to accomplish its predetermined goals.

In discussing structured exercises, we deliberately focus on a specific set of skills the group leader can employ. Indeed, almost any repetitious leader behaviors could be construed as techniques. Some of these behaviors—honesty, integrity, patience, courage, flexibility, warmth, empathy, timing are considered more global in character and as more a function of the approach or orientation of the leaders than as techniques per se. These characteristics of leadership were delineated in Chapter 6. It is expected that a well-trained, ethical leader who employs structured exercises will do so with honesty, integrity, and empathy.

CHARACTERISTICS OF STRUCTURED EXERCISES

Structured exercises and techniques are defined in this chapter as *relatively short-term, voluntary* group experiences which are *instituted or sanctioned by group leaders* for a *specific purpose.* These experiences *must be well timed* and must have *clearly determined starting and ending points,* and their effects must be *discussed in detail* by members as soon as they are terminated.

Relatively Short Term

For each of the structured exercises described in this chapter (and many more that are presented in the appropriate reference), the total group time expended is less than two hours. Frequently the exercises, especially the nonverbal ones, are completed in less than 15 minutes. Discussion of group members' reactions may take much longer, up to several hours of group process.

Voluntary

Group members should have the right to refuse to participate in any exercise, as they do for any other individual component of the group. Often novice group leaders get so caught up in completing the exercise that group members are forced into participation which they resent and from which they gain no benefits. Such resentment can seriously affect subsequent learning in the group. The group therapist should explicitly acknowledge members' rights to refuse to participate in any group activity during the screening and introductory stages of the group.

Instituted or Sanctioned by Group Leaders

These exercises are employed by group leaders to accomplish a specific goal. Often, in the course of a group, a member will recommend that the group try a particular technique. Unless the leader agrees to its application, such a suggestion cannot be considered as being within the purview of this definition.

Specific Purpose

Perhaps the most important factor in determining the value of a technique is the extent to which it fulfills a specific need in the group process. Group leaders may institute a particular technique to elicit members' feelings, to increase or decrease the level of anxiety extant in the situation, to clarify a particular piece of group process, to increase the level of trust and sharing in the group, and so on. Unless the leader has a particular goal in mind before employing a technique, he or she can develop a tendency to throw in a technique at any point where the group process is not understood. Such casual and extravagant use of exercises can undermine the group process and increase members' dependency on the leader. Indiscriminate use of techniques in this manner—typically by lay group facilitators—is a major drawback in the pop psychology and human potential movement types of groups.

Well Timed

It is extremely important that exercises be presented in such a manner as to enhance group process. Poorly timed, a technique can cut off the natural process of the group and be destructive. It is very important for a leader to be aware of the ongoing process for the group and for each member before introducing a new piece of process such as a technique. There also must be enough time available to complete the exercises and discussion of members' reactions to them during the sessions in which they are introduced. Indeed, it can be dangerous to members if time runs out in the middle of an exercise.

Clearly Determined Starting and Ending Points

It is important for group leaders to make it clear that a technique is beginning and to request members' participation. Termination of a technique is marked by the leader's invitation to members to discuss their experiences during the exercise.

Discussion

Perhaps the most important aspect of participation in an exercise is the group members' reactions to this participation. In order to integrate the experience into a larger personal framework, members must verbalize their feelings, thoughts, and sensations; hear reactions of others who have shared their experiences; and then incorporate their new learning into their cognitive maps and behavioral repertoire.

FUNCTIONS OF STRUCTURED EXERCISES

The number and variety of structured group exercises is nearly infinite. They range from verbal to nonverbal, from active to passive, from observation to direct participation, from humorous to serious, from giving feedback to giving massages, from reacting to management simulations to touching nude bodies, and from children's games to high-level cognition.

Structured exercises serve two broad functions in the group setting: *Diagnostic* and *treatment*. As a diagnostic tool, these techniques provide an environment in which a group leader can understand the dynamics and behaviors of individual members better. They also help the leader understand group process issues and highlight them for the group members. As treatment, these techniques help ease the way for individual members to try out new behaviors, to experience themselves in novel ways, to face their fears, to stand up to deal with authority, and to practice new behaviors learned in the group setting.

Several authors have indicated the merits of such exercises. These include supplementing the natural spontaneity of the group members (Russell, 1971), reducing the barriers between members and increasing their willingness to self-disclose (Cooper & Bowles, 1973), facilitating openness (Verny, 1975), and providing flexibility in the levels of structure employed by the leaders (Pfeiffer & Jones, 1974a, 1974b).

Denny (1969, 1972), discussing art therapy groups, suggests that art materials facilitate the release of feelings, promote self-understanding, and lead to constructive action. Bender and Woltmann (1936), Beiser (1955), and Axline (1969) all suggest the use of play therapy with children in groups for both diagnostic and therapeutic goals. Bobula (1969) has used drama techniques in breaking down barriers in hospitalized patients. Everett (1968), using a variation of role playing, has shown how to set up an adversary system in married couples' group therapy. This technique makes it easier to understand and deal with angry impasses. Verny (1975) classified these techniques into three major categories and presents several arguments for the use of a variety of techniques in groups.

Several excellent compendiums or summary descriptions of techniques are available and will not be replicated here. For listings and descriptions of a wide variety of group exercises, readers are encouraged to investigate the resources listed in Table 8–1. These resources provide hundreds of structured exercises for use in groups. Before elaborating on a few of the techniques I have preferred, the dangers of employing these exercises in a therapy or encounter group will be addressed.

Lieberman, Yalom and Miles (1973), in their classic study of encounter groups, concluded that leaders who used large numbers of structured exercises were significantly lower on outcome measures than those who used fewer such exercises. The high-exercise leaders, however, were generally seen as more competent and effective by members. These apparently paradoxical findings suggest that the more directive and structured an encounter group leader is, the more likely is she or he to be viewed as a "star" leader. However, the more the leader structures the group experience, the less chance members have to develop sequentially towards meeting workable therapeutic goals. A fast-moving, multiple-exercise approach to leadership can produce a guru-type leader, who, as was pointed out in chapter 6, leaves a lot to be desired and is more apt to produce casualties in the group.

TABLE 8–1: Selected Compendiums of Group Techniques

M. Bates & C. Johnson. *Group Leadership.* Denver: Love Publishing, 1972.

A. M. Cohen & R. D. Smith. *The Critical Incident in Growth Groups: A Manual for Leaders.* La Jolla, Calif.: University Associates, 1976.

C. Hills & R. Stone. *Conduct Your Own Awareness Sessions.* New York: Signet Books, 1970.

H. Lewis & H. Streitfeld. *Growth Games.* New York: Bantam Books, 1972.

H. A. Otto. *Group Methods to Actualize Human Potential.* Beverly Hills, Calif.: Holistic Press, 1970.

J. W. Pfeiffer & J. E. Jones. *A Handbook of Structured Experiences for Human Relations Training* (Vols. 1–5 and Reference Guide). La Jolla, Calif.: University Associates, 1969–1974.

J. W. Pfeiffer & J. E. Jones. *Annual Handbooks for Group Facilitators, 1972–1975.* La Jolla, Calif.: University Associates, 1972–1975.

J. Russell. "Personal Growth through Structured Group Exercises." *Voices: The Art and Science of Psychotherapy,* 1971, 7, 28–36.

W. C. Schutz. *Joy: Expanding Human Awareness.* New York: Grove Press, 1967.

W. C. Schutz. *Here Comes Everybody.* New York: Harrow Books, 1972.

J. E. Zweben & K. Hamman. "Prescribed Games: A Theoretical Perspective on the Use of Group Techniques." *Psychotherapy Theory Research and Practice,* 1970, 7 (1), 22–27.

REQUIRED CONDITIONS

One of the first requests novice leaders make is for a "bag of tricks," a set of techniques they can use when they get stuck. While the possession of such a set of tools can be reassuring to student leaders, its maladaptive use can be destructive. Verny (1975) describes leaders who "become preoccupied with techniques. . . . Every hour on the hour a new exercise is introduced. Not only is such a leader insensitive to the needs of his group, but by triggering feelings and not providing enough time to deal with them, he is literally creating a time bomb without defusing it" (p. 142). Verny (1975) and others have noted the likelihood of this time bomb going off when the leader is not present. Such out-of-group or postgroup explosions frequently result in therapeutic emergencies. We are not saying that the eschewal of techniques will always produce fewer group casualties. The critical point is to employ the exercises in a timely and sparse fashion and to instigate them at appropriate developmental group stages in which the members' ego strength and abilities to deal with the revelations produced by such techniques will be optimal.

It is a great temptation for group leaders to employ a technique to "get something going" or to introduce one whenever movement in the group seems stilted or slow. I believe strongly that several conditions should pertain before any such action is taken.

The Test of Timeliness

Before employing any structured exercise, it is imperative that the leader be aware of current group process. Techniques should not suddenly appear as if inspired by divine intervention. Rather, they should be introduced naturally in the course of group events.

The Test of Appropriateness

Instigation of a technique should not require a sharply discrepant set of behaviors of the members. In requesting members' participation, certain new behaviors may be necessary. However, they should not be so discrepant as to surprise or shock members or to be contrary to current group norms in any major way.

The Test of Consent

Prior to commencing any structured exercise, a brief description of the expectations of members' behaviors should be given and their consent should be requested. If members are unwilling to participate voluntarily, the group will need to discuss this and determine how it wants to handle the situation—allowing unwilling participants to sit out or to veto the activity, discussing the unwillingness in place of using the exercise, forcing participation, and so on.

The Test of Theory

Before employing any technique, the group leader needs to ask several questions of himself or herself:

1. What's happening now in the group process?
2. What would I like to have happen?
3. Why am I looking to change the level of the group functioning?

Is it because of my personal discomfort or something needed by the group members?

4. If I did nothing different, what would occur?
5. How long before these issues would naturally emerge?
6. Which technique will I employ?
7. Is it appropriate to this group now?

Only after all of these questions have been considered by the leaders can an exercise be recommended effectively to the group. The group leader, much like the individual psychotherapist, needs to be well practiced in the theoretical and cognitive aspects of therapy as well as sensitive to process variables and flexible in his intervention strategies.

In discussing the optimal use of structured experiences, Pfeiffer and Jones (1975) recommend a five-stage process: experiencing, publishing reactions to the experience, integrating the sharing with other participants, generalizing from the experience, and behavioral application. This formulation very much follows our own recommendations for all group process and is valuable as a means of incorporating structured experiences into the body of the group.

THE GOLDEN RULE OF STRUCTURED EXPERIENCES

It is far less important to complete the exercise than to deal with whatever behaviors and feelings are generated by the exercise or the suggestion of the exercise. This is the principal rule to be followed in presenting structured experiences to a group.

All too often, novice group leaders change all their leadership skills when they introduce a structured technique. They become technique centered as opposed to process centered and will attempt only to complete the technique or will follow certain rules to the exclusion of other group leadership behaviors. An example of this occurred early in a therapy group. Following a fairly long silence and fairly low levels of interpersonal trust, the group leader attempted to increase the trust levels in the following ways.

LEADER: I'd like to suggest a game for us now, since nobody's bringing up anything. It's called "secret." I'm going to hand out 3 by 5 cards and I want each person to *print* some secret in their life on it. Be sure not to identify yourself.

Mel: I don't have any secrets.

LEADER: Just choose something that most people don't know about you.

Mel: I'm just an open book—I got nothing to hide.

LEADER: Well, just do the best you can. (After each member had written something); OK, now let's put all the cards in this box and shake them up. Then we'll draw them out one at a time and read the secrets and discuss them.

Sandy (whispering to Bob): I wonder if we have the same secret.

Bob (turning red): Bitch! If you. . . .

LEADER: Could you hold it down? OK, who'll draw the first card? How about you, Nancy?

In this situation, the technique does not seem particularly well timed or appropriate, and consent was not really considered. Even more crucial was the leader's decision to ignore an apparently explosive piece of process in order to complete the sequence of his technique. If the leader's goal was to increase levels of spontaneity and trust, this decision would have an opposite effect. In this particular group, this decision reinforced members' feelings that it was very important to say and do the "right" thing and to adhere to the rules. This produced cautious behaviors by the members, with little spontaneity or openness.

By contrast, the following interaction demonstrates an example in which the ultimate goal of the technique was reached by discarding the technique. This process occurred in a training group of mental health professionals and advanced students in training (psychiatric residents, psychology interns). The group was approximately in Phase II. Stage 15 had just about been completed when several members noted that they were feeling very untrusting in this group and asked if the leaders would be willing to suggest a technique. Sensing that there were still lots of leadership challenges left in this group, the leaders were hesitant at first.

Peg: JoAnne, what about a technique? I'd really like to feel close to these people.

JOANNE (LEADER 1): Do you have any particular idea in mind?

Peg: No, but I was hoping you and Jerry could kind of lead us in one.

JOANNE: Well, I'm not sure I'd like to suggest anything just yet. Could you share some of your feelings of mistrust?

Peg: Just feel like everyone here is being the therapist and I want us all to be patients for this time.

JOANNE: How do other people feel about this?

Don: I'm aware that I'm watching and analyzing more than participating.

Vic: Yeah, I guess I'm not too ready to be a patient.

Dick: I'd feel more open if *everyone* were equal (staring at the leaders).

JOANNE: You'd like there to be no leaders?

Dick: No, there's got to be leaders with *this* group.

JERRY (LEADER 2): OK, well let's try an exercise and see how it goes. Since people are concerned about building trust, maybe we could try a blind walk. Does everyone know how that works?

Dick: (angrily): That is so typical of your idiotic thinking, you're so fucking simpleminded. (In a mocking voice): OK team, now we're going to fucking take a fucking blind fucking shit walk. I can't fucking believe you.

JOANNE: Dick, it sounds like you've got something going regarding Jerry, and I'm not sure it's completely related to this exercise.

Dick: That's it, stick up for your fucking buddy. I should have expected that anyhow. You're just his fucking lackey anyhow. You do whatever he says.

JERRY (angrily): OK, what do you want from me?

Dick: Why don't you just get off the stick and get a competent leader in here? Shit, anyone here could do a better job than you two assholes, excuse me, asshole and assistant.

Don: Dick, I don't agree with you. It seems to me that you're avoiding by attacking.

Dick: Well, I suppose I could have expected that from you. You and they have worked together for a long time.

JERRY: I don't know what you want from me, but I'd be willing to hash it out between us if someone else would facilitate (looking directly at Barry, another therapist in the group).

Barry: I'd be willing to do that.

Dick: Why should I let that happen, you're not much fucking better than they are. If anyone should be the leader it should be me, dammit.

At this juncture other group members began to step in and discuss their feelings about the leaders, their feelings about being members, and their feelings about Dick's leadership plans. Thus they began the arduous journey toward mutual trust. The "Blind Walk" exercise was never mentioned again, nor was it necessary. The outburst precipitated by the suggestion of the exercise was far more important in terms of the group's process than the exercise could have been. Furthermore, the goal of the proposed exercise was more than accomplished by the working through of the leadership challenge and the participation of all members in that process.

A Word of Caution

As a general rule, structured exercises are used most effectively when they do not have to be used. With this perspective, and the caution that *the following exercises may be hazardous to the health of your group,* a sample of the techniques I and my colleagues have used quite often is given in the balance of this chapter.

Structured Exercises

Introductory Exercises

    Purpose: Introduction, entry into group.
    Group type: Therapy, encounter.
    Age limits: No specific limits.
    Caution: None.

1.   *Standard Introduction*
     Time: 5–20 minutes.
     LEADER: Let's start by giving our names and saying briefly why we're here. (Turning to the person on immediate left or right): Could you begin?

1a. (option)
     LEADER: After giving your name, please share what you hope to get out of this group and what you fear from this group.

1b. (option)
     LEADER: Please choose a name you'd like to be called during this group. It can be a real name or something you've always wanted to be called. Don't tell why you've chosen this name or whether it's your real name or not. Write the name on a 4 by 6 card and put the card in front of you.

1c. (option) *Alliterative Introduction*
    Each person gives a first name and a personality descriptive adjective or adverb beginning with the same letter, such as "Sexy Sadie," or "Angry Arnie." Each person will then say the names and adjectives of each preceding individual, in reverse order. For example, "I'm 'Good Guy' and this is 'Sexy Sadie,' and this is 'Horrible Harmon,' and this is" and so on. Introductions end when the first person gives the names of all others.

2. *Nonverbal Introduction: Hand Jive*
   Time: 15–45 minutes.
   LEADER: I'd like everyone to get up and begin to mill around the room. *Do not speak,* but make eye contact and look at everyone else. As you go around find someone you'd like to communicate with nonverbally. (When everyone has a partner, leader continues): Now, using only your hands, say hello to this person (approximately 30 seconds). Okay, now express competition with this person (30 seconds). Okay, now express cooperation with this person (about 30 seconds). Okay, now express cooperation with one hand and competition with the other (30 seconds). Now, nonverbally express what this contact has meant (30 seconds), and now say goodbye.

This is repeated two or three times and then discussed in detail, particularly with reference to getting names of people and discussing the relative ease of the different steps. Was competition or cooperation more difficult? Was it easy or difficult to express things nonverbally? This technique is not recommended with groups of children and younger adolescents.

3. *Introduction for Shy People: Building Up to It*
   Time: 30–45 minutes.
   LEADER: Since several members of this group have talked about how difficult it is to talk in a group setting, we thought we'd begin this group by easing into it. Since it's easier to begin talking to one person than a group of people, please choose one partner. Somebody here you don't know or someone you would like to get to know better. (When everyone has paired off, the leader continues): Okay, now decide who will talk first and who will talk second. The person who will talk second is to interview the first person for 10 minutes. When you're the interviewer, try to get to know the person in a personal way, not just status or occupation but values, attitudes, feelings, likes, dislikes, and so on. When this is done you'll be asked to introduce your partner to the group.

After everyone has introduced his or her partner, each individual is allowed to correct, elaborate on, or agree with the information regarding himself or herself. Discussion frequently focuses on problems of choosing a partner or waiting to be chosen (avoid rejection, but take a chance on not getting whom you want), the embarrassment or comfort of having someone else talk about you, and so on. Often successful with groups of administrators, businessmen, and schoolteachers, this technique usually generates much discussion in the early there-and-then stages.

3a. (option)

For very frightened people, move from dyads to groups of four, eight, and so on, until everyone has met in a group smaller than the total group.

Trust Exercises

Purpose: Increasing levels of interpersonal communication and trust.

Group type: Encounter.

Age limits: 17 years old and up.

Caution: Match people of roughly equal size. Not for children or adolescents.

Materials: None.

1. *Trust Fall*

    Time: 5–15 minutes.

    LEADER: Choose a partner of approximately similar size to yourself. Now both of you face the same direction. The person in front is to close his eyes and hold his arms out like this (demonstrates with arms spread parallel to floor). Then as you feel your body moving, let yourself fall backward and your partner will catch you. After you do this, reverse roles.

This relatively simplistic exercise is a favorite among encounter group enthusiasts. It is often seen as a game by participants but does not really affect levels of trust to any great extent. It works better as a classroom demonstration exercise than a group technique.

1a. (option) *Rocking or Lifting*

The leader chooses one member of the group who feels left out or mistrustful.

    LEADER: Would everyone be willing to form a close circle facing inward and would you (identified member) stand in the middle, close your eyes, and let your body fall toward other members of the circle?

Often members keep moving the central person from one to another until they gently lower him to the floor. Then the group gently lifts the person to the waist, shoulder, or above head level and supports and rocks him.

This exercise is a little less simplistic than the simple trust fall and seems to have a moderate impact on the individual. It does seem to help a member open up to being touched physically and to feel like the center of attention in a group. This technique is strongly contraindicated for therapy groups. The physical contact can be very threatening, and the type of trust that has people assured that they won't be dropped is substantially different from the type of trust that involves sharing of feelings, attitudes, and thoughts, which is necessary for patients in a therapy group.

2.   *Blind Walk*

   Purpose: Increasing levels of trust, heightening nonvisual, non-verbal senses.

   Group type: Encounter, therapy (particularly couples' groups).

   Age limits: 17 years old and up.

   Caution: A good exercise for the leader to observe and not participate in. Can be a bad idea if there are angry participants or psychopathic individuals (see example below). Call it a Blind Walk, not a trust walk, for maximum effectiveness.

   Materials: One blindfold for each two participants.

   Time: Approximately 1½–2 hours. Each walk can take from 15 to 30 minutes.

   LEADER: This exercise is called a blind walk. It is designed to help people get in touch with senses besides seeing. Each person should choose a partner. After you have a partner choose who will be blindfolded second. Place the blindfold across the eyes of one person. From now on there should be no verbal communication until the entire exercise is completed. Your task is to lead the blindfolded person around, giving him as full a sensory experience as you can, safely. Each person will lead for 20 minutes. Everyone should be back in this room in 40 minutes and we'll discuss this experience.

Discussion is usually active, and people generally seem able to express many feelings during this period. Themes that often come up are the relative comfort of leading vs. being led (dependence-independence), fears of being inadequate, concern about being responsible for another person, and so on.

This exercise has both therapeutic and diagnostic value. The therapeutic value is evidenced in participants' enhanced levels of trust, feelings of altruism, and sense of sharing a fearful yet enjoyable experience. There are also relatively high levels of diagnostic value in this exercise. As in most exercises, the leader can learn much by observing the interactions between members. Similarly, the discussion period frequently highlights particularly troublesome areas for members. Once identified, these areas can be approached and altered therapeutically.

Sometimes this exercise can identify previously unconscious dynamics that inhibit individuals in a group from interacting clearly. One such example occurred in a training group for psychiatric social workers. One woman (Martha) in this group was consistently given feedback by other members that they thought she was nonverbally disapproving of many of their statements. She denied this without vehemence but did not alter her behavior, particularly toward two of the more active male members. On returning from the blind walk, the following interaction occurred.

BRUCE (LEADER 1):   Well, any reactions to the exercise?

Charles: I have a very strong reaction; I am so pissed off at Martha I feel like punching her out (glaring at Martha).

BRUCE: What happened?

Charles (to Martha):   I saw what you did. I can't believe you tried to hurt someone who was so helpless. You deliberately walked Wilfred into those bushes when he was blindfolded.

Wilfred (hesitantly):   No, I don't think it was deliberate (fingering some mild scratches on his face and arms). Was it?

Charles: Damn right it was. I was ready to come over and take you away from her and walk you and Sandy (indicating his own partner) together.

Martha: He didn't get hurt.

Wilfred (looking confused):   Did you walk me into the bushes on purpose?

Martha (mocking):   Did the big man get hurt?

Charles (shouting):   You bitch!

Martha: You can't hurt him. He's a man. He doesn't have any feelings. All of you bastards are like that. Just use a woman and dump her. Well I just began to get even.

PAM (LEADER 2):   You've got something to get even with Wilfred for?

Martha: Wilfred, Bruce, Charles, Joe, my ex-husband. You're all pigs. I just had my chance with him.

This process, which continued for several hours of group time, allowed several of the members to deal with their sexual feelings, fears, prejudices, and attitudes. The technique was effective in bringing Martha's very strong negative attitudes into the open, and it gave the group and Martha a chance to deal with them.

3. *I've Got a Secret*
   Purpose: Increasing levels of trust and self-disclosure, improving interpersonal communication, enhancing perceived similarities between members.
   Group type: Encounter, therapy.
   Age limits: None.
   Caution: Tell people they won't have to reveal their secret. Should occur later in group, not before Phase III. Not for use with paranoid patients.
   Materials: None.
   Time: 60–90 minutes.

This is another exercise which has diagnostic as well as therapeutic value.

LEADER: I'd like each person to think of a secret. Something about yourself that you've never told anyone. *You will not have to tell us your secret.* Just keep it in mind.

Leader waits until each person has a secret. If one or two people cannot think of one, leader can ask them to respond to the questions as if they had a secret.

LEADER: Okay, beginning with (indicating a member to the immediate right of the leader and going counterclockwise), I'd like you to indicate who in the group would be most critical of you if they knew your secret.

Members and leaders in turn choose that member (or leader) they feel would be most critical of them. This is then discussed, and feedback regarding reasons for selection is encouraged. After this discussion is terminated, the leader continues;

LEADER: This time we'll go around clockwise (turning to member on immediate left). Indicate the member you feel would be most accepting of you if they knew your secret.

Members and the leader indicate their choices, and feedback as to reasons for choices is again requested. In addition, members are asked to express their feelings about being (or not being) chosen. After this discussion is terminated, the leader continues;

> LEADER: Now, being careful not to reveal your secret, please indi-
> cate why you have kept it a secret. Let's begin with Joe (indicating
> a member located halfway around the group from the leader).

Members will give a variety of reasons for keeping secrets. When a member simply says "I don't know" or "I never got around to telling anyone," the leader must ask the member to explain further until they share a feeling or concern. There may also be a brief discussion of reactions to this phase of the exercise.

> LEADER: This time let's go around and choose one person in the
> room whose secret you'd most like to know. We'll begin with
> Mary (another member).

This stage frequently elicits a lot of laughter and joking. It also has some diagnostic value. People often choose someone they want to get to know better outside the group. After this phase ends, the leader asks, "Would anyone like to share their secret?" Depending on the group and the nature of the secrets, somewhere between zero and 60 percent of the members share secrets. After the sharing, discussion of the entire technique should include members' feelings about their secrets (often dramatically different) and about other members. Often members' secrets lose their negative valence through this exercise. The key to this technique, as with most others, is the talk interspersed with the structured components of the exercise. The impact of being chosen as accepting or unaccepting (critical) by one or more fellow group members can be substantial. The impact of not being chosen can be equally powerful.

In one group, all the other members chose one woman as the person who'd be most "critical." When questioned about her feelings, she responded,

> *Member:*   It doesn't bother me. We're used to that sort of reaction.
> LEADER: We?
> *Member:*   All undercover policewomen.

The group responded to her by telling her that they hadn't known her profession, but she seemed always to be taking mental notes and evaluating them. Ultimately she was able to understand that she was maintaining her professional behaviors in her personal life and alienating people she wished to befriend. Incidentally, her own secret was that she had a twin sister who died when she was 13, and she'd never had a close friend she felt she could trust since then. The obvious connection was very helpful to her in developing some insight and behavior change.

The content of the secrets that people do share is interesting. The greatest percentage (over half) of all reported secrets is extramarital affairs. This is followed in frequency by aggressive and illegal secrets, homosexuality, and so on. One secret we've heard only once was a man who confessed that he was a priest. He kept this secret in the group because he feared others would react differently to him if they knew. The subsequent dialogue suggests his perception was accurate:

Keith: Well, my secret is that I'm a priest.
Sue: Really? I never would have guessed that.
Keith: I just wanted people to react to me as Keith, not as Keith in my religious role.
Pat: Well, I don't think that's fair, father. I think you could.

At this point the group interrupted with laughter, but it took Pat at least two minutes to understand what he had said that was so humorous.

4. *The Nonverbal Sensuous Lunch (Dinner, Breakfast)*

    Purpose: Increasing interpersonal communication and trust, increasing closeness between members, exposing dependence/independence needs.

    Group type: Encounter, therapy (with well-functioning members only).

    Age limits: Adolescents to adults.

    Caution: Should occur later in groups (Phase III). Not for use in groups with obsessive-compulsive, paranoid, or hyperaggressive patients. Works best in marathon format.

    Materials: Meal consisting of food defined as sensuous by each member, some kind of floor covering.

    Time: 60–120 minutes.

This technique, which works well in marathon sessions, needs some preparation. Prior to the session in which it will be used, instructions should be given to each member. "Please bring to the session some food that you consider sensuous, for lunch (breakfast, dinner). We'll all be sharing the food that everybody brings."

It is often a good idea to delay the commencement of this exercise

until it is past normal mealtime, to ensure that participants have ap-
petites. The leader begins:

> LEADER: Okay, let's get ready for lunch. We'll take a short break
> to clean up and do any necessary preparations. Let's all get our
> food and bring it back here to the middle of the room. Please put
> your food in front of you, and let's not nibble until we can all
> begin.

After the food is ready and a floor covering is laid down, members
form a circle with their food on the inside.

> LEADER: Let's begin by going around the circle and having each
> person indicate what they brought, what makes this food sensuous
> for them, and how the food is representative of them. How does
> this food represent some aspect of your personality?

Often leaders will have to encourage members to answer all these questions:

1. What did you bring?
2. What makes it sensuous?
3. How does it represent you?

After all members have responded to these questions, the leader
continues:

> LEADER: Okay, now we're ready to eat. From now on until the
> end of the meal we'll proceed nonverbally. Please feed one another.
> Try to use as few utensils as possible. Please do not talk until
> the meal is completely over. We'll discuss this all afterwards.

During the meal the leaders should participate but also should observe
interactions between members. As soon as the meal is over and cleared
away, the discussion begins. A request for feelings about the exercise;
saying no to people offering food; acceptance or rejection of one's own
offerings; manner in which food is proffered, and so on will typically
yield an array of reactions.

Discussion of this exercise often lasts for 60 minutes or longer and
frequently leads into other major issues such as dependency needs and
fears of intimacy.

5. *Truth Pillow*

> *Purpose:* Increasing communication between members, increasing levels of feedback, increasing trust.
>
> *Group type:* Encounter, therapy.
>
> *Age limits:* None.
>
> *Caution:* Can be introduced in Phase II, but is recommended for Phase III. If introduced prematurely, can provide feedback that cannot be heard adequately by members.
>
> *Materials:* Scatter pillow, whiffle ball, any small stuffed animal, or other soft, throwable, inanimate object.
>
> *Time:* 30–60 minutes.

LEADER: As a way of increasing our communication I'd like to recommend this exercise. (Picking up the pillow): This pillow will have special qualities for awhile. If someone throws this pillow to you, you're required to give them positive and negative feedback. Say something you like and something you don't like about them in this group. For example, if I were to throw this to Tom, he would have to give me feedback. Then Tom could throw it to whomever he wanted to receive feedback from. Okay, let's begin (throwing it to a member).

After a while it becomes clear that some people have had the pillow several times and others seem left out entirely. This can be discussed if a member brings it up, or the leader can suggest at any time;

LEADER: Let's hold the pillow for a few minutes and open up discussion. Is there anyone here who would like to give feedback to or receive feedback from anyone else?

This exercise often drifts away rather than terminating crisply. Often members get bored and bring up other, more meaningful issues, or the feedback leads people to confront one another and this develops into more meaningful interactions. Discussion of feelings about being chosen by several people or by few or none is of value. Also, discussion of feelings engendered by the specific content of the feedback received is frequently important in self-concept development and group trust levels.

The preceding are only a few of the hundreds of trust and communication exercises. They represent a sampling of exercises I and my colleagues employ in some group settings. Each of these exercises has both diagnostic and therapeutic value. The next section will focus on exercises with primary diagnostic value. These techniques can all be used with children's groups.

Diagnostic Exercises

1.   *Tinker Toys*

    Purpose: Increased understanding of group dynamics, team building.

    Group type: Encounter, therapy, organizational development.

    Age limits: 7 years old and up.

    Caution: None.

    Materials: Set of Tinker Toys (Lincoln Logs, Erector set).

    Time: 30–60 minutes.

This is a three-phase exercise as presented here. Each of the phases can be instituted independently with success. The full sequence seems to work well as a whole. The leader introduces the exercise: "I'd like to try an exercise. Now, could I have X (number of) volunteers?" The leader specifies one half the total number of group members; if there are 10 members in the group, 5 volunteers are requested, for example. Frequently one or two members volunteer immediately, then several minutes can pass before the requisite number is obtained. As soon as there are enough volunteers, the first phase of the exercise is completed and discussed. Questions such as what led some members to volunteer and some to refrain provide valuable information as to members' receptivity to new experiences, charactertistic response styles, trust and so on. When this discussion is complete, the leader continues: "Will the volunteers please form a small circle inside the larger one?"

Once there are two circles, an inner one and an outer one, the leader empties a box of Tinker Toys on the floor (table) inside the inner circle. Addressing the volunteers, he says, "Your task is to build something with these materials. You have 10 minutes to complete the task." Addressing the outer circle, the leader says, "While they do this, your job is to observe and try to understand the group process."

When this is completed, members' feelings regarding participation or nonparticipation, styles of approach to the task, teamwork, and observations and analysis of the observers are discussed. This section can take several minutes. When it is completed, the leader proceeds to the third phase.

    LEADER: Now let's change places. Those of you who were in the inner circle switch to the outer circle, and those in the outer circle switch into the inner circle. (Once the move is made): For you in the inner circle now, your task is to alter the Tinker Toy structure in whichever way you like. You have 10 minutes. You who are now in the outer circle, please observe the group process for later discussion.

Some of the issues that can be highlighted by this exercise are cooperation vs. competition, work styles, ego needs ("I made this and they changed it; therefore that's a criticism of me"). Some of the most interesting diagnostic information can be depicted by the following examples:

1. In a group of "hyperactive" adolescents, one member took all the round parts (wheels) and built his own movable designs, oblivious of the rest of his group.
2. In a group of military personnel, one member took charge and assigned each member a task. He then supervised and critiqued their progress.
3. In a group of couples, one woman concealed three vital pieces of connections in the bosom of her dress and coyly suggested a game to look for them.
4. In a group of businessmen, one member dismantled the entire structure and began to rebuild it, with less than a minute left in the time limit.

Such behaviors, and observations of their effects on the group process, often have a great impact on individuals in the group. When these behaviors occur, other members also learn how to deal with them in more effective ways by practicing and observing tentative solutions.

2.   Group Artwork

Art materials have been therapeutically in a variety of settings (see Denny, 1969, 1972; Foy, 1961; Kwiatkowska, 1962). Several techniques have been used successfully in group and family therapy. There is a journal devoted exclusively to papers on art therapy (*The Journal of Art Therapy*). Art materials can be especially valuable for use with less verbal groups, "psychotic" groups, groups of younger members, and natural groups in which members have known each other for a substantial time.

Any art materials can be used in creating the artwork. With children, the use of crayons rather than finger paints is recommended, for practical reasons. Complaints from parents regarding sending a white (black, brown) child to school and getting a blue (green, purple) one back raise unnecessary problems.

2a. *The Group Drawing*

Purpose:	Provide information regarding group dynamics, increase intermember communication.
Group type:	Therapy, encounter, organizational development.
Age limits:	None.
Caution:	Old clothes are recommended. Remind members that they do not have to draw well to participate.
Materials:	Large box of crayons, large pieces (roll) of construction paper.
Time:	60–120 minutes. Art session can last from 20 to 60 minutes.

The leader lays out a large piece of construction paper and a large box of crayons.

> LEADER: Today I'd like to suggest that we do a group drawing. Please use these crayons and draw a picture of the group. I know that you may feel that you're not a good enough artist, but this doesn't have to be a masterpiece. Just try your best. You'll have 20 minutes to complete the drawing. Please begin now.

As with the Tinker Toy exercise above, much diagnostic information can be gleaned from group members' participation in this exercise. Cooperation, competition, passive and active aggression, compliance, a hierarchical work structure, alliances between members, ego needs, and work styles all become evident while members work on their projects. Some of these characteristics are evident in the following examples:

1. In a group of "underachieving" grade-schoolers, one boy took all the colored crayons for his own purposes, leaving the other five members of the group with the achromatic black, white, and gray crayons.
2. In a group of "problem" children, one 9-year-old girl took all the red crayons and tried to eat them.
3. In a group of intermediate school students, one boy drew a picture of another boy, exaggerating certain physical characteristics, and proceeded to show several other members this caricature. Their subsequent teasing and laughter precipitated a fight between the "artist" and his "victim."
4. In a group of mental health professionals, one psychiatrist did no drawing of her own but was extremely critical of the artistic merits of the finished product.
5. In a group of outpatients at a mental health clinic, one man took all the crayons and doled them out to others at his whim.
6. In a couples group, a husband criticized his wife's drawing ability,

choice of colors, inabilities to use perspective and shading, and overuse of the materials. She agreed with him on each count and then accidentally spilled coffee on the paper and, in cleaning it up, tore it in half. This entire episode was accompanied by profuse apologies.

One of the most dramatic uses of this technique occurred in a family group. While such a group does not completely fit into the purview of this text, the example demonstrates the value of the technique for diagnostic and therapeutic purposes. The family consisted of five members, and the incident occurred in the sixth session. There was one male and one female co-therapist. The family members included:

1. Dad, a 40-year-old, 6'4", 250-pound former football player, now a career officer in the military, very soft spoken and quiet.
2. Mom, a 40-year-old, 4'11", 90-pound school teacher and house-wife. Seemed nervous and angry constantly, spoke quickly and loudly. One notable characteristic was a habit of baring her teeth when she wasn't speaking.
3. Kathy, a 13-year-old, attractive 8th-grader. Just beginning puberty, and appeared very well adjusted.
4. Mary, an 11-year-old 6th-grader, the identified patient. Seemed sullen, uncommunicative, responded to father and male therapist more readily than to anyone else present.
5. Jonathan, aged 6, the baby of the family. Seemed happy and appeared to get along with everyone.

Not present at the sessions was the family's pet dog, "Scout."

The initial referral was for Mary, from the school counselor. Her schoolwork had fallen off precipitously in the past five months, and she seemed to be disinterested in classes. After two sessions alone, the therapist decided to see the whole family with a co-therapist. Through the first five sessions the family got comfortable with the situation and began to blame Mary a great deal for the problems and for her "attitude." In the sixth session the therapists asked the family members to collaborate on a family drawing. After some initial reticence, they entered the task avidly and worked together for approximately 35 minutes. An artist's depiction of their work appears in Figure 8–1.

After confirming that they all agreed that Figure 1 was an accurate representation, one of the therapists noticed the absence of the family pet. She mentioned this, and Mary grabbed a crayon and drew "Scout" in beside herself and Dad. At this point Kathy angrily said, "Now Mary, you put Scout right here by Mother where he belongs." The resultant argument provided the therapist an opportunity to comment on the

FIGURE 8–1: Artist's Depiction of "Before" Drawing

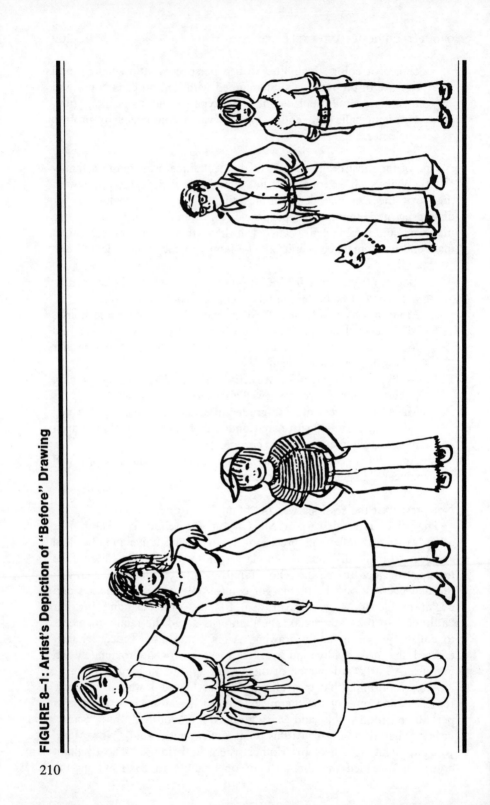

FIGURE 8–2: Artist's Depiction of "After" Drawing

two separate factions in the family, the distance between them, and the relative larger size of Mom and Kathy by comparison to Dad and Mary (despite the opposite physical size of Mom and Dad).

This diagnostic information led to several discussions and some major work. Employing the same technique in the eighth session, the therapists requested the family to draw another picture of the way they'd like it to be. An artist's depiction of this result appears as Figure 8–2. Once this family could compare where they were to where they wished to be, the therapeutic steps were relatively quickly attained. It may be valuable to note that the member of the family most resistant to change was Kathy.

2b. *The Group Drawing* (option)
The group need not work together on this task. Often leaders prefer to have each member work independently and then have all members look at the drawing as a whole and at the component parts.

2c. *The Group Drawing* (option)
The group need not draw itself. Requesting that they draw whatever they like can produce much diagnostic information. There is also a cathartic effect to drawing that can be of great value in certain group settings.

3. *Group Sculpture*
This technique follows all the rules of the group drawing except that it provides different materials (typically clay), and uses the sculpture technique. It seems particularly effective with hospitalized groups.

One diagnostic exercise that seems to work particularly with higher level groups is statuing.

4. *Statuing*

Purpose:	Understanding group process, depicting interpersonal communication for feedback.
Group type:	Encounter, organizational development, therapy (rarely).
Age limits:	Adults.
Caution:	Involves some physical contact. Groups of people who are uncomfortable with such contact may find it too threatening.
Materials:	None.
Time:	15–30 minutes.

4a. *Group Statue*
In this exercise, members are chosen to place their fellow members in positions where they pose as statues to depict the group process.

LEADER: I'd like to suggest that we all could understand this process better if we could see it. (Turning to a member who generally understands process): Pris, would you be willing to move people around in such a way as to make a statue out of them that would depict the process?

Once this is done, the group discusses the statue and their feelings about it.

4b. *Interaction Statue*

Where two people profess to want to communicate more effectively but consistently seem blocked, the leader can choose the more frustrated of the pair and ask him or her to create a picture of the interaction by posing the other one.

LEADER: I wonder if you two would be willing to try something to break this impasse. (After gaining consent from both parties): Okay, Pat, would you be willing to create a statue of your relationship with Marvin? Move him into a position that depicts his relationship to you. (As soon as they begin): What material are you using—clay, granite, wood, or what?

Once the statue is complete, both the sculptor and statue are asked how they feel about the work and their positions. After they respond, the leader then requests of the sculptor:

LEADER: Would you now place yourself into the statue assuming a position which represents how you perceive the relationship between you? (As soon as this is done): Please hold that pose for a moment and check out your feelings about it. Any alterations? Okay, let's discuss it.

Discussion centers on different perceptions of the relationship by the two parties involved, feedback from the group, and the difficulties of maintaining the relationship in its current form.

In one instance, a male member of a mental health professional training group sculpted a female member into a pose with one knee up, one arm extended with fingers spread, and the other hand formed into a fist in front of her chest. When he placed himself into the statue, he rested his testicles against the uplifted knee and the outstretched hand and fingers against his neck. He was also cowering away from her. She responded to this by suggesting another statue where the roles were reversed. She then sculpted herself on the floor with his foot on her throat and his fists beating his chest, as if in victory. The resultant discussion of these two perceptions allowed the participants to begin talking about their mutual attraction for one another and their fears of being dominated in such a relationship. One particularly interesting facet of this exercise was that the other group members were able to acknowledge that *both* statues seemed appropriate to them. This was a major impetus for the two sculptors to understand the mutuality of their relationship.

5. *Card Games*

Understanding hierarchical structure of group, depicting interpersonal relationships.

Group type: Therapy, activity, play, encounter.
Age limits: Most effective for children and adolescents, sometimes for adult groups.
Caution: None.
Materials: One or more standard decks of playing cards.
Time: 15–30 minutes.

A deck of cards may bring as many as a hundred exercises to the group. There are several advantages to techniques generated by these stimuli: they are almost universally familiar to group members, and are low cost, easily transportable, and safe. Complete lists of techniques using cards can be found elsewhere; a few samples are given below.

5a. *Pecking Order*
Placing a deck of cards in the center of the group, the leader says, "We'll spend 15 minutes today playing a card game. Go ahead and I'll tell you when time is up."
The diagnostic value of this technique is indicated by the following examples:

1. In a group of teenage inmates at a reform school, one 15-year-old boy tore the top three cards in half and threw the remaining cards onto the floor.
2. In a group of third graders, one girl took all the aces, kings, and queens and then dealt out the remainder of the other members for a game of "war."
3. In a group of intermediate school children, one girl consistently was unable to learn the rules of any game, thereby making it impossible for others to complete one.
4. In a family group, one 10-year-old child took the 10 of spades and ate it, while his parents helplessly pleaded with him to desist.
5. In a group of teenagers, one 14-year-old decided to teach each

member how to play a complex game, despite their numerous objections.

Discussion of fears of losing, implications of winning and losing, the pecking order of the group, power by active and passive aggression and so on is of great import in understanding the group process and responding therapeutically to it.

5b. Teach and Learn

In this exercise the leader requests each member to find a partner. He then gives each pair a deck of cards and requests that they determine a teacher and learner. The teacher is instructed to teach the learner a card game in 10 minutes. They then switch roles.

This technique helps elucidate the issues of authority, dominance/submission, reactions to failure of self and others, self-concept, and so on.

6. Reincarnation

This is a relatively nonthreatening technique which is also typically very enjoyable for the participants.

> LEADER: If you were to die and come back as an animal, what would you most like to be? Let's each describe the animal we chose and say a few words about why we made this particular choice.

After each person chooses and describes his or her choice, the choices can be examined relative to high need states. Animals chosen tend to reflect the need for power (elephants, rhinos, lions, sharks), cosmetics (leopards, minks, purebred show dogs), affection (koala bears, puppies), freedom (eagles, hawks, jaguars). In discussing these needs, members can often begin to expose their desires for changes in their lives. Thus this simple exercise can have some substantial diagnostic value.

6a. (option)

Use inanimate objects instead of animals.

Individual Depth Exercises

These exercises represent intrapsychic approaches and have a primarily therapeutic function. They are often dramatic and require excellent timing and closing skills. They typically open people up quickly, and there must be time for closing. All can be done by the group as a whole or by an individual in the group.

These exercises require group members to allow the leader to suggest images, thoughts, and feelings while they are in a state of heightened receptivity, relaxation, or mild hypnosis. In each of the following five techniques, the member is asked to relax and then to accept direction of his mind's images from the leader. The techniques described below are presented in order of increasing depth. *These techniques all require special skills and cannot be treated as games. The results of such techniques can be substantial and can require reconstructive professional treatment.*

Purpose:	Insight into repressed areas of unconscious, discovering and removing defenses and blocks to understanding, elicitation of feelings and noncognitive experiences.
Group type:	Therapy, encounter.
Age limits:	Adolescents and adults.
Caution:	Should only be instituted by qualified professionals. There should be enough time to complete exercise and discussion in a single session.
Materials:	Tape recordings of instructions.
Time:	30–120 minutes.

In the following exercises group members occasionally show great affect as a result of experiencing or reexperiencing certain feelings and concomitant thoughts and memories. It is essential that the leader work therapeutically with these individuals in the group following termination of the actual exercise.

1. *Focusing or Centering*
This technique, requiring the members to focus on internal bodily states and affect, is often done by the whole group simultaneously. The following instructions are intended only as a guide and are interchangeable with several other sets.

LEADER: (In a smooth monotone, slowly and calmly): Please lie down and find yourself a comfortable spot on the floor. Try and get really comfortable and try not to be so close to someone else that you touch them or can feel their closeness. Okay now, as I tell you let's even out our breathing. Inhale . . . Exhale . . . Inhale . . . Exhale. Now, if your eyes are still open I'd like you to close them and continue to focus on your breathing . . . Inhale . . . Exhale . . . Inhale . . . Exhale. Keep your breathing regular, not very deep breaths, just normal inhaling and exhaling. Okay, now I'd like you to focus your attention on your feet. If you find any tension at all let it flow out through the bottom of your feet and dissipate in the floor and air. Just let any tension or tightness ease out of your feet . . . Now let's move up to your ankles . . . Any tension at all, just let it flow out . . . so your ankles and feet will be just relaxed and easy, no tightness left at all. Just feeling relaxed, mellow, easy. . . .

This continues in the same leisurely way until the entire body—legs, thighs, buttocks, stomach, chest, head, face, arms, fingers—is relaxed. This process takes approximately 15 minutes. After the entire body has been relaxed the leader continues:

LEADER: Now you're feeling really relaxed and calm and easy. Just do a brief search inside your body and see if there's any tension or tightness anywhere. If there is, let it ease out, let it go, and you're now reaching a state of total relaxation. Focus on your breathing, keeping it regular, and observe how relaxed you feel.

These relaxation exercises are used in all of the techniques in this section. The following instruction is unique to *focusing* (see Gendlin, Beebe, Cassens, Klein, & O'Berlander, 1968).

LEADER: (Slowly, with 10- or 15-second silences between sentences): Okay, now I'd like you to focus on that part of your body in which you usually feel fear or pain or anger (guilt, sadness, etc.). Just let all your attention drift into that area inside you. After a few moments you'll probably discover that something is occurring in that area. If it is, just let it occur and focus on it. If it is not, just keep focusing on the area. As a feeling develops, let it grow and move about. You may find it moving within you. If so, just follow it. Keep the feeling as the center of your attention. As you follow this feeling, see if any words or pictures come to mind to describe it. If so, focus on those words and pictures. See what's happening to the feeling now. If it changes, let it change and follow it in its new form. If new pictures develop or new words occur, follow them.

This continues for a short period of time. Then the leader concludes:

LEADER: Okay, now let's just let the feeling go. Think about this experience and the feelings, and keeping your relaxation prepare to leave your internal trip and come back to the group. When you do, you'll feel as rested and alive as if you've had a four hour nap. . . . OK, now when you're ready come back to the group, sit up and open your eyes and we'll discuss this experience.

Occasionally a member falls asleep and must be awakened. The discussion generally involves exploration of the images and feelings encountered. Members may show great affect as a result of experiencing or reexperiencing certain feelings and the concomitant thought-memory processes. The leader should work with these individuals.

2. *Guided Fantasy*

This technique is related to and similar to the focusing exercise; the relaxation component is identical to that described above for centering. This first phase of the exercise will not be repeated here; we will assume that the relaxation phase has been completed. The leader then adds:

LEADER: (slowly, with silence between the sentences): "Now that you're relaxed, I'd like to take you on a special fun trip. In a moment you'll be able to imagine that you're back again at age 9 or 10 or 11. Try to picture your bedroom at that age. Imagine that you're lying in your bed just daydreaming, drifting away. Now imagine that you get up and go to that special place that you kept your special things in when you were young. It may be a closet, or corner, or box, or drawer.

For this trip you have the power to change size. Imagine yourself becoming smaller and smaller, so small that you can walk into that place where you kept your special things. As you near the back, you discover a passageway. Go through it. As you emerge you come to a landing and see an elevator ready to take you down into a new adventure. Look inside the elevator. It's padded and carpeted in a beautiful soft material. It's your favorite color. Look inside.

Now enter. It reads 20th floor, but as soon as you enter the door closes and it begins to descend. Feel the material and relax in anticipation as it goes down to the 19th, 18th, 17th, 16th floors. Prepare yourself for a beautiful experience. Now it's at the 15th, 14th, 13th, 12th, 11th floors, and now you become ready as it slows, 10, 9, 8, 7, 6, 5, 4, 3, 2, 1.

The doors open and you see a beautiful field. It may be a field you remember. Feel the grass and the dirt. Look up, you can feel the warmth of the sun on your forehead. Let yourself feel the warmth. Now begin walking across the field. Feel how exhilarating it is. There's a nice breeze, and it's a beautiful day. As you keep walking you begin to go up a rise. You can feel your leg muscles working as you climb a small hill and come to a plateau on the top. Across the plateau at the very far end you see an old, old man. As you see him you become instantly aware that he knows everything and you realize that you can ask him one question and he'll answer it for you. Walk up to him now and ask your question. Listen to his answer and remember both the question and answer. . . . Now you can see the sun going down and you know it's time to leave and return home. Say goodbye to the old man, start back across the plateau . . .

The leader retraces all the steps, through the field, elevator, special place, bedroom. Then the leader says, "Now come back to this room. You're normal size again. Prepare to discuss the experience."

Again some members may need to be gently awoken. A discussion of what parts of the exercise people experienced (wind, sun, color of elevator), what questions they asked and the answers and so on follows. It is not necessary to complete all the steps above; any parts of it (child in bedroom, old man, field) can be independently employed successfully.

2a. (option). *Object in Water*

This is virtually the same, only instead of visiting the old man, the suggestion is that members come to a stream (pool) of water and see something at the bottom. Mentally taking off their clothes, they jump in and feel the excitement of the water and chill. They pick up the object and return it. The object is then discussed.

Often the object is symbolic. In one group, one woman found a gold ring which she interpreted as her innocence which she had "lost very long ago." Retrieving it gave her the impetus to talk about an abortion she had undergone several years ago.

Several other options of this exercise are favored by other group leaders: going through a cave, to a deserted island, and so on.

3. *Regression Fantasies*

These techniques are similar to the guided fantasy techniques and employ a similar process of induction. The major differences are that members are always encouraged to go back to earlier times in their lives and to recreate the feelings that were extant at that time. Such experiences are frequently highly affect laden and are often done with individual members rather than the group as a whole (the "hot seat" procedure).

In these procedures, the leader typically asks one member to come to the center of the group and then works with this member individually, relaxing him and then regressing him to an earlier time of his life where there was some unresolved conflict. Thus a member who cannot relate effectively to other adults for fear of rejection can be brought back via regression fantasy to a time when he was young and felt rejected or deserted by his parents. Working through the previous rejection in fantasy can free the individual to confront his current fears with greater psychic energy and in an adult manner.

In a couples group, one of the husbands was able to confirm that he didn't know why, but sometimes he became unreasonably angry with his wife of three years. He acknowledged that he felt that this was the sole reason for their current difficulties. He was regressed to fantasize a similar scene with his first wife, and he became markedly enraged. The subsequent insight, that he became unreasonably angry with his second wife when he perceived her as having characteristics in common with his first wife, helped both of them adapt to this situation and improve their relationship.

Regression fantasies can serve both diagnostic and therapeutic functions. Not only do insights regarding the nature of the conflicts develop (unresolved feelings regarding the first wife, in the example above), they also can be resolved in a fantasy way, thus removing some of the blocks to behavior change.

3a. *Primals*

An extreme example of the regression fantasy is the primal regression. Here, individuals are regressed in a fantasy way to moments of birth and infancy. The essential notion of this great a regression is that trauma related to birth or the first few months of life continues to influence adult adaptation negatively. The individual is encouraged to work through these traumas by going through the process of birth and infancy for a second time and experiencing it more positively.

In general, such approaches are useful only in rare and specific situations and are of only passing interest here.

4. *Hypnosis*

Much like the fantasy approaches, hypnotherapy and group hypnosis can have a special place in the group setting. Using induction techniques similar to those in the guided fantasy and relaxation techniques, hypnosis can be employed both therapeutically and diagnostically. Hypnotherapy is a specific skill requiring specialized training. Excellent reviews of hypnosis in several settings can be found in Diamond (1974), Hilgard (1970), and Fromm and Shor (1972); these will not be duplicated here. One note of interest is that in addition to the use of hypnosis for therapeutic and diagnostic purposes, Shapiro and Diamond (1972) have also used hypnotic susceptibility as an outcome measure in encounter group research.

5. *Systematic Desensitization*

Another technique often used by group leaders to modify members' behaviors is systematic desensitization (Wolpe, 1958). This technique employs relaxation procedures (E. Jacobsen, 1938), similar to the relaxation procedure described above, and fantasy recommendations. Using an individually determined hierarchical set of anxiety-producing situations, leaders attempt to reduce members' anxiety by presenting images of these stimuli in situations inimical to anxiety (relaxation). Additional information regarding the use of systematic desensitization in different settings can be found in Davison (1968), Fishman and Nawas (1971); Lazarus (1961, 1964); Nawas, Fishman, and Pucel (1970); Paul and Shannon (1966), and Wolpe (1969).

Like hypnosis, systematic desensitization requires specialized training and is not recommended to novices.

Nudies and Touchy-Feelies

Among the exercises that have achieved the most publicity are those that involve the absence of clothing and physical contact. These exercises, which occur infrequently in encounter groups, are most dramatic and titillating, and have been terribly overplayed by the press and pop psych literature. Paul Bindrim (1968) and Martin Shepard and Marjorie Lee (1970, 1972), two of the most popular proponents of these techniques, essentially argue that clothing serves as ego defenses, and unless these defenses are removed, the individual cannot be free of their constraints. In his novels about groups, Shepard also suggests that homosexual and heterosexual activity within the group setting is a way to remove "hang-ups".

From a professional point of view, these assumptions are questionable, and the behavior they support could have serious ethical repercussions. However, it is of value to examine a few of the common techniques in this area as a way of determining their relative merit in a group setting.

Purpose: Understanding and improving body image, becoming aware of sexual and intimacy problems, reducing fears.
Group type: Encounter.
Age limits: Adult.

Cautions: Can be extremely threatening to members, can increase fears of groups, and could result in lawsuits. Informed consent is mandatory, and individual veto power should be respected. Important to discuss in detail before participation.

Materials: Swimming pool, sauna, hot baths, etc. desirable.

Time: 30–90 minutes.

1. *Body Image*

In this technique members are asked by the leader to disrobe and meet in five minutes at a specified location such as a pool. Members then stand in a circle and the leader requests each person to view his or her own body and those of the other group members. After about two minutes, the leader continues:

> LEADER: Each of us has a particular part of his or her body that we find most and least attractive. Let's go around the circle and have each person tell which part they find most and least attractive and then show what about that part they like and dislike.

After each member does this, the remaining group members are encouraged to give them feedback. It is thought that by such exposure, members' negative feelings about parts of their bodies will be reduced. This in turn will improve their self-image.

It is generally a good idea to mix such techniques with play in order to alleviate some of the anxiety. Group swims are valuable before or after activities.

1a. (option). *Positive Feedback*

In this option members mention and show the part of their body that they like the least, and other members of the group provide the most positive feedback they honestly can. In this way body image fears can be desensitized.

1b. (option). *Negative Feedback*

This option is only for members with good ego strength who are experienced in processing feedback. Opportunities for follow-up must be available.

Whereas in option 1a members responded to the show-and-tell components with positive feedback, in this technique the feedback given is preordained to be negative. In this way the individual can hear his worst fears verbalized and still not be rejected.

Paulette: The thing I hate most is my stretch marks. I think they make me look old.

Sandy: They are pretty bad.

Tom: I'd say worse than that, I've never seen stretch marks like that before.

2.   *Physical Intimacy and Massage*

Members are asked to choose a partner: someone in the group they'd like to know better. After members are paired off they are asked to disrobe and give their partner a full massage, including or omitting genitals, and with oil or dry.

The physical contact serves to decrease needs for body space and defenses against intimacy.

2a.   (option). *Nonsexual Massage*

In this option partners close their eyes and explore each other's face (hands) with their hands.

2b.   (option). *Center of Attention*

In this option, there is no pairing. Each person in turn is massaged by the remaining members.

These techniques are rarely used and can be very dangerous except in very high-functioning encounter groups. Use of such techniques in natural groups or organizational development groups can have particularly long-term negative effects.

Termination Exercises

As was suggested in Chapter 5, termination and transfer of training are two of the most difficult and critical components of the group experience. The following exercises can frequently assist in the termination process. In each of these, there are two primary goals: (1) separation and (2) relating the group experience to back-home life.

Purpose: Termination, transfer of training, generalization of group barriers.

Group type: Therapy, encounter, organizational development.

Age limits: None.

Time limit: 60–120 minutes.

1.   *Standard Termination*

This technique is an excellent, natural way to bring matters to a close. It has two major phases.

LEADER: Well, we've only got one session left after today. I'd like to recommend that we spend a little time reflecting on this experience. Before we do that, does anyone have anything they'd like to bring up at this point: any unfinished business, unresolved feelings, feedback, questions? Now would be a good time to bring them up.

Members often accept this invitation and proceed to discuss their considerations. When this unfinished business is completed, the first phase of this exercise ends. The leader then continues:

LEADER: Let's go around the group one time, and one by one share our feelings about the group and our feelings about it ending. Who'd like to begin?

When this is completed, the group normally says its goodbyes and terminates.

2.   Extended Termination

This termination takes several hours of group time and is the recommended one when possible. After a request for unfinished business (as above), the leader begins:

LEADER: Well, our time is rapidly running out, and I'm aware that I feel like I only know certain parts of people here. I'd really love to know more. I'd like to recommend an exercise. What I'd like is for us to go around the group and for each person to tell us something about himself that's important, but something that there's been no reason to bring up in the group till now.

This exercise often yields a wide variety of responses and allows people to deal with conflicts they previously thought were inappropriate. In one such group, one woman took this opportunity to share the fact that she'd had an abortion between the fifth and sixth group sessions and was concerned about its relevance for the group. Once this is completed, the leader continues by asking for the following:

LEADER: Okay, this time I'd like to suggest that each person tell the group what you got out of the group and specifically what you will do with it.

As each person speaks, the leader and members respond to their plans. Often role playing of potential danger situations is done extensively (see the examples for Stage 34 in the chronological process analysis in Chapter 5). After each person has an opportunity to describe and practice his new learning, the leader closes the group by requesting feelings, as in the standard termination.

THE RULES OF PARSIMONY

Each of the structural exercises presented above can be skillfully and effectively applied if it is used sparingly. Like most tools in a craftsman's kit, they can be used to assist or to deter the group process. Each leader must make hard decisions regarding the use of techniques, with reference to the tests recommended at the outset of this chapter.

One Minor Exception

There is one major type of group that needs to be more or less technique oriented. These are groups for children and young adolescents. There are several reasons for this. First, the normal avenue of communication for children is not sit-down conversation. Children communicate through play as well as through language. Second, most children who are referred to groups do not have a very long attention span. Third, children are often intimidated and less natural when they are forced to play a game with adults' rules. It is much easier for younger group members to have rules which suit their natural tendencies. Aronin (1972), commenting on the difficulty elementary school students have in expressing themselves and in trusting the counseling situation, suggested a technique which incorporates group discussions with gym activities. Frank and Zilbach (1968) recommend the use of activity groups in school settings as a substitute for the clinical approach. Consistent work by Axline, Gazda, Mahler, Redl, and Slavson recognizes the need for activities in groups for young group members.

It is important to provide relevant stimulus materials for children in order to get them to relate in ways that prepare them for the benefits of group therapy approaches. With these populations, it is essential for leaders to provide a vast array of novel stimulus situations with some structure (such as exercises, techniques, and activities) to keep motivation in the group at optimal levels.

THE GRANDFATHER OF THE TECHNIQUES: ROLE PLAYING

I have placed role playing in a separate category. By earlier definitions it certainly qualifies as a technique, but it also represents an entire method of group therapy. If we include psychodrama in this category, there also is a theory for its use and a wealth of research support.

Corsini and Cardone (1966), like Bennis (1964), have suggested that role playing demands a great deal of personal involvement. They argued that this makes it an especially useful technique in all forms of psychotherapy, especially with groups. Gibb (1952) has demonstrated that college students who had a T-group experience in conjunction with role playing were superior on a self-report measure of self-insight to students who had only T-group experiences. Gibb also reported that the role-playing group also showed nonsignificant greater tendencies toward "role flexibility" and ability to conceptualize a new role.

Shapiro (1970, 1971) has shown distinct augmentation of encounter group effects by use of role playing as a group technique, in comparison to control group subjects who did not role play. Siegel (1969), in an excellent review of the role-playing literature, concluded that there is strong evidence to suggest that role playing as a technique does cause attitudinal and behavioral changes. Indeed, the more active the role-playing procedure, the more effective the techniques seem to be. Furthermore, L. Mann (1967) has suggested that when degrees of active participation are compared, the more emotional the role playing, the more effective it seems.

Perhaps the study that stands out the most in this area is one by Janis and Mann (1965) and the follow-up by Mann and Janis (1968). In these studies, the authors have shown that the use of emotional role playing was far more successful in changing the behavior of smokers than was identical auditory information presented by tape recording. That is, the subjects in the role-playing group showed significantly greater reduction in smoking than did an equivalent group of subjects who listened to tapes of other subjects' role-playing sessions.

On the basis of these studies it has been assumed that the effects of role-playing programs could facilitate the effects of therapy and encounter groups.

Role Playing

Purpose: Diagnostic and therapeutic. Effective in breaking through process impasses.

Group type: Therapy, encounter, organizational development, activity.

Age limits: None.

Caution: Overuse can give group a "game playing" rather than therapeutic orientation.

Materials: None.

Time: 15–120 minutes.

Role playing can be done with one or more individuals in a group or with the entire group as a whole.

1. *Family*

   LEADER: I'd like to suggest that we try something different now. Smitty has been saying how difficult his childhood was, and I'm having a hard time grasping the problem. I would like members of the group to act like Smitty's family. Who here is like your mother?

After the member indicates a person, the leader asks that person if he or she would be willing to role play the mother. The process continues with the member's father, brother, sister, dog, cat, and so on. Once the roles are set, the member is asked to instruct each player in the intricacies of his or her role, and the representative family scene is played out.

2. *Acting As If*

This technique is designed to help individuals behave in ways that are difficult for them, for one reason or another. In cases where members claim that they would like to be more assertive (or patient, direct, sensual, e.g.) they can be encouraged to do this by acting out these behaviors in a make-believe setting. The leader requests that members behave as if they were assertive (patient, direct, sensual), in the group.

   LEADER: How would you behave if you were as assertive as you'd like? What would you say to Connie? Let's just try it. Make believe you're as assertive as you'd like. What would you say?

When member(s) begin to answer the question, the leader orchestrates and instructs the member to "tell Connie. Tell her now." Once the group member has succeeded in being assertive, patient, etc.) in the "safe" group environment, the leader can begin to help him gradually transfer these behaviors to the back-home environment.

3. *Role Reversals*

This role-playing technique is especially effective in groups of families, couples and other natural groups. It is particularly dramatic when two or more members have a difficult time listening to each other and communicating openly. With married couples the husband is asked to role play the wife, and vice versa.

   LEADER: Jim, I'd like you to try something. Be Judy. Act like you are her. Present her point of view, her emotions, everything. And Judy, you be Jim. Use his words, his gestures, etc. Try it now.

Both members of the couple are now forced to deal with the impact of their own behavior. They typically respond as emotionally to their own behavior as they did to that of their partners. This experience often leads to greater understanding of each other's feelings and thoughts and motives, and greater communication ensues.

4. *Behavioral Rehearsal*

One particularly utilitarian procedure in the transfer-of-training phase of group therapy is behavioral rehearsal. This procedure involves practicing newly acquired behaviors in the safer group environment via simulation, and receiving feedback from the other group members and leaders. Thus members are requested to role play their next discussion or confrontation with their boss, spouse, parents, and so on.

> LEADER: Let's try the situation where you share your feelings with your boss. Who will play the boss? OK, describe the setting, situation, and so on, and then tell him how you feel (what you're thinking, wishing, etc.).

5. *Doubling*

One special form of role playing is called doubling. In this technique, a leader or member of the group can speak for another person. This is especially helpful if the individual in question is having difficulty expressing his true feelings or blocking feedback from other members.

> LEADER: If you feel that anyone is having great difficulty expressing himself and you feel empathic, you can move behind that person, place your hand on his shoulder, and speak (with his permission) for him, as if you were this person. It is valuable to keep such statements short and restricted to feelings.

One example of this occurred when one member was discussing her recent divorce from another group member.

> *Candy:* I really find it hard to talk in here with Jack present. I feel like you'll feel bad for us, and I don't want any pity.
> *Rick:* Well, I don't have pity. I feel a bit uncomfortable hearing either of you put the other one down, but I think your divorce was a good thing. I think you were really courageous.
> *Candy:* Do you really think it was courageous?
> *Millie* (doubling): I don't feel very strong now.
> *Candy:* Yeah.
> *Joe:* Well, why don't you tell us how you do feel?
> *Candy:* I guess I'd feel bad if I began to talk about how much I'm hurting and you'd blame Jack. It's not only his fault.

Millie (doubling):   I'm scared if I tell you how I really feel, you'll all reject me too.

At this point Candy burst into tears and acknowledged her fear. In this particular group, the leader waited for her to be comforted and then gave her permission to avoid discussing the divorce in the group if she didn't want to. This allowed her to share her fears without attacking Jack defensively. Thus, instead of dividing the group into two camps, other members were able to listen and help both Jack and Candy. Millie's empathic *doubling* had a very powerful effect on the group process.

The most fascinating phenomenon of the role-playing procedures is the rapidity with which members become truly emotionally involved. Even though the techniques begin as a game, members quickly project their own affects, values, and attitudes into their roles, and in a sense they become the character they're playing. In this emotion-laden state they are susceptible to rapid learning.

As a set of techniques, these role-playing procedures provide members with a means of viewing their maladaptive behaviors in cognitive, affective, and sensory ways. This occurs in a supportive environment in which reinforcement is readily available. In this way these techniques can help to maximize learning in the group setting.

Scope

Chapter 9

Applications of
Group Psychotherapy

Group therapy has been used in almost every form of treatment and training. The examination of representative literature in this chapter leads to the conclusion that very few aberrations of mind or behavior have not been treated by some variety of the group method. This chapter will survey some of the uses of group psychotherapy, with the following items serving as a guide for discussion:

1. Diagnostic uses.
2. Applications to somatic conditions and neuroses.
3. Applications in drug and alcohol abuse.
4. Uses in corrections.
5. Major behavior pathologies: Institutionalized populations.
6. Sex, marriage, and the family applications.
7. Uses for children, adolescents, and schools.
8. Training and supervision applications.
9. Miscellaneous.

The reference citations in the following sections, while considerable, are not intended to be comprehensive; such an endeavor would require a book in itself. Instead, the intention is to demonstrate the scope of the group therapy movement by presenting a representative sample of the applications and findings that have been reported in the literature.

DIAGNOSTIC USES OF GROUP PSYCHOTHERAPY

In psychology a diagnosis may refer to etiological conditions which have brought some present condition to fruition, or it may refer to a pattern of interaction which has behavioral manifestations. Despite advances in diagnosis, there has been a reaction against formal typing. The psychiatrist of several decades ago was primarily interested in identifying and labeling the patient, since there was little else that could be done. The mental health professional of today, however, understands the gross unreliability of diagnostic labels and has a more optimistic outlook as a result of advances in psychotherapy and the use of somatic methods in the treatment of psychoses. Therefore the professional is less concerned with differential diagnoses than with treatment interventions and tends to view the whole person on a continuum of illness or discomfort. Thus the present tendency is to devalue labeling, but diagnosis is still undertaken, and new techniques for more accurate classifying are being introduced. Therefore the traditional taxonomy is used for purposes of convention and ease of presentation in this section, despite its obfuscating qualities.

The data the diagnostician uses come from various sources: from case histories, from test results, from observation of the patient's interactions with others, or (as it most often does) from an interview. Ideally, a diagnosis would be based on material from all these sources.

It has been suggested by many that the group situation gives the diagnostician a unique insight into the individual patient's interactions with others in unstructured situations. Among those who have written on this point are Bell (1948), Gula (1944), Redl (1944), Symonds (1947), Atterbury (1945), and Bierer (1948a). The various arguments go somewhat as follows: The patient in a group is more natural and less guarded than in an interview; that is, he is more himself. Observing individuals in groups with their varied tensions gives greater insights into areas of strain. Individual observation is generally of short duration, but the same amount of time per person will give the diagnostician more time to observe all members of the group. Individuals who have periodic flare-ups can be seen more readily over prolonged observation. And people who do not verbalize well can be seen in behavioral interaction with others.

Furthermore, Shapiro (1972c) has noted that a group allows the individual patient to influence and react to several diverse personalities, not just one therapist or other person with greater authority. In this way, more typical interaction patterns can be viewed, and diagnosis in the group setting can have an environmental as well as an intrapsychic focus. By way of contrast, Kaplan and Sadock (1971) argue that diagnosis cannot be done in a group setting. This orientation is primarily maintained by leaders trained in psychoanalysis, which focuses primarily on individual therapy; it seems to represent a minority opinion.

Diagnosis comes directly from medical tradition; it is generally maintained in medicine that treatment is contingent on diagnosis. But in psychotherapy, diagnosis may not affect the nature of the treatment; that is to say, people with diverse diagnoses may get essentially the same kind of treatment, and those with the same diagnosis may get very different treatments. Corsini (1957) argues the psychotherapy *is* diagnosis, and an individual analysis may be considered one long diagnostic interview. In effect, diagnosis, particularly with group therapy, has generally been an informal and less frequently employed art in recent years.

However, it can be reported that some new forms of diagnosis treatment have been employed recently. Hodgman and Stewart (1972) report great success with an adolescent screening group in reaching and treating teenagers, as does Churchill (1965) with child guidance groups. Intake screening groups such as those used by Abrahams and Enright (1965) and Lederman (1958) are also increasing in numbers. Tabaroff, Brown, Dorner, Reiser, Talmadge, Goates, and Stein (1956) and Tyler, Truumaa, and Henshaw (1962) have dealt with intake diagnosis in groups, and D'avanzo (1962) and Jordan, Campbell, and Hodge (1957) have used groups to diagnose family pathologies.

APPLICATIONS TO SOMATIC CONDITIONS

One of the several applications of the group method which have merged into group psychotherapy as it is known today is the treatment of somatic conditions. When J. H. Pratt started his first group he was interested in instructing patients in the efficient management of their disease; he appears to have been naive of any concept of what is today called psychosomatic medicine. Other workers saw different possibilities in the group method and began to apply it as *the* therapeutic agent. There were on the one hand some enthusiastic ministers, who, feeling that the church had a healing function, began to treat a variety of diseases using traditional religious techniques: prayer, sermons, and hymns. Certainly the expectancy effects of the other members of the congregations led to some very real placebo cures. On the other hand there were some physicians who, perhaps misreading Pratt's papers, felt that there might be some therapeutic quality to groups. Among these were Smilie (Pratt, 1922), who used group therapy for diabetics; Harris (1939), who experimented with cardiac and prenatal cases; Buck (1937), who worked with hypertension; and Emerson (1910), who treated undernourished children.

It gradually became evident that group psychotherapy per se had little if any effect on the course of a strictly somatic disease, but it might be of considerable value for four separate purposes: (1) helping people with a somatic disease to make adjustment to the disease itself, (2) affecting the attitudes of relatives of patients with disease, (3) bringing about improvement when the condition is totally or parially based on psychosomatic reactions, and (4) relieving symptoms of a hysterical nature.

Adjustment to Illness

Piskor and Paleos (1968) have used groups to help patients adjust to strokes, and Strauss, Burrucker, Cicero, and Edwards (1967) recommend a variety of group procedures for stroke patients and their families. Dalzell-Ward (1960) has instituted group procedures with male VD patients, and Murray (1962) emphasizes the uses of group procedures for orthopedic patients. Goldner and Kyle (1960) and Mone (1970) both have used short-term groups to help postcardiac patients adjust to their illnesses. Adsett and Bruhn (1968), working with postcardiac patients, Bardach (1969), working with aphasic patients, and D'afflitti and Wertz (1974), working with stroke patients, all recommend involving family members in their therapy groups. Hollon (1972), citing the role of denial in patients with chronic hemodialyses, recommends a physician-led group therapy approach.

Deutsch and Zimmerman (1948), Kihn (1959), Randall and Rogers (1950), and Scarborough (1956) worked with epileptics; they illustrate the use of group therapy to help sick persons make better adjustments to seizures. Santiago, Treant, and Sanchez (1964) also recommend group therapy for mothers of adolescent epileptics. Thus, even if the epilepsy itself cannot be cured by group therapy, a person with this disease may make a better adjustment to the environment. Some recent thinking in the area of psychosomatic medicine suggests that if such an adjustment were successfully made, the incidence of stress-induced seizures would also diminish.

Reports of the use of group therapy have been given by Day, Day, and Hermann (1953), Barnes, Busse, and Dinken (1954) and Mally and Strehl (1963), with reference to multiple sclerosis; and by Lubin and Slominiski (1960) for cerebral palsy. Turnbloom and Myers (1952) and Blackman (1950) have used groups in treating aphasics. Group therapy has also been recommended for prenatal (Colman, 1971), postpartum (Smith, 1971), and postabortion patients (Bernstein & Tinkham, 1971; Burnell, 1972), as well as for the blind (Manaster, 1971; Manaster & Kucharis, 1972; Shlensky, 1972) and the deaf (Stinson, 1971, 1972). Myocardial infarction (Bilodeau & Hackett, 1971; Rahe, 1973), and cystic fibrosis patients (Farkas & Schwachman, 1973) have also been found to benefit from group therapy.

It is possible to get patients to adjust to physical diseases and to accept their ailments with better attitudes. Perhaps the best example

is seen with senile persons; surely group therapy will not affect physiological changes that are the result of aging. However, Case (1951),
Linden (1953, 1956), Manaster (1972), Silver (1950), and Smith,
Bryant, and Twitchell-Allen (1951) have reported on the use of group
methods with those so aged they had to be hospitalized. Smith et al.,
working with 43 elderly women, reported that communications between
patients increased and there was a decrease in problem behavior and
a general improvement in morale while the group activities existed.
When the program was stopped, however, conditions went back quickly
to the previous equilibrium.

More recent studies with groups for the aged include Burnside's
(1971) report on long-term group work with the aged, Euster's (1971)
study of groups for the institutionalized aged, and Goldfarb's (1971)
article exploring the use of groups for therapy both within institutions
and outside. Linden's (1953) initial description of group psychotherapy
and his (1956) review of the use of groups for the aged point out a
number of special problems in this area. A primary example is the
fact that old-age home and nursing home operators have no illusions
about rehabilitation for discharge; people come there to live until they
die. This type of situation is a low motivation condition at best. Goldfarb notes that groups in such settings cannot be successful unless the
limitations are accepted and expectations are not set too high. Even
brain-damaged patients who cannot remember the content of the discussion or the members from the last session can carry some feelings
of goodwill from the sessions, and this can be beneficial. Wolff (1967)
has pointed out the value of simple sociability and social integration
through identification with the group and encouragement of self-
expression. In a major study of hospitalized psychiatric hospital patients
over 65 years of age, Wolk and Goldfarb (1967) have demonstrated
major changes in depression, anxiety, self-concept, and interpersonal
relationships by comparison to a control group. Two other recent
descriptions of group therapy for the aged in hospitals are by Lehrman
and Friedman (1970) and Williams (1976). In discussing process in
groups for the aged, Burnside (1970) specifies the areas of loss as a
major issue. Recent groups dealing with diabetics (Leeman, 1970),
arthritics (Valentine, 1970), cardiac patients (Mone, 1970), kidney
patients (Wilson, Muzekari, Schneps & Wilson, 1974), the deaf (R. E.
Geller, 1970), and presurgical patients (Mezzanotte, 1970) all point
to the wide-ranging value of group therapies for patients.

Relatives of Patients

Group psychotherapy has been given to parents or spouses of patients with various mental and physical diseases in the hope that they
would get comfort from communication with relatives of other per-

sons similarly afflicted and might learn how to deal with the patients and with their own feelings. Wendland (1955) has discussed a group of husbands and wives of poliomyelitic patients; Mattsson and Angle (1972), groups for parents of hemopheliacs; Gordon and Bowman (1953), group therapy with husbands of psychotic women; Bice and Holden (1949), group counseling with mothers of children with cerebral palsy; Ross (1948) describes group therapy with relatives of psychotic patients; Santiago et al. (1964), group treatments for mothers of adolescent epileptics; and Hefferman (1959), for mothers of diabetic children.

More recently, Haley (1971), Speck (1967), and others have discussed the transfer-of-illness phenomenon in schizophrenic families. In these cases, the family survival patterns require one member to be an identified "victim" or "patient." If this patient is treated successfully and then returned to the family, frequently the result is a complete reversion to sick behavior by the patient, or a developing illness in another family member. With a family pattern like this, it is essential for therapy to include the entire family. Unless the relatives are treated, they will undo any therapeutic progress.

Treating Psychomatic Conditions

Psychomatic symptoms are distinguished from purely somatic symptoms by the nature of the inducement of the illness. Both involve some physical malady. Somatic conditions are generated by physical means; exposure to bacteria, incorporation of germs or virus, contusions, abrasions, and so on. Psychosomatic conditions are generated by psychological stimuli; fear, anxiety, stress, and so on. Both types of symptoms are displayed physically.

Another type of psychogenic symptom is also apparently displayed physically. These are called conversion reactions; they can be distinguished from somatic and psychosomatic symptoms in that there is no actual physical deterioration. For example, a person who suffers from hysterical blindness has had no actual damage to the visual system. A person who has a psychosomatically induced ulcer, however, has a definite, measurable, painful digestive problem.

It is known that some diseases have predisposing psychological components, stomach ulcers, colitis, and allergic conditions being prime examples. It appears reasonable that if these diseases have their origin in psychological tensions, relief of these tensions should lead to improvement, if not cure, of the condition. The evidence for this point of view with respect to group psychotherapy is growing and impressive.

Several authors have discussed the use of groups for psychosomatic disorders. Deutsch (1964), Igersheimer (1959), Sternleib (1963), Stein

(1971b), and Wittkower (1964) have all provided rationalizations for the use of group psychotherapy for these disorders and evidence of at least moderate success.

Allergies. Baruch and Miller (1951), a psychologist and an allergist, have used group therapy with allergy patients who had a variety of conditions, including hay fever, asthma, and gastrointestinal disturbances. They used a permissive form of group therapy, eclectic in nature, which featured the analysis of projective drawings. In one of their papers (1946) they state that 22 out of 23 patients improved, 6 to the point of complete remission of all symptoms. All 23 patients had allergies that had been confirmed by positive skin reactions to tests; none had benefited from medical care; and none had received any help from other procedures.

Clapham and Sclare (1958) also reported success in getting asthmatics to deal successfully with affect-laden material without symptom increase. Additional work on asthmatics in group therapy has been reported by Abramson and Peshkin (1960, 1961), Barendregt (1957), Bastiaans (1958) Cain, Charpin, and Planson (1959), Groen and Pelser (1960) and Reed (1962). Stein (1971a) confirms these data with his own work of over a quarter of a century at Mt. Sinai Hospital, New York. Similarly, Shoemaker, Guy, and McLaughlin (1955) report reductions in allergic skin reaction symptoms with group therapy.

Ulcers. In one of the earliest but most influential investigations of psychosomatic conditions, Chappell et al. (1937) formed two groups of carefully matched patients who had subjective and objective symptoms of peptic ulcer. One group was given a course of treatment which included group psychotherapy, while the control group had no group psychotherapy. Results were impressively in favor of the experimental group, with a majority of patients losing subjective and objective symptoms. Similar results have been reported by Curtis, Clarke, and Abse (1967), Fortin and Abse (1956), Karush, Daniels, O'Conner, and Stern (1968, 1969), Stein (1971b), and Stein, Steinhardt and Cutler (1955).

Overweight. Grant (1951) calls obesity America's No. 1 problem in preventive medicine. Certainly, if the advertising that promises to help people lose weight serves as a criterion, the 80 million people in this country who are stated to be overweight do have a great interest in shedding excess poundage. Overweight may be due to many causes, but compulsive overeating appears to be the most important. The major problem for a person with such a compulsion is not to reduce but to remain at a lower weight once the poundage has been lost.

Individual psychotherapy has been used to control weight; according to Nicholson (1946), "Psychotherapy leads to a higher percentage of successful cures in reducing weight than any other method." Kotkov (1953a), reporting on a group therapy approach for the control of obesity, concluded, "Although no amazing overall weight loss occurred, it is concluded that group psychotherapy served as an invaluable relationship experience for the maintenance of weight loss in 48 percent of the patients who did not succeed by other methods."

In more recent work, Glomset (1957), Freyberger (1958), Mees and Kenter (1967), Holt and Winnick (1961) and Dorfman, Slater, and Gottlieb (1959) have all demonstrated success with obese patients via group therapy. Spango (1966), using group methods with other treatments in a summer camp for obese girls, demonstrated excellent results. Hanley (1967), however, noted that psychotherapy alone, without attention to the eating habits of obese individuals per se, was typically not successful. Wagonfeld & Wolawitz (1968) investigated a self-help program (TOPS) which employed some group techniques and reported that it was successful as long as the members remained in the program. These results are similar to those reported by Alcoholics Anonymous and drug addiction treatment programs.

Similar results have been reported by Wollersheim (1970), using learning theory–based group therapy; Collum (1972), using a modified group involvement feedback technique; and Bailey (1972), using a "visual-sensory-commitment-action group therapy." Bornstein and Sipprelle (1973) have claimed success by an "induced anxiety" technique. Snow and Held (1973) have worked with obese adolescent females, and Rohrbacher (1973) has conducted a special camp program for obese boys.

Hypochondriacal Symptoms. Pratt's clinic started at the Boston Dispensary in 1930 was for individuals with somatic complaints but no demonstrable symptoms (see Chapter 2). His study (1934) of 2,000 consecutive admissions showed that 36 percent had unjustifiable complaints as far as physical examinations could ascertain. Instead of dealing with frank disease, as he had in 1906, he was concerned with neurotics who simulated illness.

In the Thought-Control Class, as the clinic came to be known, the purpose was not to teach people how to manage their disease but rather to get them to give up unfounded symptoms. Members were referred to this clinic when their symptoms could not be supported or corroborated by physical examination. New members were given individual interviews at which the purpose of the group was explained. When they entered the session, they found the members sitting classroom style, and they were asked to sit in the front row. Long-standing members sat on the "honor bench" with the therapist, facing the rest of the group. The director called the roll; in this way members got to know each other by name. A secretary passed slips of paper on which members wrote about any progress they had made. The collected slips were read by the director without mentioning names. Those who did not report improvements were interviewed privately. There was a relaxation period during which everyone was to close his eyes. This lasted from five to seven minutes. The director then gave a short inspirational message, after which testimonials were solicited from patients.

Pratt (1934) reported that the rate of improvement varied from 60 to 90 percent. He stated that patients who attended this group did much better than patients who saw him privately.

With hypochondriacal patients, the most difficult task seems to get them to accept psychological therapies (group) for their imagined "physical" illnesses. Once in therapy, their needs for such symptoms can be explored and corrective behavior taken. If the needs (attention, companionship, dependence, etc.) are met by having the imagined symptoms relieved in less debilitating ways, the symptoms likewise vanish.

Neuroses. The neuroses comprise a group of psychological disorders which are judged to be mild. They are considered to be characterized by the presence of anxiety and symptomatic evidence of excessive defense activities. Unlike the psychoses, they present no evidence of gross disorientation, distortions, or disorganization. Most patients in outpatient clinics and private clinics are neurotics who comprise the majority of members of nonspecialized groups. For this reason, it is rare for groups to be set aside specifically for certain types of neurotic symptoms. When a private practitioner opens a group to his patients, it is likely to filled by people with diagnoses of neuroses (and situational reaction disorders). The major categories of neurotic symptomatology include: the phobias, obsessive-compulsive reactions, anxiety reactions, dissociative and conversion hysteria, hypochondriasis (discussed above), and depressive reaction.

Several authors have indicated that the group therapy situation is an optimal one for understanding and explicating the neuroses (Abell, 1959; Genevard, Schneider, Jordi, Delaloye, Genton, Gloor, & Villa, 1961; Jackson & Grotjahn, 1958). For the most part, group therapy with neurotics is done on an outpatient basis. However, Bovill (1972) and Guyer (1956) have both worked with hospitalized groups of neurotics. Kass and Abroms (1972) have also worked with hospitalized patients in their behavioral approach to group treatment of hysterics. Behavior modification has also been successfully employed in group treatment of phobias (Lazarus, 1961), and test anxiety (Crighton & Jehu, 1969; Katahn, Strenger, & Cherry, 1966; Mitchell & Ingham, 1970; Mitchell & Ng, 1972, and Suinn, 1968). Gilbreath (1968) has applied traditional group counseling approaches to test anxious under-achievers, with some success. Mitchell and Ng did not replicate these data but found that a combination of Gilbreath's procedure and desensi-tization had maximum effectiveness. Dawley and Wenrich (1973a, 1973b), have recommended implosive group therapy for test anxiety.

Barron and Leary (1955) found reduced MMPI profiles as a result of group therapy with neurotics. Jackson and Grotjahn (1958) worked with a marriage neurosis successfully in group, and Lee (1960) worked with neurasthenics. Scott (1961) has discussed the development and management of the phobias, and Schwartz (1972a, 1972b) has pro-duced two papers dealing with obsessive disorders in group therapy. Solyom (1973) used group therapy to reduce fear of flying.

ADDICTION: DRUG AND ALCOHOL ABUSE

Alcoholism

The rubric of alcoholism contains a wide variety of people with extremely diverse problems. Alcohol addiction can be a symptom of an underlying problem (i.e., dependency) a problem in and of itself, or a combination of these. Calling a person an alcoholic does not help us treat her or him as a person; all kinds of people misuse alcohol. In this section we will focus only on research which deals directly with the elimination of alcohol abuse and not with therapy for the whole person who happens to be an alcoholic.

The fact that there are several hundred articles on the use of group therapy with alcoholics and at least three journals which deal exclusively with this problem suggests the ubiquity of this problem. Stein and Fried-man (1971) conclude their review of group therapy approaches to alcohol abuse with the observation that "with individual psychotherapy, most writers agree, 20–40 percent of alcoholics improve . . . . With group psychotherapy the figures reported in the literature are considera-bly higher." Their conclusion seems to be shared by most researchers and therapists in this area. Thus from Alcoholics Anonymous (AA) to marathons to Delancey Street (Hampden-Turner, 1976), all novel approaches to reducing alcoholism seem to stress group treatment and interpersonal interactions.

Group therapy as a form of treatment for alcoholics has been used since the 1930s. Thomas (1943) has documented the success of those early groups, as has Bales (1944) in his account of Alcoholics Anonym-ous. Other early group therapy approaches to alcoholism are reported by Pfeffer, Friedland, and Wortis (1949), Allison (1952), Mueller (1949), McCarthy (1946), and Lerner (1953a). The reports of the latter two may be of greater interest because they contain long transcriptions of actual sessions. One learns from these reports that alcoholics are like everyone else, and they express themselves in much the same way as other persons do. Feldman (1956) has reviewed all treatment programs for alcoholics and has recommended group treatments, as has Fox (1962). Weiner (1966) also provides an overview of group therapy approaches.

The recent review by Stein and Friedman (1971) discusses several theories of treatments of alcoholism. They focus on both AA and other group techniques and argue that group treatment is superior to individual approaches. While AA has generally been considered the most successful treatment, Ends and Page (1957), McGinnis (1963), and Curlee (1971) have found improvement in the AA treatment when additional group therapy procedures are also employed. That AA is still important as treatment is borne out by Moore and Buchanan's (1966) survey indicating that AA is in use in 88 percent of state hospitals, and group therapy is in use in 78 percent of them.

One major trend noted in the literature is the inclusion of spouses, families, and significant others in the treatment programs. Cork (1956), Ewing, Long, and Wengel (1961), Gliedman (1957), Gliedman, Nash, and Webb (1956), Gliedman, Rosenthal, Frank, and Nash (1956), Igersheimer (1959), MacDonald (1958), Sands and Hanson (1971), Pixley and Stiefel (1963), and Whalen (1953) all have provided arguments for combined or concurrent group treatment of male alcoholics' wives or relatives.

Bruner-Orne and Orne (1956) have demonstrated particular effectiveness with hospitalized alcoholics. Other researchers who have also focused on hospitalized alcoholic groups include Hoy (1969), Jensen (1962), Schual, Saller, and Paley (1971), Voth (1963), and Wolff (1967). Blume, Robins, and Branston (1968) have demonstrated improvements with group psychodrama techniques. Haberman (1966) has described factors related to increased sobriety in group psychotherapy, and marathon techniques are reported anecdotally by Dichter, Driscoll, Ottenberg, and Rosen (1971) and by Gazda, Parks, and Sisson (1971). Yalom (1970) has summarized much of the current thought on the problem by suggesting that if alcoholics are to be put in a therapy group, it should be in a homogeneous group with other alcoholics.

Drug Abuse

Like alcoholism, drug abuse can be looked at as a particular form of symptom which some persons, for unknown reasons, assume. Drug addiction appears to be growing in importance and increasing statistically, in terms of use of the whole range of habit-forming drugs and existence in a wide variety of population groups.

Two presidential commissions, newspaper and magazine articles galore, and the popularization of drugs by Vietnam War veterans and college groups have made the public aware that drug abuse is a major social and health problem exists. Any estimate of the number of drug abusers is guesswork, but without a definition of which substances are considered hard drugs and which are considered harmless, even guesswork is of little value. For example, popular surveys on marijuana usage suggest that 50–80 percent of students between the ages of 13 and 20 have at least tried it. Heroin abuse in certain sections of the country (like New York City's Harlem district) is rampant. Most studies do not even consider prescription drug abuse in their surveys. Treatment typically involves total environmental changes (i.e., institutionalization) and voluntary participation.

Early work on narcotics abuse has been discussed by Buck (1952), who used psychodrama, Johnston (1951), and Thorpe and Smith (1952). The biggest impetus in work with narcotics addicts came with Chuck Diederich's Synanon and the notions that heroin addiction is a manifestation of underlying character disorders, and laymen and peers, especially reformed addicts, could be most helpful in treatment. The two most famous residential treatment centers are Synanon, founded in 1958, and Daytop Village, established in New York in 1963. Several other houses following similar models have also been formed; typically, they employ Synanon veterans. Phoenix House and Odyssey House are two of the most famous. The Synanon "game" or encounter has formed a classic model for all such treatment, and "cold turkey" has been used to motivate rapid detoxification and subsequent commitment to behavior change.

Several studies on these residential treatment centers have demonstrated their varied degrees of success (Calof, 1967, 1969; Collier, 1970; Kramer, Bass, & Berecochea, 1968; Markoff, 1969; Ramirez, 1961). A major critique of these programs is their lack of commitment to transfer of training. Thus patients do get off drugs while in the house but typically cannot seem to leave the house and maintain themselves in nonaddicted ways. Another treatment for heroin addicts is the methadone treatment, or methadone maintenance program. These programs provide a drug to eliminate narcotic craving without increased toxicity. A major goal of these treatment programs is social functioning in the community. High rates of staying in treatment have been reported by Gewirtz (1969), Langrad, Lowinson, Brill, and Joseph (1971), and Lowinson and Zwerling (1971). Evaluations of these programs are still new, but preliminary results are promising (Joseph & Dole, 1970; Logan, 1972).

Self-help groups and peer counseling are at the core of many group therapy programs for drug addicts (Kaufman, 1972; Ketai, 1973; Rachman & Heller, 1976). Drug addicts' families have been included by Brown (1973). Adolescent amphetamine users have been treated by therapeutic community approaches (Brook & Whitehead, 1973), as were former addicts (Weppner, 1973). Freudenberger and Marrero (1972–73) used a marathon approach with returning Vietnam veteran addicts.

Binot (1973) and Sorenson (1973) have provided interesting reviews of group therapy treatment programs. The trend in the area of treatment of narcotic addiction seems to be away from analytic therapy and toward increased group work, milieu treatment, voluntary participation, and return to the community. Medical treatments and behavioral approaches also seem to provide some promise, but critical studies are still lacking.

Smoking

One other form of addiction that has been attacked in a group setting is smoking. In recent years, a plethora of approaches have been applied to the voluntary elimination of tobacco addiction. Four major approaches have been used: emotional role playing (Janis & Mann, 1965), psychodynamic (Tamerin, 1972), behavioral (Whitman, 1972), and corrective (Crosbie, Petroni, & Stitt, 1972).

The "corrective" group employs regular group therapy methods emphasizing peer social pressure and conformity to a non-smoking norm. Crosbie et al., using a four-group design emphasizing differential levels of social pressure, indicate that smoking reduction was linked to increased social pressure. J. L. Schwartz (1969) and Lawton (1967) have summarized this literature.

Koenig and Masters (1965) found equal effectiveness with three different techniques: systematic desensitization, aversion therapy, and supportive counseling. An interesting finding of their study was that the more successful patients viewed their therapists more negatively than did unsuccessful patients. Whitman (1972) successfully used an aversion technique which paired a bitter-tasting pill with cigarettes for at least six months.

Studies by Bozzetti (1972) and Guilford (1972), and a review of the literature by Keutzer, Lichtenstein, and Mees (1968), also have recommended the use of groups.

CORRECTIONS

Correctional institutions—jails, penitentiaries, training schools, reformatories, prisons—can be regarded as being intended to serve a therapeutic function. Prisoners are sent to these institutions not only for punishment but also for correction. That little correction actually takes place is a serious social problem. Considering the concept of punishment may promote understanding of this fundamental problem in the treatment of people who commit crimes.

Criminals are stigmatized, and those who view them with sympathy are usually derided for being soft. It may be "natural" to regard the criminal as "bad," but it is not logical in view of the fact that the insane, the retarded, tubercular and epileptic patients, the deaf, lepers, alcoholics, and gamblers were once looked on as evil, or filled with the devil, and were consequently treated cruelly and inhumanely. Deeply ingrained in our laws and mores is the concept that the criminal offender is evil, and our mounting fears for safety, particularly in the big cities, reinforce this idea. These feelings are sustained and developed by the mass information media which publicize and glamorize the exploits of professional criminals (who, as a matter of fact, rarely go to prison). If we consider the criminal as sick or at least in need of resocialization, advances may be made in treating criminosis, just as they have been made in treating psychoses.

A basic question is whether it is possible to punish and to correct at the same time. A basic prerequisite of psychotherapy is acceptance, but in a prison inmates are not accepted as individuals by the guards or administrators. The traditional use of numbers instead of names in prisons is both a cause and a symptom of such nonacceptance. Furthermore, the prison culture has its own system of rules, regulations, and justice which is particularly degrading and is geared to maintain the established power system. A striking aspect of the prison environment is the fear that troubles every inmate and pervades every corner within the walls. My experience in working clinically with male inmates is that they are socially deficient, interpersonally inept, and very frightened. All these characteristics typically retard the effects of therapy.

The literature on individual psychotherapy in prisons is sparse. Accounts given by Lindner (1944) and Karpman (1940) do not manage to overcome Brancale's (1943) pessimism about psychotherapy in prisons. Perhaps the major reason for the failure of individual psychotherapy in prisons is the "unsymmetry" of individual therapy, using J. L. Moreno's terminology. Two common undesirable aspects of individual psychotherapy are resistance and dependency. If an insecure person is put into therapeutic association with a secure person, it is quite likely that the weaker, who is supposed to confess to the stronger, may resist the process, even if he is paying for the privilege. Later, as the association continues, the weaker may feel he needs the stronger person, and a dependency relation develops. Fidler (1951) states that the deeper levels of personality cannot be handled until anxieties and hostilities, which are other names for resistance, are settled. Lipschutz (1952) says, "I believe I can safely state that the majority of failures in psychotherapy are essentially due to the factor of resistance."

It is not surprising that individual psychotherapy, as ordinarily practiced by psychoanalysts and those who assume semiauthoritarian roles, has not been successful in prisons, since in such circumstances the resistance generally encountered in patients who come to therapists of their free will in a free situation is multiplied by the nature of the institution. (Some exceptions to this rule of thumb can be found in the recent use of behavior modification techniques in prison settings. These programs have led to major behavior changes, at least initially in several settings.) However, the capacity of group psychotherapy to reduce resistance appears to be well established. Lipschutz, quoted above, also states, "It was found that the usual resistances met in psycho-analytic therapy are more readily broken with the aid of group therapy." On this same point, Wolf, Locke, Rosenbaum, Hillpern, Goldfarb, Kadis, Obers, Milberg, and Abell (1952), also representing the psycho-analytic point of view, state:

> It is largely the interactive atmosphere of a group session,
> deliberately cultivated by the therapist but increasingly acted
> upon by one patient after another, that enables those more blocked
> to engage in the emotional give and take . . . even these severely
> immobilized analysands can frequently be reached by the
> explosive atmosphere of the group.

We can make the following conclusion: If resistance is a problem in psychotherapy, and if resistance to therapy is greater in a prison than outside, then, in a free (outside) situation, if resistance to therapy is lowered by the group form it appears that group therapy will be more successful in correctional work than individual therapy. Such seems to be the situation, since practically the entire literature of successful therapy in correctional institutions is about group methods.

Arnold and Stiles (1972), summarizing the use of group methods in correctional institutions, state that group . . . methods have become one of the major tools of correctional personnel working with inmates in a sizable majority of our penal institutions. Almost 4 out of 5 of these institutions apply such methods to at least a few of their inmates; and in 26% of the institutions practically all the inmates are in group programs (p. 77).

Summarizing surveys by McCorkle (1953), and McCorkle and Elias (1960), as well as their own survey, Arnold and Stiles (1972) suggest that more institutions are using group therapy methods, that groups are being led by a wider range of personnel, and that the types of therapy offered have become more diversified as the years have passed. Ackman, Normandeau, and Wolfgang (1968) support these data with their own survey of group treatments in corrections from 1945 to 1967.

Delinquents

It is difficult to conceive of a group more resistant to psychotherapy than delinquents who are also mentally retarded. Yonge and O'Connor (1954), who engaged in group therapy in a British correctional institution, have summarized an experiment utilizing two matched groups of boys, ranging from 16 to 21 years old. One group was made the control and was treated exactly like the other, except that the experimental group had one hour of group therapy once a week for 32 weeks. The two groups were observed and recorded in their various activities. The group method used was a variant of the circular discussion method originally employed by Burrow but based on the writings of Foulkes. Results indicated that members of the experimental group developed more positive attitudes to authority figures and peers, greater appreciation, better attitudes toward themselves and group mates, less masochism, and less unsatisfactory work behavior. No such changes occurred for control group members.

Although the statistical significance of these results was not given, the trend is unmistakable and tends to support the contention of the efficacy of group psychotherapy. Many recent studies seem to confirm these data. Snyder & Sechrest (1959), comparing group therapy to placebo and no treatment, found greatest improvement with the group treatment for "dull normal delinquents."

Persons (1966) has reported reduced pathology and anxiety for juvenile delinquents through group therapy, in comparison to controls, and Truax (1968) has shown that delinquents in vicarious (group) therapy pretraining developed both improved self-concepts and reduced MMPI profiles. Similarly, Feder (1962) has found that delinquents in group therapy had increased therapeutic readiness, and McDavid (1964) has demonstrated increased social awareness.

Furthermore, Yong (1971) has discussed several advantages of group over individual treatment for delinquents, and Truax (1971) has demonstrated that positive behavior change through group therapy is related to negative transference toward the therapist. Redfering (1971) used groups with institutionalized delinquent females. Franklin and Nottage (1969) used psychoanalytically oriented groups meeting five times a week for severely disturbed juvenile delinquents, as did Lievano (1970) for delinquent boys.

Training Schools

Youthful multiple offenders who are adjudged delinquent by the courts are sent to training schools which are given a variety of names, such as protectories, reform schools, industrial schools, or parental schools. The inmates of these schools may be as young as 10 and as old as 18, but the bulk of the population is among the early teens. The crimes may vary from such minor infractions as disobeying parents, running away from home, sexual promiscuity and prostitution, or playing hooky to the more serious crimes of robbery and murder. Females are usually incarcerated for lesser crimes than males.

Group therapy has been employed in several of these schools with some success. Lassner (1947), in one of the earliest reports, comments on his use of dramatics with youths in a mental hospital ward, in much the same manner as that employed by Curran and Schilder (1940). He reports clinical improvements in behavior. In a more complete report, Thorpe and Smith (1952) state that while boys reacted well to the group in the beginning, in a short time hostility developed which showed itself in negativism and criticism. This phenomenon was also found in Geller's (1950) report on analytic groups in a mental hospital (Corsini, 1957). However, this negative reaction is interpreted quite differently in "correctional" settings, and sanctions are often imposed, irrespective of their countertherapeutic impact.

The most adequate early report concerning group therapy in training schools is by Gisela Konopka (1954). Konopka, in spite of the advantage of her sex and the fact that she was not a regular member of the staff, nevertheless found the inmates difficult to deal with, primarily because of the autocratic nature of the institution. This point needs further discussion; although seen most clearly in juvenile institutions, it is a problem in all correctional institutions and represents a clear-cut philosophical conflict between the ideologies of therapy and those of "correction."

As has been noted, an essential aspect of psychotherapy is the existence and demonstration of a noncritical attitude called *acceptance* or *love*. The official attitude of a correctional institution, based securely on the demands of the public or at least on the interpretation of these demands by the administrators, is the opposite of this, as witnessed by the many, often ridiculous rules that are enforced. Thorpe and Smith, who were concerned with negative attitudes, and Konopka, who found her work difficult because of the autocratic nature of the institution, illustrate the problem in specific detail.

Corsini (1957) reported that at a particular institution for juveniles, smoking was forbidden except at certain times and certain places, and even then the cigarettes were carefully rationed out to the older boys.

All employees were cautioned to watch for unauthorized smoking and were required to report any infractions of these rules. Despite this, and maybe because of it, secret smoking took place all the time, and some employees closed their eyes to such violations of the rules. The superintendent had periodic drives against smoking and made an issue of the whole matter.

A group was formed in this institution for the purpose of therapy. It met in a secluded room under the supervision of a psychologist and a psychiatrist who had discussed in detail beforehand the philosophy, theory, and practice of the therapy. At the first session, one of the therapists was laying down the ground rules, stating,

> In this group you can say or do anything whatsoever without getting any punishment, any warnings, or any reprimands.
> We will keep everything you say and do a secret. We want you to feel free to express yourself in any way you wish. If we desire to set up rules, we will do it democratically. We will be like a little independent island. . . .

At this point one of the boys took out a cigarette, deliberately lit it, and took a great puff, slowing exhaling the smoke through his nose, looking right at the speaker. The other boys fastened their eyes on the greatly desired butt and began to beg for a puff. As the therapist went on, the cigarette moved from mouth to mouth, and no attention was being paid to his statements.

The therapists were put into the situation of having to either ignore the cigarette or do something about it. If they ignored it, they were being insubordinate, since the superintendent had established a firm no-smoking rule. If they commanded the boys to stop smoking, this would have a direct contradiction of their permissive philosophy. If they had tried to get the boys to stop smoking during the therapy by democratic vote, at least in the early life of the group, the vote would have been 12 to 2, with the therapists in the minority.

The therapists did nothing about the situation except to indicate in the vaguest terms that everybody should keep secret what happened in therapy. Very shortly other inmates began to ask to enter the group, stating quite frankly that they wanted to enter so they could smoke. At this point, the therapists dissolved the group. Advance agreements to follow rules and specifications as to certain topics which will be automatically reported to administration (running away, homicide, suicide) can inhibit some of the acting-out behavior, but the problem of the mutually exclusive demands of punishment and rehabilitation remains a serious one.

Despite such obvious problems, some positive results from group therapy have been reported in these settings. Lievano (1970), on the basis of his experiences with adolescent boys in an industrial school in Topeka, Kansas, argues that group therapy reached the boys faster and deeper than individual therapy. These results confirmed the findings of Scarborough and Novick (1962). Aitken (1970) demonstrated attitudinal changes via group guidance techniques.

Much of the recent work in training schools has focused on training the staff rather than the inmates. The assumptions behind this move include the notion that unless staff members are retrained they will sabotage new inmate behaviors, and by training staff it is possible to get wider coverage of the therapy. Fenton and Taron (1965) have presented the results of a major study on staff training for youth correctional facilities in California, and Coffey (1965), Martinson and O'Brien (1966), and Shapiro and Ross (1970, 1971) have specifically evaluated the group training component. In the Shapiro and Ross studies, major changes in staff behavior were demonstrated and maintained for at least one year. A particular advantage of these studies was the ranking of staff behaviors by inmates who were unaware of the assignment of staff to experimental and control conditions. These groups focused primarily on personal growth for staff. N. W. Ackerman (1972) also demonstrated the effectiveness of groups which focused on work problems in a women's prison.

Reformatories

The second stage of correctional institutions is represented by reformatories, which generally take inmates from the ages of 16 to 30. Curiously, very little in the way of group psychotherapy in these institutions has been reported, and what does exist is generally of a comparatively superficial kind. Probably the most distinguished effort is that at Highfields, New Jersey, where an entire segment of a reformatory was transferred to a private estate with the intention of engaging in "guided group interaction" under the direction of Lloyd McCorkle. This project has been favorably reviewed by Weeks (1953), but little is known of its long-term effectiveness.

Plowitz (1950) has experimented with group therapy at the reformatory at Elmira, New York, and reports favorable results in its early use. Gula (1944) has used an institution for the main purpose of evaluating youths held in detention, and also for therapy. A doctoral thesis published by Gerstenlauer (1950) referred to the use of group therapy in delinquency.

One of the more informative and hopeful reports in this area is by Kennedy (1951), who was in the position of reorganizing an entire institution through creating a number of overlapping commissions to inquire into various aspects of the institution. One of the commssions investigated the potentialities of group therapy, and later such a program was put into effect. As a result of the total reorganization, there was a decided drop in institutional infractions and an improvement in morale. In their recent survey, Arnold and Stiles (1972) indicated 67 percent of reformatories reported some type of group work, but details are still sketchy and generally unreported.

Prisons

It would appear that the major use of group therapy in correctional work is in the prisons. The first report in the literature about group methods with adult offenders seems to be Abrahams and McCorkle (1946). Their procedure, called *guided group interaction,* has been used at various times with military and civilian prisoners, as described by McCorkle (1949, 1952, 1953). In essence, it is, as its name implies, a circular, discussional type of therapy in which the inmates initiate and discuss issues under the general direction of the therapist. It is quite similar to the procedure used by McCarthy (1950) and Lerner (1953b) with alcoholics.

Psychodrama in prisons was first used by Lassner (1950) at San Quentin. On the basis of his observations and follow-ups, Lassner concluded that psychodrama is of considerable value in helping prisoners. Further reports of the use of psychodrama at the same institution were published by Corsini (1951a), who felt that this method was uniquely valuable for the rapid dissolution of resistances and the attainment of "immediate therapy". Using a combined lecture-testimonial method, Corsini (1954) also treated inmates who were at first actively hostile to group therapy. Despite initial resistance, and after some early struggles, the members of this forced group began to function and apparently got some value out of the proceedings.

Bromberg and Franklin (1952) have reported the use of psychodrama in a correctional setting in a mental hospital. They also have reported enhanced group cohesion as a function of administrative oppression, with the therapist identified as part of the group rather than being linked to the administration.

Among others who have discussed group psychotherapy in prisons are Fenton (1951), Janney and Bemis (1954), Hadden (1948), Clarke (1952), Cavanagh and Gerstein (1949), Deberker (1963), Jew (1973), Moore (1972), and O'Brien (1950). Hadden more or less summarizes general opinion about the value of group methods in adult correctional institutions: "Group psychotherapy has been studied sufficiently to be appreciated as being more effective than any other method in the treatment of certain neurotic states. Some of its dynamics are unique properties which make it highly effective in penal situations." Referring to the problems of conducting what is essentially a democratic form of treatment in an autocratic environment, Hadden says, "Psychiatric services in a prison can be effective only when prison personnel is cooperative and sympathetic."

One of the relatively few critical comments about group psychotherapy is with reference to prison use. O'Brien deprecates its value, considering it only a supplement to individual therapy. However, O'Brien's understanding of the term seems to be quite different from its usual definition, since he equates it with any kind of group work, including academic classes and recreational teams.

In recent years the use of chaplain-led groups and groups conducted by lay leaders have become popular. Grand (1965) speaks highly of his own program for 16–21-year-old male inmates, as does Ramer (1971). However, Arnold and Stiles (1972), summarizing the wide use of groups in correctional institutions, warn against the employment of unqualified personnel. A few studies seem to demonstrate some attitude and behavior change in prison groups. Baumgold (1970), using a marathon technique, and Reinstein (1970), working with military prisoners, both have suggested the value of this method. Hampton (1971) and Rappaport (1971) also have demonstrated the effectiveness of group therapy on attitude changes.

Two recent innovations are reported by Neussendorfer (1969) and Shapiro (1976). Neussendorfer did marriage counseling at the St. Cloud, Minnesota, Reformatory for inmates and their wives. Shapiro conducted two groups for convicted rapists in which five inmates were each paired for individual counseling with a female graduate student in a mental health field. After one hour of individual discussion, the entire group (five inmates, five graduate student counselors, and a group therapist) met for an additional hour. Attitude and behavior change seemed to occur with this format; and inmates' self-concept also improved. As in the Neussendorfer study, however, no hard data were collected, and thus these results have only heuristic value at this time.

Parole

The parolee has just come from prison, where he has been subjected to all the disadvantages of monosex associations and has been carefully conditioned to lose all his initiative, since any display of unique behavior is a signal for trouble in prison. With no recent experience in meeting social problems, and with a crushing understanding that the rest of the free world regards him as an ex-convict, he is thrown into a

society full of dangers and temptations. His parole officer, who is sometimes unsympathetic and always overworked, is usually regarded with
some fear and suspicion, especially since he can return the parolee to
the institution.

In some states, since ex-convicts on parole cannot associate with
each other, conducting therapeutic groups for this population may
actually be a violation of the law. M. R. King (1953) has suggested
group therapy as a means of helping parolees make a better social
adjustment, and so has Fuller (1952), but it was Yablonsky (1955)
who made the first attempts to treat parolees with psychodrama through
a community agency. Ghaston and Wells (1965) have made one
attempt to conduct therapy groups with parolees; their results suggest
that group members made better adjustments to the outside world.
Belford (1971) has compared role playing and group therapy on
socialization in parolees, and Rest and Ryan (1970) have used groups
for vocational counselors for parolees and probationers.

Jails

Jails are a unique kind of institution, primarily intended to hold
prisoners in temporary custody. For the most part, no programs of any
kind are held for men or women in jails. One of the very few reports in
this area has been provided by Lerner (1953b), with extended transcriptions of remarks. Using a discussional method quite similar to that
of McCorkle, he has dealt extensively with alcoholics. Illing (1951) has
also discussed group psychotherapy in jails. Youmans (1968) has
demonstrated that residents of the San Diego County Jail became more
positive toward authority and less recidivistic when they had group
experience.

Predelinquents

In every community, the police and others, including school teachers
and community leaders, know of youths who are definitely heading for
correctional institutions. Many juvenile courts, as a matter of policy,
tend to return youths found guilty of infractions for the first time to
the custody of their parents. Among those who have discussed the use
of group methods with predelinquents are Schulman (1952), Buck
and Grygier (1952), Hill (1953), and Gersten (1952). Actually, in
many community agencies, such as those described by Slavson (1947b)
and Dreikurs (1951a), a sizable proportion of the youths express their
disturbances by antisocial behavior.

Predelinquents find the world a hostile place. On the one hand they
are desperately seeking to find a place in society, wanting to become an
adult, and on the other hand they are often treated by parents and

other adults as a child who should be in school and whose major task is to conform. The inadequacy of programs for after-school recreation for such youths, especially in crowded sections of cities, is well known. Many of them have no place to discuss their problems nor any person who will listen to them seriously; they have no opportunities for real communication with others. Rap groups and drug clinic groups have begun to fill this void in the seventies, but the quality of group leadership often limits the effectiveness of these groups. Some of this work will be described below under the heading of "Children, Adolescents, and Schools," and addiction groups were discussed above.

One particular problem facing group leaders in corrections that is different from that faced by workers in psychiatric settings is that improvement does not necessarily lead to noticeable rewards. While a mental patient may be released on the basis of successful group therapy, an inmate may have no chance of environmental change for several months or years. In these terms it is hard to tell potential correctional group members what a group has to offer, given the reality of their situation. Even with these problems, however, the increasing use of groups in correctional institutions from 1950 to 1966, according to Arnold and Stiles (1972), is astronomical.

MAJOR BEHAVIORAL PATHOLOGIES

Perhaps the most important applications of group psychotherapy have been with persons who are institutionalized because they are incapable of making adequate social adjustments. More than one half of all the hospital beds in this country are filled by mental patients at the present time, and more than 200,000 people live in institutions for the mentally retarded. The social importance of rehabilitating this huge population should be evident.

Mental Defectives

Mental defectives can be classified into three groups: the endogenous, who were born deficient; the exogenous, who became deficient mentally because of injuries or disease; and the pseudo defectives, who appear to be mentally inferior but are not. Only the last of the three groups can be helped with respect to improvement of intelligence. It is possible through group therapy, however, to help the mentally retarded make better institutional adjustments. Fisher and Wolfson (1953), Cotzin (1948), Lipnitzky (1940), Mehlman (1953), Myers (1971), Sarbin (1945), Taylar, Strickland, and Lindsay (1948), Wilcox and Guthrie (1957) and Zifstein and Rosen (1973), have discussed the use of group methods with mental defectives. In general, the findings are that mental defectives are readily affected by such group experiences, and as a result of treatment they frequently are able to make better adjustments to institutional conditions. Forman (1971) has discussed using groups to mediate patient needs and institutional needs. Whalen and Henker (1971) look at long-term effects of groups via their "pyramid therapy," and Broms (1971) specifies the value of groups for the preschool retarded child. Appell, Williams, and Fishel (1964), Cummings and Stock (1962), Sugar (1971), and Lewis (1972) have demonstrated the effectiveness of working with the parents of retarded children, and Payne and Williams (1971) examine the considerations in working with groups of all retardates, or mixed groups of retardates and non-retardates.

Two interesting studies by Fisher and Wolfson (1953) and Mann, Beaber, and Jacobson (1969) indicate attempts to get group behavior to generalize to extragroup behavior. Working with mentally deficient girls and boys, respectively, they have demonstrated self-concept and behavior changes.

Psychotics

The earliest workers with therapeutic groups in mental hospitals appear to have been Marsh and Lazell. Neither of these pioneers, who began their work about 1910 and who, according to Pratt, probably were not influenced by his work, had any intention of "curing" schizophrenia or any other mental disease (Corsini, 1957). They wanted to bring some cheer and joy into the lives of the mentally ill. It is difficult to say who was the first to conceive of group psychotherapy as a specific treatment for the insane. The most probable explanation is that a concatenation of the work of Schilder, Burrow, Marsh, Lazell, Wender, Moreno, Klapman, and Low resulted gradually in the acceptance of the idea that psychotics could be expected to improve with group therapy as the primary treatment agency.

Many techniques have been used with institutionalized psychotics: the repressive-inspirational method, group analysis, psychodrama, textbook-mediated therapy, round-table psychotherapy, mechanical group therapy, ABC, motivation incentive therapy, rational-emotive therapy, behavior modification, and so on.

Altshuler, an enthusiastic proponent of the value of music in psychotherapy for psychotics, has used a method called Rhythm Therapy. Groups of from 35 to 50 patients are formed. The theory of the method, according to Altshuler (1940), is to establish a temporary parent-child relationship between the therapist and the patients, using the mechanisms of catharsis, transference, and substitution. The objective of the method is "The development and strengthening of rapport, the stimulation of self-confidence, the creation of opportunities for self-expression, the cultivation of work habits and education of the reason coupled with training in morals and ethics." The ultimate aim of the method is "to offer reality so attractively and abundantly that the ego will lose its desire to remain in seclusion with the subconscious."

Essentially, patients are involved in the group process by clapping wooden blocks in time to marching music. By maintaining the patients' attention in this way and providing them with a common experience, the therapist was able to get them to sing, talk about events, and ultimately to discuss their concerns. Thus music served Altshuler in the same way textbooks served Klapman (1946) in his textbook method and the blackboard and chalk served Jacobson and Wright (1942) in their ABC method—as a means of gaining the attention of highly distractible patients.

Contemporary uses of music therapy for schizophrenic patients have been reported by Lehrer-Carle (1971) and Szelenberger (1971).

Geller (1949) used discussional groups with psychotic patients. Groups of from 10 to 15 were reported to be optimal. Patients were nominated by ward physicians, based on their judgments of who was most likely to benefit. Each patient selected was screened by a psychiatrist who explained the nature and purpose of the groups. Sessions lasted for one hour and were held weekly. Individual interviews were also given at irregular intervals.

Procedures involved discussions and interpretations along dynamic lines. Analyses were carried out not only by the therapists but also by the patients, who were encouraged to participate. The therapist might agree or disagree with any interpretation. The therapist took a permissive attitude and allowed a maximum of initiative for the patients. This method is essentially similar to that initiated by Burrow (1927a) and used also by Schilder (1937) in dealing with neurotics.

The following results were noted in Geller (1949). Expressions of resentment and hostility toward the hospital and its personnel were common. New patients who entered already-formed groups tended to be silent at first, but when they did begin to participate, they generally were critical. Such expressions were regarded as a "testing" of the group. Hostile feelings subsided quickly, either as a result of ventilation or because the therapist tended to answer all complaints and to explain the situation complained about. Favorable attitudes were not confined to the group; other patients on the wards also began to change their attitudes as communications spread throughout the hospital. Feelings of acceptance and of security began to develop. It was noted that patients were affected more by the opinions of their mates than by those of the therapist. Anxiety was reduced by discussions of symptoms. A sense of unity began to develop in the group. Although Geller states that results in terms of any single person did not approach the depth to be found in individual analysis, in some cases remarkable insights were obtained.

In addition to these therapeutic groups, other group activities were established in which educational and recreational activities predominated. A convalescent-status orientation group, assembled for patients who were about to leave, was designed to help them make the precarious adjustment to the world outside. These meetings, held daily, consisted for the most part of lectures with opportunities for questions.

Another group method used in treating psychotic patients is represented by the therapeutic social clubs conceived by Bierer (1948a, 1948b). Bierer's basic postulates, which stem out of Adlerian philosophy, are the following:

1. Patients should be treated as normal, with no more being done for them than is absolutely necessary.
2. Treatment is under "field" conditions, or, as Moreno puts it, "on the spot."
3. Situational treatment is considered to be aimed at a result intermediate between insight and fulfillment, or between intellectual and emotional changes.
4. Associability, or loss of contact with others, is the most common maladjustment.
5. Treatment depends not on transference but on the full range of social tensions and attractions.
6. The personality and experience of the psychiatrist determine the success of the treatment.
7. The club can serve as a prophylactic instrument.
8. The method is socially efficient and available to many.

Bierer's basic attitude is that psychotics have motivations, and institutional personnel can be manipulated by patients who will accept help even when it is not needed. This contention is validated by Braginsky, Braginsky, and Ring (1969). The major purpose of the clubs is to aid patients in recovering their initiative under democratic circumstances. The therapy is hidden, or indirect, since there are none of the usual activities seen in therapeutic groups, such as interpretation of symptoms, analysis of part history, and direct advice.

This method can be compared with Moreno's early philosophy of every man being the therapeutic agent of the other. In 1931 Moreno suggested that prisoners be classified into groups of such composition that the interactions between the individuals would be beneficial to all members. Bierer's procedure is similar to McCann's (1953) method of round-table psychotherapy in that, in each case, the therapist is absent. In a more recent study, Aleksondrowicz and Gaye (1971) reported effectiveness of the use of a therapeutic social club for adolescent schizophrenics. Certainly the opportunity for a patient to be altruistic and help another patient has beneficial effects for both. The helper feels some self-gratification and has a success experience in interpersonal relationships, and the one helped gains a sense of lesser pathology by receiving help from a peer rather than from the omniscient-seeming therapist. The same basic assumptions underlie the Synanon and AA approaches to substance abuses.

It is generally believed by psychiatrists that major changes in schizophrenics and other psychotic patients will not be forthcoming through any known treatment mode. Typically, psychotics are treated medicinally and institutionally. Yalom (1970), for example, recommends against including psychotics in therapy groups because of the effects on other patients, problems for the therapists, and lack of effectiveness of the group itself.

However, some studies have produced positive changes. A wide variety of approaches, from highly structured didactic lectures to more traditional, feeling-oriented types of groups, has been investigated. While results are still inconclusive, several authors have demonstrated constructive personality changes in psychotic populations through group therapy. Semon and Goldstein (1957), for example, found that schizophrenic patients in a therapy group demonstrated improved ratings on the hospital adjustment scale when compared to controls. Similarly, Sachs and Berger (1954) demonstrated that schizophrenic patients in groups showed greater movements to less disturbed wards, and Williams, McGhee, Kittleson, and Halperin (1962) found significant improvement, using TAT measures, for schizophrenics in a group program. In addition, Kraus (1959), Fairweather and Simon (1963), and Fairweather, Simon, Gebhard, Weingarten, Holland, Sanders, Stone, and Reahl (1960) found improvements in psychotic patients via group therapy. Becker (1971), comparing group vs. nongroup preparation for discharge of 58 chronic schizophrenic women prior to community placement, found significantly greater patient improvement during preparation and higher discharge rates for the group participants. Similarly, O'Connor (1969) showed that a group of chronic schizophrenic women led by a student nurse showed increased socialization and reduced alienation after 60 meetings. Rueveni and Speck (1971) and Bowers, Banquer, and Bloomfield (1974) have recommended nonverbal and touching exercises with schizophrenics in helping break through the multiple resistances found in psychotic groups. Payn (1974), on the other hand, has recommended pharmacotherapy for the same purpose.

McGee, Starr, Powers, Racusen, and Thornton (1965) and Miller (1972) have used combinations of psychodrama and group therapy effectively. Battegay (1965) has used group therapy to train schizophrenics for posthospital release, and Alikakos (1965) worked with posthospital schizophrenics. Sculthorpe and Blumenthal (1965) conducted combined patient-relative groups, and Kibel (1968) reported success with a combination of group therapy and milieu treatment.

Several modern approaches to groups of psychotics continue to be developed and empirically tested. The critical factors in the success of these groups seem to be patience on the part of the therapist and a willingness to work with limited expectancies for rapid change. One thing does seem likely, however; the placement of psychotic patients in groups, and hence paying attention to them, can have a moderating effect on their symptoms.

Pedophiles and Other Sex Offenders

An account of group psychotherapy with pedophiles (adults who seduce or criminally attack children) was written by Corsini (1954). The members of the group, when interviewed individually, refused to participate. Questions arose concerning whether it would be a violation of ethics to force treatment on these adults, and whether it would do any good to do so. A rationalization used to "answer" the first question is that there is plenty of precedence for treating people against their will: Mental hospitals are a prime example. The answer to the second question came from the experience. Although the majority of the group was initially hostile, by the end of the term of the group all but one had participated in telling about their crimes, and several asked for the group to be continued.

In later work, Illing and Miles (1969) have reported positive results with sex offenders in long-term groups, and Cabeen (1961), Cabeen and Coleman (1961), and R. E. Anderson (1969) have demonstrated effective programs with institutionalized sex offenders in group psychotherapy. Anderson's technique involved the exchange of tape recordings between inpatients at the sex crimes facility of Wisconsin State Prison and university students. These recordings served as a catalyst for the group process. Group therapy has also been used with exhibitionists (Mathis & Collins, 1970a), voyeurs (Freese, 1972), sexually acting-out girls (Friedman, 1971), and rapists (Shapiro, 1976).

SEX, MARRIAGE AND THE FAMILY

The use of group therapy to resolve domestic problems is growing rapidly. As more and more people become alienated by divorce and other breakdowns in family relations, the group becomes an increasingly greater substitute for family relationships and an important treatment modality.

Sexual Problems

Sexual disorders which involve crimes and hospitalization have been discussed above, but several sexual problems do not involve the community at large. These problems cause discomfort, discontent, and feelings of inferiority for individuals. Unless treated, they can develop into long-term patterns of unhappiness and insecurity.

Preorgastic Sexual Dysfunctions. Kaplan (1974) calls orgastic difficulties the most prevalent sexual complaint of women. If this is the case, surprisingly few authors have written of group approaches to this problem. Most frequently, orgastic difficulties have been treated in couples therapy (i.e., Masters & Johnson, 1970). Two studies dealing with this problem have been reported in the group literature (Stone & Levine, 1950; Van Emde Boas, 1950).

Stone and Levine used the following approach. Wives met for three 2-hour sessions, and later the husbands came for one 2-hour session. One of the therapists conducted the group and the other acted as an observer. The therapist started with a short lecture, answered questions, and then led a discussion. The discussions, according to the authors, were, from the first, amazingly free and frank. By the third and last session, any evident feeling of constraint had disappeared. However, anxiety and other emotional reactions were found.

To evaluate the results of these eight hours of therapy, a six-month follow-up was held for members of either sex. Significant changes in attitude were noted by these clinicians. Some of the wives had achieved orgasm for the first time. Some couples reported that they were now capable of talking to each other, for the first time, about sensitive matters. In addition, the members stated that they had lost a sense of feeling isolated from others, and the release of feelings in talking about sex before others without condemnation or disapproval had created a sense of greater ease. Considerable insight was engendered by these few hours: understanding occurred for many with reference to the background causes of the behavior, and the understanding led to better attitudes toward their mates and toward sex.

In general, in therapy groups in which there are one or more preorgasmic women, discussion of this topic in the group often leads to some relaxation and an attendant remission of symptoms. In my experience, the introduction of this subject in a group setting often provides impetus for members to seek individual therapy in this area.

Male Sexual Disorders. Even less has been written on male sexual dysfunction. Indeed, men seem much less likely to acknowledge such problems in a public setting. Betlheim (1959) has discussed the treatment of impotence in group therapy, and Kaplan (1974) mentions treatment of premature ejaculation in couples groups.

Homosexuality. Probably no other condition has been so seriously misunderstood as homosexuality. The multiplicity of theories and plain distortions of fact about sexual inversion, the emotional attitudes of so-called normal persons, and the exhibitionist tendencies of some transvestites have created a folklore about homosexuality which modern authors, such as Ellis (1954), have vainly attempted to correct. A person with a sexual liking or preference for one of his own sex usually suffers because of this liking. Since there is a strong desire on the part of all people to be accepted, and since those who are known to be homosexual are commonly regarded with contempt by others, homosexual individuals often present themselves for treatment of their "condition." Generally, mental health professionals view any nonheterosexual behavior as pathological and attempt to assist the individual to make behavior change. It is generally assumed that while there may be some biological determinants of this condition, it seems likely that much homosexual behavior is learned, and what is learned can be unlearned.

Among the early writers who have discussed group therapy with homosexuals are Eliasberg (1954), Ellis (1956), and F. K. Taylor (1950). Eliasberg reports on the psychoanalytic group treatment of two groups, each consisting of six men on probation.

Hadden (1958) organized a "homosexual" group in 1955 with the goal of increasing heterosexuality. He was successful for two of his three initial members. He also reports success with individual and group therapy. Kaye (1967) has had success in treating lesbians, and Mintz (1966), Hadden (1966), and Fried (1955) have all had success in combining group. and individual treatment. Litman (1961) and Singer and Fischer (1967) have discussed the treatment of homosexuals in mixed groups. Moore and Query (1963) and Ward (1958) have worked with institutionalized homosexual psychiatric patients and delinquents, respectively.

Other approaches have recently been demonstrated to be successful with homosexuals. Pittman and DeYoung (1971) for example, have mixed male and female homosexuals in four groups with excellent success. Johnsgard and Schumacher (1970) have reported on intimacy in groups with male homosexuals. Warner (1971) has also reported successful effects of behavioral group counseling with homosexuals. Forester and Swiller (1972) claim success with a potential transsexual via group therapy. Bieber (1971), summarizing the literature on homosexuals in groups, states "homosexuals can be treated successfully in groups . . . combined therapy with homogeneous groups has been described as the treatment of choice."

Most authors (e.g., Slavson, 1964; Hadden, 1966) have argued that because homosexuals are so threatening to others, they should be treated in homogeneous groups. Pittman and DeYoung (1971), however, have demonstrated that heterogeneous groups can be effective, although the heterosexuals in their groups all had had prior experience with homosexuals, and this would naturally reduce any anxiety-shock reaction.

One major problem in this area is that most group leaders define "success" as a movement toward heterosexuality. An important consideration may be to strive for a different kind of success—acceptance and comfort of homosexuality or bisexuality. Enhanced self-acceptance has been commonly found as a result of group participation.

Transsexuals. Until recently, transsexualism was an extremely infrequently observed phenomenon. However, with the popularization of Christine Jorgenson's experience, *Myra Breckenridge,* and the tennis career of Renee Richards, reports of this condition have increased. Forester and Swiller (1972) write, "Transsexualism is characterized by an individual's intense desire for sexual transformation by surgical and/or hormonal means, based on his or her identification with the gender role of the opposite sex" (p. 343). A transsexual biological male considers him/herself to be a woman and feels that his/her male genitalia are a mistake of nature. Forester and Swiller report a case of transsexualism who decided to forego the operation as a result of insight gained from a therapy group.

Miscellaneous Sex-Related Groups. Bernstein and Tinkham (1971) report success on postabortion groups with married and single women. They report less success with a group of only single women. Braen (1970) discusses three types of group therapy programs with school-age pregnant girls. Obler (1973) used systematic desensitization for sexual disorders, Romano (1973) employed groups for sex counseling, and Rosenberg and Chilgren (1973) reported on sex education groups in a medical setting. Horn (1975) also has described a procedure (Lopicolo and Milles) to help couples with sexual problems.

The Family

Another area of burgeoning group activity is in the application of group techniques to family and marital problems. The large area of problems connected with the family can be separated into marital problems, child-parent relationships, and problems of children in the home. Special concern with this area derives out of theory and logic: Almost all later problems of life have their origin in the home. If every family followed the principles of mental hygiene implicit in all group therapy, it is possible that the incident of mental disturbance would be very much smaller than it is at present.

Couples. For the most part in Western culture, people are free to marry whom they wish. Since this important decision is usually made with great consideration, it is surprising and shocking to learn that approximately three quarters of all marriages can be classified as unsuccessful; that is, they end in divorce or desertion, or the husband and wife live together with minimal communication or in a state of misery. Recent statistics indicate that as many as 50 percent of all marriages end in divorce.

The causes of marital unhappiness and disequilibrium have been extensively examined. They vary, extending from cultural differences to differences in personality patterns. Sometimes a single shocking event in the family, such as unfaithfulness on the part of one of the mates, can upset a marriage's equilibrium to such an extent that it is never again the same. For many years there have been centers and private counselors available to help couples reconcile their differences and learn to live together more comfortably.

Moreno (1952a) has described psychodrama in the treatment of a marital conflict of the triangle sort; Redwin (1955) has used the behind-the-back technique; Ruskin (1953) has used analytic group therapy; and Solby (1941) has used psychodrama.

Papanek (1970b) has argued that marriage pathology is the result of individual pathology, and psychoanalytically oriented authors tend to support this notion (e.g., Jackson & Grotjahn, 1958). Many modern-day therapists working toward marital conflict resolution, however, believe that the family unit forms a synergistic unit (Fullmer, 1972), and changes in one partner lead inevitably to changes in the other. The major thrust in intervention is thus on the interpersonal communication patterns. Jay Haley, perhaps the most influential spokesman for this point of view, delineates communication patterns and mechanisms of control as critical to therapeutic intervention (Batesson, Jackson, Haley, & Weakland, 1956; Haley, 1963b; Haley & Hoffman, 1967). Another leader in this field, Satir (1964), also supports these notions. A few summaries can be found—Bowen (1971), Boszormenyi-Magi (1962) and N. W. Ackerman (1956).

Other recent studies also demonstrate great advances in the use of group therapy for marital problems. Gottlieb and Pattison (1966), for example, have reported the use of groups for people who have marital problems but who function well outside of this area, and Leichter (1962) offers multiple family group therapy for crisis situations.

Blinder and Kirschenbaum (1967) also provide techniques for married couple group therapy. McClellan and Stieper (1971) have used a combination of methods (programmed instruction, rational-emotive therapy, and psychodrama), and Kohn (1971) has treated several married couples in groups with success. Marital therapy with aging patients (Lynch & Waxenberg, 1971), and couples orientation groups (Giberti, 1971) are also on the upswing. In this area, Otto (1959) and Glendening and Wilson (1972) have all worked with premarital couples groups. Beukenkamp (1960) reports on anxiety activated by the idea of marriage.

Conjoint marital therapy is reported by Aldous (1973), McGhee & Kostrubala (1964), and Wadeson (1972). Gauron, Breeden, and Brightwell (1975) compared the effects on couples of being in the same or separate groups. Gottlieb (1960) investigated the responses of married couples in a singles group. Hinkle and Moore (1971) have developed couples workshops for students.

Additional studies of intensive marital groups are presented by Boas (1960), Emde-Boas (1962), Hooper, Sheldon, and Koumens (1968-1969), Hooper and Sheldon (1970), Kagan and Zaks (1972), Leichter (1963), and Reckless (1969). Encounter approaches are recommended by Pilder (1972). An excellent summary of the literature is provided by Gurman (1971). Cochrane (1973) provides some interesting reflections on an unsuccessful group.

Finally, the use of marathons with marital groups has recently been encouraged (Andrews, 1970; Worthen & Maloney, 1972), and Kessler (1976) has begun divorce adjustment groups.

Child-Parent Relations. An observer of the social scene could be forgiven for considering children and parents in our society to be locked in a death struggle for supremacy. In clinics more and more is learned about the independence shown by some children, their lack of respect to parents, and their winning of battles with parents. There is also testimony to the almost shocking forms of behavior by parents designed to win over their children or to punish them. Some parents become completely lost; they feel that the battle is over, and they no longer have any self-confidence. For these cases, group therapy, which enables parents to meet and to learn that they are not unique in their family problems, is a means of relief, first because of the universalization effects, and second, because they learn new and psychologically effective techniques for handling children.

The methods used in child guidance or parent guidance centers vary somewhat, but most of them tend to be of the circular discussional type (for small groups) or of the lecture sort. A rather unique method is that initiated by Alfred Adler and developed by Rudolf Dreikurs which was briefly described in Table 3–1. Among those who have written on the topic are Lowrey (1944), Buchmueller and Gildea (1949), Kadis and Lazarfeld (1945), Kolodney (1944), Konopka (1947), and Spotnitz and Gabriel (1950). Kahn, Buchmueller, and Gildea (1951) is a rare article because it describes a failure of the method.

Gottsegen and Grasso (1972) report on a group approach to mother and daughter relationships. Groups of parents and their children have also been reported by Endres and Evans (1968) and Perkins and Wicas (1971). Ginnott (1961) argues that children can only sustain therapeutic gains if their parents have undergone an "emotional reorganization" as well.

Parents of retarded children have been provided with group experiences by Appell, Williams, and Fishel (1964), Cummings and Stock (1962), Bricklin (1970), Gerber and Singer (1969), Rankin (1957) and Weingold and Hormuth (1953). Grunewald and Casella (1958) and Southworth (1968) have reported on groups with parents of children who are adjustment problems and underachievers. Other recent studies have reported success in teaching parents methods to manage children's acting-out behavior (McPherson & Samuels, 1971), and to deal with sexually acting-out girls (Friedman, 1971), schizophrenic children (Krider, 1971; Lurie & Ron, 1971), self-induced seizures (Libo, 1971), and delinquency (O'Neil, 1971). Multiple family therapy techniques and issues were demonstrated by Ackerman (1970), Paul and Bloom (1970) and MacGregor (1970).

CHILDREN, ADOLESCENTS, AND SCHOOLS

Children

Groups are frequently the recommended treatment of choice for children. Socialization, communicating, and empathy skills are most easily learned in groups, and these are the most common deficits for children. There are literally thousands of reports on group therapy and counseling for children and adolescents. Only a few representative groups will be reviewed here.

Therapeutic groups for disturbed children have been reported by many. The procedures are usually of an activity kind, taking place in playrooms, on trips, in playgrounds, and so on. Hawkey (1951) has made use of puppets, as have Bender and Woltman (1936). E. Papanek (1945) has used a democratic social club kind of procedure, reminiscent of the earlier procedures used by Lewin, Lippitt, and White (1939). Lippitt and Clancy (1954) have used psychodramatic techniques with children in the kindergarten and nursery school levels, and Rosenthal (1951), Burlingham (1938), Wineman (1949), and Kraft (1971) have offered further descriptions of methods of dealing with disturbed children in groups.

The two major influences in working with groups of disturbed children are Slavson (1951, 1964), and Axline (1947, 1969). Slavson has been given credit for coining the phrases *activity group therapy* and *play therapy*. In these groups, it is claimed that children are permitted to express their "dammed-up hostilities and sibling hatreds." Slavson (1948) recommends the use of play groups for preschool-age children. If Slavson coined the phrase *play therapy,* Axline is responsible for developing and popularizing this treatment. Unlike Slavson, Axline has used play therapy for older children as well as younger ones. She argues that play therapy is based on the fact that play is the child's natural medium of self-expression. In play therapy a child is given the opportunity to play out his feelings and problems just as an adult would talk them out. Axline recommends a nondirective, accepting, warm, friendly, nonjudgmental, and permissive atmosphere in play therapy, to encourage the child to feel free to express himself in whichever way he feels is most comfortable. Support for the use of play therapy with disturbed children has come from Cox (1953), Dorfman (1958), Hendricks (1972), Moustakas (1969), and Seeman and Ellinwood (1964).

Ginnott (1961) has developed his own similar play therapy groups and has developed these into a whole system of child-adult communication (cf. *Between Parent and Child,* 1973). Support for activity group therapy comes from Frank and Zilback (168), and Van Scoy (1972), among others. Pasnau, Williams, and Tallman (1971) report success with this method in a 12-year research project for the Montebello (California) school system. While their research relied heavily on subjective evaluations, the results are instructive and recommend continued use of this method. Komechak (1971) reports on her use of an activity interaction group as a short-term counseling procedure with elementary school children. Glaser (1971) has used psychodrama and other activity therapy techniques in child care centers, and C. H. King (1959) has reported success with a schizophrenic boy in group therapy.

Group therapy for psychotic children has also been reported by Gratton and Rizzo (1969), J. Harper (1973), Eisenberg (1967), Schecter, Shurley, Sexauer, and Toussieng (1969), Coffey and Wiener (1967), Jensen, Boden, and Multari (1965), and Straight and Werkman (1958). Studies have also been reported for group treatment of resistant children (Joseph & Heimlich, 1959); nonverbalizing elementary school children (Tosi, Swanson, & McLean, 1970); alienated children (Frey & Kolodney, 1966); retardates (Fisher & Wolfson, 1953; Neham, 1951; Stubblebine & Roadruck, 1956); underachievers (Esterson, 1973; Gurman, 1969); and drug abusers (Galbis, 1970). Children with physical problems (Dubo, 1951); foster children (Watson & Boverman, 1968); emotionally disturbed children (Bardell, 1972); antisocial children (Wodonski, 1973); hyperactive children (Cermak, 1973), and feminine boys (Green & Fuller, 1973) have all been found to benefit from group therapy.

Several theories are represented in the literature on group psychotherapy for children. Barabasz (1973), Graziano (1972), and Hinds and Roehlke (1970) have used learning theory approaches. Boulanger (1961), Leal (1966), and Scheidlinger and Rauch (1972) have approached it from a psychoanalytic framework. Platt (1971) and Stormer and Kirby (1969) have discussed groups from an Adlerian viewpoint. Developmental group counseling is represented by Dinkmeyer (1970), gestalt therapy by Wiesenhutter (1961), and nondirective group therapy by R. M. House (1970), Kraak (1961), and Moulin (1969). In the past few years, several reviews and studies of groups for latency-age children have appeared (Bardell, 1972; Dannefer, Brown, & Epstein, 1975; Epstein & Altman, 1972; Kraft, 1971; Rhodes, 1973; Strunk & Witkin, 1974).

Adolescents

Greene and Crowder (1972) have suggested that group psychotherapy with adolescents has some unique advantages: similar maturational conflicts, common problems, prominence of peer influence, and so on. They suggest that the group is an uniquely appropriate environment in which adolescents can work on these problems. Group therapy with adolescents has been excellently reviewed by N. W. Ackerman (1955), Kraft (1968), MacLennan and Felsenfeld (1968), and Berkowitz (1972).

Because of the social implications and visibility of the problem, a predominant focus of group therapy with adolescents has been on the problem of delinquency. The juvenile delinquent (adolescent psychopath) is characterized by repeated antisocial behavior with apparently no attendant guilt. Included in these dissocial behaviors are such acts as truancy, stealing, sexual promiscuity, aggression, mugging, and running away from home. Many authorities have argued that such problems are particularly resistant to group therapy (e.g., Yalom, 1970). However, some positive results, especially with homogeneous groups of delinquents, have been reported.

In order to be effective, therapy groups for delinquents must address an obvious problem early in the group process. In essence, the delinquent's problem is based on his or her opposition to the rule of authority in society. In a group setting, this is often displayed by multiple leadership challenges. Schulman (1959) notes that the basis of establishing a therapeutic relationship with the delinquent revolves around the resolution of this problem. Two divergent approaches to this issue seem dominant: impressing the adolescent with the leaders' authority by setting limits (Shellow, Ward, & Rubenfeld, 1958), and nondirectiveness, warmth, and understanding (Thorpe & Smith, 1952).

An additional problem in dealing with adolescents is discussed by Kraft (1971). He notes that since delinquents are frequently seen in institutional settings, the therapist's normal roles of impartiality passivity, and authority are disrupted. Schulman (1959) notes the importance of reestablishing an authority-dependency relationship of a more healthy nature than the adolescent has previously experienced. Schulman (1959) addresses the problem of resistance.

In general, isolated group therapy with this population is not very successful (Kraft, 1971). Several authors, however, have indicated successful alteration of deviant social patterns for juvenile delinquents as a function of combinations of group therapy and other treatments. Schneer, Gottesfeld, and Sales (1957) used group therapy as an aid to other therapies in a special school. Similarly, S. M. Feder (1961), B. Feder (1962), Franklin (1959), Franklin and Nottage (1969), Jacks (1963), Odenwald (1964), and Wolk and Reid (1964) all report on the use of group therapy with treatments in institutional settings.

Lievano (1970) has reviewed the process of a 42-session group with institutionalized delinquent boys and has delineated dynamic developmental stages. He summarizes by arguing that group therapy reaches boys faster than individual therapy; that the subjects are less anxious, lonely, and defensive in groups; and that the therapist becomes more of a "real" person to the boys. Hersko (1962), Patterson (1950), and Redfering (1972, 1973) have all focused on delinquent girls in institutions and have claimed success for the group therapy method, as has Brian (1971), working with the same population in foster homes.

Pregnant high schoolers have also come under the purview of the group therapists (Black, 1972; Dailey, 1972). S. Anderson (1971) and Eliasoph (1965) have used groups for drug-abusing teenagers, as have Rachman and Heller (1976). In their approach, Rachman and Heller propose a peer group psychotherapy program for drug abuse. Similar programs of peer help are reported in the literature on Daytop, Delancey Street, and Synanon. Hilgard (1969) also recommends the use of better adjusted peers as resources in group therapy.

Groups for jobless adolescents have been reported by MacLennan and Klein (1965). Obsessional (E. K. Schwartz, 1972a), neurotic (Krevelon, 1962), and hospitalized (Rybak, 1963) adolescents have also been treated in groups. Groups for unwed mothers (Kaufmann & Deutsch, 1967); obese adolescent girls (Zakus & Solomon, 1973) and emotionally disturbed girls (Parrish, 1962) have also been reported.

High school underachievers have been treated with group counseling by Baymur and Pattison (1969), Benson and Blocker (1967), Carr (1971), Finney and Van Dalsem (1968), Gilbreath (1968), Gurman (1969), and Thoma (1964). Groups with underachieving junior high school students have been reported by Collins (1964) and Cook (1971). Clements (1963) has noted the value of group and individual approaches for 5th-, 8th-, and 10th-grade boys.

College and College-Age Students

Colleges and universities have been the centers for most of the encounter group research, and college students have been the major recipients of the benefits of such groups. Literally hundreds of outcome studies attest to the value of encounter group training for such factors as enhanced self-actualization and self-concept, increased spontaneity, acceptance of aggression, capacity for intimate contact, and assertiveness. Several of these studies are reviewed in Chapter 10 and will not be replicated here. Since this chapter deals with applications of group therapy procedures and not with outcome per se, we will focus on the use of group methods for specific populations within this age group.

Berman (1972) has profiled the use of group techniques in university counseling centers and has suggested their ubiquitous presence. Some of the most frequent problems treated in groups are those of test anxiety, dating anxiety, vocational problems, and underachievement. Test anxiety was discussed above.

Dating Anxiety

McGovern, Arkowitz, and Gilmore (1975) have compared a discussion group to two behavior rehearsal groups and have found reduction of dating inhibition in all three groups. Curran, Gilbert, and Little (1976) have compared a tape recorder–led sensitivity group to a behavioral replication program and have claimed moderately better success with the latter approach. Similarly, Gitter (1976) has compared live encounter groups to behavioral rehearsal groups and found no differences in efficacy in reducing heterosexual dating anxiety. However, Gitter suggests that a combined encounter–skills rehearsal group might be effective in future work. The effect of group procedures on reducing dating anxiety has not yet been conclusively proven in any one study, but there seems to be great promise for longer term, extended approaches.

Vocational Problems

Several authors have recommended the use of group vocational counseling (Aiken, 1970; Aiken & Johnston, 1973; Kagan, 1966; Thoreson, 1969; Westbrook, 1974). Zimpfer (1968) suggested that to that date no true group procedures had been reported, and the extant studies had simply used individual procedures in a group setting.

Aiken and Johnston, using "group reinforcement counseling," have reported an increase in career information-seeking behaviors and some movement toward more adequate skills in independent action. Westbrook has claimed success for group vocational counseling approaches using test and occupational information in group settings.

Underachievement

Teahan (1966) has demonstrated significant increases in college grades of university students as a function of group treatment. Gilbreath (1967) has reported changes in ego strength, but no concomitant behavioral measure changes were indicated. Mitchell and Piatkowska (1974), reviewing 31 relevant studies, noted that significant increases in grades were reported by Abel (1967), Dickenson and Truax (1966), Gilbreath (1968), Heaps, Rickabough, and Fuhriman (1972), Roth, Mauksch, and Peiser (1967), Spielberger, Weitz, and Denny (1962), and Teahan (1966). Mitchell and Piatkowska have concluded that unstructured treatments, lengthy treatments, and voluntary participation are superior, and there is no consistent relationship between treatment type and outcome.

In other studies on college populations, Jackson (1974) used groups to improve students' study habits, and R. L. Anderson (1956), Spielberger and Weitz (1964), Webster and Harris (1958), and Zytowski (1964) all worked with adjustment of college freshmen. Rosenberg and Fuller (1957) had groups for student nurses, and Hedquist and Weinhold (1970) used behavioral group counseling with anxious and unassertive college students.

TRAINING

Group methods have been employed in the training of a wide variety of fields. The NTL and organizational development group approaches have been used in a plethora of business organizations to increase job satisfaction and productivity, to improve relations between levels of management, and to train managers (Cooper & Mangham, 1971; Rogers, 1973). Groups have also been used to train police (Bahn, 1972; Diamond & Lobitz, 1974; Porpotage, 1972), resident assistants

(Schroeder, 1973), teachers (Lett, 1973; Lindenauer and Caine, 1973; Shapiro, 1971), and hospital administrators (Weitz & Boganz, 1952).

Nowhere has the implementation of group techniques been as great as with providers in the health care services. If the people doing groups truly believe in the value of this method, it is natural for them to use the techniques in their own training programs. Early reports of such use were by Wender and Stein (1949), for training psychiatric residents; Berman (1953), for other mental health professionals; Patton (1954), for hospital staff; Glenn (1951), for nurses and psychiatric aides; and Whitaker (1953), for medical students. In recent years, most training programs for mental health professionals have included group training as an integral component (Yalom, 1975; also see Chapter 7 of this text). Groups with counselors and counselors in training have been reported by Apostal and Muro (1970), Emener (1973), Gazda (1959), Gazda and Ohlsen (1961), A. E. Harper (1961), Ohlsen (1977), Ormont (1962), and Shapiro and Gust (1974). Nurses and nursing students have received much training via group methods; efforts have been reported by Gladstone (1962), L'Acoursiere (1974), Parker (1958), Rueveni (1971), Shapiro (1970), and Spitz and Sadock (1973).

Psychiatric residents' training also often includes groups, as reported by Grossman and Karmiol (1973), Hadden (1947), Latendresse and Kennedy (1961), Ross, Block, and Silver (1958), E. K. Schwartz (1972), Slavson (1956), and Yalom (1975). Medical student groups have been discussed by Cath (1965), Ganzarain, D'avanzo, Flores, and Ester (1959), Golden and Rosen (1975), E. K. Schwartz (1972b) and Seguin (1965).

Group training for hospital aides, attendants, and paraprofessionals has been reported by Carkhuff and Truax (1966), Christmas (1966), M. F. Cohen (1974), Ebersole, Leiderman, and Yalom (1969), Guerney (1969), Pattison (1974), Sata (1974), Terrell, McWilliams, and Cowen (1972), True (1974) and Wiedorn (1957).

In addition, Beatman (1964) and Papell (1972) have recommended group training for social workers, as have Blumberg and Lockhart-Mumery (1972), for mental health personnel; Kramer (1972), for pupil personnel counselors; Blank, Wilker, and Grundfest (1972), for employment counselors; Casella (1972), for seminarians; Shapiro and Ross (1970), for corrections staff; and Lyon (1956), for clinical psychology students. Dellis and Stone, (1960) have recommended it for all therapists; Langen (1963), Leichter (1963), and Levin and Kanter (1964), for group therapists; and Boenheim (1971), for doctors.

Thus group methods have become a primary source of training for a wide variety of professions.

MISCELLANEOUS

Groups also have been applied to a myriad of other populations. A few of these are briefly noted in this section.

The women's liberation movement has brought attention to special problems of women and women's consciousness-raising groups. Articles on special needs for women in groups have been presented by Fried (1974), Glatzer (1974), Mintz (1974), and Scheidlinger (1974). Hartsook, Olch, and de Wolf (1976) present a study of women's assertiveness training groups.

Consciousness raising (CR) groups are described by Arnold (1970), Bird (1970), and Sarachild (1970, 1971). Resistances to consciousness are discussed by Pislikis (1970), and an account of a CR group is provided by Nancy (1970).

Groups for culturally disadvantaged populations are also on the rise. Groups for minority populations have been discussed by Felton and Biggs (1973), for black underachievers; Koegler and Williamson (1973), for Spanish-speaking people; Williams (1972), for black college freshmen; and Kehres (1972), for black male adolescents. Racial awareness and cross-cultural factors are discussed by Kaneshige (1973), for Asian Americans; Anderson and Love (1973), and Walker and Hamilton (1973). Ayers (1970), Curry (1967), A. S. Samuels (1971), and Shapiro and Siu (1976) write of the effects of the race of the group leaders, and Slavson (1956), Dubois and Li (1971), and Vassiliou and Vassiliou (1974) discuss additional cultural factors.

Chen (1972) has written of group therapy in Taiwan, and Ziferstein (1972) has written of groups in the Soviet Union. Problems of culturally disadvantaged youth have been addressed by Allgeyer (1970), Duncan and Gazda (1967), MacLennan (1968), Puick (1970), and Savenko and Winder (1970).

Several authors have written of group approaches for older people and geriatric patients. Two excellent summaries are provided by Berger and Berger (1973) and Goldfarb (1971). Early work in this field was done by Linden (1956), who took a psychoanalytic approach. A greater variety of approaches today provide for greater participation by older people. Hospitalized geriatrics have been studied in groups by Atkinson, Field, and Freeman (1955), Benaim (1957), and Rustin and Wolk (1963).

Berger and Berger (1973) recommend activity groups for both inpatients and outpatients. Burnside (1971) provides an interesting personal account of a long-term group with hospitalized aged in which she claims success in reducing boredom.

In other specialty groups, Comstock and McDermott (1975) have reported on a group for patients who are suicidal and Weisberg (1973) has conducted groups for suicidal college students. B. J. Wilson (1971) has described a group for creative persons, Lowen (1971), has reported on his bioenergetic group therapy, Slavson and MacLennan (1956) have described groups with unmarried mothers, and H. M. Ruitenbeek (1970) has summarized reports on nude groups and theme groups.

This survey of the literature, though not exhaustive, makes it clear that group therapy methods are being widely used. They are having a major impact on mental health and on society today and are apparently here to stay.

Chapter 10

Evaluating
Group Psychotherapy

The progress of any method of therapy, psychological or somatic, depends on continued evaluation. To persist in the use of any method of treatment without understanding its effectiveness is unscientific and potentially dangerous. For this reason, almost every psychotherapist who has discussed this matter has commented on the importance of scientific evaluation.

However, it is one thing to desire measurement or evaluation; it is quite another to actually measure and evaluate methods of psychotherapy. There are several reasons why it has been difficult to come to a satisfactory understanding of the value of group therapy procedures. First, it is difficult to specify the independent variable. Group psychotherapy is composed of a variety of methods and theories and thus has no uniform basis for comparison. Second, outcomes have rarely been specified. Third, measurement techniques and instruments have frequently been insensitive and imprecise. Fourth, at least for encounter groups, there has been a strong antiscientific bias among practitioners. Fifth, the representativeness of the group being studied is limited. Sixth, evaluation procedures have been cumbersome, time-consuming, complex, and expensive.

Practitioners are often called on to answer questions such as "Do you think group therapy will be useful in this agency?", "I would like to refer a patient to a therapeutic group; do you believe he will benefit?", "I would like to join a group; do you think it will do me any good?" To answer these and other specific questions which in essence are questions as to whether group psychotherapy can accomplish therapeutic changes, the practitioner should have as broad a knowledge of

275

the field as possible and should be aware of current trends. In this chapter, some of this information will be summarized.

METHODS OF EVALUATION

There are five common approaches to information about the value of group psychotherapy: testimonials, reports and group histories, personal experiences, statistics and research. While each type has its advocates, a combination of methods is typically superior to any single one.

One way to evaluate group psychotherapy is with the *testimonials* of interested parties. It is a readily available method, and it may be the most deceptive. Testimonials can come from all kinds of people: from eminent psychotherapists, such as Paul Schilder, who are very much impressed with the potentialities of the field; from practitioners such as S. H. Foulkes, who report on their experiences; and from patients, who indicate what the group experience has meant to them. Testimonials vary in quality and intensity, and the person who is interested in second-hand evaluations will, of course, evaluate the testifier as well as the content presented. One matter of interest is the extent to which such an opinion reflects the common consensus.

A second method of evaluation depends on vicarious participation in a group through the reading or observing of objective summaries or *reports* of group sessions, whether transcriptions, written reports, videotapes, or audiotapes. Many such reports are currently available.

For other people, *personal observation* through participation in groups is the best method. They can participate as observers, patients, or therapists. In this way one's own eyes and ears are the source of information; one does not have to depend on indirect or second-hand sources.

A fourth procedure for evaluating group psychotherapy is to analyze *statistics* of improvement. Some people want facts and believe that numbers are the best kind of facts; for them, objective data are most impressive.

For some people, the best kind of evidence depends on careful *research* in which hypotheses are examined and tested for an indication of their worth. This type of information is more generalizable, more respected in the scientific community, and less fraught with inadequacies than other methods.

Testimonials

Some statements that have been made about the value of group psychotherapy amount to testimonials. In effect, they comprise a judgment of group therapy procedures based on personal experience.

Simon, Holzberg, Solomon, and Saxe (1947), who worked with military psychoneurotics, state that: "group therapy is selected [by patients] as the most valuable treatment in the hospital . . . here is a consistently positive attitude towards group therapy. . . . ." But Sarlin and Berezin (1946), who, like Simon et al. worked in a military hospital, appear to come to quite different conclusions. They say, "If the standard for evaluation of the results of this work is to be established on the basis of patients returned to useful military service, then it is obvious that the treatment was entirely unsatisfactory."

An atypically enthusiastic testimonial is provided by Rudolf Dreikurs (1952), who comments, "The understanding of the patient's psychodynamics is greatly facilitated by group therapy. . . . The facility with which the patient can gain insight through group therapy is remarkable."

As early as 1921, E. W. Lazell described group psychotherapy with schizophrenics:

> The advantages of the group method are many . . . the patient
> is socialized with reference to the fear of death and the sexual
> problem, and feels that there are so many others in the same
> condition as himself, he cannot be so bad. It was found that many
> patients apparently absolutely inaccessible heard and retained
> much. . . . (p. 170)

Carl Rogers has suggested that as a result of encounter groups, individuals

> . . . come to know themselves and each other more fully than is
> possible in the usual social or working relationships; the climate
> of openness, risk taking and honesty generates trust which enables
> a person to recognize and change self-defeating attitudes, test out
> and adopt more innovative and constructive behavior, and
> subsequently to relate more adequately and effectively to others
> in his everyday life. (1969b, p. 1)

Maliver (1973) has said that encounter groups are "a callous exploitation and a sham group therapy." Beymer entitles his (1969) article "Confrontation Groups: Hula Hoops?" and Koch (1971) has referred to them as "a threat to dignity and individuality." Robertiello (1970), also writing on encounter groups, adds: "Encounters really are sublime for some people and really are ridiculous for others. This is basically what explains the very strong polarization of reactions to them." Yokotsuji (1972), however, commenting on Robertiello's article, says,

> . . . it seems that Dr. Robertiello has rationalized his
> uncomfortableness in groups and has come out with these

fantastic criteria as to who should participate or not in groups.
If the group is for the purpose of awakening the human potential
to feel, then I would tend to think that those who like to
verbalize and see emotional demands in groups are the kinds of
people who would most benefit from the group experience.
I suppose this comes from my personal experience for I saw
the same things happening as Dr. Robertiello in my first
experience with a group, but I got over it and am happier for it.

John Black (1970), defining encounter groups in education, states: "people often ask whether the benefits of encounter groups are lasting. There is no definitive answer to this question." He adds, "But is the question a fair one in the first place? Do we apply the same stringent criterion to a course in history, a trip to Europe, reading a book or seeing a movie?"

All of these statements were made by group therapists. Another source of testimonials is group members. The following examples represent common testimonials from members.

From the journal of a patient in a couples group:
    . . . it's just been the only way . . . my marriage was being
    destroyed, my role as a parent falling apart, I was on the verge
    of a nervous breakdown when we entered the group. Now
    I feel like I've just turned the corner and my life is going to
    come out.
Her husband wrote:
    Marie and I were ready for divorce when the group began.
    Now I feel like our relationships are strong and my desire for her
    and us tremendous.
Another patient wrote about an outpatient therapy group:
    The group ruined my life . . . took three years in therapy to
    recover.
Reactions to one encounter group included:
    This was the most important, most wonderful experience of my
        entire life.
    It's made a new woman of me.
    This group has freed me from myself and from my terror.
    Before the group, we were all up tight, now we walk around with
        only towels on and share the same bathroom.
    I didn't get much out of it, wasn't really deep or intimate for me,
        kinda felt left out.
    All I can say is, thank you.

Perhaps the most succinct response was made by a 1972 group member who subsequently became a leader:

As soon as the group ended and everyone began to leave,
I felt the need to reach out to someone without being
preposterous and mushy. I felt awkward so I walked away—
alone. This I didn't like doing but have felt myself
doing many times due to awkwardness and fear of putting
myself on someone else or fear of rejection. I felt lonely
and rather lost for awhile. About two hours later I had
exuberant feelings. I felt good toward myself as well as
toward the group. I felt as though I had come to grips with
myself—had a good look at myself—an opportunity to check
myself and plan a future course of action. I also had a
fear that no action might take place once the group disbanded.
When I now look at the group I am hesitant to take
everything which came out of it so readily. Perhaps we really
got to see just parts of a total picture and reacted to just one side
or part, and one side or one part does not validate change.
Anyway, it's up to the individual to decide. . . .

The fact that most of the reports quoted are favorable is not entirely due to my own biases, since most reports are found to be distinctly favorable. However, this does not necessarily mean that all experiences in groups are successes. There is a common tendency to put only favorable material into print, and it is quite possible that a good many unsuccessful groups are not made known. In recent years interest in the failures and casualties has increased, and more cautious statements about groups are appearing.

Reports

Inherent in a testimonial is a personal evaluation: Someone tells whether he thinks whatever he is testifying about is good or bad. A more objective procedure is the written report. There are many reports in the literature: summaries of groups, details of experiments tried out in groups, case histories, and so on. Like testimonials, however, most reports tend to create a favorable impression. No one likes to write about failures.

A number of reports are summarized below. They fall into two kinds: case histories of individuals, and histories of groups.

Individuals. One example of a case history is reported by Miller and Baruch (1948), who worked with people with allergic difficulties. The subject was a 23-year-old female with a skin condition, diagnosed by the allergist as neurodermatitis, probably psychogenic in origin. The condition was present in childhood and had not responded to medical treatment.

The patient stated in the group that her major problem was that her parents overpowered her. It was noticed in a conference held with the girl and her mother that the mother dominated the interview. After every session, her father picked up his daughter. The mother phoned the therapist, frequently asking that the therapist insist her daughter get eight hours of sleep.

For five sessions the subject did not participate in the group. At the sixth session she spoke only one sentence. At the seventh session she began to talk, complaining that her parents would not allow her to have music lessons. "They both try to take too much care of me. They don't think I am grown up. They try to keep me a baby."

Later, when she participated in psychodrama, she acted in an inhibited manner, she listened to others discussing their hostile feelings toward their parents. One patient stated that she wanted to poison her father. The girl saw how much acceptance the group and the therapist showed for such hostile feelings; and she saw besides how, even in the group, members were able to express animosity toward each other—and still obtain liking and acceptance.

She began to express her own resentments about her parents' treatment. As more negative feelings were expressed, more positive ones emerged. She was able to get her father to stop calling for her. She smoked, for the first time, in front of her parents. Members of the group commented that she looked happier and that her skin condition had improved. By the 18th session she reported that whereas previously she had had difficulty holding a job, now she had been given a raise.

This report is typical of a good many "success stories" to be found in the literature of group psychotherapy. There is a plethora of testimonies of individuals obtaining relief from problems through membership in therapeutic groups.

Another kind of report has to do with "critical incidents," that is, a particular event which occurred in a group and which appeared to be a turning point in an individual's life. A report of this kind is presented here for the first time.

Scott, a 25-year-old male college graduate, entered a psychotherapy group as his part of a pact made with his wife. She simultaneously joined another group which met at the same time. During the first three sessions, he was active in helping others, humorous, and attentive. Generally, the therapists and other members responded to him as a person with considerable ego strength.

During the fifth session, a female member of the group began to discuss the failure of her marriage. Two other women in the group, both recent divorcees, began to empathize with her. As this continued, strong feelings of hurt, fear and a sense of failure were expressed, both affectively and verbally, and all of the other group members except Scott seemed intimately involved in the process. At an appropriate time, the leaders turned to Scott:

MARTY (LEADER 1):   Scott, what's happening with you?

Scott: Oh, I'm OK.

MARTY: I guess I see everyone in the group reacting pretty emotionally, and you seem aloof to me.

Scott: I just don't see any need to get all upset just because a marriage breaks up.

Lois: (incredulously):   What kind of marriage do *you* have?

Scott: It's a decent marriage.

TOM (LEADER 2):   But . . .

Scott: No buts, we have a perfectly comfortable agreement.

TOM: Would you be willing to share that with the group?

Scott: Well, it's really no big thing. Cindy and I have an agreement. She does what she wants and I do what I want and when we want each other—we're together—and when we don't we aren't. It works fine—open marriage—have you read the book?

This nonaffective description of the relationship continued for some time. Scott denied having any jealousy about his wife's activities with other men or any feelings of happiness or unhappiness in either being with her or away. He also insisted that it was better to not be involved; that way nobody got hurt. Several group members then pointed out the apparent paradox of Scott's attendance in the group and his desire to remain uninvolved emotionally. The leaders invited him to try to become involved in the group setting. After receiving his consent, the male co-leader engaged Scott in a hypnotic regression and had Scott experience himself as a five-year old boy who was being ignored by his parents. He was encouraged to call out to them. The resultant outpouring of affect was intense and dramatic. The patient cried, expressed rage at not getting what he wanted, and remained agitated for several minutes.

On returning from the altered state, Scott was shy and reticent to engage other group members. The group leaders requested that he ask for feedback from each other member. Five of the other seven members told Scott that they felt closer to him than they ever had before and genuinely wished friendship with him. The other two patients confessed that they were frightened by his vulnerability. Following these interactions, the leaders continued:

TOM: Scott, what are you feeling now?
Scott: Scared, powerless.
MARTY: You're also smiling.
Scott: It's neat to have so many people care about me.
MARTY: It's good to let others get close.
Scott: Fantastic . . . but I'm scared now.
TOM: Cindy?
Scott: Yeah, what if she doesn't want it?

Subsequent to this critical incident, Scott endeavored to form closer relationships with the other group members and with significant others in his life, including his parents. He and Cindy entered marriage counseling as a couple.

Group Histories. Another type of report commonly found in the literature is the natural history of a group. An example is the report of McCann's round-table group method given in McCann and Almada (1953).

First, McCann expounds the philosophy that determines the form of the group. He states that mental conditions are not problems; rather they are answers. However, often the answers are incorrect, and it is the role of the therapist to help people find correct answers. Therapy is a procedure that enables people to find new answers to old problems.

Four wards in a state mental hospital were set aside for research: two for controls, the other two for the experimental evaluation of the round-table method. Patients were selected for the various wards in such a way that the groupings of types of illness were approximately equated. Then for a period of five months, no oftener than three times a week, patients in the experimental groups participated in the round-table procedure. Some partial statistics are quoted, since at the time of the report the experiment was still in progress. Of 22 female patients, 5 showed a remission of symptoms, while only 2 of the 22 control female patients showed such remissions. Of 10 male experimental patients, 7 showed remissions, but this was true of only 1 of the 10 control patients.

McCann refuses, on the basis of such partial statistics, to make any conclusions about the value of the method, but he does report that in his experience, two principles for wholesome living emerge. The first principle is that he who would find himself must lose himself in the problems of others, which appears to be about the same as the mechanism of altruism. And the second principle is essentially the same: He who would help himself must begin by helping others.

There are two conclusions from a survey of case histories, critical incidents, and histories of groups: In all cases, what appears to be quite impressive work is being done. However, everyone accomplishes the work in a somewhat different manner and interprets success in a different way.

Personal Impressions

Another avenue of exploration is through personal impressions. Of course, this means that every person who investigates this subject must come to her or his own conclusions. In summarizing my own participation in and observations of over 200 groups, the following impressions and conclusions can be stated.

Need. Anyone in a helping profession regularly receives requests for help from people with problems of personal unhappiness, feelings of inferiority, fears, somatic complaints that have no organic origin, anxieties, compulsions, social maladjustments, family conflicts, and so on. There is no dearth of such personal and social maladjustments. Whether a therapist is in private practice, a social agency, or an institution, the demand for his or her services far outstrips the amount of time available. Individual psychotherapy is frequently a long-term, time-consuming, uneconomical procedure. Group psychotherapy seems to be a solution which enables a therapist to allocate the available time more efficiently. Even if a group method were demonstrably inferior to individual therapy for any one person, it might still have a place if individual therapy were completely impossible for this person and she or he could be given some relief through group therapy.

Therefore, the first conclusion to be drawn is that on economic grounds alone, group psychotherapy is a valid procedure because it apparently meets a social demand. That is, people who want attention can get it in this manner when no other possibility exists.

Problems. Many people who demand psychotherapy do not react favorably to the idea of group therapy. When these attitudes are explored, they seem generally to be based on fears of rejection by other members.

However, when a group is assembled and after the initial hesitation is overcome, members almost always experience feelings of universality. Statements such as these are common:

My problem is like yours.

I am surprised to find you think as I do.

It seems to be that we are all in the same boat.

I've always thought I was the only one who thought that way.

I thought I was really messed up because I had those
feelings—now I can see I'm not so bad.

Group members experience a great, evident relief when they finally expose their sensitive areas and find that the others in the group can and do accept them, in spite of their previous fears that they would be rejected when they told about themselves. Patients often find it difficult to believe that others can have tolerance and respect for them when they know who they "really" are. They may also find it quite difficult to understand that others can be so upset over problems that seem relatively minor to them.

Processes.   In therapeutic groups members go through various stages. At first there is generally a reluctance to participate. Then there is an expression of dissatisfaction, and then attempts at solutions. The group may combine and recombine into cliques and give attention at various times to various persons. Some members may incur the displeasure of the group, and the members may experiment with various techniques of handling group problems. The therapist serves as the agent of each individual and also of the group as a whole, helping the individuals to express themselves and the group to persist toward its goal of individual advancement.

The group movement can be viewed as a movement of individuals, each of whom proceeds toward vague goals; the more any individual advances, the more he helps others to advance. There sometimes seem to be levels in the group: as one patient advances to a particular level of feeling or accomplishment, others get courage to go ahead. In any event, it is difficult for the therapist to evaluate all that goes on in the group. A rather quiet member who seems to be making little progress may suddenly report startling advances, crediting them to the group, and no one, including the therapist, can see how the change was accomplished or what part the group played in it.

Achievements.   The ultimate purpose of group psychotherapy is to improve the individual. These improvements are of two kinds: subjective and objective. Some of the subjective improvements that have taken place in my own and my colleagues' groups are examined here, and objective improvements are described in the research section.

Judy claims that she cannot find an honest man. Every man is out to take advantage of her. She repeats this assertion, with varied evidences of the validity of her viewpoint. Two men in the group respond that she puts them down unless they approach her aggressively. She is encouraged by the group members to try out new behaviors. She subsequently reports meeting a "nice" man.

Karl complains that he cannot study. He feels there is little purpose in life. He has contemplated suicide. He feels no one loves him. Group members point out that they are interested in him. Later he informs the group that his grades are improving and that life seems worthwhile.

Jake complains of chronic fatigue, which he cannot understand. As he ventilates about business problems in the group, he comes to understand that they are related to his subjective feelings.

Alice presents herself as a spontaneous, here-and-now oriented woman, trying to get the most out of each situation. She also describes herself as happy-go-lucky but is terrified of loneliness and keeps active constantly. The group gets her to make a commitment to other members, and she begins being more planful, less frenetic, and less lonely.

Harvey complains that nobody is interesting in his life and that he'd rather be alone than with anyone dull or boring. The group provides him the opportunity to be involved with several other individuals, and his boredom ceases.

Patricia, a recent divorcee, feels like there's no meaning in her life. Her career is unsatisfactory, her feelings of being physically attractive low. Group members are attracted to her and respect her. Her self-concept improves.

Individual vs. Group. Evidence concerning the value of group and individual psychotherapy also comes from patients who are in both simultaneously, or who have been at various times in one or the other.

One patient said, "I liked individual therapy better in one way. I had you all to myself, and I felt more comfortable in discussing very personal problems. But, overall, I felt that the group was more important, since they were many people and they represented a transition to society as a whole."

Another patient put it this way: "In individual therapy I feel I can learn more about myself; in group therapy I can learn more about others."

Still another patient made this remark: "First, as I see it, I must make a relationship to one person, then I have to make it to others. It is much more difficult to learn to belong to a group than to one person."

And another patient, with rare insight, said, "I am the kind of person who is always out to confuse and fool people. I think I can fool you, but I can't fool other people in the group. They don't let me get away with things. They represent social reality."

Several former group members have expressed another thought so well: "I knew I had to leave you, but I could keep the group. By the end of therapy, we could function without you and stay together as real friends."

Statistics

Suppose you read an article about the use of group psychotherapy in a mental hospital which stated that 70 percent of the patients eventually improved. This might create the impression that the patients improved because of group psychotherapy, but when one considers the claims that approximately 67 percent of all patients recover from neurotic states without any treatment whatever (Eysenck, 1952), this apparently high percentage of success could be actually quite low. For this reason, research studies with appropriate control groups are preferred as indices of success of a given method. Some statistics on recovery on the basis of group psychotherapy are of interest, however.

Pratt (1945), writing about his clinic, states, "Among all patients attending classes, 187, or 68 percent, reported having been helped." Johnson (1950), writing about the same clinic, reports, "Statistical studies indicate that 60 to 90 percent are notably helped to recovery." Abrahams and McCorkle (1947) found that 78 percent of their subjects made satisfactory adjustment for three months in the military service subsequent to group treatment. Kahn, Buchmueller, and Gildea (1951) state that 80 percent of subjects in parental group therapy showed behavior improvement. Altshuler (1940) states that his careful statistics indicate improvement in 72 percent; Friedman and Gerhart (1947) found that 60 percent of patients claimed improvement; Lerner (1953b) cites 80 percent of alcoholics as stating that they benefited from group therapy; Smith and Hawthorne (1949) state that 80 percent of relatives of people in group therapy claim that their family members had improved.

Shapiro (1970) reports 93 percent improved self-concept after an encounter group. Lieberman, Yalom, and Miles (1973) report that for subjects who completed 1 of 10 encounter groups, 65 percent considered them pleasant, 78 percent reported them constructive, and 61 percent claimed that it was a good learning experience. Instruments measuring several dependent measures for these same subjects indicated that 39 percent of the subjects underwent significant positive changes as a function of group participation, and these changes persisted at least six months. In the same study, 16–19 percent of the group members had significant measurable negative changes.

Some more conservative statistics have also been reported. Wright (1946) found 56 percent improvement; Barton (1946), 50 percent; Jacobson and Wright (1944), 49 percent; Sequin (1947), 48 percent. It seems, then, that using the therapists' or the patients' judgments, improvements are found in from 5 to 8 out of 10 people in the typical group.

Some other figures may be of interest. Schwartz and Goodman (1953) state that all of their 19 patients who were overweight and had diabetes lost weight while in group therapy. Klein (1949) reports that 7 out of 13 patients with skin disease were symptom-free at the end of therapy. Baruch (1945) found that 15 out of 18 members felt that an easing of personality problems had taken place as the result of group therapy. Wender and Stein (1949) state that 11 out of 14 patients who had group and individual therapy improved remarkably. Buchmueller and Gildea (1949) state that 9 out of 13 children improved as a result of group therapy. Kotkov (1953a) found that 48 percent of over-weight patients who had not been able to lose weight in any other manner made weight reductions as a consequence of group therapy. Becker (1948) reports that 17 out of 26 children with sibling rivalry resolved their problems through therapy in an activity group. Solomon and Axelrod (1944) discovered that 8 out of 11 girls who were withdrawn neurotics made rapid improvements.

In a sense these statistics prove nothing, but they should be considered as evidence that the therapists who report them find them impressive. The subjectivity of the patients and of the therapists is at issue. We may see what we look for, and we may give answers that are expected. Moreover, therapists are ego involved in their work, and it can hardly be expected that they will tend to be ultraconservative when it comes to reporting their own successes. And yet, if I were asked to indicate the percentage of people in my own experience who have made improvements because of group psychotherapy, I too would feel inclined to say that the percentage is above 70. What percentage of improvement would have taken place without therapy is impossible to say, because the common, garden variety of problems that come to therapeutic groups outside of institutions have not been studied sufficiently in terms of spontaneous cures.

Indeed, the most striking statistics would be a simple report of the total number of groups and group members. Can the facts that over a million people have been in groups, and the group movement is growing in popularity, be taken as anything less than success of the method?

In summary, the reader is left with the task of interpreting the value of such statistics. With the exception of the Shapiro (1970) and Lieberman et al. (1973) studies cited above, no confirming objective measures have been produced. It is also clear that most studies citing percentages alone were conducted before the middle 1950s. Since that time, many empirical studies have involved research.

Research Studies

Several excellent reviews of the group therapy and encounter group literature have been written in the past 25 years. The group therapy literature has been reviewed by Corsini (1957), Pattison (1965), Stotsky and Zolih (1965), Meltzoff and Kornreich (1970), Bednar and Lawlis (1971), Frank (1975b), and Grunebaum (1975). The encounter group literature has been reviewed by Buchanan (1965), Campbell and Dunnette (1968), Gibb (1971), Hampden-Turner (1976), Harrison (1967), R. J. House (1967), Knowles (1967), and Stock (1964).

These reviews will not be replicated here, but several studies will be cited. The methodological difficulties in group research will be defined, and efforts toward effective outcome research will be described. The model experimental paradigm proposed in the section that follows was partially conceptualized by Michael Jay Diamond, whose basic work is represented here to a considerable extent. Earlier forms of these sections can be found in Diamond and Shapiro (1975a).

Methodological Inadequacies. Despite the plethora of research on therapy and encounter groups in the past 25 years, major methodological and design inadequacies have generally not been overcome. The vast majority of studies have been all too easily satisfied with the "Your group made a new man of me, Doc!" or "What happened to me was just too beautiful to describe" type of testimonial data. Several investigators have noted numerous methodological flaws in this group research (Campbell & Dunnette, 1968; Cooper, 1969; Foster, Marks, & Conry, 1972; Gibb, 1971; Harrison, 1967; R. J. House, 1967; Stock, 1964).

The Problem of the Independent Variable. One major problem, the adequate specification of the independent variable (i.e., the nature of the group experience), has been neglected by researchers and most methodological critics. Although labels like *encounter, group therapy, group method, sensitivity,* and *T group* are applied to differentiate groups, there is limited consensus as to the relationship between the label and the process or content of the group experience. Thus, for some authors, a sensitivity group consists of a wide variety of body awareness exercises and communion-oriented activities, while for others, a sensitivity group is limited to verbal interaction oriented toward the understanding of group communication (Gottschalk and Davidson, 1971).

Confusion also exists as to the intrapersonal or interpersonal orientation within the group (Lakin, 1972; Shapiro & Diamond, 1972), the activity or passivity of the leader (Yalom, (1970), or the amount of structured experience (Lieberman, Yalom & Miles, 1973). There are also differences in the emphasis on the application of the group learning to the back-home environment (Campbell & Dunnette, 1968), the temporal (e.g., short-term vs. long-term; spaced vs. massed) and spatial arrangements of the group (Gibb, 1971), and the member composition of the group in terms of variables such as embedded or open, horizontal or vertical, homogeneous or heterogeneous, cohesiveness, and compatibility (Cooper & Mangham, 1971).

In view of the multitude of critical parameters, generic terms like *therapy, sensitivity, encounter,* and *T group* are inadequate as defining operations. At this stage, it is most important for researchers and theoreticians to isolate and specify exactly what goes on in their groups, at least in terms of the above dimensions.

Additional major methodological flaws in group outcome research include: (1) a lack of adequate base rate or pretraining measures, (2) failure to include a matched-control group, (3) a lack of truly independent observers, (4) failure to control adequately for test reactivity and obtrusive observer effects, (5) failure to employ quantitative dependent measures consistent with the group goals, (6) failure to employ adequate statistical analyses, (7) unwarranted extrapolations, and (8) with few exceptions, failure to include follow-up as well as transfer-of-training (i.e., generalization) testing. Similar methodological problems beset group process research.

The Problem of Measuring Group Outcome. Group therapy and encounter have most frequently been investigated generically. Bednar and Lawlis (1971) note that though there are great differences among leadership styles and abilities, these differences have been largely ignored as variables related to group outcome. The most common research design has compared outcome measures of group therapy and a no-treatment control group, or has compared post–group therapy measurements to pre–group therapy measurements. Bednar and Lawlis note that,

> the interpretation of these data depends on the standard of research employed. ... The demanding critic can point out that few of the better experiments have been replicated. Furthermore, evidence based on follow-up investigations suggests that positive treatment effects are short-lived and tend to dissipate with time.

In addition, other methodological inadequacies make even consistently positive data questionable. An excellent example of this occurred in a study of a T group by Burke and Bennis (1961). Using a semantic differential technique, they noted that subjects perceived actual self, others' perception, and ideal self as being closer at the end of training than at the beginning, and the T group was seen as the change medium. However, this T group took place within the laboratory context and hence was coincident with several other training procedures. Furthermore, when Carson and Lakin (1963) replicated this study, adding a control group, pretreatment-posttreatment differences were not significant.

Bunker (1965), employing matched control subjects (no group), found three clusters of changes affected by human relations laboratory training: increased openness, increased skill in interpersonal relations, and improved understanding. However, these data were based on recollections of changes a full year after the group ended, and no premeasures were discussed.

In comparing sensitivity groups to lecture-type groups, Argyris (1965) used tape analyses from early, middle, and late sessions. These provided some suggestive data, including evidence that membership of the sensitivity T groups showed the most behavioral change. Argyris argued that the lecture groups created the same processes that caused on-the-job problems, whereas the T group approach, which emphasized self-exploration and confrontation, was responsible for the greater behavioral change. Similarly, Greening and Coffey (1966) have suggested that significant learnings occur as a result of sharing feelings about difficulties in relating to others. This sharing was more common for sensitivity groups than discussion groups.

Cabeen (1961) used Minnesota Multiphasic Personality Inventory (MMPI) and staff judgments as dependent measures for a group of sex offenders. He reported lower recidivism and a positive correlation between amount of group therapy and improvement. However, he did not use a control group. Similarly, Rashkis and Shaskin (1946) found reduced MMPI scale scores for war neurosis patients, but no external comparisons were made. In studies that did use no-treatment controls, Persons (1966) found reduction of anxiety and MMPI scale scores with juvenile delinquents. Kadis and Heimlich (1959) reported greater reduction in MMPI scale scores for psychiatric patients in groups than for those who were not in groups. Feifel and Schwartz (1953), using staff judgments as the dependent measure, found similar results.

Lifton and Smolen (1966), working with schizophrenic children in two-hour groups meeting three times a week, noted lessened withdrawal; a decrease in psychotic fantasies, delusions, and bizarre behavior; better self-control; and more interpersonal modes of relating. No control group was evaluated, however. Cooper (1971), using Shostrom's (1966) Personal Orientation Inventory (POI) as a measure of self-actualization, found group members becoming more independent, spontaneous, and accepting of aggression as a function of two one-week, one-leader groups. No control group was reported.

Cohen, Johnson, and Hanson (1971), applying a four-week human relations training program to psychiatric patients, found increases in expressed hostile and angry feelings on the MMPI and interpersonal checklist, and Bok (1969) and Brudno (1968) got improved functioning in hospitalized geriatric patients, but neither of these studies included adequate controls. Berger, Sherman, Spaulding, and Westlake (1968), using videotapes with groups of severely disturbed and prerelease patients, reported several positive behavior changes. They too did not report controls or any statistical treatment, however.

Chambers and Ficek (1970) using a control group, external raters, and the marathon group technique with females between the ages of 16 and 21, found differences in ratings which favored marathons. Unfortunately, subjects were not randomly assigned. Foulds, Gerona, and Guinan (1970), also using marathon groups with college students and adequate controls, reported that 15 of 16 participants in the marathon showed significant positive changes. No such changes were reported for matched control subjects.

Rueveni, Swift, and Bell (1969), and Culbert, Clark, and Bobele (1968), as well as Shapiro (1970), have all demonstrated increases in POI scales (Shostrom, 1966) as a function of group participation, at least for subjects whose pretest scores were in the normal range. Increases on POI scales reflect increases in self-actualization. Thus subjects in groups reported by these studies became more able to live in the present, more flexible in the application of their values, more spontaneous, and more able to have intimate contacts.

Boyd and Elliss (1962) and Underwood (1965) reported greater positive and negative changes in postgroup on-the-job situations. This finding of increased variability was also reported by Fairweather et al. (1960) in his study comparing the effects of group psychotherapy, individual psychotherapy, no therapy, and group living for psychiatric patients. Several other authors (Frank, 1975a; Lieberman, Yalom & Miles, 1975) have also commented on this result of psychotherapy.

Negative Outcomes. Not all of the research has been positive, however. Schein and Bennis (1965), for example, noted that certain laboratory participants demonstrated increased tension on the job after their group experience.

Casualties of any therapeutic program are always a serious problem. It is alarming to discover, for example, that a new medicine which provides help to a vast number of people is fatal to others. Similarly, psychotherapists have known for years that some prospective clients would do better without therapeutic intervention, and such intervention could have harmful results. It is within this context that we examine the few studies which have had distinctly negative findings.

Bass (1967) and Deep, Bass, and Vaughn (1966) created simulated companies comprised of either multiple group members or single group members and then had them play the Carnegie Tech Management Game (a simulated business enterprise experience). Companies comprised of members who were all in one T group reported less internal conflict, more ease of contact, and more openness. They also lost over five million simulated dollars, while companies comprising members with multiple group membership broke even or made money. While these negative results were in terms of simulation games, there is great concern for such negative outcomes of group therapy and encounter.

Bergin (1967) and Truax and Carkhuff (1967) have demonstrated that individual psychotherapy clearly helps people change. Such change can, unfortunately, be for the better or for the worse. Truax (1966b), in a large-scale investigation of group therapy outcomes, was able to rank order 16 psychotherapists with regard to average standard scores of patient change. His results were startling. The range of averaged standard scores was +0.54 to —0.52, a clear indication that some group therapists were ineffective, even toxic, to their patients.

The deterioration effects in encounter groups have too often not been measured or have been referred to in terms of a spur to growth. In an exception to this tendency, Lieberman, Yalom, and Miles (1973), in their major study of 10 encounter group methodologies, reported that approximately 8 percent of the group members became more psychologically distressed or disturbed as a function of group participation. Gottschalk (1966), using his own observation, reported 47 percent of the members showed "psychopathological reactions."

Hartley, Roback, and Abramowitz (1976) reviewed nine studies indicating "casualties" from encounter group participation and found that, for the most part, the incidence of casualties across all groups was relatively low. Summarizing the incidence and types of casualties, they have argued that certain variables indicate high-risk situations; members with previous psychological disturbances, unrealistically high expectations, and low self-esteem are more likely to become casualties, especially in coercive groups demanding high levels of intimacy and having high-charismatic, high-authoritarian, nonsupportive leaders. These characteristics, however, are based on data from less than ideal studies.

Four outcome studies have commonly been cited as supporting the hypothesis that encounter group experience leads to positive changes in job behavior. These studies (Boyd & Elliss, 1962; Bunker, 1965; Miles, 1965; Valiquet, 1964) all used "perceived change" measures as the basic external criterion. Estimates of change were typically obtained from results to open-ended questionnaires in which respondents reported changes in subjects' behaviors over a specified period of time. All of these data were obtained several months after the completion of training. In the Boyd and Elliss study, "substantial change" was seen by the observers for 64 percent of the experimental subjects and only 23 percent of the control subjects (no-group and "conventional" training programs combined). Across all studies, between two and three times as many changes were reported for the experimental as compared to the control subjects. The types of changes which seemed most discriminative showed T group subjects as more sensitive, more open with their communications, and more flexible behaviorally. However, as noted for the Deep et al. (1966) study cited above, these changes are not necessarily related to successful job performance.

It seems somewhat of a paradox that the bulk of studies in an area that has led to far-reaching generalizations as to the value of such training have been so deficient in adequacy of research design. R. J. House (1964) has made a strong plea for halting the proliferation of T groups until more adequate empirical research has been done. Taylor (1967) has been far less gentle in his comments. He has noted that the majority of research has been on behavior in the training group, and little work has focused on the vital question of transfer of training. Indeed, the studies which have explored the issues of transfer have relied on highly unsatisfactory self-report data. Taylor comments: "workers in this field have been too easily satisfied with the 'your-course-made-a-new-man-of-me' brand of testimony." Porter (1966) has acrimoniously pointed out that

> ... in the section of Stock's chapter devoted to 'the impact
> of the T group on individual learning and change,' 21 references
> were cited, but only four of these had been published. Since
> T group training has been going on for 15 years, this averages
> out to one fourth of a published evaluation article per year!
> (p. 408).

Toward Effective Outcome Research.   Harrison (1967) has distinguished several problems in the design and interpretation of research in human relations training. The first problem is that of finding or designing adequate control groups. Harrison argues that the fact that a person knows that he is in a control group biases his self-image and the perception of him that others have. The fact that a person is in a control group creates an expectancy for no change or negative changes relative to the treatment groups. Conversely, the fact that a person is in a training group "inclines him and others to look for change in his behavior" (Harrison, 1966, p. 2).

At least two studies have eliminated this source of bias. Byrd (1966) compared subjects in a T group to subjects who received "personal growth" experiences in a nongroup situation. Since both groups had been through a training experience, the design eliminated the biasing of perception which occurs when an untrained control group is used. Unfortunately, this design also eliminated the opportunity to evaluate treatment results relative to no treatment.

Massarik (1965) used another acceptable procedure that is customarily seen in psychotherapy outcome studies: a waiting list control group. However, since the determination of who was to wait was made by the subjects themselves, self-selection to the waiting list may have been due to some reticence or ambivalence, and this could be related to poorer outcome. If assignments to the waiting list condition were made by administrative fiat and a reasonable rationale was presented to the waiting list subjects, it is possible that an important source of bias could thus be eliminated.

A more formidable problem has been the lack of elucidation and prediction of dimensions and directions of change. Typically, studies in this area have been content with post hoc statements as to the ways change has taken place and the amounts of change that have occurred in subjects.

Three classes of outcome or behavioral change studies have been reported in the literature. The most common approach is the wide-focus, free-response type. Studies by Bunker (1965), Miles (1965), and Valiquet (1964) exemplify this approach.

In these studies, subjects and their self-nominated raters were asked to give open-ended accounts describing any changes which had taken place in the participant's behavior during the preceding year. The obtained responses were then classified on a post hoc basis, and the changes for subjects in the training groups were compared to control group subjects. Aside from the general problem of expectancy artifacts, such open-ended hypotheses allow for descriptive data only. Furthermore, since the dimensions and directions of change were not specified, a change in a negative direction is as meaningful as one in a positive direction.

In each of these studies, the external observers were chosen by the participants themselves, and the observers were always aware that the participants had been in the group. Given this knowledge of participants and the open-ended questionnaire, it would indeed be surprising if they did not report some changes in participants' behavior.

The second approach is represented by Harrison and Oshry's (1967) study of changes in organizational behavior following a T group experience. Deriving three scales from Argyris's (1967) two-dimensional theory of organizational behavior (technical competence and interpersonal competence), they predicted changes only on these three dimensions. They also predicted the direction of these changes. Thus their study was both prescriptive and unidirectional. However, the predictions were normative in the sense that changes toward middle values on these dimensions were predicted as positive. Given the statistical phenomenon of regression toward the mean, it is not surprising that these studies generally reported positive results.

The third position regarding the appropriate way to study therapy outcome was suggested by Bennis (1962) in an article on the goals of laboratory training. Bennis argued that the critical study of T groups and the laboratory method must look at "general improvement in adaptive capability." Hence, for an encounter group to be maximally effective, it must allow each individual member to show change on the dimensions and directions he or she chooses. Shapiro (1970) provides one example of this in a study of encounter group–induced changes using a perceived self–ideal self adjective checklist discrepancy score. This method allowed each subject, in a sense, to choose the dimensions along which experimentally predictive changes would occur. That is, each subject completed a perceived self-description and ideal self-description form of the Shapiro Adjective Check List (SACL), both before beginning and after completion of training. Changes in self-description from pre- to posttreatment in the direction of the ideal self were considered positive. This satisfies Bennis's (1962) suggestion that each subject should be evaluated on her or his own adaptive capability.

The use of adjective checklists to indicate pretreatment to posttreatment personality change is supported by the work of Gough (1960), Gough and Heilbrun (1965), Gough and Meschieri (1967), Gough and Riva (1967), Shapiro (1967), and Shapiro and Ross (1971).

As a way of elucidating the dimensions and directions of group-induced change, Diamond and Shapiro (1975a) have presented a four-fold classification of learning outcomes. This classification is consistent with recent theoretical developments in social learning theory (e.g., Bandura, 1969), and cognitive-affective theory (e.g., Schacter & Singer, 1962). The learning in groups can be conceptualized in the frameworks of personal awareness (i.e., self- and other-awareness), cognitive structuring, arousal enhancement and reduction, and behavioral expression. Table 10–1 presents these potential learning modalities with reference to leadership (intervention) style.

These four categories clearly cover the hypothesized T group outcomes summarized by Campbell and Dunnette (1968). Moreover, it is useful to consider these learning outcomes with reference to the leader's intervention style. A useful continuum of intervention has been the intrapersonal-interpersonal formulation (Lakin, 1972; Shapiro & Diamond, 1972). In intrapersonal intervention, members are dealt with in a one-to-one fashion, with a major goal being to improve a member's relationship to himself. The "hot seat" technique used in gestalt therapy

TABLE 10–1: Potential Encounter Group Learning Outcomes with Reference to Intervention Style

Intrapersonal Style	Interpersonal Style
1. *Personal Awareness* Self-awareness (feelings, cognitions verbal and nonverbal behavior, sensory awareness, expanded consciouness)	1. *Personal Awareness* Self and other awareness (feelings, cognitions verbal and nonverbal behavior, sensory awareness, expanded consciousness)
2. *Cognitive Structuring* Humanistic world view, increased acceptance of others' views, prejudice reduction, flexibility in value application, increased cognitive complexity, self-acceptance, appreciation and use of primary process thinking	2. *Cognitive Structuring* Humanistic world view, increased acceptance of others' views, prejudice reduction, flexibility in value application, cognitive complexity, cognitive discrimination
3. *Arousal Enhancement and Reduction* Fear (sexual and sensual behavior, evaluation failure, rejection, aggression, ambiguity, spontaneity, fear of fear, self-reflection and expression) Anger, rage, loneliness, sadness	3. *Arousal Enhancement and Reduction* Fear (sexual and sensual behavior, evaluation failure, rejection, aggression, ambiguity, spontaneity, responses to authority figures, feedback from others, self-exposure, disclosure) Anger, rage, love, attraction
4. *Behavioral Expression* Risk taking, spontaneity, symptom reduction, activity preferences	4. *Behavioral Expression* Risk taking, spontaneity, activity preferences, symptom reduction (interpersonal behaviors), cooperation and sharing, problem solving, conflict resolution, self-expression

is one example. An interpersonal intervention focuses on the relationships between members, with a major goal being enhanced interpersonal relations within the group. National Training Laboratory (NTL) groups are representative of this end of the continuum. These leadership styles were discussed in greater detail in Chapter 6.

THE SEARCH FOR AN EMPIRICAL PARADIGM

Most of the empirical work evaluating the effectiveness of the group method has focused on the encounter group. The reasons for this include: accessibility of subjects, ethical considerations, university support, and ease of matching and defining the subject population on independent variables. However, the encounter (sensitivity training) group is still somewhat resistant to outcome measurement.

In the early days of the T group, these groups occurred in the context of a wide variety of educational experiences, often referred to as a "laboratory" or "human relations institute." Warren Bennis 1964), a leader in the National Training Laboratory approach, lists experiences that were customary in different laboratories. In addition to T groups, there was group therapy, psychodrama, role playing, group discussions, case studies, lectures, and movies. He arranges these on a continuum stretching from there and then to here and now. The basic construct appears to have been personal involvement with here-and-now experiences representing greater levels of involvement. Thus Bennis arranged the training procedures in terms of increasing involvement with lectures and movies at the there-and-then, or low, end, discussions and role playing at intermediate levels, and the sensitivity group, representing the highest level of personal involvement, at the here-and-now end of the continuum.

Because of the wide variety of these training experiences, Baumgartel and Goldstein (1967) have suggested that it was extremely difficult to ascribe any part of the learning process to the group itself. Similarly, Stock (1964) has argued, "it is difficult to separate out any single aspect of a laboratory and say that *this* is what influenced learning. The laboratory typically includes lectures on theory and demonstration, and practice sessions, on the assumption that these plus the T-group constitute an integrated whole" (p. 421).

Because the inclusion of the T-group experience is the only commonality across laboratories, it has generally been assumed that this is the critical element that produces change in the laboratory setting. Since group training has so often been included in fairly comprehensive in-service training programs, such as those for mental health professionals, educators, and businessmen, it is critical to evaluate both the effects of the entire program and the differential effects of its parts. Careful attempts to accomplish this have only begun to be successfully completed.

Three methods of circumventing this problem of differentiating the effects of the group training from other laboratory experiences seem possible: (1) study of T-group training outside of the laboratory situation, (2) study of an entire laboratory in which only the group experience is varied and all other aspects of training are held constant, and (3) study of the effects of manipulating varying amounts of different types of nongroup laboratory procedures in the sensitivity training itself.

One example of the first method, studying the effects of sensitivity training alone, is represented by Shapiro's (1971) study of sensitivity training for teachers and teachers to be. In this study, subjects were matched for age, sex, previous experience in groups, and pretest scores and were randomly assigned to one of four conditions. The four groups varied in the manner in which conflicts were resolved. The sensitivity group employed confrontation and the here-and-now context to resolve conflicts. The role-playing resolution groups employed role-playing procedures to resolve conflict. The attention placebo control group—a cognitive discussion group—attempted to resolve conflict through an understanding of issues involved in the conflict and through methods of behavior change. Another control group, a waiting list group, did not meet until the entire project had been concluded. Since the groups all met on five consecutive days, and since pretests were taken immediately before the groups began and posttests immediately after they were concluded, systematic extraneous training effects were eliminated. Thus the results, which overwhelmingly favored the sensitivity group, could be interpreted without concern for this bias.

An example of the application of the second method, holding extra group training constant, is represented by Shapiro and Ross's (1970) study of the effects of T-group training on the performance of line staff at a girls' training school in Ontario. In this study, all of the line staff (supervisors) were engaged in an educational training program which included lectures and movies describing new techniques for dealing with patients. All of the supervisors were asked to fill out a self-description adjective checklist, and, on the basis of the responses, they were matched and randomly assigned to an additional (encounter group) training procedure or to a no-group control condition. The encounter group met twice a week for three months. At the conclusion of the groups, all supervisors again completed a self-report form. In addition, a set of independent observers (the inmates) also completed adjective checklist descriptions of all of the supervisors.

Those supervisors who had had the sensitivity training were described with a significantly greater number of positive adjectives both by themselves and by the independent observers than were the matched control subjects. Furthermore, these results were maintained over a full year, even when there was a 100 percent turnover of independent observers (Shapiro & Ross, 1971). The fact that only those subjects who were included in the sensitivity group showed such changes suggested that the encounter group experience was responsible for these significant differences. However, since these authors did not employ a pseudo sensitivity control group, it is impossible to conclude that a different type of training, such as discussion groups, would not have yielded similar results. Furthermore, it is not known if, and to what extent, the additional training experiences (lectures and movies) augmented the T-group experience.

An example of the third approach, systematically varying the extra group experiences, can be seen in Shapiro's (1970) study of nine varieties of group training procedures. In this study, four sensitivity and four discussion groups were combined with role playing, videotape playback, audiotape playback, or nothing as an auxiliary training procedure. Thus there were role playing–sensitivity, role playing–discussion, videotape-sensitivity, videotape-discussion, audiotape-sensitivity, audiotape-discussion, sensitivity alone, and discussion alone conditions. A ninth group, a waiting list control group, received no training but took the pre- and posttests. With this design, it was possible to compare the effects of sensitivity procedures to those of discussion procedures and also to examine the relative effects of the most common auxiliary procedures in a sensitivity training laboratory.

A Model Experimental Paradigm

Diamond and Shapiro (1975b) have proposed an eight-step paradigm for encounter group research. This research model should be equally effective for therapy group research. The eight steps are graphically presented in Table 10–2.

Step 1 involves the determination and operational specification of group goals for experimental and control groups. For example, is the group designed to produce increased job effectiveness, reduction of phobic reactions, personal growth, or increased assertiveness? Whatever the goal, careful operationalization is important, as is the provision of adequate control groups. Thus if the goal of the group is reduced aggressions in a prison setting, this might be operationalized in terms of number and quality of reported incidents of aggressive behavior, and matched control groups would include a waiting list (no-training) condition and an attention placebo comparison group.

Step 2 includes the *screening* of members to ensure against casualties (Reddy, 1972) and to assure voluntary and informed participation. Individuals in crisis situations, hysterics, schizoids, drug addicts, psychopaths, individuals undergoing psychotherapy or holding goals that are incongruent to the specific group goals, and "institutionalized groupies" may be screened out.

Step 3 includes pretesting, matching, and assignment to the various groups as delineated in Step 2. This is the *pretesting* phase. Biographical and subjective expectational scales, standardized self-report tests, unobtrusive behavioral measures, psychophysiological measures, independent observers' reports, and independent observers' self-reports are admin-

TABLE 10–2: A Model Experimental Paradigm

	EXPERIMENTAL Group Encounter and Therapy	CONTROL Group: Attention Placebo	CONTROL Group: Waiting List
Step 1	Determination of group goals	Determination of group goals	Determination of group goals
	Designation of comparison groups	Designation of comparison groups	Designation of comparison groups
Step 2	Screening	Screening	Screening
Step 3	Pretesting	Pretesting	Pretesting
Step 4	Treatment occurs	Irrelevant experience occurs	No group experience
	Process measures recorded	Process measures recorded	
Step 5	Posttesting occurs	Posttesting occurs	Posttesting occurs
	Subjective reactions elicited	Subjective reactions elicited	Subjective reactions elicited
	Demand characteristics evaluated	Demand characteristics evaluated	relevant unscheduled experiences explored
Step 6	3- to 6-month follow-up testing	3- to 6-month follow-up testing	3- to 6-month follow-up testing
Step 7	1- to 3-year follow-up testing	1- to 3-year follow-up testing	1- to 3-year follow-up testing
Step 8	Report results to members	Report results to members	Group experience (most effective treatment offered)

istered. These tests are then independently scored, and subjects are matched on critical variables and randomly assigned to each of the groups.

Data are normally collected from the group members themselves, significant others, and independent observers, and relevant measures are also obtained on the leaders. It is recommended that collected pretest data represent (1) self and other perceptions, (2) arousal level, (3) cognitive structuring, and (4) behavioral expression (Diamond & Shapiro, 1975b).

Experimental treatment occurs in Step 4. Accordingly, the treatment and attention placebo groups run their course in identical settings. During this time, process measures are recorded. Thus, developmental measures of empathy, congruence, cohesion, interpersonal facility, and physiological measures (Loomis, 1976) are recorded, to be subsequently related to outcome dependent measures.

Step 5, the *posttesting phase,* immediately follows the conclusion of Step 4 and is identical to the pretesting phase (Step 3), with the exception that subjects' subjective perceptions of their group experiences in the form of diaries, journals, or interviews are solicited. Additionally, an assessment of experimental demand characteristics is made by means of an interview in order to partial out compliance or negativity effects from group learning effects. Carefully worded questions should be used, with well-stated demands for honesty (cf. Bowers, 1967).

Step 6 involves follow-up *retesting* at a three- to six-month interval following the conclusion of the posttesting phase. The procedure is identical to that in the posttesting phase. This testing is particularly sensitive to any hibernation effects or sharp learning decrements.

Step 7 involves a *long-term follow-up* testing administration one to three years following the conclusion of the posttesting phase, in order to determine more permanent learning effects. The procedure is again identical to the posttesting phase.

Finally, in Step 8, *data are analyzed* with respect to discovering the optimal treatment, and this treatment is then offered to *waiting list* group subjects.

Diamond and Shapiro were cognizant of the ethical considerations involved in withholding treatment for the waiting list group for such an extended period of time. Naturally, provisions need to be made for control group subjects, as they are deemed clinically viable. This model was designed for experimental purity, not clinical exigencies.

In line with the research model in Table 10–2 and the conceptual scheme delineating types of group outcomes in Table 10–1, the following survey of research is presented as an example of work from a single laboratory. This work is not intended to represent all relevant research but is suggested as a description of developing knowledge in this area. Similar descriptions of the laboratories at Stanford University Medical School under Irvin Yalom, at Cincinnati under Brendan Reddy, and at Bowling Green University under Melvin Foulds could be equally instructive.

A SUMMARY OF GROUP OUTCOME RESEARCH

In these investigations, data were regularly collected in three areas of endeavor: groups for clinical and community consultation purposes, groups for graduate training and supervision, and groups designed for basic research. A wide range of dependent measures was employed including:

1. Self-report questionnaires. Examples are Shostrom's (1966) POI; the Teacher's Counseling Questionnaire (Shapiro, 1970); Rotter's (1966) I–E locus of control scale, and Taft's (1969) Peak Experience Inventory, as well as selected scales measuring trust, dogmatism, prejudice, and so on.
2. Independent observer reports. Examples are behavior rating scales, adjective checklists, and a measure of rigidity.
3. Behavioral measures such as hypnotic susceptibility.
4. Subjective reports and follow-up inquiries.

Parameters such as group type, member and leader style, and setting influences served as independent variables.

A wide variety of participants was studied, including teachers, prison inmates, correctional workers, policemen, agricultural inspectors, civil service workers, undergraduate students, psychiatric nurses, aides and paraprofessional workers, and graduate students in the mental health field. In addition, group members were selected from a wide range of ethnic and subcultural backgrounds.

The first study (Shapiro & Ross, 1970) was completed at the Galt, Ontario correctional facility for girls who had been judged delinquent. The group was conducted with the "houseparents" (guards). Approximately one third of the guards were members of a semiweekly group which met for three months. Dependent measures included both self-report and independent observer data. Members of the encounter group reported significant increases in self-confidence and self-perception. Similarly, the inmates, who were unaware of which staff were group members and which were controls, also reported significant increases in the number of positive descriptive adjectives for group members. No changes were found for control group subjects.

In a one-year follow-up study (Shapiro and Ross, 1971), results indicated that the group effects were long-lasting. Subjects who had been in the encounter groups remained superior to control subjects. An important aspect of these data was that there was a complete turnover of inmates during the year; thus a *new set* of independent observers also detected the differences in staff behavior a full year after the group had ended. These results are particularly meaningful in that there were no pretraining differences.

The next study (Shapiro, 1970) was conducted with nurses, aides, and attendants at the Hamilton, Ontario, Psychiatric Hospital. The goal of these groups was to improve staff-patient and staff-staff relationships. In addition, the effects of pretraining on encounter group outcome were studied. Nine groups were run simultaneously, with volunteer subjects randomly assigned to the nine conditions. Voluntary participation was substantially enhanced by the generous offer of the nursing supervisory staff to allow all participants to work only days during the duration of the groups.

There were four sensitivity groups, four discussion groups, and one waiting list control. Four types of pretraining were employed: role playing, videotape playback of role playing, audiotape (only) playback, and none. Thus there was a role playing–sensitivity group, a role–playing discussion group, a videotape–sensitivity group, and so on. Results indicated that sensitivity group training led to major changes for participants, and role playing was the most enhancing type of pretraining. Significant increases were found on several POI scales, self-percept scales, information about therapy scales, and so on. The placebo (discussion) groups showed moderate increases over control subjects, but significantly less change than sensitivity group subjects.

It was concluded that sensitivity training was a valuable and valid training procedure for psychiatric nurses, aides, and attendants, and that as involvement in pretraining increased, the effects were augmented. Furthermore, the primary goal of enhanced staff-patient and staff-staff relationships was achieved, as indicated in reports from patients and staff members who served as independent observers. These observers were not aware of the specific treatment that members received.

Working with a different population, Diamond and Lobitz (1974) demonstrated similar results. Subjects in this study were policemen and students during a campus uprising following the Cambodian invasion of 1970. Three interpersonal communication experiences were employed: (1) rap groups, (2) squad car riding, and (3) encounter groups. All three produced significant attitudinal depolarization of one group toward the other group, as well as more harmonious behavioral intentions, in comparison with a no-treatment control group. This study was conducted at Stanford University in the spring of 1970. A follow-up study was completed a year later in Honolulu during a noncrisis period. In this study, students and police met in an encounter minithon; similar depolarization trends resulted. The kinds of behaviors and attitudes that changed via these encounter group experiences seem socially desirable.

Weekly encounter group experiences were also shown to facilitate personal growth as measured by changes on Shostrom's (1966) POI scale for inmates at Oahu State Prison and students in a local community college. These groups indicate a successful application of encounter group procedures to populations that were neither primarily Caucasian nor middle class. Members of both groups communicated primarily by means of "pidgin" instead of standard English. Even standard group terminology (e.g., "How do you feel?") became modified (e.g., "Howzit Brah?"). Despite the language and population differences, significant increases in interpersonal functioning and self-percept were reported.

Shapiro (1971) specifically investigated the effects of training in four types of groups. In this study, a confrontation sensitivity group, a role-playing group, a cognitive discussion group, and a waiting list control group for identical populations were compared. Group members were teachers and teachers in training. The differences between the groups were particularly evident in the way conflict resolution took place. In the confrontation group, conflict resolution was achieved by working out problems directly with other group members, whereas role playing and cognitive discussion were employed for resolution in the other two groups.

Results as perceived by members and nominated observers indicated that the confrontation-sensitivity group was the most effective. Members in this group showed significantly greater within-group and between-group differences compared to those in the other groups. They became more sensitive to their own and others' needs, more accepting of aggression and intimacy, had better self-percepts, became more like their ideal selves, developed better abilities in interpersonal interaction, and generally were better liked by both themselves and the nominated observers. Subjective follow-up reports further suggested that their subsequent relationships with their students also improved. These results were taken as an indication of the primacy of this confrontation encounter model.

Additional behavioral confirmation was reported in Shapiro and Diamond's (1972) study of hypnotic susceptibility and encounter. In this investigation, hypnotic susceptibility, largely a function of interpersonal trust, was shown to increase dramatically from pretest to posttest for graduate students in encounter groups, where it did not do so for untreated control group subjects. In addition the amount of increasing susceptibility was related to the group leader's orientation. Interpersonally oriented leaders (those who primarily facilitate interactions in group process) augmented hypnotizability to a significantly greater extent than did intrapersonally oriented leaders (those who primarily work therapeutically on individuals' intrapsychic conflicts).

These results were further replicated by Shapiro, Marano, and Diamond (1973) in a comparative study of experienced and inexperienced leaders. The authors demonstrated that greater trust was engendered by interpersonal and experienced leaders than by novice (graduate student) leaders. However, greater increases in capacity for intimacy and acceptance of aggression were demonstrated by members of groups with inexperienced leaders. It was argued that modeling played a major role in these differences.

The value of encounter group approaches for professional training has also been investigated in our laboratories at the University of Hawaii. Shapiro and Gust (1974) have demonstrated that as a function of group participation, graduate student in counseling psychology became more competent in several counseling endeavors. Over a two-semester period, 61 students were enrolled in six encounter groups. These subjects were compared to 30 control group students who were enrolled in the counseling program but not in the group experience. Results for the two semesters indicated that group subjects produced increased scores on several POI scales, the Taft experience questionnaire, and a test of interviewing skill. They also demonstrated enhanced self-concept and greater hypnotic susceptibility, and they became significantly more internal on Rotter's (1966) locus of control scale. The internal locus of control is associated with less anxiety, less dogmatism, less suspiciousness and defensiveness, and greater trust and adjustment. All are important qualities in effective counseling.

These last results were confirmed by Diamond and Shapiro (1973a). Graduate student group members were shown to demonstrate greater movement toward an internal orientation by comparison to control subjects. These results pertained for members of groups led by experienced professionals as well as graduate student leaders.

Loomis (1976), working in the same laboratory, has compared the relative effectiveness of marathon and time-extended groups. His research suggests the value of both approaches, with some comparative advantages being displayed by the time-extended format. Loomis has further investigated a process variable in encounter groups. He measured galvanic skin response (GSR) during both marathon and time-extended groups and related these physiological data to the learning attained. Of special note was his finding of significant higher resistance for marathon group members, a finding contrary to the theoretical notions of Bach (1966) and Stoller (1972). These results have implications for the quality and extent of learning that occurs in the group setting. Future work in which arousal levels are specifically manipulated is planned.

Finally, Shapiro and Siu (1976) have demonstrated cultural modeling patterns in encounter groups. In these studies, group members became more like their leaders in several dimensions. This was especially noticeable when leaders and members came from different cultures.

In summary, the model for empirical research in groups suggested here has been effectively applied to measure group effectiveness. It is expected that future research employing similar and more sophisticated models will enable us to answer more scientifically the questions posed at the beginning of this chapter.

References

Abel, W. H. Group counseling and academic rehabilitation of probationary transfer students. *Journal of College Student Personnel,* 1967, *8,* 185–188.

Abell, R. G. Personality development during group psychotherapy: Its relation to the etiology and treatment of the neuroses. *American Journal of Psychoanalysis,* 1959, *19,* 53–72.

Abrahams, D., & Enright, J. D. Psychiatric intake in groups: A pilot study of procedures, problems and prospects. *American Journal of Psychiatry,* 1965, *122,* 170-174.

Abrahams, J. Preliminary report of an experience in the group psychotherapy of schizophrenics. *American Journal of Psychiatry,* 1948, *104,* 613–617.

Abrahams, J. Group psychotherapy: Implications for direction and supervision of mentally ill patients. In T. Muller (Ed.), *Mental health in nursing.* Washington, D.C.: Catholic University Press, 1950.

Abrahams, J., & McCorkle, L. W. Group psychotherapy of military offenders. *American Journal of Sociology,* 1946, *51,* 455–464.

Abrahams, J., & McCorkle, L. W. Group psychotherapy at an Army rehabilitation center. *Diseases of the Nervous System,* 1947, *8,* 50–62.

Abramson, H. A., & Peshkin, M. M. Psychosomatic group therapy with parents of children with intractable asthma. II: Adaptation mechanisms. *Annals of Allergy,* 1960, *18,* 87–91.

Abramson, H. A., & Peshkin, M. M. Group psychotherapy of the parents of intractably asthmatic children. *Journal of Child Asthma Research Institute Hospital,* 1961, *1,* 77–91.

Ackerman, N. W. Group therapy from the viewpoint of a psychiatrist. *American Journal of Orthopsychiatry,* 1943, *13,* 678–687.

Ackerman, N. W. Group psychotherapy with veterans. *Mental Hygiene,* 1946, *30,* 559–570.

Ackerman, N. W. The diagnosis of neurotic marital interaction. *Social Casework,* 1954, *35,* 139–145. (a)

Ackerman, N. W. Some structural problems in the relation of psychoanalysis and group psychotherapy. *International Journal of Group Psychotherapy,* 1954, *4,* 131–145. (b)

Ackerman N. W. Group psychotherapy with a mixed group of adolescents. *International Journal of Group Psychotherapy,* 1955, *5,* 249.

Ackerman, N. W. Interlocking pathology in family relationships. In S. Rado & G. E. Daniels (Eds.), *Changing concepts in psychoanalytic medicine.* New York: Grune & Stratton, 1956.

Ackerman, N. W. *Psychodynamics of family life: Diagnosis and treatment of family relationships.* New York: Basic Books, 1958.

Ackerman, N. W. *Encyclopedia of mental health* (Vol. 2, p. 612). New York: Franklin Watts, 1963. (a)

Ackerman, N. W. Psychoanalysis and group psychotherapy. In M. Berger & M. Rosenbaum (Eds.), *Group psychotherapy and group function.* New York: Basic Books, 1963. (b)

Ackerman, N. W. *Treating the troubled family.* New York: Basic Books, 1966.

Ackerman, N. W. Family psychotherapy today. *Family Process*, 1970, 9, 123–126.

Ackerman, N. W. *Family therapy: An introduction to theory and technique.* Los Angeles: Wadsworth, 1972.

Ackerman, P. H. A staff group in a woman's prison. *International Journal of Group Psychotherapy*, 1972, 29, 364-373.

Ackman, D.D., Normandeau, A., & Wolfgang, M. E. The group treatment literature in correctional institutions: An international bibliography, 1945–1967. *Journal of Criminal Law, Criminology, and Police Science*, 1968, 59, 41–57.

Adsett, C. A., & Bruhn, J. G. Short-term group psychotherapy for post myocardial infarction patients and their wives. *Canadian Medical Association Journal*, 1968, 99, 577–581.

Aiken, J. L. *Group vocational counseling.* Unpublished doctoral dissertation, University of Missouri, Columbia, 1970.

Aiken, J. L., & Johnston, J. A. Promoting career information seeking behaviors in college students. *Journal of Vocational Behavior*, 1973, 3, 81–87.

Aitken, J. R. A study of attitudes and attitudinal change of institutionalized delinquents through group guidance techniques. *Dissertation Abstracts International*, 1970, 30, 4762a.

Aldous, W. R. Mechanisms of stalemate in conjoint marital therapy. *Canadian Psychiatric Association Journal*, 1973, 18, 191–199.

Aleksondrowicz, D. R., & Gaye, Z. A therapeutic club for schizophrenic adolescents. *Bulletin of the Menninger Clinic*, 1971, 35(3), 199–220.

Alexander, F., & French, T. M. *Psychoanalytic therapies: Principles and applications.* New York: Ronald Press, 1946.

Alikakos, L. C. Analytic group treatment of the post-hospital schizophrenic. *International Journal of Group Psychotherapy*, 1965, 15, 492–504.

Alkens, W. R. The life skills program: Structured counseling for the disadvantaged. *Personnel and Guidance Journal*, 1970, 49.

Allgeyer, J. M. The crisis group: Its unique usefulness to the disadvantaged. *International Journal of Group Psychotherapy*, 1970, 2, 211–219.

Allison, S. G. Non-directive group therapy of alcoholics in a state hospital. *Quarterly Journal of Studies in Alcohol*, 1952, 13, 596–601.

Allport, G. *Personality: A psychological interpretation.* New York: Holt, Rinehart, & Winston, 1937.

Altshuler, I. M. One year's experience with group psychotherapy. *Mental Hygiene*, 1940, 24, 190–196.

Altshuler, I. M. The organism-as-a-whole and music therapy. *Sociometry*, 1945, 465–470.

Anderson, B. N., Pine, I., & Mee-Lee, D. Resident training in cotherapy groups. *International Journal of Group Psychotherapy*, 1972, 22(2), 192–198.

Anderson, N. J., & Love, B. Psychological education for racial awareness. *Personnel and Guidance Journal*, 1973, 51, 666–670.

Anderson, R. E. Exchange of tape recordings as a catalyst in group therapy with sex offenders. *International Journal of Group Psychotherapy*, 1969, 19(2), 214–220.

Anderson, R. L. *An experimental investigation of group counseling with freshmen in a women's college.* Unpublished dissertation, New York University, 1956.

Anderson, S. Group counseling in drug awareness. *School Counselor*, 1971, 19, 123–126.

Andrews, E. E. The group marathon method with married couples: Summary of workshops. *Newsletter of the American Orthopsychiatric Association*, 1970, 14(2), 16.

Anthony, E. J. Reflections on twenty-five years of group psychotherapy. *International Journal of Group Psychotherapy*, 1968, 18, 277–283.

Anthony, E. J. The history of group psychotherapy. In H. I. Kaplan & B. J. Sadock (Eds.), *Comprehensive group psychotherapy.* Baltimore: Williams & Wilkins, 1971.

Apostal, R., & Muro, J. Effects of group counseling on self-reports and on self-recognition abilities of counselors in training. *Counselor Educa-*

tion and Supervision, 1970, *10,* 56–63.

Appell, M. J., Williams, C. J., & Fishel, K. N. Changes in attitudes of parents of retarded children effected through group counseling. *American Journal of Mental Deficiency,* 1964, *68,* 807–812.

Appley, D. G., and Winder, A. E. *Groups and therapy groups in a changing society.* San Francisco: Jossey-Bass, 1973.

Argyris, C. *Interpersonal competence and organizational effectiveness.* Homewood, Ill.: Dorsey Press, 1962.

Argyris, C. On the future of laboratory education. *Journal of Applied Behavioral Science,* 1967, *3*(2), 153–183.

Arnold, J. *Consciousness raising women's liberation: Blueprint for the future.* New York: Ace Books, 1970.

Arnold, W. R., & Stiles, B. A summary of increasing use of group methods in correctional institutions. *International Journal of Group Psychotherapy,* 1972, *22,* 77–92.

Aronin, E. Activity group counseling in the gym. *Elementary School Guidance and Counseling,* 1972, *6,* 220–221.

Atkinson, S., Field, S. P., & Freeman, J. G. An intensive treatment program for state hospital geriatric patients. *Geriatrics,* 1955, *10,* 111.

Atterbury, G. P. Psychodrama as an instrument for diagnostic testing. *Sociometry,* 1945, *8,* 79–81.

Axline, V. M. *Play therapy.* New York: Houghton Mifflin, 1947; Ballantine Books, 1969.

Ayers, G. E. The white counselor in the black community: Strategies for effecting attitude changes. *Journal of Rehabilitation,* 1970, *36,* 25.

Bach, G. R. *Intensive group psychotherapy.* New York: Ronald Press, 1954.

Bach, G. R. The marathon group: Intensive practice of intimate interaction. *Psychological Reports,* 1966, *18,* 995–1002.

Bach, G. R. Marathon group dynamics. II: Dimensions of helpfulness: therapeutic aggression. *Psychological Reports,* 1967, *20,* 1147.

Bach, G. R. Discussion. *International Journal of Group Psychotherapy,* 1968, *18,* 244.

Back, K. Interpersonal relations in a discussion group. *Journal of Social Issues,* 1948, *1,* 61–65.

Back, K. *Beyond words.* New York: Russell Sage Foundation, 1972.

Bahn, J. J. Value of the action lab in police training. *Group Psychotherapy and Psychodrama,* 1972, *25,* 27–29

Bailey, W. L. A comparison of the effects of visual-sensory-commitment action group therapy with commitment action group therapy and no-treatment control group of obese university females. *Dissertation Abstracts International,* 1972, 3773A.

Bales, R. F. The therapeutic role of Alcoholics Anonymous as seen by a sociologist. *Quarterly Journal of Studies in Alcohol,* 1944, *5,* 267–278.

Bales, R. F., & Slater, P. Role differentiation in small decision-making groups. In T. Parsons, R. F. Bales, J. Olds, M. Zelditch, Jr., & P. E. Slater (Eds.), *Family socialization and interaction process.* Glencoe, Ill.: Free Press, 1955.

Bandura, A. *Principles of behavior modification,* New York: Holt, Rinehart & Winston, 1969.

Bandura, A., & Walters, R. H. *Social learning and personality development.* New York: Holt, Rinehart & Winston, 1963.

Barabasz, A. F. Group desensitization of test anxiety in elementary schools. *Journal of Psychology* 1973, *83,* 295–301.

Bardach, J. L. Group sessions with the wives of aphasic patients. *International Journal of Group Psychotherapy,* 1969, *19,* 361.

Bardell, D. R. Behavior contracting and group therapy with pre-adolescent males in a residential setting. *International Journal of Group Psychotherapy,* 1972, *22,* 333–342.

Barendregt, J. T. A psychological investigation of the effect of group psychotherapy in patients with bronchial asthma. *Journal of Psychosomatic Research,* 1957, *2,* 115–119.

Barnes, R. H., Busse, E. W., & Dinken, H. The alleviation of emotional problems in multiple sclerosis by group psychotherapy. *Group Psychotherapy*, 1954, *6*, 193–201.

Barron, F., & Leary, T. F. Changes in psychosomatic patients with and without psychotherapy. *Journal of Consulting Psychology*, 1955, *19*, 234–245.

Barton, W. B. Convalescent reconditioning program for neuropsychiatric casualties in the United States Army. *Research Publication of the Association for Mental and Nervous Diseases*, 1946, *25*, 271–284.

Baruch, D. W. Description of a project in group therapy. *Journal of Consulting Psychology*, 1945, *9*, 271–280.

Baruch, D. W., & Miller, H. Group and individual psychotherapy as an adjunct in the treatment of allergy. *Journal of Consulting Psychology*, 1946, *10*, 281–284.

Baruch, D. W., & Miller, H. The use of spontaneous drawings in group therapy. *American Journal of Psychotherapy*, 1951, *5*, 45–58.

Bass, B. M. The anarchist movement and the T-group. *Journal of Applied Behavioral Science*, 1967, *3*, 211–226.

Bastianns, J. Psychodynamic aspects of group therapy for asthmatics. *Ned. T. Geneesk*, 1958, *120*, 257–260.

Bates, M., & Johnson, C. *Group leadership*. Denver: Love Publishing, 1972.

Bateson, G., Jackson, D., Haley, J., & Weakland, J. H. Toward a theory of schizophrenia. *Behavior Science*, 1956, *1*, 257–259.

Battegay, R. Psychotherapy of schizophrenics in small groups. *International Journal of Group Psychotherapy*, 1965, *15*, 316–320.

Baumgartel, H., & Goldstein, J. W. Need and value shifts in college training groups. *Journal of Applied Behavioral Science*, 1967, *3*, 87–101.

Baumgold, J. Prison notes. *Voices: The Art and Science of Psychotherapy*, 1970, *6*(2), 37–41.

Baymur, F. B., & Patterson, C. H. A comparison of three methods of assisting underachieving high school students. *Journal of Counseling Psychology*, 1960, *7*, 83–89.

Beatman, F. L. The training and preparation of workers for family-group treatment. *Social Casework*, 1964, *45*, 202–208.

Becker, M. The effects of activity group therapy on sibling rivalry. *Journal of Social Casework*, 1948, *29*, 217–221.

Becker, R. Group preparation for discharge and group placement of chronically hospitalized schizophrenic patients. *Diseases of the Nervous System*, 1971, *32*, 176–180.

Bednar, R. L., & Lawlis, G. F. Empirical research in group psychotherapy. In A. E. Bergin & S. L. Garfield, (Eds.), *Handbook of psychotherapy and behavior change*. New York: John Wiley, 1971.

Beiser, H. R. Play equipment for diagnosis and therapy. *American Journal of Orthopsychiatry*, 1955, *25*(4), 761–770.

Belford, R. Q. An evaluation of the relative effectiveness of role playing and group therapy on the subsequent socialization of parolees. *Dissertation Abstracts International*, 1971, 551B.

Bell, J. E. *Projective techniques*. New York: Longman, 1948.

Bell, J. *Family group therapy* (Public Health Monograph No. 64). Washington, D.C.: U.S. Department of Health, Education and Welfare, 1961.

Benaim, S. Group psychotherapy within a psychiatric unit: An experiment. *International Journal of Social Psychiatry*, 1957, *3*, 123–132.

Bender, L. Group activities on a children's ward as methods of psychotherapy. *American Journal of Psychiatry*, 1937, *93*, 151–173.

Bender, L., & Woltman, A. G. The use of puppet shows as a psychotherapeutic measure for behavior problem children. *American Journal of Orthopsychiatry*, 1936, *6*, 341–354.

Benjamin, S. E. Cotherapy: A growth experience for therapists. *International Journal of Group Psychotherapy*, 1972, *22*(2), 199–209.

Benne, K. D. History of the T-group in the laboratory setting. In L. P. Bradford, J. R. Gibb, & K. D. Benne (Eds.), *T-group theory and labora-*

tory method: Innovation in re-education. New York: John Wiley, 1964.

Benne, K. D. *Education for tragedy: Essay in disenchanted hope for modern man.* Lexington: University of Kentucky Press, 1967.

Bennis, W. G. *The relationship between some personality dimensions and group development.* Unpublished manuscript, Boston University, Human Relations Center, 1956.

Bennis, W. G. Goals and meta-goals of laboratory training. *Human Relations Training News,* 1962, *6,* 1–4.

Bennis, W. G. Patterns and vicissitudes in T-group development. In L. P. Bradford, J. R. Gibb & K. D. Benne, (Eds.), *T-group theory and laboratory method:* Innovation in re-education. New York: John Wiley, 1964.

Bennis, W. G. Organic populism: A conversation with W. G. Bennis and T. G. Harris. *Psychology Today,* 1970, *3*(9), 48.

Bennis, W. G., & Slater, P. E. *The temporary society.* New York: Harper & Row, 1968.

Benson, R., & Blocker, D. Evaluation of developmental counseling with groups of low achievers in a high school setting. *The School Counselor,* 1967, *14,* 215–220.

Berger, L. F., & Berger, N. M. A holistic group approach to psychogeriatric outpatients. *International Journal of Group Psychotherapy,* 1973, *23,* 432–444.

Berger, M. M., Sherman, B., Spaulding, J., & Westlake, R. The use of videotape with therapy groups in a community mental health service program. *International Journal of Group Psychotherapy,* 1968, *18,* 504–515.

Bergin, A. E. An empirical analysis of therapeutic issues. In D. Arbuckle (Ed.), *Counseling and psychotherapy: An overview.* New York: McGraw-Hill, 1967.

Berkowitz, I. H. (Ed.). *Adolescents grow in groups: Clinical experiences in adolescent group psychotherapy.* New York: Bruner/Mazel, 1972.

Berman, A. L. Profile of group therapy practice in university counseling centers. *Journal of Counseling Psychology,* 1972, *19,* 353–354.

Berman, L. Mental hygiene for educators: Report on an experiment using a combined seminar and group psychotherapy approach. *Psychoanalytic Review,* 1953, *40,* 319-325.

Berne, E. *Principles of group treatment.* New York: Oxford University Press, 166.

Bernstein, N. R., & Tinkham, C. B. Group therapy following abortion. *Journal of Nervous and Mental Disease,* 1971, *152*(5), 303–314.

Berzon, B., & Solomon, L. N. The self-directed therapeutic group: Three studies. *Journal of Counseling Psychology,* 1966, *13,* 221–233.

Betlheim, S. [Concerning group therapy of psychologically impotent married men.] *Newsletter of Diagnostic Psychology,* 1959, *5,* 251–259.

Bettis, M. C. A method of group therapy. *Diseases of the Nervous System,* 1947, *8,* 235–246.

Beukenkamp, C., Jr. Anxiety activated by the idea of marriage as observed in group psychotherapy. *Mental Hygiene,* 1960, *43,* 532–538.

Beymer, L. Confrontation groups: Hula hoops? *Counselor Education and Supervision,* 1969, *9,* 75–86.

Bice, H. V., & Holden, M. Group counseling with mothers of children with cerebral palsy. *Journal of Social Casework,* 1949, *30,* 104–109.

Bieber, T. Acting-out in homosexuality. In L. E. Abt & S. L. Weissman (Eds.), *Acting.* New York: Grune & Stratton, 1965.

Bieber, T. B. Group therapy with homosexuals. In H. I. Kaplan & B. J. Sadock (Eds.), *Comprehensive group psychotherapy.* Baltimore: Williams & Wilkins, 1971.

Bierer, J. Psychotherapy in mental hospital practice. *Journal of Mental Science,* 1940, *86,* 928–947.

Bierer, J. A new form of group therapy. *Mental Health* (London), 1944, *5,* 23–26.

Bierer, J. Modern social and group therapy. In M. G. Harris (Ed.), *Modern trends in psychological medicine.* New York: Hoeber, 1948(a).

Bierer, J. (Ed.). *Therapeutic social clubs.* London: Lewis, 1948(b).

Bilodeau, C. B., & Hackett, T. B. Issues raised in a group setting by patients recovering from myocardial infarction. *American Journal of Psychiatry,* 1971, *128,* 105–110.

Bindrim, P. A report on a nude marathon. *Psychotherapy,* 1968, *5,* 3.

Binot, E. Group therapy for hospitalized drug addicts: Review of four years of experience. *Toxicomanies,* 1973, *5,* 31–45.

Bion, W. R. The leaderless group project. *Bulletin of Menninger Clinic,* 1946, *10,* 77–81.

Bion, W. R. *Experiences in groups.* New York: Basic Books, 1959.

Bion, W. R. *Experiences in groups and other papers.* New York: Basic Books, 1961.

Bion, W. R., & Rickman, J. Intragroup tensions: Their study as a task of the group. *Lancet,* 1943, pp. 678–681.

Bird, C. *Born female.* New York: David McKay, 1970.

Bixby, F. L., & McCorkle, L. W. Guided group interaction in correctional work. *American Sociological Review,* 1951, *16,* 455–460.

Black, J. D. An opinion: Encounter groups. *Mademoiselle,* May 1970, p. 56.

Black, S. Group psychotherapy for pregnant and nonpregnant adolescents. *Child Welfare,* 1972, *51,* 514–518.

Blackman, N. W. Experiences with a library club in the group treatment of schizophrenics. *Occupational Therapy and Rehabilitation,* 1940, *19,* 293–305.

Blackman, N. W. Group psychotherapy with aphasics. *Journal of Nervous and Mental Diseases,* 1950, *111,* 154–163.

Blake, R. R., & Mouton, J. S. Reactions to intergroup competition under win-lose conditions. *Management Science,* 1961, *7,* 420–435.

Blake, R. R., & Mouton, J. S. The intergroup dynamics of win-lose conflict and problem solving in union-management relations. In M. Sherif (Ed.), *Intergroup relations and leadership.* New York: John Wiley, 1962.

Blake, R. R., & Mouton, J. S. Union-management intergroup laboratory: Strategy for resolving intergroup conflict. *Journal of Applied Behavioral Science,* 1965, *1*(1), 25.

Blake, R. R., Mouton, J. S., Barnes, L. B., & Greiner, L. E. Breakthrough in organization development. *Harvard Business Review,* 1964, *42*(6), 133–135.

Blank, L., Wilker, P., & Grundfest, S. The value of intense encounters in interactional and group process training. *Comparative Group Studies,* 1972, *12,* 51–76.

Blinder, M. G., & Kirschenbaum, M. The technique of married couple group therapy. *Archives of General Psychiatry,* 1967, *17,* 44–52.

Bloch, J. A preschool workshop for emotionally disturbed children. *Children,* 1970, *17,* 10–14.

Blumberg, R. W., & Lockhart-Mummery, L. Training for mental health workers. *Psychological Reports,* 1972, *30,* 379–382.

Blume, S. R., Robins, J., & Branston, A. Psychodrama techniques in the treatment of alcoholism. *·Group Psychotherapy,* 1968, *11,* 241–246.

Boas, C. V. E. Intensive group psychotherapy with married couples. *International Journal of Group Psychotherapy,* 1960, *12,* 142–153.

Bobele, H. K. *A rater's guide to the Problem Expression Scale.* Unpublished manuscript, University of California at Los Angeles, Graduate School of Business Administration, 1965.

Bobula, J. A. The theatre of spontaneous man. *Group Psychotherapy,* 1969, *22,* 47–64.

Boenheim, C. Some reflections about contemporary dynamic psychotherapy. *International Journal of Group Psychotherapy,* 1971, *21,* 239–243.

Bok, M. H. A motivation model of participation in group activities among chronic geriatric mental patients. *Dissertation Abstracts International,* 1969, *30,* 819.

Borgatta, E. F. Research: Pure and applied. *Group Psychotherapy,* 1955, *8,* 263–277.

Boring, R. O., & Deabler, H. L. A simplified psychodramatic approach in group therapy. *Journal of Clinical Psychology*, 1951, *7*, 371–375.

Bornstein, P. H., & Sipprelle, C. N. Group treatment of obesity by induced anxiety. *Behavior Research and Therapy*, 1973, *11*, 339–341.

Boszormenyi-nagi, I. The concept of schizophrenia from the perspective of family treatment. *Family Process*, 1962, *1*, 103–111.

Boulanger, J. B. Group psychoanalytic therapy in child psychiatry. *Canadian Psychiatric Association Journal*, 1961, *6*, 272.

Bovill, C. A trial of group psychotherapy for neurotics. *British Journal of Psychiatry*, 1972, *120*, 285–292.

Bowen, M. Family psychotherapy. *American Journal of Orthopsychiatry*, 1961, *30*, 40–47.

Bowen, M. Family psychotherapy with schizophrenia in the hospital and in private practice. In I. Boszormenyi, I. nagi, & J. L. Framo (Eds.), *Intensive family therapy: Theoretical and practical aspects*. New York: Harper & Row, 1965.

Bowen, M. The use of family therapy in clinical practice. *Comprehensive Psychiatry*, 1966, *7*, 345–353.

Bowen, M. The use of family therapy in clinical practice. In J. Haley (Ed.), *Changing families*, New York: Grune & Stratton, 1970.

Bowen, M. Family therapy and family group therapy. In H. I. Kaplan & B. J. Sadock (Eds.), *Comprehensive group psychotherapy*. Baltimore: Williams & Wilkins, 1971.

Bowers, K. The effects of demands for honesty on reports of visual and auditory hallucinations. *International Journal of Clinical and Experimental Hypnosis*, 1967, *15*, 31–36.

Bowers, N. D., & Soar, R. S. Evaluation of laboratory human relations training for classroom teachers. In E. S. Knowles, Research since 1960: a bibliography on research on human relations training. Washington, D.C.: National Training Laboratories, 1967.

Bowers, P. F., Banquer, M., & Bloomfield, H. H. Utilization of nonverbal exercises in the group therapy of outpatient chronic schizophrenics.

International Journal of Group Psychotherapy, 1974, *24*, 13–21.

Boyd, J. B., & Elliss, J. D. *Findings of research into senior management seminars*. Hydro - Electric Power Commission of Ontario, Toronto, 1962.

Bozzetti, L. P. Group psychotherapy with addicted smokers. *Psychotherapy and Psychosomatics*, 1972, *20*, 172–175.

Bradford, L. P. *Explorations in human relations training*. Washington, D. C.: National Education Association, 1953.

Bradford, L. P. (Ed.). *Group development* (National Training Laboratories Selected Reading Series, Vols. 1–4). Washington, D.C.: National Training Laboratories and National Education Association, 1961.

Bradford, L. P. Trainer intervention: Case episodes. In L. P. Bradford, J. R. Gibb, & K. D. Benne (Eds.), *T group theory and laboratory method: Innovation in re-education*. New York: John Wiley, 1964.

Bradford, L. P. Biography of an institution. *Journal of Applied Behavioral Science*, 1967, *3*, 127–135.

Bradford, L., Gibb, J., & Benne, K. D. (Eds.). *T group theory and laboratory method: Innovation in re-education*. New York: John Wiley, 1964.

Bradford, L. P., Gibb, J. R., & Lippitt, G. L. Human relations training in three days. *Adult Leadership*, 1956, *4*, 11–26.

Braen, B. B. The evolution of a therapeutic group approach to school-age pregnant girls. *Adolescence*, 1970, *18*, 171–186.

Braginsky, B. M., Braginsky, D. J., & Ring, K. R. *Methods of madness*. New York: Holt, Rinehart, & Winston, 1969.

Brancale, R. Psychotherapy of the adult criminal. *Journal of Criminal Psychopathology*, 1943, *4*, 472–483.

Brian, W. J. Group therapy with adolescent girls in foster care. *Adolescence*, 1971, *6*, 299–316.

Bricklin, P. M. Counseling parents of children with learning disabilities. *Reading Teacher*, 1970, *23*(4), 331–338.

Bromberg, W., & Franklin, G. The treatment of sexual deviates with group psychodrama. *Group Psychotherapy*, 1952, *4*, 274–289.

Broms, D. S. Group process and the preschool retarded child. *Group Process*, 1971, *4*, 39–51.

Brook, R. C., & Whitehead, P. C. "414": A therapeutic community for the treatment of adolescent amphetamine abusers. *Corrections, Social Psychiatry and Journal of Applied Behavior Therapy*, 1973, *19*, 10–19.

Brown, B. S. Methadone and abstinent clients in group counseling sessions. *International Journal of Addiction*, 1973, *8*, 309–316.

Brudno, J. J. Resocialization therapy through group process with senile patients in a geriatric hospital. *Gerontologist*, 1968, *8*, 211–214.

Brunner-Orne, M. Ward group sessions with hospitalized alcoholics as motivation for psychotherapy. *International Journal of Group Psychotherapy*, 1959, *9*, 219–224.

Brunner-Orne, M., & Orne, M. T. Alcoholics. In S. R. Slavson (Ed.), *The field of group psychotherapy*. New York: International Universities Press, 1956, 576–595.

Buber, M. *Between man and man*. London: Kegan Paul, 1947.

Buchanan, P. C. Evaluating the effectiveness of laboratory training in industry. In *Exploration in human relations training and research* (Vol. 1). Washington, D.C.: National Training Laboratories, 1965.

Buchmueller, A. D., & Gildea, M. C. A group therapy project with parents of behavior problem children in public schools. *American Journal of Psychiatry*, 1949, *106*, 46–52.

Buck, A. E., & Grygier, T. A new attempt in psychotherapy with juvenile delinquents. *American Journal of Psychotherapy*, 1952, *6*, 711–721.

Buck, B. Psychodrama of drug addiction. *Group Psychotherapy*, 1952, *4*, 310–321.

Buck, R. W. The class method in the treatment of essential hypertension. *Annals of Internal Medicine*, 1937, *11*, 514–518.

Buckley, C. F. The Emmanuel movement and its affinities. *Alienist Neurology*, 1910, *31*, 70–79.

Bunker, D. R. Individual applications of laboratory training. *Journal of Applied Behavioral Science*, 1965, *1*, 131–148.

Burchard, E. M. L., Michaels, J. J., & Kotkov, B. Criterion for the evaluation of group psychotherapy. *Psychosomatic Medicine*, 1948, *10*, 257–274.

Burke, R. L., & Bennis, W. G. Changes in perception of self and others during human relations training. *Human Relations*, 1961, *14*, 165–182.

Burlingham, S. Therapeutic effects of a playgroup for pre-school children. *American Journal of Orthopsychiatry*, 1938, *8*, 627–638.

Burnell, G. M. Post abortion group therapy. *American Journal of Psychiatry*, 1972, *129*, 220–223.

Burnside, I. M. Loss: A constant theme in group work with the aged. *Hospital and Community Psychiatry*, 1970, *21*, 173–177.

Burnside, I. M. Long term group work with hospitalized aged. *Gerontologist*, 1971, *11*(3), 213–218.

Burrow, T. The group method of analysis. *Psychoanalysis Review* 1927, *14*, 268–280. (a)

Burrow, T. The problem of transference. *British Journal of Medical Psychology*, 1927, *7*, 193–199. (b)

Burrow, T. The basis of group analysis. *British Journal of Medical Psychology*, 1928, *8*, 198–206.

Burton, A. *Encounter: Theory and practice of encounter groups*. San Francisco: Jossey-Bass, 1969.

Byrd, R. E. *Training clergy for creative risk taking: A preliminary evaluation*. Paper presented at the annual meeting of the Society for the Study of Scientific Religion, October 1966, at the Center for Continuing Education, University of Chicago.

Cabeen, C. W., & Coleman, J. C. Group therapy with sex offenders: Description and evaluation of group therapy in an institutional setting. *Journal of Clinical Psychology*, 1961, *17*(2), 122–129.

Cabeen, C. W., & Coleman, J. C. The selection of sex-offender patients for group psychotherapy. *International*

Journal of Group Psychotherapy, 1962, *12,* 326–334.

Cain, J., Charpin, J., & Planson, C. Psychosomatic considerations in 50 cases of allergic asthma: Attempted group psychotherapy. *Acta Allergia* (KBH) 1959, *14,* 134–145.

Calof, J. A study of four voluntary treatment and rehabilitation programs for New York City's narcotics addicts. New York: Community Service Society of New York, 1967.

Calof, J. Life line to tomorrow: A study of voluntary treatment programs for narcotics addicts. New York: Community Service Society of New York, 1969.

Campbell, J. P., & Dunnette, M. D. Effectiveness of T-group experiences in managerial training and development. *Psychological Bulletin,* 1968, *70*(2), 73–104.

Camus, J., & Pagniez, P. *Isolement et psychotherapie.* Paris: Alcan, 1904.

Carkhuff, R. R., and Berenson, B. *Beyond counseling and therapy.* New York: Holt, Rinehart, & Winston, 1967.

Carkhuff, R. R., & Truax, C. B. Toward explaining success and failure in interpersonal learning experiences. *Personnel and Guidance Journal,* 1966, *45,* 723–728.

Carr, R. J. A comparison of the effects of three types of intervention with underachieving high school seniors. *Dissertation Abstracts International,* 1971, *32,* 4A.

Carson, R. C., & Lakin, M. Some effects of group sensitivity experience. Paper presented at the meeting of the Southeastern Psychological Association, Miami, Florida, 1963.

Case, M. E. The forgotten ones. *Smith College Studies in Social Work,* 1951, *21,* 199–231.

Casella, B. M. Group process in training Catholic seminarians. *International Journal of Group Psychotherapy,* 1972, *12*(3), 384–389.

Cath, S. H. The student-teacher alliance and the formation of professional ego: An experiment in small group seminars in the second year of medical school. *International Journal of Group Psychotherapy,* 1965, *15,* 303–315.

Cavanagh, J. R., & Gerstein, S. Group psychotherapy in a naval disciplinary barracks: Preliminary report. *Naval Medical Bulletin,* 1949, *49,* 645–654.

Cernak, S. A. Hyperactive children and an activity group therapy model. *American Journal of Occupational Therapy,* 1973, *27,* 311–315.

Chambers, W. M., & Ficek, D. E. An evaluation of marathon counseling. *International Journal of Group Psychotherapy,* 1970, *20,* 372–379.

Chappell, M. H., Stefano, J. J., Rogerson, J. S., & Pike, H. S. Value of group psychological procedures in the treatment of peptic ulcers. *American Journal of Digestive Diseases and Nutrition,* 1937, *3,* 813–817.

Chen, Chu Chang. Experiences with group psychotherapy in Taiwan. *International Journal of Group Psychotherapy,* 1972, *22,* 210–227.

Christmas, J. J. Group therapy with the disadvantaged. In J. Masserman (Ed.), *Current psychiatric therapies* (Vol. 6) New York: Grune & Stratton, 1966.

Churchill, S. R. Social group work: A diagnostic tool in child guidance. *American Journal of Orthopsychiatry,* 1965, *35,* 581–583.

Clapham, H. I., & Sclare, A. B. Group psychotherapy with asthmatic patients. *International Journal of Group Psychotherapy,* 1958, *8,* 44–54.

Clark, J. V., & Culbert, S. A. Mutually therapeutic perception and self awareness in a T-group. *Journal of Applied Behavior Science,* 1965, *1*(2), 180–194.

Clark, T. C., & Miles, M. B. Human relations training for school administrators. *Journal of Social Issues,* 1954, *10,* 25–39.

Clarke, E. K. Group therapy in rehabilitation. *Federal Problems,* 1952, *16*(4), 28–32.

Clements, T. A. *A study of the effectiveness of individual and group counseling approaches with able underachievers where counseling is held constant.* Unpublished doctoral dissertation, University of California, 1963.

Cochrane, N. Some reflections on the unsuccessful treatment of a group of married couples. *British Journal of Psychiatry*, 1973, *123*, 395–401.

Coffey, H. S. Group psychotherapy. In L. A. Pennington & I. A. Berge (Eds.), *An introduction to clinical psychology.* New York: Ronald Press, 1954.

Coffey, H. S. Instruction of middle management staff in sensitivity training methods. In N. Fenton & E. A. Taron (Eds.), *Training staff for program development in youth correctional institutions.* Sacramento, Calif.: Corrections Press, 1965.

Coffey, H. S., Freedman, M., Learg, T., & Ossorio, A. Social implications of the group therapy situation. *Journal of Social Issues*, 1950, *6*(1), 44–61.

Coffey, H. S., & Wiener, L. L. *Group treatment of autistic children.* Englewood Cliffs, N.J.: Prentice-Hall, 1967.

Cohen, A. M., & Smith, R. D. The critical incident approach to leadership intervention in groups. In W. G. Dyer (Ed.), *Modern theory and methods in group training.* New York: Von Nostrand Reinhold, 1972.

Cohen, A. M., & Smith, R. D. *The critical incident in growth groups: A manual for leaders.* La Jolla, Calif.: University Associates, 1976.

Cohen, A. M., & Smith, R. D. *The critical incident in growth groups: Theory and technique.* La Jolla, Calif.: University Associates, 1976.

Cohen, C. P., Johnson, P., & Hanson, D. Interpersonal changes among psychiatric patients in human relations training. *Journal of Personality Assessment*, 1971, *35*, 472–479.

Cohen, M. F. Group methods and the new careerists. *International Journal of Group Psychotherapy*, 1974, *24*(4), 393–399.

Cohen, R. R. Factors in adjustment to Army life. *War Medicine*, 1944, *5*, 83–89.

Cohen, R. R. Visual aids in group psychotherapy: Puppetry. *Group Psychotherapy*, 1945, *8*, 311–314.

Cohen, R. Military group psychotherapy. *Mental Hygiene*, 1947, *31*, 94–102.

Cohn, R. Therapy groups: Psychoanalytic, experiential, and gestalt. In J. Fagan & I. L. Shepherd (Eds.), *Ges-*

talt therapy now. Palo Alto, Calif.: Science and Behavior Books, 1970.

Collier, W. V. *An evaluation report on the therapeutic program of Daytop Village, Inc.* Daytop Village, New York, 1970.

Collins, J. E. *A comparative guidance study: Group counseling methods with selected underachieving ninth-grade students.* Unpublished doctoral dissertation, University of Southern California, 1964.

Collum, H. L. An investigation of a group approach to weight reduction involving modified group involvement feedback training. *Dissertation Abstacts International*, 1972, 4937A.

Colman, A. Psychology of a first-baby group. *International Journal of Group Psychotherapy*, 1971, *21*, 74–83.

Comstock, B. S., & McDermitt, M. Group therapy for patients who attempt suicide. *International Journal of Group Psychotherapy*, 1975, *25*(1), 44–49.

Cook, F. The use of three types of group procedures with ninth-grade underachieving students and their parents. *Dissertation Abstracts International*, 1971, *31*, 3869A.

Cooper, C. L. The influence of the trainer on participant change in T-groups. *Human Relations*, 1969, *22*, 515–521.

Cooper, C. L. T-group training and self-actualization. *Psychological Reports*, 1971, *2*, 391–394.

Cooper, C. L., & Bowles, D. Physical encounter and self disclosure. *Psychological Reports*, 1973, *33*, 451–454.

Cooper, C. L., & Mangham, I. L. *T-groups: A survey of research,* London: Wiley Interscience, 1971.

Corbin, M. L. Group speech therapy for motor aphasia and dysarthria. *Journal of Speech and Hearing Disorders*, 1951, *16*, 21–34.

Cork, R. M. Case work in a group setting with wives of alcoholics. *Social Work* (Ottawa), 1956, *24*(3), 1–6.

Corsini, R. J. The method of psychodrama in prison. *Group Psychotherapy*, 1951, *3*, 321–326. (a)

Corsini, R. J. Psychodramatic treatment of a pedophile. *Group Psychotherapy*, 1951, *4*, 166–171. (b)

Corsini, R. J. The "behind-your-back" technique in group psychotherapy and psychodrama. *Group Psychotherapy*, 1953, *6*, 102–109.

Corsini, R. J. Group psychotherapy with a hostile group. *Group Psychotherapy*, 1954, *6*, 168–173.

Corsini, R. J. Towards a definition of group psychotherapy. *Mental Hygiene*, 1955, *39*, 647–656.

Corsini, R. J. *Methods of group psychotherapy.* New York: McGraw-Hill, 1957.

Corsini, R. J., & Cardone, S. *Roleplaying in psychotherapy: A manual.* Chicago: Aldine, 1966.

Corsini, R. J., & Lundin, W. H. Group psychotherapy in the Midwest. *Group Psychotherapy*, 1955, *8*, 316–320.

Corsini, R. T., & Rosenberg, B. Mechanisms of group psychotherapy. *Journal of Abnormal Social Psychology*, 1955, *51*, 406–411.

Cotton, J. M. The psychiatric treatment program at Welch Convalescent Hospital. *Research Publication of the Association for Mental and Nervous Diseases*, 1946, *25*, 316–321.

Cotton, J. M. Group psychotherapy: An appraisal. In P. Hoch (Ed.), *Failures in psychiatric treatment.* New York: Grune & Stratton, 1948.

Cotzin, M. Group psychotherapy with mentally defective problem boys. *American Journal of Mental Deficiency*, 1948, *53*, 268–283.

Coulson, W. R. *Groups, gimmicks and instant gurus.* New York: Harper & Row, 1972.

Cox, F. W. Sociometric status and undivided adjustment before and after play therapy. *Journal of Abnormal and Social Psychology*, 1953, *48*, 354–356.

Crighton, J., & Jehu, D. Treatment of examination anxiety by systematic dissertation or psychotherapy in groups. *Behavior Research and Therapy*. 1969, *7*, 245–248.

Crosbie, P. V., Petroni, F. A., & Stitt, B. G. The dynamics of corrective groups. *Journal of Health and Social Behavior*, 1972, *13*, 294–302.

Culbert, S. A. *Trainer self-disclosure and member growth in a T-group.* Unpublished doctoral dissertation, University of California, Los Angeles, 1965.

Culbert, S. A. Trainer self-disclosure and member growth. *Journal of Applied Behavioral Science*, 1968, *4*, 47–74.

Culbert, S. A., Clark, J. V., & Bobele, H. K. Measures of change toward self-actualization in two sensitivity training groups. *Journal of Counseling Psychology*, 1968, *15*, 436–440.

Cummings, S. T., & Stock, D. Brief group therapy with mothers of retarded children outside of the specialty clinic setting. *American Journal of Mental Deficiency*, 1962, *66*, 739–748.

Curlee, J. Combined used of Alcoholics Anonymous and outpatient psychotherapy. *Bulletin of the Menninger Clinic*, 1971, *35*, 368–371.

Curran, F. J. The drama as a therapeutic measure in adolescents. *American Journal of Orthopsychiatry*, 1939, *9*, 215–231.

Curran, F. J., & Schilder, P. A constructive approach to the problems of childhood and adolescence. *Journal of Criminal Psychopathology*, 1940, *2*, 125–142; 305–320.

Curran, J. P., Gilbert, F. S., & Little, L. M. A comparison between behavioral replication training and sensitivity training for heterosexual dating anxiety. *Journal of Counseling Psychology*, 1976, *23*, 190–196.

Curry, A. E. Large therapeutic groups: A critique and appraisal of the literature. *International Journal of Group Psychotherapy*, 1967, *17*, 536–547.

Curtis, T. E., Clarke, M. G., & Abse, D. W. Etiological factors in peptic ulcer as revealed in group analytic psychotherapy. *International Record of Medicine*, 1967, *73*, 92–96.

D'afflitti, J. G., & Weitz, G. W. Rehabilitating the stroke patient through patient family groups. *International Journal of Group Psychotherapy*, 1974, *24*(3), 323–332.

Dailey, A. L. Group counseling parameters for pregnant nonresidential high school students. *Dissertation Abstracts International*, 1972, 6123A.

Dalzell-Ward, A. J. Group discussion with male V. D. patients. *British Journal of Venereal Disease*, 1960, *36*, 106–112.

Dannefer, E., Brown, R., & Epstein, N. Experience in developing a combined activity and verbal group therapy program with latency age boys. *International Journal of Group Psychotherapy*, 1975, *25*, 331–337.

D'avanzo, H. The family group in dynamic psychiatric diagnosis. *International Journal of Group Psychotherapy*, 1962, *12*, 496–502.

Davison, G. C. Systematic desensitization as a counter-conditioning process. *Journal of Abnormal Psychology*, 1968, *73*, 91–99.

Dawley, H. H., Jr., & Wenrich, W. W. Group implosive therapy in the treatment of test anxiety: A brief report. *Behavior Therapy*, 1973, *4*, 261–263. (a)

Dawley, H. H., Jr., & Wenrich, W. W. Treatment of test anxiety by group implosive therapy. *Psychological Reports*, 1973, *33*, 383–388. (b)

Day, M. The natural history of training groups. *International Journal of Group Psychotherapy*, 1967, *17*, 436–444.

Day, M. E., Day, E., & Hermann, R. Group therapy of patients with multiple sclerosis. *Archives of Neurology and Psychiatry*, 1953, *68*, 193–196.

Day, M. E., & Semrad, E. Group therapy with neurotics and psychotics. In H. I. Kaplan & B. J. Sadock (Eds.), *Comprehensive group psychotherapy*. Baltimore: Williams & Wilkins, 1971.

Deberker, D. Group counseling in penal institutions: The problem of communication. *British Journal of Criminology*, 1963, *4*(1), 62–68.

Dee, G. H. The effects of parent group counseling on children with school adjustment problems. *Dissertation Abstracts International*, 1970, *31*, 1008A.

Deep, S., Bass, B. M., & Vaughn, J. A. Some effects on business gaming of previous quasi-T group affiliations (Technical Report 12, O.N.R.). Pitts-

burgh: University of Pittsburgh, Management Research Center, 1966.

Dejerine, J., & Gauckler, E. The psychoneuroses and their treatment by psychotherapy (S. E. Jelliffe, trans.). Philadelphia: Lippincott, 1913.

Dellis, N. P., & Stone, H. K. (Eds.). The training of psychotherapists. Baton Rouge: Louisiana State University Press, 1960.

Denny, J. M. Art counseling in educational settings. *Personnel and Guidance Journal*, 1969, *40*, 221–224.

Denny, J. M. Techniques for individual and group art therapy. *American Journal of the Art of Therapy*, 1972, *11*, 3.

Denny, J. M., & Fagen, A. C. Group art therapy with university students: A comparative case analysis. *Psychotherapy Theory Research and Practice*, 1970, *7*(3), 201–214.

Deutsch, A. A., & Zimmerman, J. Group psychotherapy as adjunct treatment of epileptic patients. *American Journal of Psychiatry*, 1948, *109*, 783–785.

Deutsch, A. L. Group psychotherapy for patients with psychosomatic illness. *Psychosomatics*, 1964, *5*, 14–20.

Diamond, M. J. *Encounter groups and behavior change: Toward a social learning approach.* Paper presented at the 80th annual convention of the American Psychological Association, Honolulu, September 1972.

Diamond, M. J. Modification of hypnotic ability: A review. *Psychological Bulletin*, 1974, *81*, 180–198.

Diamond, M., & Lobitz, W. When familiarity breeds respect: The effects of an experimental depolarization program on police and student attitudes toward each other. *Journal of Social Issues*, 1974, *29*, 95–109.

Diamond, M. J., & Shapiro, J. L. Changes in locus of control as a function of encounter group experiences: A study and replication. *Journal of Abnormal Psychology*, 1973, *83*(3), 514–518. (a)

Diamond, M. J., & Shapiro, J. L. Toward the long-term scientific study of encounter group phenomena. I. Methodological considerations. Paper presented at the 53rd annual meeting of the Western Psychological

Association, Anaheim, Calif., April 1973. (b)

Diamond, M. J., & Shapiro, J. L. An expedient model of encounter group learning. *Psychotherapy: Theory, Research and Practice,* 1975, *12*(1), 56–60. (a)

Diamond, M. J., & Shapiro, J. L. Method and paradigm in encounter group research. *Journal of Humanistic Psychology* 1975, *15,* 59–70.

Dichter, M., Driscoll, G. Z., Ottenberg, D. J., & Rosen, A. Marathon therapy with alcoholics. *Quarterly Journal of Studies in Alcohol,* 1971, *32*(1), 66–77.

Dickenson, W. A., & Truax, C. B. Group counseling with college underachievers. *Personnel and Guidance Journal,* 1966, *45,* 243–247.

Dickoff, H., & Lakin, M. Patient's view of group psychotherapy. *International Journal of Group Psychotherapy,* 1964, *14*(1), 61–73.

Diedrich, R. C., & Dye, H. A. *Group procedures: Purposes, processes and outcomes.* New York: Houghton Mifflin, 1972.

Dinkmeyer, D. Developmental group counseling. *Elementary School Guidance and Counseling,* 1970, *4*(1), 267–272.

Dorfman, E. Personality outcomes of client centered therapy. *Psychological Monographs,* 1958, *72,* 3.

Dorfman, W., Slater, S., & Gottlieb, N. Drugs and placebos in the group treatment of obesity. *International Journal of Group Psychotherapy,* 1959, *9,* 345–350.

Dreikurs, R. *Challenge of parenthood.* New York: Duell, Sloan, & Pearce, 1948.

Dreikurs, R. Techniques and dynamics of multiple psychotherapy. *Psychiatric Quarterly,* 1950, *24,* 788–799.

Dreikurs, R. Family group therapy in the Chicago Community Child Guidance Centers. *Mental Hygiene,* 1951, *35,* 291–301. (a)

Dreikurs, R. The unique social climate experienced in group psychotherapy. *Group Psychotherapy* 1951, *3,* 292–299. (b)

Dreikurs, R. General review. In *Comptes rendus des seances.* Premier congres mondial de psychiatrie. Paris: Hermann, 1952.

Dreikurs, R. Early experiments with group psychotherapy. *American Journal of Psychotherapy,* 1959, *13,* 219–255.

Dreikurs, R., Sonstegard, N., Corsini, R., & Low, R. *Adlerian family counseling,* Eugene: University of Oregon Press, 1959.

Dreyfus, E. A., & Kremenliev, E. Innovative group technique: Handle with care. *Personnel and Guidance Journal,* 1970, *49,* 279–283.

Dubo, S. Opportunities for group therapy in pediatric service. *International Journal of Group Psychotherapy,* 1951, *1,* 235–242.

Dubois, R. D., & Li, M. S. Reducing group tensions. *Reducing social tension and conflict with group conversation method.* New York: Association Press, 1971.

Duncan, J. A., & Gazda, G. M. Significant content of group counseling sessions with culturally deprived ninth-grade students. *Personnel and Guidance Journal,* 1967, *46,* 11–16.

Dunnette, M. D. People feeling: Joy, more joy and the laugh of despond. *Journal of Applied Behavioral Science,* 1969, *5,* 25–44.

Durham, L. E., Gibb, J. R., & Knowles, E. S. *A bibliography of research: Esalen programs.* San Francisco: East Wind Printers, 1967, 1969, 1970.

Dusay, J. Response. *Transactional Analysis Bulletin,* 1966, *5,* 36.

Dusay, J. Proceedings of the eighth annual meeting of the International Transactional Analysis Association. *Transactional Analysis Bulletin,* 1970, *9,* 36.

Dusay, J. Transactional analysis in groups. In H. I. Kaplan & B. J. Sadock (Eds.), *Comprehensive group psychotherapy,* Baltimore: Williams & Wilkins, 1971.

Dusay, J., & Steiner, C. Transactional analysis in groups. In H. I. Kaplan & B. J. Sadock (Eds.), *New models for group therapy.* New York: Dutton, 1972.

Ebersole, G. E., Leiderman, P. H., & Yalom, I. D. Training the nonprofessional group therapist: A controlled study. *Journal of Nervous and Mental Disease*, 1969, *149*, 293–302.

Egan, G. *Encounter: Group process for interpersonal growth.* Monterey, Calif.: Brooks/Cole, 1970.

Eisenberg, L. Psychotic disorders. I: Clinical features. In A. M. Freedman & H. I. Kaplan (Eds.), *Comprehensive textbook of psychiatry.* Baltimore: Williams & Wilkins, 1967.

Eliasberg, W. G. Group treatment of homosexuals on probation. *Group Psychotherapy*, 1954, *7*, 218–226.

Eliasoph, E. A group therapy and psychodrama approach with adolescent drug addicts. *Group Psychotherapy*, 1965, *8*, 161–168.

Ellis, A. *American sexual tragedy.* Boston: Twayne, 1954.

Ellis, A. The effectiveness of psychotherapy in individuals who had severe homosexual problems. *Journal of Consulting Psychology*, 1956, *20*, 191.

Ellis, A. A weekend of rational encounter. In A. Burton (Ed.), *Encounter theory and practice of encounter groups.* San Francisco: Jossey-Bass, 1969.

Emde-Boas, C. V. Intensive group therapy with married couples. *Review of French Psychoanalysis*, 1962, *26*, 446–465.

Emener, W. G. A prepracticum laboratory training experience. *Counselor Education and Supervision*, 1973, *12*, 212–220.

Emerson, W. R. P. The hygienic and dietetic treatment of delicate children. *Boston Medical and Surgical Journal*, 1910, *163*, 326–328.

Endres, M. P., & Evans, M. J. Some effects of parent education on parents and their children. *Adult Education*, 1968, *18*, 101–111.

Ends, E. J., & Page, C. W. A study of three types of group psychotherapy with hospitalized male inebriates. *Quarterly Journal of Studies in Alcohol*, 1957, *18*, 263–277.

Epstein, N., & Altman, S. Experiences in converting an activity group into verbal group therapy with latency aged boys. *International Journal of*

Group Psychotherapy, 1972, *22*, 93–100.

Esterson, H. Time-limited group counseling with parents of preadolescent underachievers: A pilot program. *Proceedings of the 81st Annual Convention of the American Psychological Association, Montreal*, 1973, *8*, 703–704.

Euster, G. L. A system of groups in institutions for the aged. *Social Casework*, 1971, *52*, 523–529.

Everett, H. C. The adversary system in married couples' group therapy. *International Journal of Group Psychotherapy*, 1968, *18*, 70–74.

Ewing, J., Long, V., & Wengel, G. Concurrent group psychotherapy of alcoholic patients and their wives. *International Journal of Group Psychotherapy*, 1961, *11*, 329–338.

Eysenck, H. The effects of psychotherapy: An evaluation. *Journal of Consulting Psychology*, 1952, *16*, 319–324.

Ezkiel, H. A psychoanalytic approach to group treatment. *British Journal of Medical Psychology*, 1950, *23*, 59.

Fairweather, G. W., & Simon, R. A further follow-up comparison of psychotherapeutic programs. *Journal of Consulting Psychology*, 1963, *27*(3), 186.

Fairweather, G. W., Simon, R., Gebhard, M., Weingarten, E., Holland, J. L., Stone, G. B., & Reahl, J. E. Relative effectiveness of psychotherapeutic programs: A multidimensional criteria comparison of four programs for three different patient groups. *Psychological Monographs*, 1960, *74* (5, Whole No. 498).

Farkas, H., & Schwachman, H. Psychological adaptation to chronic illness: A group discussion with cystic fibrosis patients. *American Journal of Orthopsychiatry* 1973, *43*, 259–260.

Feder, B. Limited goals in short-term psychotherapy with institutionalized delinquent adolescent boys. *International Journal of Group Psychotherapy*, 1962, *12*, 503–507.

Feder, S. M. *Limited goals in short-term group psychotherapy with institutionalized adolescent delinquent boys.* Unpublished doctoral dissertation, Columbia University, 1961.

Feifel, H., & Schwartz, A. D. Group psychotherapy with acutely disturbed psychotic patients. *Journal of Consulting Psychology,* 1953, *17,* 113–121.

Feldman, D. J. The treatment of chronic alcoholism: A survey of current methods. *Annals of Internal Medicine,* 1956, *44,* 78–87.

Felton, G. S., & Biggs, B. E. Psychotherapy and responsibility: Teaching internalization behavior to black low achievers through group therapy. *Small Group Behavior,* 1973, *4,* 147–156.

Fensterheim, H. Behavior therapy: Assertive training in groups. In C. J. Sager & H. S. Kaplan (Eds.), *Progress in group and family therapy.* New York: Brunner/Mazel, 1972.

Fenton, N. The potential treatability of prison inmates of different custodial levels. *Proceedings of the American Prison Association,* 1951, 279–285.

Fenton, N., & Taron, E. A. *Training staff for program development in youth correctional institutions.* Sacramento, Calif.: Corrections Press, 1965.

Fidler, J. W. The concepts of levels in group therapy with psychotics. *International Journal of Group Psychotherapy,* 1951, *1,* 51–54.

Fiebert, M. S. Sensitivity training: An analysis of trainer intervention and group process. *Psychological Reports,* 1963, *22*(8), 829–838.

Finney, B. C., & Van Dalsem, E. Group counseling with underachieving high school students. *Journal of Counseling Psychology,* 1968, *16,* 87–94.

Fisher, L., & Wolfson, I. Group therapy of mental defectives. *American Journal of Mental Deficiency,* 1953, *57,* 463–476.

Fishman, S. T., & Nawas, M. M. Standardized desensitization method in group treatments. *Journal of Counseling Psychology,* 1971, *18*(6), 520–523.

Flach, F. F. Group approaches in medical education. In H. I. Kaplan & B. J. Sadock (Eds.), *Comprehen-*

sive group psychotherapy, Baltimore: Williams & Wilkins, 1971.

Forester, B. M., & Swiller, H. Transsexualism: Review of syndrome and presentation of possible successful therapeutic approach. *International Journal of Group Psychotherapy,* 1972, *22,* 343–351.

Forman, N. The alienated resident and the alienating institution: A case for peer group intervention. *Social Work,* 1971, *16,* 47–55.

Fortin, J. N., & Abse, D. W. Group psychotherapy with peptic ulcer: A preliminary report. *International Journal of Group Psychotherapy,* 1956, *6,* 383–391.

Foster, S., Marks, S., & Conry, R. Critical analysis of methodological problems associated with the evaluation of marathon groups. *Proceedings of the 80th Annual Convention of the American Psychological Association,* 1972, *7,* 575–576.

Foulds, M. L. Changes in locus of internal-external control. *Comparative Group Studies,* 1971, 293–300.

Foulds, M. J., Gerona, R., and Guinan, J. F. Changes in ratings of self and others as a result of marathon groups. *Comparative Group Studies,* 1970, *1,* 349–355.

Foulkes, S. H. Principles and practice of group therapy. *Bulletin of the Menninger Clinic,* 1946, *10,* 85–89.

Foulkes, S. H. *An introduction to group analytic psychotherapy.* London: Heinemann, 1948.

Foulkes, S. H. *Therapeutic group analysis.* New York: International University Press, 1965.

Foulkes, S. H., & Anthony, E. J. *Group psychotherapy: The psychoanalytic approach.* London: Penguin, 1957.

Fox, R. Group psychotherapy with alcoholics. *International Journal of Group Psychotherapy,* 1962, *12,* 56–63.

Foy, J. L. Problem areas in art therapy. *Bulletin of Art Therapy,* 1961, *1,* 22–27.

Frank, J. D. *Persuasion and healing* (Rev. ed.). New York: Shocken, 1974.

Frank, J. D. Group psychotherapy research 25 years later. *International*

Journal of Group Psychotherapy, 1975, *25*(2), 141–146. (a)

Frank, J. D. Some problems of research in group psychotherapy. *International Journal of Group Psychotherapy,* 1975, *25*(2), 141–146. (b)

Frank, J. D., & Powdermaker, F. B. Group psychotherapy. In S. Arieti (Ed.), *Handbook of Psychiatry* (Vol. 2). New York: Basic Books, 1962.

Frank, M. B., & Zilbach, J. Current trends in group therapy with children. *International Journal of Group Psychotherapy,* 1968, *28,* 447–460.

Franklin, G. H. Group psychotherapy with delinquent boys in a training school setting. *International Journal of Group Psychotherapy,* 1959, *9,* 213–218.

Franklin, G. H., & Nottage, W. Psychoanalytic treatment of severely disturbed juvenile delinquents in a therapy group. *International Journal of Group Psychotherapy,* 1969, *19,* 165–175.

Freeman, R. V., & Schwartz, A. A motivation center: A new concept in total neuropsychiatric hospital care. *American Journal of Psychiatry,* 1953, *110,* 139–142.

Freese, A. L. Group therapy with exhibitionists and voyeurs. *Social Work,* 1972, *17*(2), 44-52.

French, T. M. *The integration of behavior* (Vols. 1, 2). Chicago: University of Chicago Press, 1952.

Freud, S. *Group psychology and analysis of the ego.* London: International Psychoanalytic Press, 1922.

Freud, S. *Collected Papers: Volume II.* New York: International Psychoanalytic Library, 1924.

Freudenberger, H. J., & Marrero, F. A therapeutic marathon with Vietnam veteran addicts at S.E.R.A. *Voices: The Art and Science of Psychotherapy,* 1972–1973, *4,* 34–41.

Frey, I. A., & Kolodney, R. L. Group treatment for the alienated children in the school. *International Journal of Group Psychotherapy,* 1966, *16* (3), 321–337.

Freyberger, H. Problem of group psychotherapy in primary organic diseases represented by constitutional adiposity. *Acta Psychotherapy,* 1958, *6,* 327–348.

Fried, E. Combined group and individual therapy with passive narcissistic patients. *International Journal of Group Psychotherapy,* 1955, *5,* 194–198.

Fried, E. Does woman's new self-concept call for new approaches in group psychotherapy? *International Journal of Group Psychotherapy,* 1974, *24* (3), 265–273.

Friedman, A. S. *Therapy with families of sexually acting-out girls.* New York: Springer, 1971.

Friedman, J. H., & Gerhart, L. The question box method of group therapy. *Mental Hygiene,* 1947, *31,* 246–256.

Fromm, E., & Shor, R. E. *Hypnosis: Research developments and perspectives.* Chicago: Aldine-Atherton, 1972.

Fuller, J. K. Extension of group therapy to parolees. *Prison World,* 1952, July–August, 8–11.

Fullmer, D. W. Family group consultation. *Elementary School Guidance and Counseling,* 1972, *7,* 130–136.

Gadpaille, W. J. Observations on the sequence of resistances in groups of adolescent delinquents. *International Journal of Group Psychotherapy,* 1959, *9,* 279–286.

Galbis, R. Quoted in *Medical Tribune,* January 5, 1970, *11,* 5.

Gans, R. W. The use of group cotherapists in the teaching of psychotherapy. *American Journal of Psychotherapy,* 1957, *9,* 618–628.

Gans, R. W. Group co-therapists and the therapeutic situation: A critical evaluation. *International Journal of Group Psychotherapy,* 1962, *12,* 82–90.

Ganung, C., Lakin, M., & Thompson, U. D. *Interpersonal involvement and sensitivity training.* Unpublished manuscript, Duke University, 1966.

Ganzarain, R., D'avanzo, H., Flores, O., & Ester, D. Study of effectiveness of group psychotherapy in the training of medical students. *International Journal of Group Psychotherapy,* 1959, *9,* 475–487.

Gauron, E. F., Breeden, S. A., & Brightwell, U. R. A married couple in separate therapy groups. *Journal of*

Family Counseling, 1975, *3*(1), 24–28.

Gazda, G. M. *The effect of short-term group counseling on prospective counselors.* Unpublished doctoral dissertation. University of Illinois, 1959.

Gazda, G. M. (Ed.). *Innovations to group psychotherapy.* Springfield, Ill.: Charles C Thomas, 1968.

Gazda, G. M., & Ohlsen, M. The effects of short-term group counseling on prospective counselors. *Personnel Guidance Journal,* 1961, *39,* 634–638.

Gazda, G., Parks, J., & Sisson, J. The use of a modified marathon in conjunction with group counseling in a short-term treatment of alcoholics. *Rehabilitation Counseling Bulletin,* 1971, 97–105.

Geitgey, D. A. *A study of some effects of sensitivity training on the performance of students in associate degree programs of nursing education.* Unpublished doctoral dissertation, University of California, Los Angeles, 1966.

Geller, J. J. A program of group psychotherapy in the treatment of chronic mental illness. *Psychiatry Quarterly,* 1949, *23,* 425–438.

Geller, J. J. Current status of group psychotherapy: Practice in the state hospitals for mental disease. *Group Psychotherapy,* 1950, *3,* 231–240.

Geller, J. J. Concerning the size of therapy groups. *International Journal of Group Psychotherapy,* 1951, *1,* 118–120.

Geller, R. E. Reaching the deaf: Report of an in-hospital group. *Mental Hygiene,* 1970, *54,* 388–392.

Gendlin, E. T., Beebe, J., III, Cassens, J., Klein, M., & Oberlander, M. Focusing ability in psychotherapy, personality and creativity. In J. M. Schlein (Ed.), *Research in psychotherapy* (Vol. 3). Washington: American Psychological Association, 1968.

Genevard, G., Schneider, P. B., Jordi, P., Delaloye, R., Genton, M., Gloor, C., & Villa, J. L. Contribution of group psychotherapy *to the comprehension of neurosis. Evolution Psychiatry* (PAR), 1961, *26,* 399–416.

Gerber, S. A., & Singer, D. Dynamic group counseling with mothers of students in special classes. *Corrective Psychiatry and Journal of Social Therapy,* 1969, *15,* 25-33.

Gersten, C. Group therapy with institutionalized juvenile delinquents. *Journal of Genetic Psychology,* 1952, *80,* 35–64.

Gerstenlauer, C. Group therapy with institutionalized male juvenile delinquents. Unpublished doctoral dissertation, New York University, 1950.

Getty, C., & Shannon, A. M. Cotherapy as an egalitarian relationship. *American Journal of Nursing,* 1969, *69,* 767–771.

Gewirtz, D. Methadone maintenance for heroin addicts. *Yale Law Journal,* 1969, *1175,* 78–79.

Ghaston, J. F., & Wells, H. G. A pilot project in parole group counseling. *American Journal of Corrections,* 1965, *3,* 14–18.

Gibb, J. R. Effects of role playing upon (a) role flexibility and upon (b) ability to conceptualize a new role. *American Psychologist,* 1952, *7,* 310.

Gibb, J. R. *Defense level and influence potential in small groups* (Research Reprint Series No. 3). Washington, D.C.: National Training Laboratories, 1960.

Gibb, J. R. The present status of T group theory. In L. P. Bradford, J. R. Gibb, & K. D. Benne (Eds.), *T group theory and laboratory method: Innovation in reeducation.* New York: John Wiley, 1964.

Gibb, J. R. Effects of human relations training. In A. Bergin & S. Garfield (Eds.), *Handbook of psychotherapy and behavior change.* New York: John Wiley, 1971.

Gibb, J. R., & Gibb, L. M. Emergence therapy: The TORI process in an emergent group. In G. M. Gazda (Ed.), *Basic approaches to group psychotherapy and group counseling.* Springfield, Ill.: Charles C Thomas, 1968. (a)

Gibb, J. R., & Gibb, L. M. Leaderless groups: Growth-centered values and potentials. In H. A. Otto & J. Mann (Eds.), *Ways of growth: Approaches to exploratory aware-*

ness. New York: Grossman, 1968. (b)

Gibb, J. R., & Gorman, A. W. *Effects of induced polarization in small groups upon accuracy of perception.* Paper read at American Psychological Association convention, September 1954.

Giberti, E. [Orientation Groups for Couples.] *Revista Lat-Americano Psicologia,* 1971, *3,* 145–162.

Gilbreath, S. H. Group counseling, dependence and college male underachievement. *Journal of Counseling Psychology,* 1967, *14,* 449–453.

Gilbreath, S. H. Appropriate and inappropriate group counseling with academic underachievers. *Journal of Counseling Psychology,* 1968, *15,* 506–511.

Ginott, H. G. *Group therapy with children: The theory and practice of play-therapy.* New York: McGraw-Hill, 1961.

Ginott, H. *Between parent and child.* New York: Avon, 1973.

Gitter, O. K. *Evaluation of three treatment approaches to dating anxiety and satisfaction.* Unpublished doctoral dissertation, University of Hawaii, 1976.

Gladstone, H. P. Educative psychotherapy with student nurse classes: An investigation of socially shared conflicts and value distortions. *Mental Hygiene,* 1962, *46,* 408–419.

Glaser, R. L. An experimental program of activity therapy in a child care center. *Child Welfare,* 1971, *1,* 290–297.

Glatzer, H. T. Discussion. *International Journal of Group Psychotherapy,* 1974, *24*(3), 281–287.

Glendening, S. E., & Wilson, A. J., III. Experiments in pre-marital counseling. *Social Casework,* 1972, *53,* 551–562.

Glenn, J. Values of group discussions with psychiatric aides in a mental hospital. *International Journal of Group Psychotherapy,* 1951, *1,* 254–263.

Gliedman, L. H. Concurrent and combined group treatment of chronic alcoholics and their wives. *International Journal of Group Psychotherapy,* 1957, *7,* 414–424.

Gliedman, L. H., Nash, H. T., & Webb, W. L. Group psychotherapy of male alcoholics and their wives. *Diseases of the Nervous System,* 1956, *17,* 90–93.

Gliedman, L. H., Rosenthal, D., Frank, J. D., & Nash, H. T. Group therapy of alcoholics with concurrent group meetings of their wives. *Quarterly Journal of Studies in Alcohol,* 1956, *17,* 655–670.

Glomset, D. Group therapy for obesity. *Journal of the Iowa Medical Society,* 1957, *47,* 496–501.

Golden, J. S., & Rosen, A. C. A group dynamics course for medical students. *International Journal of Group Psychotherapy,* 1975, *25*(3), 305–314.

Goldfarb, A. I. Group therapy with the old and aged. In H. I. Kaplan & B. J. Sadock (Eds.), *Comprehensive group psychotherapy.* Baltimore: Williams & Wilkins, 1971.

Goldner, R., & Kyle, E. A. A group approach to the cardiac patient. *Social Casework,* 1960, *41,* 346–349.

Gordon, G., & Bowman, K. The auxiliary treatment of psychotic women—Group therapy for their husbands. *California Medicine,* 1953, *78,* 303–308.

Gordon, T. Some theoretical notions regarding changes during group psychotherapy. *Group Psychotherapy,* 1951, *4,* 172–178.

Gordon, T. *Parent effectiveness training.* New York: Peter H. Wyden, 1970.

Gorer, G. *The revolutionary ideas of the Marquis de Sade.* London: Wishart, 1934.

Gorlow, L., Hoch, E. L., & Telschow, E. *The nature of non-directive group psychotherapy.* New York: Columbia University Press, 1952.

Gottlieb, A., & Pattison, E. M. Married couples group psychotherapy. *Archives of General Psychiatry,* 1966, *14,* 151–155.

Gottlieb, S. B. Response of married couples included in a group of single patients. *International Journal of Group Psychotherapy,* 1960, *10,* 143–159.

Gottschalk, L. A. Psychoanalytic notes on T groups at the Human

Relations Laboratory, Bethel, Maine. *Comprehensive Psychiatry*, 1966, *7*, 472.

Gottschalk, L. A. Some problems in the evaluation of psychoactive drugs, with or without psychotherapy, in the treatment of nonpsychotic personality disorders. In D. N. Efron, J. O. Cole, J. Levine, & J. R. Wittenborn (Eds.), *Psychopharmacology: A Review of Progress, 1957–67* (Public Health Service Publication No. 1836). Washington, D. C.: U. S. Government Printing Office, 1968.

Gottschalk, L. A., & Auerbach, A. H. *Methods of research in psychotherapy.* New York: Appleton-Century-Crofts, 1966.

Gottschalk, L. A., & Davidson, R. Sensitivity groups, encounter groups, training groups, marathon groups, and the laboratory movement. In H. I. Kaplan, & B. J. Sadock (Eds.), *Comprehensive group psychotherapy.* Baltimore: Williams & Wilkins, 1971.

Gottschalk, L. A., Glesser, C. C., & Stone, W. N. Studies of psychoactive drug effects on nonpsychiatric patients. In W. Evans & N. Kline (Eds.), *Psychopharmacology of the normal human.* Springfield, Ill.: Charles C Thomas, 1968.

Gottschalk, L. A., & Pattison, E. M. Psychiatric perspectives on T groups and the laboratory movement: An overview. *American Journal of Psychiatry*, 1969, *126*(6), 91–107.

Gottsegen, M. G., & Grasso, M. Group treatment of the mother-daughter relationship. *International Journal of Group Psychotherapy*, 1973, *23*, 69–81.

Gough, H. G. The adjective check list as a personality assessment technique. *Psychological Reports*, 1960, *6*, 107–122.

Gough, H. G., & Heilbrun, A. B. *The adjective check list manual.* Palo Alto, Calif.: Consulting Psychologists Press, 1965.

Gough, H. G., & Meschieri, L. Applicazioni d'ell adjective check list allo studio de fenomini economici e politici. *Estracto dell ballettino di psicologia applicanta*, N 79, 80, 81, 82, 1967.

Gough, G. H., & Riva, A. L'applicazioni dell adjective check list allo studio dell successo scolastico. *Estracto dell ballettino di psicologica applicata.* N 79, 80, 81, 82, 1967.

Grand, S. A. Lay group counseling. *American Journal of Corrections*, 1965, *27*(1), 14–16.

Grant, M. The group approach for weight control. *Group Psychotherapy*, 1951, *4*, 156–165.

Gratton, I., & Rizzo, A. E. Group therapy to young psychotic children. *International Journal of Group Psychotherapy*, 1969, *19*, 63–71.

Graziano, A. M. *Group behavior modification of children.* New York: Pergamon Press, 1972.

Green, R., & Fuller, M. Group therapy with feminine boys and their parents. *International Journal of Group Psychotherapy*, 1973, *23*, 54–68.

Greenbaum, H. Discussion of group psychotherapy with married couples. *Journal of Psychoanalysis in Groups*, 1966, *2*, 43–48.

Greene, R. J., & Crowder, D. L. Group psychotherapy with adolescents: An integrative approach. *Journal of Contemporary Psychology*, 1972, *5*, 55–61.

Greening, T. C., & Coffey, H. S. Working with an "impersonal T group." *Journal of Applied Behavioral Science*, 1966, *2*, 401–411.

Groen, J. J., & Pelsar, H. E. Experience with, and results of, group psychotherapy in patients with bronchial asthma. *Journal of Psychosomatic Research*, 1960, *4*, 191–205.

Grossman, W. K., & Karmiol, E. Group psychotherapy supervision and its effects on resident training. *American Journal of Psychiatry*, 1973, *130*, 920–921.

Grotjahn, M. The process of maturation in group psychotherapy and in the group therapist. *Psychiatry*, 1950, *13*, 63, 67.

Grotjahn, M. Special problems in the supervision of group psychotherapy. *Group Psychotherapy*, 1951, *3*, 308–313.

Grotjahn, M. Supervision of analytic group psychotherapy. *Group Psychotherapy*, 1960, *13*, 161, 222–240.

Grotjahn, M. Analytic group therapy with psychotherapists. *International Journal of Group Psychotherapy,* 1969, *19,* 326.

Grotjahn, M. Laughter in group psychotherapy. *International Journal of Group Psychotherapy,* 1971, *21,* 234–238. (a)

Grotjahn, M. The qualities of the group therapist. In H. I. Kaplan & B. J. Sadock (Eds.), *Comprehensive group psychotherapy.* Baltimore: Williams & Wilkins, 1971.

Grune, R. J., & Crowder, D. L. Group psychotherapy with adolescents: integrative approach. *Journal of Contemporary Psychotherapy,* 1972, *5,* 55–61.

Grunebaum, H. A soft-hearted review of hard-nosed research on groups. *International Journal of Group Psychotherapy,* 1975, *25*(2), 185–198.

Grunebaum, H., & Christ, J. Interpretation and the task of the therapist with couples. *International Journal of Group Psychotherapy,* 1968, *18,* 495–507.

Grunebaum, H., Christ, J., & Huber, N. Diagnosis and treatment planning for couples. *International Journal of Group Psychotherapy,* 1969, *192,* 185–201.

Grunewald, H., & Casella, B. Group counseling with parents. *Child Welfare,* 1958, *37,* 11–17.

Guerney, B. G. *Psychotherapeutic agents: New roles for nonprofessionals, parents, and teachers.* New York: Holt, Rinehart, & Winston, 1969.

Guilford, J. S. Group treatment versus individual initiative in the cessation of smoking. *Journal of Applied Psychology.*

Gula, M. Boy's house: The use of a group. *Mental Hygiene,* 1944, *28,* 430–437.

Gunther, B. *Sense relaxation below your mind.* New York: Macmillan, 1968.

Gunther, B. Sensory awakening and relaxation. In H. Otto & J. Mann, *Ways of growth approaches to expanding awareness.* New York: Viking Press, 1969.

Gunther, B. *How the West Is One.* New York: Macmillan, 1971.

Gurman, A. S. Group counseling with underachievers: A review and evaluation of methodology. *International Journal of Group Psychotherapy,* 1969, *19*(4), 463–473.

Gurman, A. S. Group marital therapy: Clinical and empirical implications for outcome research. *International Journal of Group Psychotherapy,* 1971, *21,* 174–189.

Gustaitis, R. *Turning on.* New York: Macmillan, 1969.

Guyer, E. G., Jr. *The effect of varying a therapeutic technique in group psychotherapy with hospitalized psychoneurotic patients.* Unpublished doctoral dissertation. Pennsylvania State University, 1956.

Haberman, P. W. Factors related to increased sobriety in group psychotherapy with alcoholics. *Journal of Clinical Psychology,* 1966, *22,* 229–234.

Hadden, S. B. Group psychotherapy. *Transactions of the American Neurology Association,* 1943, *69,* 132–135.

Hadden, S. B. Group psychotherapy: A superior method of treating larger numbers of neurotic patients. *American Journal of Psychiatry,* 1944, *101,* 68–72.

Hadden, S. B. The utilization of a therapy group in teaching psychotherapy. *American Journal of Psychiatry,* 1947, *103,* 644–651.

Hadden, S. B. Group therapy in prisons. *Proceedings of the American Prison Association,* 1948, 178–183.

Hadden, S. B. Dynamics of group psychotherapy (abstract). *Archives of Neurology and Psychiatry,* 1951, *65,* 125. (a)

Hadden, S. B. Group psychotherapy in general hospitals. *International Journal of Group Psychotherapy,* 1951, *1,* 31–36. (b)

Hadden, S. B. Historic background of group psychotherapy. *International Journal of Group Psychotherapy,* 1955, *5,* 162–168.

Hadden, S. B. Treatment of homosexuality by individual and group psychotherapy. *American Journal of Psychiatry,* 1958, *114,* 810–815.

Hadden, S. B: Treatment of male homosexuals in groups. *International Journal of Group Psychotherapy*, 1966, *16*, 13–18.

Haley, J. Marriage therapy. *Archives of General Psychiatry*, 1963, *8*, 213–222. (a)

Haley, J. *Strategies of psychotherapy.* New York: Grune & Stratton, 1963. (b)

Haley, J. *Changing families: A family therapy reader.* New York: Grune & Stratton, 1971.

Haley, J. Beginning and experienced family therapists. In A. M. Ferber, M. Mendelsohn & A. Napier (Eds.), *The book of family therapy.* New York: Jason Aronson, 1972.

Haley, J., & Hoffman, L. *Techniques of family therapy.* New York: Basic Books, 1967.

Hampden-Turner, C. The dramas of Delancey Street. *Journal of Humanistic Psychology*, 1976, *16*(1), 5–54.

Hampton, K. R. Comparison of the behavior of recidivists and non-recidivists during group psychotherapy in prison as reflected by therapist ratings. *Dissertation Abstracts International*, 1971, 560B.

Hanley, F. W. The treatment of obesity by individual and group procedures. *Canadian Psychiatric Association Journal*, 1967, *12*, 549–551.

Harari, C., & Harari, C. The co-therapist encounter: A catalyst for growth. In L. Blank, G. B. Gottsegen, & M. G. Gottsegen (Eds.), *Confrontation.* New York: Macmillan, 1971.

Harper, A. E., Jr. Role playing in the training of counselors. *Group Psychotherapy*, 1961, *14*, 129–137.

Harper, J. Embracement and enticement: A therapeutic nursery group for autistic children. *Slow Learning Child*, 1973, *20*, 173–176.

Harper, R. A. *Psychoanalysis and psychotherapy: 36 systems.* Englewood Cliffs, N. J.: Prentice-Hall, 1959.

Harper, R. A. *The new psychotherapies.* Englewood Cliffs, N. J.: Prentice-Hall, 1975.

Harris, H. I. Efficient psychotherapy for the large outpatient clinic. *England Journal of Medicine*, 1939, *221*, 1–15.

Harrison, R. The impact of the laboratory on perceptions of others by the experimental group. In C. Argyris (Ed.), *Interpersonal competence and organizational effectiveness.* Homewood, Ill.: Dorsey Press, 1962.

Harrison, R. Cognitive change and participation in a sensitivity-training laboratory. *Journal of Consulting Psychology*, 1966, *30*, 517–520.

Harrison, R. Problems in the design and interpretation of research on human relations training. In *Explorations in human relations training and research* (Vol. 1). Washington, D.C.: National Training Laboratory, 1967.

Harrison, R., & Oshry, B. J. *The impact of laboratory training on organizational behavior: Methodology and results* (mimeographed technical report). Washington, D.C.: National Training Laboratory, 1967.

Harrow, G. S. Psychodrama group therapy. *Group Psychotherapy*, 1952, *5*, 120–172.

Hartley, D., Roback, H. B., & Abramowitz, S. I. Deterioration effects in encounter groups. *American Psychologist*, 1976, 247–255.

Hartsook, J. E., Olch, D. R., & de Wolf, V. A. Personality characteristics of women's assertiveness training group participants. *Journal of Counseling Psychology*, 1976, *23*(4), 322–326.

Hawkey, L. The use of puppets in child psychotherapy. *British Journal of Medical Psychology*, 1951, *24*, 206–214.

Head, W. A. Sociodrama and group discussion with institutionalized delinquent adolescents. *Mental Hygiene*, 1962, *46*, 127–135.

Heaps, R. A., Rickabough, K., & Fuhriman, A. Academic recovery and client perceptions of group counselors. *Psychological Reports*, 1972, *30*, 691–694.

Hedquist, F. J., & Weinhold, B. K. Behavioral group counseling with socially anxious and unassertive college students. *Journal of Counseling Psychology*, 1970, *17*, 237–242.

Hefferman, A. An experiment in group therapy with mothers of diabetic children. *Acta Psychotherapy*, 1959, *7*, 155–164.

Heilfron, M. Co-therapy: The relationship between therapists. *International Journal of Group Psychotherapy*, 1969, *19*, 366–381.

Hendricks, S. J. A descriptive analysis of the process of client centered play therapy. *Dissertation Abstracts International*, 1972, 3689A.

Hersko, M. Group psychotherapy with delinquent adolescent girls. *American Journal of Orthopsychiatry*, 1962, *32*, 169–175.

Hewer, V. H. Group counseling, individual counseling and a college class in vocations. *Personnel and Guidance Journal*, 1959, *13*, 660–665.

Hilgard, J. R. Better adjusted peers as resources in group therapy with adolescents. *Journal of Psychology*, 1969, *73*, 75–100.

Hilgard, J. R. *Personality and hypnosis: A study of imaginative involvement.* Chicago: University of Chicago Press, 1970.

Hill, B. An experiment in treating seriously disturbed juvenile delinquent boys. *Psychiatry Quarterly Supplement*, 1953, *27*, 105–119.

Hinds, W. C., & Roehlke, H. J. A learning theory approach to group counseling with elementary school children. *Journal of Counseling Psychology*, 1970, *17*(1), 49–55.

Hinkle, J. E., & Moore, M. A student couples program. *The Family Coordinator*, 1971, *20*, 153–158.

Hobbs, N. Group psychotherapy in preventative mental hygiene. *Teachers College Records*, 1948, *50*, 170–178.

Hobbs, N. Insight in short-term psychotherapy (abstract). *American Psychology*, 1949, *4*, 273.

Hobbs, N. Group-centered psychotherapy. In C. R. Rogers, *Client centered psychotherapy.* Boston: Houghton Mifflin, 1951.

Hobbs, N. Client-centered psychotherapy. In J. L. McCary & D. E. Sheer, *Six approaches to psychotherapy.* New York: Dryden Press, 1955.

Hodgman, S. J., & Stewart, W. H. The adolescent screening group. *International Journal of Group Psychotherapy*, 1972, *22*, 177–185.

Hollon, T. H. Modified group therapy in the treatment of patients on chronic hemodialysis. *American Journal of Psychotherapy*, 1972, *26*, 501–510.

Holt, H., & Winick, C. Group psychotherapy with obese women. *Archives of General Psychiatry*, 1961, *5*, 156, 160.

Hooper, D., & Sheldon, A. A study of group psychotherapy with married couples. II: Evaluating the changes. *International Journal of Social Psychiatry*, 1970, *16*, 299–305.

Hooper, D., Sheldon, A., & Koumens, A. J. R. A study of group psychotherapy with married couples, I. *International Journal of Social Psychiatry*, 1968–1969, *15*(1), 57–68.

Hora, T. Existential group psychotherapy. *American Journal of Psychotherapy*, 1959, *13*, 83–92.

Hora, T. Existential psychiatry and group psychotherapy. In H. M. Ruitenbeek (Ed.), *Psychoanalysis and existential philosophy.* New York: Sutton, 1962.

Horn, P. How to enhance healthy sexuality: Behavior modification in the bedroom. *Psychology Today*, November 1975, pp. 94–95.

Horney, K. *Self Analysis.* New York: Norton 1942.

House, R. J. T group training: *A review of the empiric evidence and an appraisal.* Unpublished manuscript, University of Michigan, Bureau of Industrial Relations, 1964.

House, R. J. T group education and leadership effectiveness: A review of the empiric literature and a critical evaluation. *Personnel Psychology*, 1967, *20*, 1–32.

House, R. M. The effects of nondirective group play therapy upon the sociometric status and self-concept of selected second-grade children. *Dissertation Abstracts International*, 1970, *31*, 268A.

Houts, P. S. & Serber, M. (Eds.), *After the turn on, what? Learning perspectives on humanistic groups.* Champaign, Ill.: Research Press, 1972.

Howard, J. *Please touch.* New York: McGraw-Hill, 1970.

Hoy, R. M. The personality of impatient alcoholics in relation to group psychotherapy as measured by the I.G.P.F. *Quarterly Journal for Studies on Alcohol,* 1969, *40,* 401–407.

Hulse, W. Group psychotherapy with soldiers and veterans. *Military Surgery,* 1948, *103,* 116–121.

Hulse, W. C. The social meaning of current methods of group psychotherapy. *Group Psychotherapy,* 1950, *3,* 56. (a)

Hulse, W. C. The therapeutic management of group tension. *American Journal of Orthopsychiatry,* 1950, *20,* 834–838. (b)

Hulse, W. C. International aspects of group psychotherapy. *International Journal of Group Psychotherapy,* 1951, *1,* 172–177.

Hulse, W. C. Group psychotherapy at the 4th International Congress on Mental Health, Mexico City, December 11–19, 1951, *International Journal of Group Psychotherapy,* 1952, *2,* 270–272.

Hulse, W. C., Ludlow, W. V., Rindsberg, B. K., & Epstein, N. B. Transference relations in a group of female patients to male and female co-leaders. *International Journal of Group Psychotherapy,* 1956, *6,* 430–435.

Igersheimer, W. W. Analytically oriented group psychotherapy for patients with psychosomatic illness. I: The selection of patients and the forming of groups. *International Journal of Group Psychotherapy,* 1954, *9,* 71–92.

Igersheimer, W. W. Group psychotherapy for nonalcoholic wives of alcoholics. *Quarterly Journal of Studies in Alcohol,* 1959, *20,* 77–85.

Illing, H. A. The prisoner in the group. *Group,* 1951, *13*(4), 3–8.

Illing, H. A., & Miles, J. E. Outpatient group psychotherapy with sex offenders. *International Journal of Social Psychiatry,* 1969, *15,* 258–263.

Jacks, I. Accessibility to group psychotherapy among adolescent offenders in a correctional institution. *American Journal of Orthopsychiatry,* 1963, *33,* 567–568.

Jackson, B., & Van Zoost, B. Self-regulated teaching of others as a means of improving study habits. *Journal of Counseling Psychology,* 1974, *21*(6), 489–493.

Jackson, D. The marital quid pro quo. In G. Zuk & I. Boszormenyi-nagi (Eds.), *Family therapy for disturbed families.* Palo Alto, Calif.: Science and Behavior Books, 1966.

Jackson, D. (Ed.). *Communication, family and marriage* (Vol. 1). Palo Alto, Calif.: Science and Behavior Books, 1968.

Jackson, E. N. The therapeutic function in preaching. *Pastoral Psychology,* 1950, *1,* 36–39.

Jackson, J., & Grotjahn, M. Re-enactment of the marriage neurosis in group psychotherapy. *Journal of Nervous and Mental Diseases,* 1958, *127,* 503–510.

Jacobsen, E. *Progressive relaxation.* Chicago: University of Chicago Press, 1938.

Jacobson, J. R. Group therapy in the elementary schools. *Psychiatric Quarterly,* 1945, *19,* 3–16.

Jacobson, J. R., & Wright, K. W. Review of a year of group psychotherapy. *Psychiatric Quarterly,* 1942, *16,* 744–764.

Jacobson, J. R., & Wright, K. W. Review of a year of group psychotherapy. *Elgin State Hospital Papers,* 1944, *5,* 26–44.

Janet, P. *Psychological healing.* New York: Macmillan, 1925.

Janis, I. L., & Mann, L. Effectiveness of emotional role playing in modifying smoking habits and attitudes. *Journal of Experimental Research in Personality,* 1965, *1,* 84–90.

Janney, H. M., & Bemis, C. E. Efficient use of the prison psychiatrist. *Prison World,* January–February 1954, p. 4.

Jensen, S. E. A treatment program for alcoholics in a mental hospital. *Quarterly Journal of Studies in Alcohol,* 1962, *23,* 315–320.

Jensen, S. E., Roden, F. K., & Multari, G. Treatment of severely disturbed children in a community. *Canadian*

Psychiatric Association Journal, 1965, *10*, 325–330.

Jew, C. C., Clanon, T. L., & Mattocks, A. L. The effectiveness of group psychotherapy in a correctional institution. *American Journal of Psychiatry,* 1972, *129*, 114–117.

Joel, W., & Shapiro, D. Some principles and procedures for group psychotherapy. *Journal of Psychology,* 1950, *29*, 77–88.

Johnsgard, K. W., & Schumacher, R. M. The experience of intimacy in group psychotherapy with male homosexuals. *Psychotherapy: Theory, Research and Practice,* 1970, *7*, 173–176.

Johnson, P. E. Introduction. In J. H. Pratt & P. E. Johnson, *A 20 year experiment in group therapy.* Boston: New England Medical Center, 1950.

Johnson, P. E. *Psychology of religion.* New York: Abington Press, 1959.

Johnston, M. Experiment with narcotic addicts. *American Journal of Psychotherapy,* 1951, *5*, 24–31.

Jones, F. D., & Peters, H. N. An experimental evaluation of group psychotherapy. *Journal of Abnormal and Social Psychology,* 1952, *47*, 345–353.

Jones, M. Group psychotherapy. *British Medical Journal,* 1942, *2*, 276–278.

Jones, M. Group treatment with particular reference to group projective methods. *American Journal of Psychiatry,* 1944, *101*, 293–299.

Jones, M. Emotional catharsis and re-education in the neuroses with the help of group methods. *British Journal of Medical Psychology,* 1948, *21*, 104–110.

Jordan, P. H., Campbell, M., & Hodge, E. J. A therapeutically oriented group technique for the diagnostic evaluation of parents of disturbed children. *Group Psychotherapy,* 1957, *10*, 114–128.

Joseph H., & Dole, V. P. Methadone patients on probation and parole. *Federal Probation,* 1970, *34*, 42–48.

Joseph, H., & Heimlich, E. P. The therapeutic use of music with "treatment resistant" children. *American Journal of Mental Deficiency,* 1959, *64*, 41–49.

Kadis, A. L., Krasner, J. D., Winick, C., & Foulkes, S. H. *A practicum of group psychotherapy.* New York: Harper & Row, 1963.

Kadis, A., & Lazarfeld, S. The group as a psychotherapeutic factor in counseling work. *Nervous Child,* 1945, *4*, 228–235.

Kadis, A., & Markowitz, M. The therapeutic impact of a co-therapist interaction in a complex group. In J. L. Moreno (Ed.), *The international handbook of group psychotherapy.* New York: Philosophical Library, 1966.

Kagan, E., & Zaks, M. S. Couple multicouple therapy for marriages in crisis. *Psychotherapy: Theory, Research and Practice,* 1972, *9*, 332–336.

Kagan, N. Group procedures. *Review of Educational Research,* 1966, *36*, 274–287.

Kahn, J., Buchmueller, A. D., & Gildea, M. Group therapy for parents of behavior problem children in public schools: Failure of the method in a Negro school. *American Journal of Psychiatry,* 1951, *108*, 351–357.

Kamin, S. H., Llewelleyn, C. J., & Sledge, W. L. Group dynamics in the treatment of epilepsy. *Journal of Pediatrics,* 1953, *53*, 410–412.

Kaneshige, E. Cultural factors in group counseling and interaction. *Personnel and Guidance Journal,* 1973, *51*, 407–412.

Kanzer, M. Freud: The first psychoanalysis group leader. In H. I. Kaplan & B. J. Sadock (Eds.), *Comprehensive group psychotherapy.* Baltimore: Williams & Wilkins, 1971.

Kaplan, H. I., & Sadock, B. J. *Comprehensive group psychotherapy.* Baltimore: Williams & Wilkins, 1971.

Kaplan, H. I., & Sadock, B. J. *Sensitivity through encounter and marathon.* New York: Aronson, Modern Group Books, 1972.

Kaplan, H. S. *The new sex therapy.* New York: Brunner/Mazel, 1974.

Karpman, B. Principles and aims of criminal psychopathology. *Journal of Criminal Psychopathology,* 1940, *1*, 187–218.

Karush, A., Daniels, G. E., O'Connor, J. F., & Stern, L. O. The response to psychotherapy in chronic ulcerative colitis. I: Pretreatment factors. *Psychosomatic Medicine,* 1968, *30,* 255–264.

Karush, A., Daniels, G. E., O'Connor, J. D., & Stern, L. O. The response to psychotherapy in chronic ulcerative colitis. II: Factors arising from the therapeutic situation. *Psychosomatic Medicine,* 1969, *31,* 201–221.

Kass, D. J., & Abroms, G. M. Behavioral group treatment of hysteria. *Archives of General Psychiatry,* 1972, *26,* 42–50.

Katahn, M., Strenger, S., & Cherry, W. Group counseling and behavior therapy with test-anxious college students. *Journal of Consulting Psychology,* 1966, *30,* 544–549.

Kaufman, E. A psychiatrist views an addict self-help program. *American Journal of Psychiatry,* 1972, *128,* 846–852.

Kaufman, P. N., & Deutsch, A. L. Group therapy for pregnant unwed adolescents in the prenatal clinic of a general hospital. *International Journal of Group Psychotherapy,* 1967, *17,* 309–320.

Kehres, J. E. Differential effects of group counseling methods with black male adolescents. *Dissertation Abstracts International,* 1972, 1440A.

Kennedy, M. L. The organization and administration of a group treatment program. *Journal of Correctional Education,* 1951, *3,* 14–19.

Kessler, S. Divorce adjustment groups. *Personnel and Guidance Journal,* 1976, *10,* 251–256.

Ketai, R. Peer observed psychotherapy with institutionalized narcotic addicts. *Archives of General Psychiatry,* 1973, *29,* 51–53.

Keutzer, C. S., Lichtenstein, E., & Mees, H. L. Modification of smoking behavior: A review. *Psychological Bulletin,* 1968, *70,* 520–523.

Kibel, H. D. Group psychotherapy as an adjunct to milieu treatment with chronic schizophrenics. *Psychiatric Quarterly,* 1968, *42,* 338–351.

Kiernan, J. G. Limitations of the Emmanuel movement. *American Journal of Clinical Medicine,* 1909, *16,* 1088–1090.

Kihn, B. Group therapy in epilepsy. *Acta Psychotherapy* (Basel), 1959, 7 (Suppl.) Pt. 2, 183–195.

King, C. H. Activity group therapy with a schizophrenic boy. *International Journal of Group Psychotherapy,* 1959, *9,* 184–194.

King, M. R. Trends in medical correctional work. *Newsletter of the Medical Correctional Association,* 1953, 1 ff.

Klapman, J. W. *Group psychotherapy: Theory and practice.* New York: Grune & Stratton, 1946.

Klapman, J. W. Didactic group psychotherapy. *Diseases of the Nervous System,* 1950, *11,* 35–41.(a)

Klapman, J. W. *Social adjustment.* Chicago: Resurgo Association, 1950. (b)

Klapman, J. W. Group psychotherapy: Social activities as an adjunct to treatment. *Group Psychotherapy,* 1951, *3,* 327–338.

Klapman, J. W. Psychiatric social club therapy. *Group Psychotherapy,* 1953, *6,* 43–49.

Klapman, J. W., & Meyer, R. E. The team approach in group psychotherapy. *Diseases of the Nervous System,* 1957, *18,* 95–103.

Klein, H. S. Psychogenic factors on dermatitis and their treatment by group therapy. *British Journal of Medical Psychology,* 1949, *22,* 32–52.

Kline, N. S. Psychodrama for mental hospitals. *Journal of Clinical Psychology,* 1947, *8,* 817–825.

Kline, N. Some hazards in group psychotherapy. *International Journal of Group Psychotherapy,* 1952, *2,* 111–115.

Kline, N. S., & Dreyfus, A. Group psychotherapy in Veterans Administration hospitals. *American Journal of Psychiatry,* 1948, *104,* 618–622.

Klopfer, W. G. The efficacy of group therapy as indicated by group Rorschach records. *Rorschach Research Exchange,* 1945, *9,* 207–209.

Knowles, E. S. Research since 1960: A bibliography of research on human relations training. In *Explorations in human relations research.* Washington, D.C.: National Training Laboratories, 1967.

Koch, S. The image of man implicit in encounter group theory. *Journal of Humanistic Psychology,* 1971, *11,* 109–127.

Koegler, R. R., & Williamson, E. R. A group approach to helping emotionally disturbed Spanish-speaking patients. *Hospital and Community Psychiatry,* 1973, *24,* 334–336.

Koenig, K. P., & Masters, J. Experimental treatment of habitual smoking. *Behavior Research and Therapy,* 1965, *3,* 235–243.

Kohn, R. Treatment of married couples in a group. *Group Process,* 1971, *4,* 96–105.

Kolodney, E. Group treatment of mothers as a supplement to child psychotherapy. *Mental Hygiene,* 1944, *28,* 437–444.

Komechak, M. G. The activity interaction group. *Elementary School Guidance and Counseling,* 1971, *6*(1), 1–7.

Konopka, G. Group therapy in overcoming social and cultural tensions. *American Journal of Orthopsychiatry,* 1947, *17,* 693–699.

Konopka, G. *Therapeutic group work with children.* Minneapolis: University of Minnesota Press, 1949.

Konopka, G. *Group work in the institution: A modern challenge,* New York: Whiteside, 1954.

Kotkov, B. Techniques and explanatory concepts of short-term group psychotherapy. *Journal of Psychology,* 1949, *28,* 369–381.

Kotkov, B. A bibliography for the student of group therapy. *Journal of Clinical Psychology,* 1950, *6,* 77–91.

Kotkov, B. Experiences with group psychotherapy with obese. *Psychosomatic Medicine,* 1953, *15,* 243–251. (a)

Kotkov, B. Group psychotherapy with wayward girls. *Diseases of the Nervous System,* 1953, *14,* 308–312. (b)

Kraak, B. [Nondirective group therapy with institutionalized children.] *Z. Exp. Angew. Psychology,* 1961, *8,* 595–622.

Kraft, I. A. Some special considerations in adolescent group psychotherapy. *International Journal of Group Psychotherapy,* 1961, *11,* 196–203.

Kraft, I. A. Multiple impact therapy as a teaching device. *American Psychiatric Association Research Report,* 1966, *20,* 218–222.

Kraft, I. A. An overview of group therapy with adolescents. *International Journal of Group Psychotherapy,* 1968, *18,* 461–472.

Kraft, I. A. Child and adolescent group psychotherapy. In H. I. Kaplan & B. J. Sadock, *Comprehensive group psychotherapy.* Baltimore: Williams & Wilkins, 1971.

Kramer, H. C. The microlab—uses in student personnel. *College Student Journal,* 1972, *6,* 62–65.

Kramer, J., Bass, A., & Berecochea, B. A. Civil commitment for addicts: The California program. *American Journal of Psychiatry,* 1968, *125,* 816–824.

Kraus, A. R. Experimental study of the effect of group therapy with chronic psychotic patients. *International Journal of Group Psychotherapy,* 1959, *9,* 293–302.

Krevelon, A. V. [Group psychological aspects in the treatment of neurotic youngsters.] *Zeitung Psychotherapie und Medical Psychologye,* 1962, *12,* 186–194.

Krider, J. W., Jr. Desensitizing and presensitizing the schizogenic family system. *Social Casework,* 1971, *52,* 370–376.

Kwatkowska, H. Y. Family art therapy: Experiments with a new technique. *Bulletin of Art Therapy,* 1962, *1,* 3.

L'Acoursiere, R. A group method to facilitate learning during the stages of a psychiatric affiliation. *International Journal of Group Psychotherapy,* 1974, *24*(3), 342–351.

Lakin, M. *Participant's perception of group process in group sensitivity training: A case study.* Unpublished manuscript, Duke University, 1960.

Lakin, M. Some ethical issues in sensitivity training. *American Psychology,* 1969, *42,* 923–931.

Lakin, M. *Interpersonal encounter.* New York: McGraw-Hill, 1972.

Lakin, M., & Carson, R. C. *Some effects of group sensitivity training experience.* Paper presented at the meeting of the Southeastern Psychological Association, Miami Beach, Fla., April 1963.

Lakin, M., & Carson, R. C. A participant's perception of group process in group sensitivity training. *International Journal of Group Psychotherapy*, 1964, *14*(1), 116–122.

Lakin, M., Lomranz, J., & Lieberman, M. *Arab and Jew in Israel: A case study in human relations approach to conflict*. (Middle East Area Studies, Series 1.) New York: American Academic Association for Peace in the Middle East, June 1969.

Lakin, M., Thompson, L., Thompson, V., & Lomranz, J. *The person in the sensitivity training group, change, and the training culture*. Unpublished manuscript, Duke University, Department of Psychology, 1970.

Langen, D. Difficulties in the training of group psychotherapists. *Zeitung Psychotherapie und Medical Psychologye*, 1963, *13*, 125–127.

Langrad, J., Lowinson, J., Brill, L., & Joseph, H. Methadone maintenance from research to treatment. In L. Brill & L. Lieberman (Eds.), *The treatment of drug addition and drug abuse*. New York: Behavioral Publications, 1971.

Lassner, R. Playwriting and acting as diagnostic therapeutic techniques with delinquents. *Journal of Clinical Psychology*, 1947, *3*, 349–356.

Lassner, R. Psychodrama in prison. *Group Psychotherapy*, 1950, *3*, 77–91.

Latendresse, J. D., & Kennedy, D. F. Free discussion in teaching group therapy to residents. *Diseases of the Nervous System*, 1961, *22*, 527–529.

Lawton, M. P. Group methods in smoking withdrawal. *Archives of Environmental Health*, 1967, *14*, 258–265.

Lazarus, A. A. The use of systematic desensitization in psychotherapy. *South African Medical Journal*, 1957, *31*, 934–937.

Lazarus, A. A. Group therapy of phobic disorders by systematic desensitization. *Journal of Abnormal and Social Psychology*, 1961, *63*, 504–510.

Lazarus, A. A. Crucial procedural factors in desensitization therapy. *Behavior Research and Therapy*, 1964, *2*, 65.

Lazarus, A. A. Behavior therapy in groups. In G. M. Gazda (Ed.), *Basic approaches to group psychotherapy and group counseling*. Springfield, Ill.: Charles C Thomas, 1968.

Lazarus, A. A. *Behavior therapy and beyond*. New York: McGraw-Hill, 1971.

Lazell, E. W. The group treatment of dementia praecox. *Psychoanalytic Review*, 1921, *8*, 168–179.

Leal, M. R. M. Group analytic play therapy with pre-adolescent girls. *International Journal of Group Psychotherapy*, 1966, *16*, 58–64.

Lederman, D. G. Small group observation as a diagnostic technique. *American Journal of Mental Deficiency*, 1958, *63*, 64–71.

Lee, H. The effect of recognition in the treatment of neurasthenia. *Acta Psychologica Sinica*, 1960, *1*, 36–45.

Leeman, C. P. Dependency, anger, and denial in pregnant diabetic women: A group approach. *Psychiatric Quarterly*, 1970, *44*, 1–12.

Lehrer-Carle, I. Group music with schizophrenics. *Journal of Contemporary Psychology*, 1971, *2*, 111–116.

Lehrman, N. S., & Friedman, J. H. A treatment-focused geriatric program in a state mental hospital. *Mental Health Digest*, 1970, *2*(2), 8–10.

Leichter, E. Group psychotherapy with married couples. *International Journal of Group Psychotherapy*, 1962, *12*, 151–155.

Leichter, E. Use of group dynamics in the training and supervision of group therapists in a social agency. *International Journal of Group Psychotherapy*, 1963, *13*, 74–79.

Leichter, E. Treatment of married couples groups. *Family Coordinator*, 1973, *22*, 31–42.

LeMay, M. L., & Weigal, R. G. Group counseling with high and low ability freshmen. *Journal of Educational Research*, 1966, *59*, 429.

Lerner, A. An experiment in group counseling with male alcoholic inmates. *Federal Probation,* September 1953, pp. 37–39. (a)

Lerner, A. An exploratory approach in group counseling with male alcoholic inmates in a city jail. *Quarterly Journal of Studies in Alcohol,* 1953, *14,* 427–467. (b)

Lett, W. R. The relevance and structure of human relations training in teacher education. *Australian Psychologist,* 1973, *8,* 17–27.

Levin, S., & Kanter, S. S. Some general considerations in the supervision of beginning group psychotherapists. *International Journal of Group Psychotherapy,* 1964, *14,* 318–331.

Levitsky, A., & Perls, F. The rules and games of gestalt therapy. In H. I. Ruitenbeek, *Group therapy today.* New York: Atherton, 1971.

Lewin, K. *Resolving social conflict.* New York: Harper, 1948.

Lewin, K. *Field theory in social science.* New York: Harper & Bros., 1951.

Lewin, K., Lippitt, R., & White, R. Patterns of aggressive behavior in experimentally created social climates. *Journal of Social Psychology,* 1939, *10,* 271–299.

Lewis, H., & Streitfeld, H. *Growth games.* New York: Bantam Books, 1972.

Lewis, J. Effects of group procedures with parents of MR children. *Mental Retardation,* 1972, *6,* 14–15.

Libo, S. S. Family group therapy for children with self-induced seizures. *American Journal of Orthopsychiatry,* 1971, *41,* 506–509.

Lieberman, M. A., Yalom, I. D., & Miles, M. B. The impact of encounter groups on participants. *Journal of Applied Behavioral Science,* 1972, *8,* 29–50.

Lieberman, M. A., Yalom, I. D., & Miles, M. *Encounter groups: First facts.* New York: Basic Books, 1973.

Lievano, J. Group psychotherapy with adolescents in an industrial school for delinquent boys. *Adolescence,* 1970, *5,* 231–252.

Lifton, N., & Smolen, E. M. Group psychotherapy with schizophrenic children. *International Journal of Group Psychotherapy,* 1966, *16*(1), 23–41.

Linden, M. E. Group psychotherapy with institutionalized senile women. *International Journal of Group Psychotherapy,* 1953, *3,* 150–170.

Linden, M. E. *Geriatrics in the field of group psychotherapy.* New York: International Universities Press, 1956.

Lindenauer, G., & Caine, E. Human relations training in teacher education. *Journal of Emotional Education,* 1973, *13,* 27–37.

Lindner, R. *Rebel without a cause.* New York: Grune & Stratton, 1944.

Lipkin, S. Notes on group psychotherapy. *Journal of Nervous and Mental Disorders,* 1948, *107,* 459–479.

Lipnitzky, S. J. Psychotherapy in an institution for mentally defective patients. *Lost and Found,* 1940, *3,* 5–6.

Lippitt, R. L. *Training in community relations.* New York: Harper & Row, 1949.

Lippitt, R., & Clancy, C. Psychodrama in the kindergarten and nursery schools. *Group Psychotherapy,* 1954, *7,* 262–290.

Lipschutz, D. M. Group psychotherapy as an auxiliary aid in psychoanalysis. *International Journal of Group Psychotherapy,* 1952, *2,* 316–323.

Litman, R. E. Psychotherapy of a homosexual man in a heterosexual group. *International Journal of Group Psychotherapy,* 1961, *11,* 440–451.

Logan, D. G. A pilot methadone program to introduce comprehensive addiction treatment. *Hospital and Community Psychiatry,* 1972, *23,* 76–79.

Loomis, T. P. *Skin conductance and the effects of time distribution on encounter group learning: Marathons vs. spaced groups.* Unpublished doctoral dissertation, University of Hawaii, 1976.

Low, A. A. Group psychotherapy. *Illinois Psychiatry Journal,* 1941, *1,* 3–4.

Low, A. A. *Mental health through will-training.* Boston: Christopher, 1952.

Low, P., & Low, M. Treatment of married couples in a group run by a husband and wife. *International*

Journal of Group Psychotherapy, 1975, *25*(1), 54–66.

Lowen, A. *The betrayal of the body*, New York: Macmillan, 1967.

Lowen, A. Bioenergetic group therapy. In H. M. Ruitenbeek (Ed.), *Group therapy today*. New York: Atherton, 1971.

Lowinson, J., & Zwerling, I. Group therapy with narcotic addicts. In H. I. Kaplan & B. J. Sadock (Eds.), *Comprehensive group psychotherapy*. Baltimore: Williams & Wilkins, 1971.

Lowrey, L. G. Group therapy for mothers. *American Journal of Orthopsychiatry*, 1944, *14*, 589–592.

Lubin, B., & Eddy, W. B. The laboratory training model: Rationale, method and some thoughts for the future. *International Journal of Group Psychotherapy*, 1970, *20*, 305–339.

Lubin, B., & Lubin, A. W. *Group psychotherapy: A bibliography*. East Lansing: Michigan State University Press, 1966.

Lubin, B., & Lubin, A. W. The group psychotherapy literature; 1972. *International Journal of Group Psychotherapy*, 1973, *23*, 474–513.

Lubin, B., & Slominski, A. A counseling program with adult male cerebral palsied patients. *Cerebral Palsy Review*, 1960, *21*, 3–10.

Lubin, B., & Zuckerman, M. Level of emotional arousal in laboratory training. *Journal of Applied Behavioral Science*, 1969, *5*, 483–490.

Luchins, A. S. A course in group psychotherapy: Method, content and results. *Journal of Clinical Psychology*, 1946, *2*, 231–239.

Luchins, A. S. Methods of studying the progress and outcomes of a group psychotherapy program. *Journal of Consulting Psychology*, 1947, *11*, 173–183.

Luchins, A. S. Restructuring social perceptions: A group psychotherapy technique. *Journal of Consulting Psychology*, 1950, *14*, 446–451.

Luchins, A. S. *Group therapy: A guide*. New York: Random House, 1964.

Lundin, W. H., & Aronov, B. M. The use of co-therapists in group psychotherapy. *Journal of Consulting Psychology*, 1952, *16*, 76–80.

Lurie, A., & Ron, H. Family group counseling of discharged schizophrenic young adults and their parents. *Social Psychiatry*, 1971, *6*, 88–92.

Lynch, G., & Waxenberg, B. Marital therapy with the aging: A case study. *Psychotherapy: Theory, Research and Practice*, 1971, *8*, 59–63.

Lyon, W. Group therapy for students in clinical psychology. *American Psychologist*, 1956, *11*, 290–291.

MacDonald, D. E. Group psychotherapy with wives of alcoholics. *Quarterly Journal of Studies in Alcohol*, 1958, *19*, 125–132.

MacGregor, R. Group and family therapy: Moving into the present and letting go of the past. *International Journal of Group Psychotherapy*, 1970, *20*, 495–515.

MacLennan, B. W. Co-therapy. *International Journal of Group Psychotherapy*, 1965, *15*, 154.

MacLennan, B. W. Group approach to the problems of socially deprived youth. *International Journal of Group Psychotherapy*, 1968, *18*, 481–494.

MacLennan, B. W., & Felsenfeld, N. *Group counseling and psychotherapy with adolescents*. New York: Columbia University Press, 1968.

MacLennan, B. W., & Klein, W. L. Utilization of groups in job training for the socially deprived. *International Journal of Group Psychotherapy*, 1965, *15*, 424–433.

MacLennan, B. W., & Levy, N. The group psychotherapy literature: 1969. *International Journal of Group Psychotherapy*, 1970, *20*, 372–411.

MacLennan, B. W., & Levy, N. The group psychotherapy literature: 1970. *International Journal of Group Psychotherapy*, 1971, *21*, 345–380.

Maliver, B. L. *The encounter game*, New York: Stein & Day, 1973.

Mally, M. A., & Strehl, C. B. Evaluation of a three-year group therapy program for multiple sclerosis patients. *International Journal of Group Psychotherapy*, 1963, *13*, 328–334.

Manaster, A. The diagnostic group in a rehabilitation center for visually handicapped persons. *New outlook for the blind*, 1971, *65*, 261–264.

Manaster, A. Therapy with the senile geriatric patient. *International Journal of Group Psychotherapy*, 1972, *22*, 250–257.

Manaster, A., & Kucharis, S. Experiential methods in group counseling with blind children. *New outlook for the blind*, 1972, *66*, 15–19.

Mann, J. H. The effect of role playing experience on self-rating of interpersonal adjustment. *Group Psychotherapy*, 1958, *11*, 27–32.

Mann, L. The effects of emotional role playing experience on desire to modify smoking habits. *Journal of Experimental Social Psychology*, 1967, *3*, 334–348.

Mann, L., & Janis, I. L. A follow-up study on the long-term effects of emotional role playing. *Journal of Personality and Social Psychology*, 1968, *8*, 339–342.

Mann, P. H., Beaber, J. D., & Jacobson, M. D. The effect of group counseling on educable mentally retarded boys' self-concepts. *Exceptional Children*, 1969, *35*(5), 359–366.

Markoff, E. L. Synanon in drug addiction. *Current Psychiatric Therapy*, 1969, *9*, 261–273.

Marsh, L. C. Group treatment of the psychoses by the psychological equivalent of the revival. *Mental Hygiene*, 1931, *15*, 328–349.

Marsh, L. C. An experiment in the group treatment of patients at Worcester St. Hospital. *Mental Hygiene*, 1933, *17*, 396–416.

Marsh, L. C. Group therapy and the psychiatric clinic. *Journal of Nervous and Mental Diseases*, 1935, *81*, 381–393.

Martinson, R., & O'Brien, W. J. Staff training and correctional change. Institute for the Study of Crime and Delinquency, Los Angeles, 1966.

Massarik, F. Explorations in human relations training and research. In *A sensitivity training impact model: Some first (and second) thoughts on the evaluation of sensitivity training* (No. 3). Washington, D.C.: National Training Laboratories and National Education Association, 1965.

Masters, W. H., & Johnson, V. E. *Human sexual inadequacy*. Boston: Little, Brown, 1970.

Masters, W. H., & Johnson, V. E. *Human sexual response*, Boston: Little, Brown, 1970.

Mathis, J. L., & Collins, M. Mandatory group therapy for exhibitionists. *American Journal of Psychiatry*, 1970, *126*, 1162–1167.

Mathis, J. L., & Collins, M. Progressive phases in the group therapy of exhibitionists. *International Journal of Group Psychotherapy*, 1970, *20*, 163–169.

Mattsson, A., & Angle, D. P. Group therapy with parents of hemophiliacs: Therapeutic process and observations of parental adaptation to chronic illness in children. *Journal of Child Psychiatry*, 1972, *11*, 537–557.

McCann, W. H. The round-table technique in group psychotherapy. *Group Psychotherapy*, 1953, *5*, 233–239.

McCann, W. H., & Almada, A. A. Round table psychotherapy: A technique in group psychotherapy. *Journal of Consulting Psychology*, 1950, *14*, 421–435.

McCarthy, R. G. Group therapy in an out-patient clinic for the treatment of alcoholism. *Quarterly Journal of Studies in Alcohol*, 1946, 7, 98–109.

McCarthy, R. G. Group therapy in alcoholism. *Quarterly Journal of Studies in Alcohol*, 1949, *10*, 68–108, 1950, *11*, 119–140 ff.

McClellan, T. A., & Stieper, D. R. A structured approach to group marriage counseling. *Mental Hygiene*, 1971, *55*, 77–84.

McCorkle, L. W. Group therapy in correctional institutions. *Federal Probation*, 1949, *13*(2), 34–37.

McCorkle, L. W. Group therapy in the treatment of offenders. *Federal Probation*, 1952, *16*, 22–27.

McCorkle, L. W. The present status of group therapy in U.S. correctional institutions. *International Journal of Group Psychotherapy*, 1953, *3*, 79–87.

McCorkle, L. W. Guided group interaction in a correctional setting. *International Journal of Group Psychotherapy*, 1954, *4*, 199–203.

McCorkle, L. W., & Elias, A. Group therapy in correctional institutions. *Federal Probation*, 1960, *24*, 57–63.

McDavid, J. W. Immediate effects of group therapy upon response to social reinforcement among juvenile delinquents. *Journal of Consulting Psychology*, 1964, *28*, 409–412.

McGhee, T. F., & Kostrubala, T. The neurotic equilibrium in married couples applying for group psychotherapy. *Journal of Marriage and the Family*, 1964, *26*, 77–88.

McGhee, T. F., Starr, A., Powers, J., Racusen, F. R., & Thornton, A. Conjunctive use of psychodrama and group psychotherapy in a group living program with schizophrenic patients. *Group Psychotherapy*, 1965, *18*, 127–135.

McGhee, T. F., & Schuman, B. N. The nature of the co-therapy relationship. *International Journal of Group Psychotherapy*, 1970, *20*, 25–36.

McGinnis, G. A. The effect of group therapy on the ego-strength scale scores of alcoholic patients. *Journal of Clinical Psychology*, 1963, *19*, 346–347.

McGovern, K. B., Arkowitz, H., & Gilmore, S. K. Evaluation of social skill training programs for college dating inhibitions. *Journal of Counseling Psychology*, 1975, *22*(6), 505–512.

McPherson, S. B., & Samuels, C. R. Teaching behavioral methods to parents. *Social Casework*, 1971, *52*, 148–153.

Mees, H. L., & Kenter, C. S. Short-term group psychotherapy with obese women. *Northwest Medicine*, 1967, *66*, 548–559.

Mehlman, B. Group play therapy with mentally retarded children. *Journal of Abnormal Social Psychology*, 1953, *48*, 53–60.

Meiers, J. I. Origins and development of group psychotherapy. *Sociometry*, 1945, *8*, 499–534.

Meltzoff, J., & Kornreich, M. *Research in psychotherapy*. New York: Atherton Press, 1970.

Meyer, G. G., Lieberman, M. A., & Perlmutter, J. Group psychotherapy. In H. Spiegel (Ed.), *Progress in neurology and psychiatry* (Vol. 17). New York: Grune & Stratton, 1967.

Mezzanotte, E. J. Group instruction in preparation for surgery. *American Journal of Nursing*, 1970, *70*, 89–91.

Milberg, I. Group psychotherapy in the treatment of some neurodermatoses. *International Journal of Group Psychology*, 1956, *6*, 53–61.

Miles, M. B. *Personal change through human relations training: A working paper*. Unpublished paper, Columbia University, 1957.

Miles, M. B. *Factors influencing response to feedback in human relations training*. Unpublished paper, Columbia University, 1958.

Miles, M. B. *Learning to work in groups*. New York: Teachers College, Columbia University, 1959.

Miles, M. B. Human relations training: Processes and outcomes. *Journal of Counseling Psychology*, 1960, *7*, 301–306.

Miles, M. B. Changes during and following laboratory training: A clinical experiential study. *Journal of Applied Behavioral Science*, 1965, *1*, 215–242.

Miller, D. Psychodramatic ways of coping with potentially dangerous situations in psychotic and non-psychotic populations. *Group Psychotherapy and Psychodrama*, 1972, *25*, 57–68.

Miller, H., & Baruch, D. W. Psychological dynamics in allergic patients as shown in group and individual psychotherapy. *Journal of Consulting Psychology*, 1948, *12*, 111–115.

Mintz, E. E. Transference in co-therapy groups. *Journal of Consulting Psychology*, 1963, *1*, 34.

Mintz, E. E. Male-female co-therapists. *American Journal of Psychotherapy*, 1965, *19*, 293–295.

Mintz, E. E. Group and individual treatment. *Journal of Consulting Psychology*, 1966, *30*, 193–195.

Mintz, E. E. Marathon groups: A preliminary evaluation. *Journal of Contemporary Psychotherapy*, 1969, *1*, 91–98.

Mintz, E. E. What do we owe today's woman? *International Journal of Group Psychotherapy*, 1974, *24*, 273–280.

Mitchell, K. R., & Ingham, R. J. The effects of general anxiety on group desensitization of test anxiety. *Behavior Research and Therapy*, 1970, *8*, 69–78.

Mitchell, K. R., & Ng, K. T. Effects of group counseling and behavior therapy on the academic achievement of test-anxious students. *Journal of Counseling Psychology*, 1972, *19*, 491–497.

Mitchell, K. R., & Piatkowska, O. E. Effects of group treatment for college underachievers and bright failing underachievers. *Journal of Counseling Psychology*, 1974, *21*(6), 494–501.

Mone, L. C. *Short-term group psychotherapy with post-cardiac patients.* Paper presented at the 27th annual conference of the American Group Psychotherapy Association, New Orleans, January 1970.

Moore, K. B., & Query, W. T. Group psychotherapy as a means of approaching homosexual behavior among hospitalized psychiatric patients. *Journal of the Kentucky Medical Association*, 1963, *61*, 403–407.

Moore, R. T. Program of psychotherapy for inmates at the Montana State Prison, *Psychological Reports*, 1972, *30*, 756–758.

Moore, R., & Buchanan, T. State hospitals and alcoholism: A nationwide survey of treatment techniques and results. *Quarterly Journal of Studies of Alcoholism*, 1966, *27*, 459–468.

Moreno, J. L. *Die Gottheit als Komediant.* Vienna: Anzangruber Verlag, 1911.

Moreno, J. L. *Application of the group method to classification.* New York: National Committee on Prisons and Prison Labor, 1932.

Moreno, J. L. Sociodrama of a family conflict. *Group Psychotherapy*, 1952, *5*, 20–37. (a)

Moreno, J. L. *Who shall survive?* New York: Beacon House, 1952. (b)

Moreno, J. L. Philosophy of the third psychiatric revolution, with special emphasis on group psychotherapy and psychodrama. In F. Fromm-Reichmann & J. L. Moreno (Eds.), *Progress in psychotherapy.* New York: Grune & Stratton, 1956.

Moreno, J. L. The Viennese origins of the encounter movement, paving the way for existentialism, group psychotherapy, and psychodrama. *Group Psychotherapy*, 1970, *22*, 7–11.

Moreno, Z. T. Psychodrama in the crib. *Group Psychotherapy*, 1954, *7*, 291–302.

Moulin, E. K. The effects of client centered group counseling using play media on the intelligence, achievement and psycholinguistic abilities of underachieving primary school children. *Elementary School Guidance and Counseling*, 1969, *5*, 55–98.

Moustakas, G. *Psychotherapy with children: The living relationship.* New York: Harper & Row, 1969.

Mueller, E. E. Group therapy with alcoholics in a hospital setting. *Diseases of the Nervous System*, 1949, *10*, 298–303.

Mullan, H. The group analyst's creative function. *American Journal of Psychotherapy*, 1955, *9*, 320–334.

Murase, H. T. *Kaikan therapy.* Internal document, East-West Center, Honolulu, Hawaii 1970.

Murray, N. Malunion of the femur treated by group practice and psychodrama. *Southern Medical Journal*, 1962, *55*, 921–929.

Myers, D. G. A comparison of the effects of group puppet therapy and group activity with mentally retarded children. *Dissertation Abstracts International*, 1971, *31* (10-A), 5234.

Nancy, J. H. Friday night study group events. *The Female State: A Journal of Female Liberation*, 1970, *4*, 108–110.

National Training Laboratory. *Personal growth and social change* (NTL Institute for Applied Behavioral Science pamphlet No. 1–26), 1970.

Nawas, M. M., Fishman, S. T., & Pucel, J. C. A standardized desensitization program applicable to group and individual treatments. *Behavior Research and Therapy*, 1970, *8*, 49–56.

Neham, S. Psychotherapy in relation to mental deficiency. *American Journal of Mental Deficiency*, 1951, *55*, 557–559.

Neussendorfer, S. Marriage group counseling inside. *American Journal of Corrections*, 1969, *31*, 33–34.

Nicholson, W. H. Emotional factors in obesity. *American Journal of Medical Science*, 1946, *211*, 443–447.

Obler, M. Systematic desensitization in sexual disorders. *Journal of Behavior Therapy and Experimental Psychiatry*, 1973, *4*, 93–101.

O'Brien, H. P. The use of group methods in correctional treatment. *Proceedings of the American Prison Association*, 1950, *80*, 263–268.

O'Connor, F. A group therapy experience with regressed patients. *Journal of Psychiatric Nursing and Mental Health Services*, 1969, *7*, 226–229.

Odenwald, R. P. Outline of group psychotherapy for juvenile delinquents and criminal offenders. *Group Psychotherapy*, 1964, *14*, 50–53.

Ohlsen, M. M. *Group counseling.* New York: Holt, Rinehart & Winston, 1977.

O'Neil, C. F. Family therapy in treatment of delinquency. *American Journal of Orthopsychiatry*, 1971, *41*, 295.

Ormont, L. R. The use of group psychotherapy in the training of marriage counselors and family life educators. *Marriage and Family Living*, 1962, *24*, 144–150.

Oshry, B. I., & Harrison, R. Transfer from here and now to there and then: Changes in organizational problem diagnoses stemming from T-group training. *Journal of Applied Behavioral Science*, 1966, *2*, 185–198.

Otto, H. A. The use of inter-action centered schedule in group work with pre-marital couples. *Group Psychotherapy*, 1959, *12*, 223–229.

Otto, H. A. *Human potentialities: The challenge and the promise.* St. Louis, Mo.: Green, 1968.

Otto, H. A. *Group methods to actualize human potential.* Beverly Hills, Calif.: Holistic Press, 1970.

Otto, H. A., & Mann, J. (Eds.). *Ways of growth.* New York: Grossman, 1968.

Papanek, E. Treatment by group work. *American Journal of Orthopsychiatry*, 1945, *15*, 223–229.

Papanek, H. Training in group psychotherapy: A symposium. III: Satisfactions and frustrations of a supervisor of group psychotherapists. *American Journal of Psychotherapy*, 1958, *12*, 500–503.

Papanek, H. Group psychotherapy with married couples. In J. Masserman (Ed.), *Current psychiatric therapies.* New York: Grune & Stratton, 1965.

Papanek, H. Therapeutic and antitherapeutic factors in group relations. *American Journal of Psychotherapy*, 1969, *23*, 396–404.

Papanek, H. Group psychotherapy interminable. *International Journal of Group Psychotherapy*, 1970, *20*, 219–223. (a)

Papanek, H. Group therapy with married couples. *Sandoz Psychiatric Spectator*, 1970, *6*(11), 8–9. (b)

Papell, C. Sensitivity training: Relevance for social work education. *Journal of Education in Social Work*, 1972, *8*, 42–55.

Parker, B. Psychiatric consultation for nonpsychiatric professional workers: A concept of group consultation developed from a training program for nurses. Washington, D.C.: U.S. Department of Health, Education, and Welfare, 1958.

Parrish, M. M. Group techniques with teenage emotionally disturbed girls. *Group Psychotherapy*, 1962, *14*, 20–25.

Pasnau, R. O., Williams, L., & Tallman, F. F. Small activity groups in the school: Report of a 12-year research project in community psychiatry. *Community Mental Health Journal*, 1971, *7*, 303–311.

Paster, S. Group psychotherapy in an Army general hospital. *Mental Hygiene*, 1944, *28*, 529–536.

Patterson, R. M. Psychiatric treatment of institutionalized delinquent adolescent girls. *Diseases of the Nervous System*, 1950, *11*, 227–229.

Pattison, E. M. Evaluation studies of group psychotherapy. *International Journal of Group Psychotherapy*, 1965, *15*, 382–391.

Pattison, E. M. *A brief history of the American Group Psychotherapy Association: The first twenty-five years:*

1943–1968. New York: American Group Psychotherapy Association, 1969.

Pattison, E. M. The place of new professionals in the practice of group skills: An overview. *International Journal of Group Psychotherapy,* 1974, *24*(4), 409–416.

Patton, J. D. Group psychotherapy: A training and teaching method in a private psychiatric hospital. *International Journal of Group Psychotherapy,* 1954, *4,* 419–428.

Paul, G. L., & Shannon, D. J. Treatment of anxiety through systematic desensitization in therapy groups. *Journal of Abnormal Psychology,* 1966, *71,* 124–135.

Paul, N. L., & Bloom, J. D. Multiple-family therapy: Secrets and scapegoating in family crisis. *International Journal of Group Psychotherapy,* 1970, *20,* 37–47.

Payn, S. B. Group methods in the pharmacotherapy of chronic psychotic patients. *Psychiatric Quarterly,* 1965, *39,* 258–263.

Payn, S. B. Reaching chronic schizophrenic patients with group pharmacotherapy. *International Journal of Group Psychotherapy,* 1974, *24,* 25–31.

Payne, J. E., & Williams, M. Practical aspects of group work with the mentally retarded. *Group Process,* 1971, *4,* 9–17.

Perkins, J. A., & Wicas, E. A. Group counseling of bright underachievers and their mothers. *Journal of Counseling Psychology,* 1971, *18,* 273–278.

Perls, F. S. *Gestalt therapy verbatim.* Lafayette, Calif.: Real People Press, 1969.

Perls, F. S. *In and out the garbage pail.* Lafayette, Calif.: Real People Press, 1970.

Perls, F. S., Hefferline, R. F., & Goodman, P. *Gestalt therapy: Excitement and growth in the human personality.* New York: Julian Press, 1951.

Perls, F. S., Hefferline, R. E., & Goodman, P. *Gestalt therapy.* New York: Dell, 1965.

Persons, R. W. Psychological and behavioral change in delinquents following psychotherapy. *Journal of Clinical Psychology,* 1966, *22*(3), 337–340.

Pfeffer, A. A., Friedland, P., & Wortis, S. B. Group psychotherapy with alcoholics. *Quarterly Journal of Studies in Alcohol,* 1949, *10,* 198–216.

Pfeiffer, J. W., & Jones, J. E. *A handbook of structured experiences for human relations training* (Vols. 1–5 and Reference Guide). La Jolla, Calif.: University Associates, 1969–1974. (a)

Pfeiffer, J. W., & Jones, J. E. *Annual Handbooks for Group Facilitators.* La Jolla, Calif.: University Associates, 1972–1975. (b)

Pilder, R. Encounter groups for married couples. In L. Solomon & B. Berzon (Eds.), *New perspectives on encounter groups.* San Francisco: Jossey-Bass, 1972.

Piskor, B. K., & Paleos, S. The group way to banish after-stroke blues. *American Journal of Nursing,* 1968, *68,* 1500-1506.

Pislikis, I. Resistances to consciousness. *Notes from the second year: Women's liberation.* New York: Liberation Press, 1970.

Pittman, F. S., & DeYoung, C. D. The treatment of homosexuals in heterogeneous groups. *International Journal of Group Psychotherapy,* 1971, *21,* 62–73.

Pixley, J. M., & Stiefel, J. R. Group therapy designed to meet the needs of the alcoholic's wife. *Quarterly Journal of Studies in Alcohol,* 1963, *24,* 304–314.

Platt, J. M. Efficacy of the Adlerian model in elementary school counseling. *Elementary School Guidance and Counseling,* 1971, *6,* 86–91.

Plowitz, P. E. Psychiatric service and group therapy in the rehabilitation of offenders. *Journal of Correctional Education,* 1950, *2,* 78–80.

Polansky, N. A., Miller, S. C., & White, R. B. Some reservations regarding group psychotherapy in inpatient psychiatric treatment. *Group Psychotherapy,* 1955, *8,* 254–262.

Porpotage, F. M., II. Sensitivity training. *Police Chief,* 1972, *39,* 60–61.

Porter, L. W. Personnel management. *Annual Review of Psychology,* 1966, *17,* 395–422.

Powdermaker, F., & Frank, J. D. *Group psychotherapy*. Cambridge, Mass.: Harvard University Press, 1953.

Prados, M. The use of films in psychotherapy. *American Journal of Orthopsychiatry*, 1951, *21*, 36–46 (a)

Prados, M. The use of pictorial images in group therapy. *American Journal of Psychotherapy*, 1951, *5*, 196–214. (b)

Pratt, J. H. The home sanitarium treatment of consumption. *Boston Medical Surgeon Journal*, 1906, *154*, 210–216. (a)

Pratt, J. H. The home sanitarium treatment of consumption. *Johns Hopkins Hospital Bulletin*, 1906, *17*, 140–144. (b)

Pratt, J. H. The class method of treating consumption in the homes of the poor. *Journal of American Medical Association*, 1907, *49*, 755–759. (a)

Pratt, J. H. The organization of tuberculosis classes. *Medical Communications*, Massachusetts Medical Society, 1907, *20*, 475–492. (b)

Pratt, J. H. Results obtained in the treatment of pulmonary tuberculosis by the class method. *British Medical Journal*, 1908, *2*, 1070–1071.

Pratt, J. H. The class method in the homes of tuberculars and what it has accomplished. Transactions of the American Climatic Association, 1911, *27*, 87–118.

Pratt, J. H. The tuberculosis class. *Proceedings of the New York Conference Hospital Society Service Association*. New York City, 1917, *4*, 49.

Pratt, J. H. The principles of class treatment and their application to various chronic diseases. *Hospital Society Service*, 1922, *6*, 401–411.

Pratt, J. H. The influence of emotions in the causation and cure of psychoneuroses. *International Clinics*, 1934, *4*, 1–16.

Pratt, J. H. The group method in the treatment of psychosomatic disorders. *Sociometry*, 1945, *8*, 323–331.

Pratt, J. H. The use of Dejerine's methods in the treatment of the common neuroses. Boston: New England Medical Center, 1953, *15*, 1–9.

Pratt, J. H., & Johnson, P. E. (Eds.). *A 20-year experiment in group therapy*. Boston: New England Medical Center, 1950.

Puick, C. L. Evolution of treatment method for disadvantaged children. *American Journal of Psychotherapy*, 1970, *24*, 112–123.

Rachman, A. W., & Heller, M. E. Peer group psychotherapy with adolescent drug abusers. *International Journal of Psychotherapy*, 1976, *36*(3), 373–384.

Rahe, H. Group therapy in the outpatient management of post myocardial infarctive patients. *Psychiatric Medicine*, 1973, *4*, 77–88.

Ramer, J. C. Community laymen as group participants within a prison setting. *American Correctional Association*, 1971, 57–63.

Ramirez, E. Addiction Research Center Bulletin No. 4. Puerto Rico, 1961.

Randall, G. C., and Rogers, W. C. Group therapy for epileptics. *American Journal of Psychiatry*, 1950, *107*, 422–427.

Rankin, J. E. A group therapy experiment with mothers of mentally deficient children. *American Journal of Mental Deficiency*, 1957, *62*, 49–55.

Rappaport, R. G. Group therapy in prison. *International Journal of Group Psychotherapy*, 1971, *21*, 489–496.

Rashkis, H. A., & Shaskin, D. A. The effects of group psychotherapy on personality inventory scores. *American Journal of Orthopsychiatry*, 1946, *16*, 345–349.

Reckless, J. A. A confrontation technique used with married couples in a group therapy setting. *International Journal of Group Psychotherapy*, 1969, *192*, 203–213.

Reddy, W. B. Screening and selection of participants. In L. H. Solomon and B. Berzon (Eds.), *New perspectives on encounter groups*. San Francisco: Jossey-Bass, 1972.

Reddy, W. B., Colson, D. B., & Keys, C. B. The group psychotherapy literature: 1975. *International Journal of Group Psychotherapy*, 1976, *24*, 487–545.

Reddy, W. B., & Lansky, L. M. The group psychotherapy literature: 1973. *International Journal of Group Psychotherapy*, 1974, *24*, 477–517.

Redfering, D. L. Differential effects of group counseling with Negro and white delinquent females. *Corrective Psychiatry and Journal of Social Therapy*, 1971, *17*, 29–34.

Redfering, D. L. Group counseling with institutionalized delinquent females. *American Journal of Corrections*, 1972, *26*, 160–163.

Redfering, D. L. Durability of effects of group counseling with institutionalized delinquent females. *Journal of Abnormal Psychology*, 1973, *82*, 85–86.

Redl, F. Group emotions and leadership. *Psychiatry*, 1942, *5*, 579–596.

Redl, F. Diagnostic group work. *American Journal of Orthopsychiatry*, 1944, *14*, 53–67.

Redl, F. Resistance in therapy groups. *Human Relations*, 1948, *1*, 307–313.

Redwin, E. The behind-your-back technique in marriage counseling. *Group Psychotherapy*, 1955, 8, 40–46.

Reed, J. W. Group therapy with asthmatic patients. *Geriatrics*, 1962, *17*, 823–830.

Reik, T. *Listening with the third ear*. New York: Farrar, Strauss, 1948.

Reinstein, M. Group therapy for basic trainees: A means of coping with adjustment problems. *Military Medicine*, 1970, *135*, 760–764.

Renouvier, P. Group psychotherapy in the United States. *Sociatry*, 1948, *2*, 75–83.

Rest, W. G., & Ryan, F. J. Group vocational counseling for the probationer and parolee. *Federal Probation*, 1970, *34*(2), 49–54.

Rhodes, S. L. Short-term groups of latency age children in a school setting. *International Journal of Group Psychotherapy*, 1973, *23*, 204–216.

Riesman, D. *The lonely crowd*. New Haven, Conn.: Yale University Press, 1950.

Robertiello, R. C. Encounter techniques: Ridiculous or sublime? *Voices: Art and Science of Psychotherapy*, 1970, *5*(4), 80–90.

Rogers, C. R. *Counseling and psychotherapy*. Boston: Houghton Mifflin, 1942.

Rogers, C. R. *Client-centered therapy*. Boston: Houghton Mifflin, 1951.

Rogers, C. R. *On becoming a person: A therapist's view of psychotherapy*. Boston: Houghton Mifflin, 1961.

Rogers, C. R. The process of the basic encounter group. In J. F. T. Bugental (Ed.), *Challenges of humanistic psychology*. New York: McGraw-Hill, 1967.

Rogers, C. R. Interpersonal relationships: U.S.A. 2000. *Journal of Applied Behavioral Science*, 1968, *4*, 265–280. (a)

Rogers, C. R. *The process of the basic encounter group*. La Jolla, Calif.: Western Behavioral Sciences Institute, 1968. (b)

Rogers, C. R. *On encounter groups*. New York: Harper & Row, 1969. (a)

Rogers, C. R. *Program description, The 1969 La Jolla summer encounter institute*. (b)

Rogers, C. R. The T-group comes of age. *Psychology Today*, 1969, 3(7), 27. (c)

Rogers, K. Group dynamics for marketing managers. *Journal of Advertising Research*, 1973, 13, 7–14.

Rohrbacher, R. Influence of a special camp program for obese boys on weight loss, self-concept, and body image. *Research Quarterly of the American Association of Healing Physicians*, 1973, *44*, 150–157.

Romano, M. D. Sexual counseling in groups. *Journal of Sex Research*, 1973, *9*, 69–90.

Rome, H. P. Comments on Hadden's paper. *Transcripts of the American Neurological Association*, 1943, *69*, 136.

Rome, H. P. Audio-visual aids in psychiatry. *Hospital Corps Quarterly*, 1945, *18*, 37–38. (a)

Rome, H. P. Military group psychotherapy. *American Journal of Psychiatry*, 1945, *101*, 494–497. (b)

Rosenbaum, M. Group psychotherapy and psychodrama. In B. Wolman (Ed.), *Handbook of clinical psychology*. New York: McGraw-Hill, 1965.

Rosenbaum, M. The responsibility of the group psychotherapy practitioner for a therapeutic rationale. *Journal of Group Psychoanalysis and Process*, 1969, *2*, 5–17.

Rosenbaum, M. Co-therapy. In H. I. Kaplan & B. J. Sadock, *Comprehensive group psychotherapy*. Baltimore: Williams & Wilkins, 1971.

Rosenbaum, M., & Berger, M. *Group psychotherapy and group function*. New York: Basic Books, 1963.

Rosenbaum, M., & Hartley, E. A summary review of current practises of ninety-two group therapists. *International Journal of Group Psychotherapy*, 1962, *12*, 194–198.

Rosenberg, P. P., & Chilgren, R. Sex education discussion groups in a medical setting. *International Journal of Group Psychotherapy*, 1973, *23*, 23–41.

Rosenberg, P. P., & Fuller, M. Dynamic analysis of the student nurse. *Group Psychotherapy*, 1957, *10*, 22–39.

Rosenthal, L. Group psychotherapy in a child guidance clinic. *Social Casework*, 1951, *8*, 337–342.

Ross, T. A. *The common neuroses and their treatment by psychotherapy*. London: Arnold, 1924.

Ross, W. D. Group psychotherapy with patients' relatives. *American Journal of Psychiatry*, 1948, *104*, 623–636.

Ross, W. D., Block, S. L., & Silver, H. Integrating training in group psychotherapy with psychiatric residency training. *International Journal of Group Psychotherapy*, 1958, *8*, 323–328.

Roth, R., Mauksch, H., & Peiser, K. The non-achievement syndrome, group therapy and achievement change. *Personnel and Guidance Journal*, 1967, *46*, 393–398.

Rotter, J. Generalized expectancies for internal vs. external locus of control of reinforcement. *Psychological Monographs*, 1966, *80*, (1, Whole No. 609).

Rueveni, U. Using sensitivity training with junior high school students. *Children*, 1971, *18*, 69–72.

Rueveni, U., & Speck, R. V. Using encounter group techniques in the treatment of the social network of the schizophrenic. In R. Buckhout and 81 concerned Berkeley students (Eds.), *Toward social change: A handbook for those who will*. New York: Harper & Row, 1971.

Rueveni, U., Swift, M., & Bell, A. A. Sensitivity training: Its impact on mental health workers. *Journal of Applied Behavioral Science*, 1969, *4*, 600–602.

Ruitenbeek, H. M. *Group therapy today*. New York: Atherton, 1969.

Ruitenbeek, H. M. *The new group therapies*. New York: Avon, 1970.

Ruskin, I. W. Analytic group psychotherapy for husbands and wives. *California Medicine*, 1953, *77*, 140–145.

Russell, J. Personal growth through structured exercises. *Voices: The Art and Science of Psychotherapy*, 1971, *7*, 28–36.

Rustin, S. L., & Wolk, R. L. The use of specialized group psychotherapy techniques in a home for the aged. *Group psychotherapy*, 1963, *16*, 25–32.

Rybak, W. S. Disguised group therapy: An approach to the treatment of hospitalized teen-aged patients. *Psychiatric Quarterly Supplements*, 1963, *37*, 44–55.

Rychlak, J. F. *A philosophy of science for personality theory*, Boston: Houghton Mifflin, 1968.

Sachs, J. M., & Berger, S. Group therapy techniques with hospitalized chronic schizophrenic patients. *Journal of Consulting Psychology*, 1954, *18*, 297–307.

Samuels, A. S. The reduction of interracial prejudice and tension through group therapy. In H. I. Kaplan & B. J. Sadock, *Comprehensive group psychotherapy*, 1971, *21*, 23–24.

Samuels, S. D. Stroke strategy. I: The basis of therapy. *Transactional Analysis Journal*, 1971, *1*, 23–24.

Sands, P. M., & Hanson, P. G. Psychotherapeutic groups for alcoholics and relatives in an outpatient setting.

International Journal of Group Psychotherapy, 1971, *21*, 23–33.

Santiago, D. L., Treant, R. D., & Sanchez, L. L. A group work experience for mothers of adolescents with epilepsy. *Bol. Asoc. Med. P. Rico*, 1964, *56*, 51–57.

Sarachild, K. A program for feminist consciousness raising. *Notes from the Second Year: Women's Liberation*. New York: Liberation Press, 1970.

Sarachild, K. *Consciousness raising and intuition: The radical therapist*. New York: Ballantine Books, 1971.

Sarbin, T. R. Spontaneity training of the feebleminded. *Sociatry*, 1945, *7*, 389–393.

Sarlin, C. N., & Berezin, M. A. Group psychotherapy on a modified analytic basis. *Journal of Nervous Mental Diseases*, 1946, *104*, 611–667.

Sata, L. S. Group methods, the volunteer and the paraprofessional. *International Journal of Group Psychotherapy*, 1974, *24*(4), 400–408.

Satir, V. *Conjoint family therapy: A guide to theory and technique*. Palo Alto, Calif.: Science and Behavior Books, 1964.

Savenko, N., & Winder, A. Group counseling with neighborhood youth corps trainees. *Personnel and Guidance Journal*, 1970, *18*, 561–567.

Scarborough, D. D., & Novick, A. G. (Eds.). *Institutional rehabilitation of delinquent youths*. Albany, N.Y.: Delmar, 1962.

Scarborough, L. F. Management of convulsive patients by group therapy. *Diseases of the Nervous System*, 1956, *17*, 223–225.

Schachter, S., & Singer, J. E. Cognitive, social, and physiological determinants of emotional states. *Psychological Review*, 1962, *69*, 379–399.

Schechter, M. D., Shurley, J. T., Sexauer, T., & Toussieng, P. W. Perceptual isolation therapy: A new experimental approach in the treatment of children using infantile autistic defenses. *Journal of the American Academy of Child Psychiatry*, 1969, 97–111.

Scheidlinger, S. Group therapy—its place in psychotherapy. *Journal of Social Casework*, 1948, *29*, 299–304.

Scheidlinger, S. Therapeutic group approaches in community mental health. *Social Work*, 1968, *19*, 87–98.

Scheidlinger, S. Innovative group approaches. In L. Bellak & H. H. Barten (Eds.), *Progress in community mental health*. New York: Grune & Stratton, 1969.

Scheidlinger, S. Women's role and group psychotherapy: Editor's introduction. *International Journal of Group Psychotherapy*, 1974, *24*(3), 263–264.

Scheidlinger, S., & Rauch, E. Psychoanalytic group psychotherapy with children and adolescents. In B. Wolman, *Handbook of child psychoanalysis*. New York: Van Nostrand Reinhold, 1972.

Schein, E. H., & Bennis, W. C. *Personal and organizational change through group methods: A laboratory approach*. New York: John Wiley, 1965.

Schilder, P. The analysis of ideologies as a psychotherapeutic method, especially in group treatment. *American Journal of Psychiatry*, 1937, *93*, 605–615.

Schilder, P. Introductory remarks on groups. *Journal of Social Psychology*, 1940, *12*, 83–100.

Schneer, H. I., Gottesfeld, H., & Sales, A. Group therapy as an aid with delinquent pubescents in a special public school. *Psychiatric Quarterly Supplements*, 1957, *31*, 246–260.

Schroeder, K. Systematic human relations training for resident assistants. *Journal of College Student Personnel*, 1973, *14*, 313–316.

Schual, F., Saller, H., & Paley, M. G. Thematic group therapy in treatment of hospitalized alcoholic patients. *International Journal of Group Psychotherapy*, 1971, *21*, 226–233.

Schulman, I. The dynamics of certain reactions of delinquents to group psychotherapy. *International Journal of Group Psychotherapy*, 1952, *2*, 334–343.

Schulman, I. Modifications in group psychotherapy with antisocial adolescents. *International Journal of Group Psychotherapy*, 1957, *7*, 310–317.

Schulman, I. Transference, resistance and communication problems in adolescent psychotherapy groups. *International Journal of Group Psychotherapy*, 1959, *9*, 496–503.

Schutz, W. C. *Joy: Expanding Human Awareness*. New York: Grove Press, 1967.

Schutz, W. C. *Here comes everybody*. New York: Harrow Books, 1972.

Schutz, W. C. *Elements of encounter*. Big Sur, Calif.: Joy Press, 1973.

Schutz, W. C. Not encounter and certainly not facts. *Journal of Humanistic Psychology*, 1975, *15*(2), 7–18.

Schwartz, E. K. Group psychotherapy: The individual and the group. *Acta Psychotherapy*, 1965, *13*, 142–149. (a)

Schwartz, E. K. Leadership and the psychotherapist. In B. Stokvis (Ed.), *Topical problems of psychotherapy*. Basel: S. Karger, 1965. (b)

Schwartz, E. K. Obsessional disorders in childhood and adolescence. *American Journal of Psychotherapy*, 1972, *26*, 361–371. (a)

Schwartz, E. K. The treatment of the obsessive patient in the group therapy setting. *American Journal of Psychotherapy*, 1972, *26*, 352–361. (b)

Schwartz, E., & Goodman, J. Group therapy of obesity in elderly diabetics. *Geriatrics*, 1953, *7*, 280–283.

Schwartz, E. K., & Rabin, H. M. A training group with one non-verbal co-leader. *Journal of Psychoanalysis Group*, 1968, *2*, 35–49.

Schwartz, E. K., & Wolf, A. On countertransference in group psychotherapy. *Journal of Psychology*, 1963, *57*, 131–142. (a)

Schwartz, E. K., & Wolf, A. Psychoanalysis in groups: Resistances to its use. *American Journal of Psychotherapy*, 1963, *17*, 457–463. (b)

Schwartz, E. K., & Wolf, A. The interpreter in group therapy: Conflict resolution through negotiation. *Archives of General Psychiatry*, 1968, *18*, 186.

Schwartz, J. L. A critical review and evaluation of smoking control methods. *Public Health Reports*, 1969, *84*, 483–506.

Schwartz, W. C., & Allen, V. L. The effects of a T group laboratory on interpersonal behavior. *Journal of Applied Behavioral Science*, 1966, *2*, 265–281.

Scott, M. E. The development and management of phobias. *Southern Medical Journal*, 1961, *54*, 1022, 1025.

Sculthorpe, W., & Blumenthal, I. J. Combined patient-relative group therapy in schizophrenia. *Mental Hygiene*, 1965, *49*, 504–573.

Seeman, J., & Ellinwood, C. Interpersonal assessment of play therapy outcome. *Psychotherapy: Theory, Research and Practice*, 1964, *2*, 64–65.

Seguin, C. A. Un experimento con psicoterapie colectiva. *Revista Neuropsychiatrica*, Lima, 1947, *10*, 378–379.

Seguin, C. A. Groups in medical education. *Journal of Medical Education*. 1965, *40*, 281–285.

Seidle, R. School guidance clinics in Vienna. *Journal of Individual Psychology*, 1936, *2*, 75–78.

Semon, R. C., & Goldstein, W. The effectiveness of group psychotherapy with chronic schizophrenics and an evaluation of different therapeutic methods. *Journal of Consulting Psychology*, 1957, *3*, 247–249.

Shaffer, J. B., & Galinsky, M. D. *Models of group therapy and sensitivity training*. Englewood Cliffs, N.J.: Prentice-Hall, 1974.

Shapiro, J. L. *An investigatory study into the clinical use of an adjective check list*. Unpublished manuscript, Hawaii State Hospital, Kaneohe, 1967.

Shapiro, J. L. An investigation into the differential effects of a variety of sensitivity training procedures. Unpublished doctoral dissertation, University of Waterloo, 1970.

Shapiro, J. L. Encounter groups as inservice training for teachers and teachers-to-be. *Journal of the Hawaii Personnel and Guidance Association*, 1971, *1*(2), 18–25.

Shapiro, J. L. A dimensional approach to encounter groups: Beginning of a theory. *Proceedings of the American*

Psychological Association, 1972, 7(2), 929. (a)

Shapiro, J. L. An investigation of the value of sensitivity groups in training counselors and teachers. *Proceedings of the 20th International Congress of Psychology*, 1972. (b)

Shapiro, J. L. The uses and abuses of encounter groups. Invited address at the Hong Kong Federation of Youth Groups, Hong Kong, 1972. (c)

Shapiro, J. L. Encounter in Hawaii. *Hawaii Observer*, June 26, 1973, pp. 8–9.

Shapiro, J. L. Process, progress & concerns for encounter groups. Paper presented at Hawaii Association of Humanistic Psychology convention, 1975.

Shapiro, J. L. The use of videotape in group leader training. Paper presented at the World Educators Conference, Honolulu, 1976.

Shapiro, J. L., & Diamond, M. J. Increases in hypnotizability as a function of encounter group training. *Journal of Abnormal Psychology*, 1972, 79(1), 112–115.

Shapiro, J. L., & Diamond, M. J. *Toward the long-term scientific study of encounter group phenomena*. II: Empirical findings. Paper presented at the meeting of the Western Psychological Association, Anaheim, Calif., 1973.

Shapiro, J. L., & Gust, T. Counselor training for facilitative human relationships: Study and replication. *Counselor Education and Supervision*, 1974, 13(3), 198–207.

Shapiro, J. L., Marano, P. T., & Diamond, M. J. *An investigation of encounter group outcome and its relationship to leadership experience*. Paper presented at the 19th annual meeting of the Southeastern Psychological Association, New Orleans, April 1973.

Shapiro, J. L., & Ross, R. R. Sensitivity training in an institution for adolescents. *Journal of Applied Behavioral Science*, 1971, 7(6), 710–723.

Shapiro, J. L., & Ross, R. R. Sensitivity training for staff in an institution for adolescent offenders: A preliminary investigation. *American*

Journal of Corrections, July–August, 1970. Also in J. G. Cull & R. E. Hardy (Eds.), *Law enforcement and correctional rehabilitation*. Springfield, Ill.: Charles C Thomas, 1973.

Shapiro, J. L., & Siu, P. K. *Cultural modeling patterns, racial attributes in leaders and members, and outcome in encounter groups*. Unpublished manuscript, University of Hawaii, 1976.

Shaskan, D. A. Must individual and group psychotherapy be opposed? *American Journal of Orthopsychiatry*, 1947, 17, 290–297.

Shaskan, D. A. Evolution and trends in group psychotherapy. *American Journal of Orthopsychiatry*, 1948, 18, 447–454.

Shaskan, D. A., Conrad, D., & Grant, J. D. Prediction of behavior in group psychotherapy from Rorschach protocols. *Group Psychotherapy*, 1951, 3, 218–230.

Shaskan, D. A., & Jolesch, M. War and group psychotherapy. *American Journal of Orthopsychiatry*, 1944, 14, 571–577.

Shaskan, D. A., & Lindt, H. The theme of the aggressive mother during group therapy: Analysis of a group interview. *Psychoanalytic Review*, 1948, 35, 295–300.

Shaskan, D. A., Plank, R., & Blum, H. The function of the group. *Psychoanalytic Review*, 1949, 36, 385–388.

Shellow, R. S., Ward, J. L., & Rubenfeld, S. Group therapy for the institutionalized adolescent. *International Journal of Group Psychotherapy*, 1958, 8, 264–269.

Shepard, M., & Lee, M. *Marathon 16*. New York: Putnam, 1970.

Shepard, M., & Lee, M. *Sexual marathon*. New York: Pinnacle, 1972.

Shlensky, R. Issues raised in group process with blind pre-college students. *Adolescence*, 1972, 7, 427–434.

Shoemaker, R. J., Guy, M. B., & McLaughlin, J. T. Usefulness of group therapy in management of atopic eczema. *Pennsylvania Medical Journal*, 1955, 58, 603–605.

Shor, J. A modified psychodrama technique for rehabilitation of military psychoneurotics, *Sociatry,* 1948, *1,* 414–420.

Shostrom, E. *Personal Orientation Inventory manual.* San Diego, Calif.: Educational and Industrial Testing Service, 1966.

Siegel, J. M. *Role playing: A review.* Unpublished manuscript, University of Waterloo, 1969.

Silver, A. W. Group psychotherapy with senile psychotic patients. *Geriatrics,* 1950, *5,* 147–150.

Silver, A. W. Interrelating group dynamic, therapeutic and psychodynamic concepts. *International Journal of Group Psychotherapy,* 1967, *17,* 139.

Simon, B., Holzberg, J. D., Solomon, A., and Saxe, C. H. Group therapy from the viewpoint of the patient. *Journal of Nervous and Mental Diseases,* 1947, *105,* 156–170.

Singer, M. & Fisher, R. Group psychotherapy of male homosexuals by a male and female co-therapy team. *International Journal of Group Psychotherapy,* 1967, *17,* 44–49.

Slavson, S. R. *An introduction to group therapy.* New York: Commonwealth Fund, 1943.

Slavson, S. R. The field and objectives of group therapy. In B. Gluech (Ed.), *Current therapies of personality disorders.* New York: Grune & Stratton, 1946.

Slavson, S. R. Differential dynamics of activity and interview group therapy. *American Journal of Orthopsychiatry,* 1947, *17,* 293–302. (a)

Slavson, S. R. The group in child guidance. In E. Harms (Ed.), *Handbook of child guidance.* New York: Child Care Publications, 1947. (b)

Slavson, S. R. Advances in group psychotherapy. *International Congress of Mental Health Procedures,* 1948, pp. 24–26.

Slavson, S. R. *The practice of group therapy.* New York: International Universities Press, 1951.

Slavson, S. R. Racial and cultural factors in group psychotherapy. *International Journal of Group Psychotherapy,* 1956, *6,* 152–156.

Slavson, S. R. Discussion. *International Journal of Group Psychotherapy,* 1960, *10,* 225–229.

Slavson, S. R. *A textbook in analytic group psychotherapy.* New York: International Universities Press, 1964.

Slavson, S. R., Hallowitz, E., & Rosenthal, L. In E. A. Spiegel (Ed.), *Progress in neurology and psychiatry.* New York: Grune & Stratton, 1952.

Slavson, S. R., & MacLennan, B. Unmarried mothers. In S. R. Slavson. *The fields of group therapy.* New York: Schocken Books, 1956.

Smith, D. S., & Hawthorne, M. E. Psychiatric rehabilitation: A follow-up study of 200 cases. *Navy Medical Bulletin,* 1949, *49,* 655–669.

Smith, E. Group Conference for Post-Partum Patients. *American Journal of Nursing,* 1971, *71,* 112–113.

Smith, M. R., Bryant, J. E., & Twitchell-Allen, D. Sociometric changes in a group of adult female psychotics following an extensive socializing program. *Group Psychotherapy,* 1951, *4,* 145–155.

Snow, D. L., & Held, M. L. Group psychotherapy with obese adolescent females. *Adolescence,* 1973, *8,* 407–414.

Snyder, R., & Sechrest, L. An experimental study of directive group therapy with defective delinquents. *American Journal of Mental Deficiency,* 1959, *64,* 117–123.

Solby, B. The psychodramatic approach to marriage problems. *American Sociological Review,* 1941, *6,* 523–530.

Solomon, J. C., & Axelrod, P. J. Group psychotherapy for withdrawn adolescent children. *American Journal of Diseases of Childhood,* 1944, *68,* 86–101.

Solomon, J., & Solomon, G. Group therapy with father and son as co-therapists: Some dynamic considerations. *International Journal of Group Psychotherapy,* 1963, *13,* 133–140.

Solyom, L. Treatment of fear of flying. *American Journal of Psychiatry,* 1973, *130,* 423–427.

Sorenson, A. Treating drug addicts with humanistic and behavioristic techniques: Complementary modalities in therapeutic communities. *Cornell Journal of Social Relations,* 1973, *8,* 143–154.

Southworth, R. S. Group counseling with parents of underachieving 6th-grade children. In J. J. Muro & S. Freeman (Eds.), *Readings in group counseling.* Scranton: International Textbook, 1968.

Speck, R. Psychotherapy of the social network of a schizophrenic family. *Family Process,* 1967, *6,* 208–219.

Spielberger, C. D., & Weitz, H. Improving the academic performance of anxious college freshmen: A group-counseling approach to the prevention of underachievement. *Psychological Monographs,* 1964, *78,* 1 (20, Whole No. 590).

Spielberger, C. D., Weitz, H., & Denny, J. F. Group counseling and the academic performance of anxious college freshmen. *Journal of Counseling Psychology,* 1962, *9,* 195–204.

Spitz, H., & Sadock, B. J. Small interactional groups in the psychiatric training of graduate nursing students. *Journal of Nursing Education,* 1973, *12,* 6–13.

Spitz, R. A., & Wolf, K. M. Anaclitic depression: An inquiry into the genesis of psychiatric conditions in early childhood, II. *Psychoanalytic Studies of the Child,* 1946, *2,* 313–342.

Spotnitz, H. Group therapy as a specialized technique. In G. Bychowski & J. L. Despert (Eds.), *Specialized techniques in psychotherapy.* New York: Basis Books, 1952, 85–101.

Spotnitz, H. *The couch and the circle.* New York: Alfred A. Knopf, 1961.

Spotnitz, H. *Topical problems in psychotherapy.* Basel: S. Karger, 1965.

Spotnitz, H., & Gabriel, B. Resistance in analytic group therapy: A study of the group therapeutic process in children and mothers. *Quarterly Journal of Child Behavior,* 1950, *2,* 71–85.

Stein, A. Group interaction and group psychotherapy in a general hospital. *Mount Sinai Journal of Medicine,* 1971, *38,* 89–100. (a)

Stein, A. Group therapy with psychosomatically ill patients. In H. I. Kaplan and B. J. Sadock (Eds.), *Comprehensive group psychotherapy.* Baltimore: Williams & Wilkins, 1971.

Stein, A., & Friedman, E. Group therapy with alcoholics. In H. I. Kaplan & B. J. Sadock, *Comprehensive group psychotherapy.* Baltimore: Williams & Wilkins, 1971.

Stein, A., Steinhardt, R. W., & Cutler, S. I. Group psychotherapy in patients with peptic ulcer. *Bulletin of New York Academy of Medicine,* 1955, *31,* 583–588.

Stemer, C. The stroke economy. *Transactional Analysis Journal,* 1971, *1,* 9–15.

Sternlieb, S. F. The development of group psychotherapy for psychosomatic manifestations in various existing settings. *South Dakota Journal of Medicine and Pharmacology,* 1963, *16,* 32–35.

Stinson, M. Group communication for the deaf. *Journal of Rehabilitation,* 1971, *37,* 42–44.

Stinson, M. Group communication for the deaf. *Volta Review,* 1972, *74,* 52–54.

Stock, D. The relation between the sociometric structure of the group and certain personality characteristics. Unpublished doctoral dissertation, University of Chicago, 1952.

Stock, D. A survey of research on T-groups. In L. P. Bradford, J. R. Gibb, & K. D. Benne (Eds.), *T-group theory and laboratory method: Innovation in re-education.* New York: John Wiley, 1964, 395–441.

Stock, D., & Ben-Zeev, S. Changes in work and emotionality during group growth. In D. Stock & H. A. Thelen, *Emotional dynamics and group culture.* New York: New York University Press, 1958.

Stock, D., & Luft, J. *The T-E-T design.* Unpublished manuscript, National Training Laboratories, Washington, D.C., 1960.

Stoller, F. H. The long weekend. *Psychology Today,* 1967, *1,* 28–33.

Stoller, F. H. Accelerated interaction: A time limited approach based on the brief intensive group. *International Journal of Group Psychotherapy,* 1968, *18,* 220–235. (a)

Stoller, F. H. Focussed feedback with video tape extending the group's functions. In G. M. Gazda (Ed.), *Innovations to group psychotherapy.*

Springfield, Ill.: Charles C Thomas, 1968. (b)

Stoller, F. H. Marathon groups: Toward a conceptual model. In L. N. Solomon & B. Berzon, *New perspectives on encounter groups.* San Francisco: Jossey-Bass, 1972.

Stone, A., & Levine, L. Group therapy in sexual maladjustment. *American Journal of Psychiatry,* 1950, *107,* 195–202.

Stormer, G. E., & Kirby, J. H. Adlerian group counseling in the elementary school: Report of a program. *Journal of Individual Psychology,* 1969, *25*(1), 155–163.

Stotsky, B., & Zolih, E. Group psychotherapy with psychotics, 1921–1963: A review. *International Journal of Group Psychotherapy,* 1965, *15,* 321–344.

Stoute, A. Implementation of group interpersonal relationships through psychotherapy. *Journal of Psychology,* 1950, *30,* 145–156.

Straight, B., & Werkman, S. L. Control problems in group therapy with aggressive adolescent boys in a mental hospital. *American Journal of Psychiatry,* 1958, *114,* 998–1006.

Strauss, A. B., Burrucker, J. D., Cicero, J. A., & Edwards, R. C. Group work with stroke patients. *Rehabilitation Record,* November–December 1967, pp. 30–32.

Strunk, C., & Witkin, L. J. The transformation of a latency age girls' group from unstructured play to problem focused discussion. *International Journal of Group Psychotherapy,* 1974, *24,* 460–470.

Stubblebine, J. M., & Roadruck, R. D. Treatment program for mentally deficient adolescents. *American Journal of Mental Deficiency,* 1956, *60,* 552–558.

Sugar, M. Premature withdrawal from group therapy: Parents of intellectually retarded girls. *Group Process,* 1971, *42,* 29–32.

Suinn, R. M. The desensitization of test anxiety by group and individual treatment. *Behavior Research and Therapy,* 1968, *6,* 385–387.

Sutherland, J. D. Notes on psychoanalytic group therapy: Therapy and training. *Psychiatry,* 1952, *15,* 111–117.

Symonds, P. M. Role playing as a diagnostic procedure in the selection of leaders. *Sociatry,* 1947, *1,* 43–50.

Szelenberger, W. Music therapy in the psychiatric ward. *Psychiatria Poiska,* 1971, *5,* 69–72.

Taboroff, L. H., Brown, W. H., Dorner, I. N., Reiser, D. E., Talmadge, M., Goates, B. L., & Stein, E. A note on intake diagnosis in groups. *International Journal of Group Psychotherapy,* 1956, *6,* 193–196.

Taft, R. E. Peak experiences and ego permissiveness. *Acta Psychologica,* 1969, *29,* 35–64.

Tamerin, J. S. The psychodynamics of quitting smoking in a group. *American Journal of Psychiatry,* 1972, *129,* 101–107.

Tannenbaum, R., & Davis, S. A. Values, man and organizations. In W. R. Eddy et al. (Eds.), *Behavioral science and the manager's role.* Washington, D.C.: National Training Laboratories, Institute for Applied Behavioral Science, 1969, 3–24.

Tannenbaum, R., Weschler, I. R., & Massarik, F. *Leadership and organization: A behavioral science approach,* New York: McGraw-Hill, 1961.

Taylar, E., Stickland, C. A., & Lindsay, C. S. Social clubs in the treatment of defectives. In J. Bierer, *Therapeutic social clubs.* London: Lewis, 1948.

Taylor, F. C. Effects of laboratory training upon persons and their work groups. In S. S. Zalkind (Ed.), *Research on the impact of using different laboratory methods for interpersonal and organizational change.* Washington, D.C.: American Psychological Association, 1967.

Taylor, F. K. The therapeutic factors of group analytic treatment. *Journal of Mental Science,* 1950, *96,* 976–997.

Taylor, K. F. Some doubts about sensitivity training. *Australian Psychologist,* 1967, *1,* 171–179.

Teahan, J. E. Effect of group psychotherapy on academic low achievers. *International Journal of Group Psychotherapy,* 1966, *16,* 78–85.

Teirich, H. R. Group psychotherapy in Austria. *Group Psychotherapy,* 1951, *4,* 107–111. (a)

Teirich, H. R. [What is group psychotherapy?] *Psychotherapy and Medical Psychology,* 1951, *1,* 26–30. (b)

Teirich, H. R. The use of video methods in group psychotherapy. *Group Psychotherapy,* 1955, *8,* 47–48.

Terrell, D., McWilliams, S., & Cowen, E. Description and evaluation of group work training for non-professional aides in a school mental health program. *Psychology in the Schools,* 1972, *9,* 70–75.

Thoma, E. Group psychotherapy with underachieving girls in a public high school. *Journal of Individual Psychology,* 1964, *20,* 96–100.

Thomas, G. W. Group psychotherapy: A review of the literature. *Psychosomatic Medicine,* 1943, *15,* 166.

Thoreson, G. E. Relevance and research in counseling. *Review of Educational Research: Guidance and Counseling,* 1969, *39,* 263–281.

Thorpe, J. J., & Smith, B. Operational sequences in group therapy with young offenders. *International Journal of Group Psychotherapy,* 1952, *2,* 24–33.

Thorpe, J. J., & Smith, B. Phases in group development in the treatment of drug addiction. *International Journal of Group Psychotherapy,* 1953, *3,* 66–78.

Tillich, S. R. Personal communication, 1976.

Toeman, Z. Audience reactions to therapeutic films. *Sociometry,* 1945, *8,* 493–497.

Toffler, A. *Future shock.* New York: Random House, 1970.

Tosi, D. J., Swanson, C., & McLean, P. Group counseling with nonverbalizing elementary school children. *Elementary School Guidance and Counseling,* 1970, *4,* 260–266.

Truax, C. B. *Counseling and psychotherapy: Process and outcome* (VRA research and demonstration grant No. 806–P). Fayetteville: University of Arkansas, 1966. (a)

Truax, C. B. Therapist empathy, warmth, and genuineness and patient personality change in group psychotherapy. *Journal of Clinical Psychology,* 1966, *22,* 225–228. (b)

Truax, C. B. *Antecedents to outcome in group counseling with institutionalized juvenile delinquents: Effects of therapeutic conditions* (Vol. 2, No. 14). Discussion paper, Arkansas Rehabilitation Research and Training Center No. 264, University of Arkansas, 1968.

Truax, C. B. Degree of negative transference occurring in group psychotherapy and client outcome in juvenile delinquents. *Journal of Clinical Psychology,* 1971, *27,* 132–136.

Truax, C. B., & Carkhuff, R. R. *Toward effective counseling and psychotherapy: Training and practice.* Chicago: Aldine, 1967.

Truax, C. B., Carkhuff, R. R., Wargo, D. G., & Kodman, F., Jr. Changes in self-concepts during group psychotherapy as a function of alternate sessions and vicarious therapy pretraining institutionalized mental patients and juvenile delinquents. *Journal of Consulting Psychology,* 1966, *30,* 309–314.

True, J. E. Education and work performance of associate degree mental health workers as related to group therapy. *International Journal of Group Psychotherapy,* 1974, *24*(4), 383–392.

Turnbloom, M., & Myers, J. S. A group discussion program with families of aphasic patients. *Journal of Speech and Hearing Disorders,* 1952, *17,* 393–396.

Tyler, E. A., Truumaa, A., & Henshaw, P. Family group intake by a child guidance clinic team. *Archives of General Psychiatry,* 1962, *6,* 214–218.

Underwood, W. J. Evaluation of laboratory method training. *Training Directors Journal,* 1965, *19,* 34–40.

Valentine, L. R. Self-care through group learning. *American Journal of Nursing,* 1970, *70,* 2140–2142.

Valiquet, I. M. *Contribution to the evaluation of a management development program.* Unpublished master's thesis, Massachusetts Institute of Technology, 1964.

Van Emde Boas, C. Group therapy with anorgastic women. *International Journal of Sexology*, 1950, *4*, 1–6.

Van Scoy, H. Activity group therapy: A bridge between play and work. *Child Welfare*, 1972, *51*, 528–534.

Vassiliou, T., & Vassiliou, G. Variations of the group process across cultures. *International Journal of Group Psychotherapy*, 1974, *24*, 55–65.

Verny, T. R. *Inside groups: A practical guide to encounter groups and group therapy*. New York: McGraw-Hill, 1975.

Voth, A. C. Group therapy with hospitalized alcoholics: A twelve-year study. *Quarterly Journal of Studies in Alcohol*, 1963, *24*, 289–303.

Wadeson, H. Conjoint marital art therapy techniques. *Psychiatry*, 1972, *35*, 89–98.

Wagonfeld, S., & Wolawitz, H. M. Obesity and the self-help group: A look at TOPS. *American Journal of Psychiatry*, 1968, *125*, 249–252.

Walker, J. R., & Hamilton, L. S. A Chicago black/white encounter. *Personnel and Guidance Journal*, 1973, *51*, 471-477.

Ward, J. L. Homosexual behavior of the institutionalized delinquent. *Psychiatric Quarterly Supplements*, 1958, *32*, 301–314.

Warner, G. D. A special group approach in the psychiatric hospital. *Group Psychotherapy and Psychodrama*, 1971, *24*, 131–134.

Watson, K. W., & Boverman, H. Preadolescent foster children in group discussions. *Children*, 1968, *15*, 65.

Watzlawick, P., Bearin, J. H., & Jackson, D. D. *Pragmatics of human communication*. New York: Norton, 1967.

Webster, T. G., & Harris, H. I. Modified group psychodynamics for college freshmen. *Group Psychotherapy*, 1958, *11*, 283–298.

Weeks, H. A. Preliminary evaluation of the Highfields project. *American Sociological Review*, 1953, *18*, 280–287.

Weiner, H. B. An overview of the use of psychodrama and group psychotherapy in the treatment of alcoholism in the United States and abroad. *Group Psychotherapy*, 1966, *19*, 159–166.

Weingold, J. T., & Hormuth, R. P. Group guidance of parents of the mentally retarded. *Journal of Clinical Psychology*, 1953, *9*, 118–124.

Weisberg, R. S. Intensive group therapy with college age students as suicide prevention: Groups. *Journal of Group and Dynamic Psychotherapy*, 1973, *5*, 57–61.

Weitz, P., & Boganz, C. N. Application of group psychotherapy principles to hospital administration. *International Journal of Group Psychotherapy*, 1952, *2*, 245–249.

Wender, L. The dynamics of group psychotherapy and its application. *Journal of Nervous and Mental Diseases*, 1936, *84*, 54–60.

Wender, L. Group psychotherapy: A study of its application. *Psychiatric Quarterly*, 1940, *14*, 708–718.

Wender, L. Group psychotherapy. *Sociometry*, 1945, *8*, 346–349.

Wender, L. Group psychotherapy within the psychiatric hospital. In B. Glueck (Ed.), *Current therapies of personality disorders*. New York: Grune & Stratton, 1946, 46–58.

Wender, L. Current trends in group psychotherapy. *American Journal of Psychotherapy*, 1951, *5*, 381–404. (a)

Wender, L. Reflections on group psychotherapy. *Quarterly Review of Psychiatric Neurology*, 1951, *6*, 246–248. (b)

Wender, L. Selection of patients for group psychotherapy. *International Journal of Group Psychotherapy*, 1951, *1*, 55–58. (c)

Wender, L., & Stein, A. Group psychotherapy as an aid to outpatient treatment in a psychiatric hospital. *Psychiatric Quarterly*, 1949, *23*, 415–424.

Wender, L., & Stein, A. The utilization of group psychotherapy in teaching psychotherapy. *International Journal of Group Psychotherapy*, 1953, *3*, 326–329.

Wendland, L. V. A therapeutic group with husbands and wives of poliomyelitis patients. *Group Psychotherapy*, 1955, *8*, 25–32.

Weppner, R. S. Some characteristics of an ex-addict self-help therapeutic community and its members. *British Journal of Addiction*, 1973, *68*, 243–250.

Weschler, I. R., Massarik, F., & Tannenbaum, R. The self in process: A sensitivity training emphasis. In I. R. Weschler (Ed.), *Issues in human relations training* (National Training Laboratories Selected Reading Series, Vol. 5). Washington, D.C.: National Training Laboratories and National Education Association, 1962.

Westbrook, F. D. A comparison of three methods of group vocational counseling. *Journal of Counseling Psychology*, 1974, *21*, 502–506.

Whalen, C. K., & Henker, B. A. Pyramid therapy in a hospital for the retarded: Methods, program evaluation, and long-term effects. *American Journal of Mental Deficiency*, 1971, *75*, 414–434.

Whalen, T. Wives of alcoholics. *Quarterly Journal of Studies of Alcohol*, 1953, *14*, 632–641.

Whitaker, C. A. Teaching the practicing physician to do psychotherapy. *Southern Medical Journal*, 1949, *42*, 899–904.

Whitaker, C. A. An experiment in the use of a limited objective in psychiatric teaching. Paper presented at the meeting of the American Psychiatric Association, 1953.

Whitaker, C. A., & Malone, T. *The roots of psychotherapy.* New York: Blakiston, 1953.

Whitaker, C. A., Warkentin, J., & Johnson, N. A philosophical basis for brief psychotherapy. *Psychiatric Quarterly*, 1949, *23*, 439–443.

Whitaker, D. S., & Lieberman, M. A. *Psychotherapy through the group process.* New York: Atherton, 1964.

Whitman, T. L. Aversive control of smoking behavior in a group context. *Behavior Research and Therapy*, 1972, *12*, 97–103.

Wholen, T. Wives of alcoholics. *Quarterly Journal of Studies in Alcohol*, 1953, *14*, 632–641.

Wiedorn, W. S., Jr. Modified group therapy in training psychiatric aides. *Psychiatric Quarterly Supplements*, 1957, *31*, 42–49.

Wiesenhutter, E. [Gestalt and group therapy in young subjects.] *Praxis Psychotherapie*, 1961, *6*, 155–160.

Wilcox, G. T., & Guthrie, G. M. Changes in adjustment of institutionalized female defectives following group psychotherapy. *Journal of Clinical Psychology*, 1957, *13*, 9–13.

Williams, J. R. Physical, mental, and social rehabilitation for elderly and infirm patients. *Hospital Community Psychiatry*, 1976, *21*, 130–132.

Williams, M., McGhee, T. F., Kittleson, S., & Halperin, L. An evaluation of intensive group living programs with schizophrenic patients. *Psychological Monographs*, 1962, *76* (24, Whole No. 543).

Williams, R. L. A social systems model applied to a rehabilitation program for institutionalized patients. *Journal of Rehabilitation*, 1976, *36*(4), 20–23.

Williams, W. C., Jr. The efficacy of group counseling on the academic performance of black college freshmen with low predicted grade point averages. *Dissertation Abstracts International*, 1972, 4974A.

Wilson, A. L. Group therapy for parents of handicapped children. *Rehabilitation Literature*, 1971, *32*, 332–335.

Wilson, B. J. The creative persons group. In H. M. Ruitenbeek (Ed.), *Group therapy today.* New York: Atherton, 1971.

Wilson, C. J., Muzekari, L. H., Schneps, S. A., & Wilson, D. M. Time-limited group counseling for chronic home hemodialysis patients. *Journal of Counseling Psychology*, 1974, *21*, 376–379.

Wineman, D. Group therapy and casework with ego disturbed children. *Journal of Social Casework*, 1949, *30*, 110–113.

Wittkower, E. D. Treatment of psychosomatic disorders. *Canadian Medical Association Journal*, 1964, *90*, 1055–1060.

Wolf, A. The psychoanalysis of groups: I. *American Journal of Psychotherapy*, 1949, *3*, 213–232.

Wolf, A. Short-term group psychotherapy. In L. R. Wolberg (Ed.), *Short-term psychotherapy*. New York: Grune & Stratton, 1965.

Wolf, A. Group psychotherapy. In A. M. Freedman & H. I. Kaplan (Eds.), *Comprehensive textbook of psychiatry*. Baltimore: Williams & Wilkins, 1967.

Wolf, A., Locke, N., Rosenbaum, M., Hillpern, E., Goldfarb, W., Kadis, A., Obers, S. J., Milberg, I. L., & Abell, R. G. The psychoanalysis of groups: The analysis objections. *International Journal of Group Psychotherapy*, 1952, *2*, 221–231.

Wolf, A., & Schwartz, E. K. *Psychoanalysis in groups*. New York: Grune & Stratton, 1962.

Wolf, A., & Schwartz, E. K. Psychoanalysis in groups: A creative process. *American Journal of Psychoanalysis*, 1964, *24*, 46–64.

Wolf, A., Schwartz, E. K., McCarthy, G. J., & Goldberg, I. A. *Beyond the couch*. New York: Science House, 1970.

Wolff, K. Group psychotherapy with geriatric patients in a VA hospital. *Group Psychotherapy*, 1961, *14*, 85–89.

Wolff, K. Group psychotherapy for the geriatric patients in a psychiatric hospital: Six-year study. *Journal of the American Geriatric Society*, 1962, *10*, 1077–1086.

Wolff, K. Group therapy for alcoholics. *Mental Hygiene*, 1967, *51*, 549–551.

Wolk, R. L., & Goldfarb, A. I. The response to group psychotherapy of aged recent admissions compared with long-term mental hospital patients. *American Journal of Psychiatry*, 1967, *123*, 10–19.

Wolk, R. L., & Reid, F. A study of group psychotherapy results with youthful offenders in detention. *Group Psychotherapy*, 1964, *17*, 56–60.

Wollersheim, J. P. Effectiveness of group therapy based upon learning principles in the treatment of overweight women. *Journal of Abnormal Psychology*, 1970, *70*, 162.

Wolpe, J. *Psychotherapy by reciprocal inhibition*. Stanford: Stanford University Press, 1958.

Wolpe, J. *The practice of behavior therapy*. New York: Pergamon Press, 1969.

Wolpe, J., & Lazarus, A. A. *Behavior therapy techniques*. New York: Pergamon Press, 1966.

Worcester, E., McComb, S., & Coriat, I. H. *Religion and medicine*. New York: Moffat, 1908.

Worthen, V. K., and Maloney, H. N. *A comparative study of positive and negative oriented marathon group experiences for couples*. Unpublished paper, Fuller Graduate School of Psychology, Pasadena, Calif., 1972.

Wright, K. W. Group therapy in extramural clinics. *Psychiatric Quarterly*, 1946, *20*, 322–331.

Yablonsky, L. Preparing parolees for essential social roles. *Group Psychotherapy*, 1955, *8*, 38–39.

Yalom, I. D. *Theory and practice of group psychotherapy*. New York: Basic Books, 1970.

Yalom, I. D. *Theory and practice of group psychotherapy* (2nd ed.). New York: Basic Books, 1975.

Yalom, I. D., Hounts, P. S., Newell, G., & Rand, K. H. Preparation of patients for group therapy. *Archives of General Psychiatry*, 1967, *17*, 416–427.

Yalom, I. D., Houts, P. S., Zimberg, S. M., & Rand, K. H. Prediction of improvement in group therapy: An exploratory study. *Archives of General Psychiatry*, 1967, *17*, 159–168.

Yalom, I. D., & Lieberman, M. A. A study of encounter group casualties. *Archives of General Psychiatry*, 1971, *25*, 16–30.

Yalom, I. D., & Rand, K. Compatibilities and cohesiveness in therapy groups. *Archives of General Psychiatry*, 1966, *13*, 267–276.

Yokotsuji, R. Group notes. Unpublished manuscript, University of Hawaii, 1972.

Yong, J. Advantages of group therapy in relation to individual therapy for juvenile delinquents. *Corrective Psy-*

chiatry and Journal of Social Therapy, 1971, 2, 34–40.

Yonge, K. A., & O'Connor, N. Measurable effects of group psychotherapy with defective delinquents. Journal of Mental Science, 1954, 100, 944–952.

Youmans, R. D. Group counseling in jail. American Journal of Corrections, 1968, 30(31), 35–37.

Zakus, G., & Solomon, M. The family situations of obese adolescent girls. Adolescence, 1973, 8, 33–42.

Ziferstein, I. Group psychotherapy in the Soviet Union. The American Journal of Psychiatry, 1972, 129, 107–111.

Zifstein, L., & Rosen, M. Personal adjustment training: A group counseling program for institutionalized mentally retarded persons. Mental Retardation, 1973, 11, 16–20.

Zimpfer, D. G. Some conceptualizations: Some conceptual and research problems in group counseling. School Counselor, 1968, 15, 326–333.

Zweben, J. E., & Hamman, K. Prescribed games: A theoretical perspective on the use of group techniques. Psychotherapy: Theory, Research and Practice, 1970, 7(1), 22–27.

Zytowski, D. G. Diagnostic psychodrama with a college freshman. Group Psychotherapy, 1964, 17, 123–128.

Index

Abrahams, J., 5, 24, 28
Ackerman, N. W., 4, 24, 251, 268
Acting out, 46, 100
Activity group, 267
Adjuncts to group, 47, 49, 50, 52, 55, 156–157
Adjustment to illness, 236–237
Adler, 15, 21-27; Adlerian therapy, 60–61, 67
Adolescents, 233, 245, 255, 268–270
Advantages of groups, 3, 46–47, 48–49, 50, 52, 54, 56, 247–248, 283–285
Advertising groups, 69–72, 145–146
Aged, 236–237, 273
Alcoholics Anonymous, 6, 14, 242, 243
Alcoholism and alcohol addiction, 242–243; and families, 243
Allergies, 238, 239
Aloha, 112–113
Altruism, 4, 120, 121, 258–259
Altshuler, I. M., 24, 256–257, 286
Ambiguity, 80–81, 132
American Psychiatric Association, 142
American Psychological Association, 142–143
Anxiety, 50, 80, 119–120, 132; existential, 50; neurotic, 50
Anxiety hierarchy, 50
Aphasic pts, 236
Argyris, C., 24, 290, 294
Arousal, 80–81, 99–100
Art therapy techniques, 207–212
Assertiveness, 120
Asthma, 239
Autonomous therapy, 6
Awareness continuum, 47
Axline, V., 267

Bach, G. R., 24, 36, 305
Back, K., 24–25, 34, 36
Bales, R. F., 25
Baruch, D. and Miller, H., 25
Becoming, 51
Behavioral rehearsal, 228

Behavior therapy, 6, 44, 49–50, 58–59, 245
Being in the world, 51
Benne, K., 25, 30, 31, 36
Bennis, W., 295, 297
Berne, E., 36, 52
Berzon, B., 36
Bethel, Maine, 31
Bierer, J., 25, 234, 258
Bion, W. R., 25, 55
Blind, 236
Blind walk, 195, 199–201
Bradford, L., 25
BST group, 31–32
Buber, 19
Burrow, T., 23, 248

Card games, 214–215
Carkhuff, R., 133–134
Cardiac, 235, 236
Casualties, 121, 291–292
Catalyst, 120, 122, 125–127
Caveat Emptor, 144
Cerebral palsy, 236
Child-Parent relations, 265–266
Children, 233, 255, 266–268
Client centered therapy, 43, 52, 62–63
Closed group, 68
Cohesiveness, 108
Co-leaders, 150, 157–162; see Co-therapy
College, 270
Competitiveness, 153, 161
Confidentiality, 81, 142, 143, 147
Consciousness raising, 273
Consent, 142
Content, 67, 86, 162–164
Contract, 54
Conversion reactions, 238
Corrections, 233, 245–255
Corsini, 5, 13, 25, 76, 115, 143, 226, 249–250, 252, 256
Costs, 146
Co-therapy, 157–162

Co-therapy dangers, 161–162
Counter transference, 46
Couples, 264
Courage, 135
Credentials (leaders), 115, 145
Criminals, 246
Culturally disadvantaged, 273
Cystic fibrosis, 236

Dating anxiety, 270
Daytop village, 244, 269
Deaf, 236, 237
Dederich, C., 36, 244
Definition, 4–5, 7–9
Delinquents, 248, 268–269
Depth exercises, 215–223
De Sade, 17
Desensitization, 101
Diabetics, 235, 236
Diagnosis, 233, 235
Diagnostic techniques, 189, 199, 206–215
Diamond, M. J., 36, 38, 39, 68, 120, 221, 288, 295, 299–301, 303–305
Doubling, 228–229
Dreikurs, 15, 25–26, 67, 137, 158, 277
Drug abuse, 233, 243–245, 267–268, 269
Dunnette, M., 36, 288; Campbell and, 36, 288, 295
Dusay, J., 36, 52
Dynamic group therapy, 55–56

Eclectic therapy, 44, 56–57, 62–63
Economy function of group, 3, 9
Ego states, 53
Ellis, A., 37, 262
Empathy, 130, 134, 136, 151
Enabling solutions, 56
Encounter vs. therapy: see Therapy vs. encounter
Epilepsy, 236
Esalen Institute, 16, 35, 38
Ethics, 139–149
Evaluation, 275–306
Existential therapy, 44, 50–52, 58–59
Expectancies, 82–83, 98
Experimental paradigms, 296–301
Expedient model of research, 299–301
Extinction, 49

Fairweather, G. W., 26, 291
Family, 263–266
Feedback, 98
Feelings, 81, 82, 90–92, 95

Fiebert, M., 37, 67, 126
Figure-ground, 47
Financial matters, 142
Flexibility, 135–136
Focal conflict, 55, 56, 60–61; therapy, 55–56
Focusing, 101, 216–218
Follow up, 112, 147, 289
Foulds, M., 291, 301
Foulkes, S. H., 26, 248, 276
Frank, J. D., 16, 26, 37, 55; and Powdermaker, F., 26, 138
Free association, 45
Freud, S., 17–18, 137, 138

Games and scripts, 53–54
Genuineness, 134
Gestalt therapy, 6, 44, 47–49, 57–59
Gibb, J., 25, 37, 226, 288
Ginnott, H., 267
Goal of therapy, 12, 147
Golden rule of structured exercises, 193
Good and welfare, 111
Gordon, T., 26
Greek chorus, 48
Grotjahn, M., 37, 116, 135, 158
Ground rules, 79–82
Group as reflective of natural environment, 234
Group process, 89, 94–95
Group solution, 55
Guided fantasy, 101, 218–220
Guided group interaction, 252
Gunther, B., 35, 37
Gurus, 116, 121, 144–145

Hadden, S. B., 26, 37, 116, 158, 253, 262
Haley, J., 37, 87, 165–166, 264
Harrison, R., 26, 293, 294
Hawthorne effect, 40
Help rejecting complainer, 92–95
Hemodialysis, 236
Here and now, 48, 81, 84, 89–90, 92, 95
Heroin, 244
Hobbs, N., 26
Homosexuality, 145, 262–263
Honesty, 135
Hora, T., 26, 50
Hot seat, 295–296
Hulse, W., 4, 15, 26–27, 158
Hypertension, 235
Hypnosis, 141, 220–221, 304

Hypochondriasis, 240–241
Hysterics, 241

Imitation, 98, 151
Inclusion, 102–105
Independent variable, 288
Individuation, 51
Information disseminator, 120, 122, 124–126
Integrity, 135
Institutionalized applications, 233, 245–260, 290–291
Intelligence, 136
Interpersonal, 117–119, 120–122, 295–296
Interpretation, 46
Intrapsychic (intrapersonal), 117–119, 120–122, 295–296
Introductions, 81–83
Introductory exercises, 196–198
I-Thou, 14, 51
I've got a secret, 201–203

Jails, 254
Jargon, 77, 148–149
Jones, J. E., 27

Kaplan, H. I., 37, 149, 234; and Sadock, B., 37, 149
Klapman, J. W., 15, 27
Kline, N. S., 27, 138

Laboratory groups, 14
Lakin, M., 27, 37, 116, 143–144, 289, 295
Large group method, 6
Lazarus, A. A., 27, 37, 241
Lazell, 21, 256, 277
Leader as participant, 120, 122, 125, 129–132, 151–152
Leaders closing, 111–112
Leaders personality, 133–138
Leadership, 46, 48, 50, 51–52, 54, 56, 114–138
Leadership challenge, 88–89, 250
Leadership focus, 117–119
Leadership orientation, 117–119, 120–124
Leadership roles, 99, 120–133
Levin, K., 27, 30–31, 55
Lieberman, M. A., 37, 38, 55, 116, 190, 286
Locus of control, 305
Luchins, A., 28

Male sexual dysfunction, 261–262
Managers, 271–272
Marathon, 12, 265
Marriage, 233, 264–265
Marsh, L. C., 21, 256
Maslow, A., 35
May, R., 35
McCorkle, L., 24, 28
Measurement problems of outcome, 289, 293–294
Medical students, 272
Members rights, 148
Mental defectives, 255–256
Mental health, 41
Mental health professionals, 272
Mesmer, 15, 16–17
Methadone, 244
Methodology, 288–289
Miles, M., 25, 37, 190, 286, 294
Milieu therapy, 6, 21
Minorities, 273
Model, 120, 122, 125, 129–132, 160
Model training program, 153–157
Moreno, J. L., 5, 15, 22–23, 28, 137, 259, 264
Multiple sclerosis, 236
Mutual support/self therapy, 159–160
Myocardial infarction, 236

Negative outcomes, 291–292
Neuroses, neurotic patients, 233, 241–242
Non-verbal communication, 127, 162, 163, 164–165, 259
Non-verbal sensuous lunch, 203–205
NTL, 24, 25, 30–32, 143, 153–154, 271, 296, 297
Nudity, 221–223
Nurses, 271, 272

Observation, 151
Orchestrator, 120, 122, 125, 127–129
Orgasmic dysfunction, 261
Orthopedic patients, 236
Outcome research, 289–296
Overt behavior, 49
Overweight/obesity, 239–240

Pair psychotherapy, 6
Papanek, H., 38, 264
Paraprofessionals, 272
Parents, 266
Parole, 253–254
Patience, 135
Peer help groups, 269

Perls, F., 28, 35, 38, 47, 48, 117, 138
Personal experience, 276, 283–285
Personnel, 152–153
Pfeiffer, W. J.; and Jones, J. E., 38, 191, 193
Phobic reactions, 241
Play therapy, 267
Politics and group training, 152
Population, 11–12
Pratt, 15, 19–21, 133, 137, 235, 240–241, 286
Predelinquents, 254–255
Pregnancy, 236, 263, 269
Preparatory phase, 68, 69–79
Primal regression, 220
Prisons, 246, 252–253
Privileged communication, 143
Problem solving, 106
Process, 67
Professional training, 142
Professionalism, 142
Projection, 48
Psychiatric residents, 272
Psychoanalysis, 43, 45–47, 57, 58–59
Psychodrama, 101, 244, 252
Psychosomatic disorders, 236, 238–241
Psychotics, 256–260, 267
Publicity, 69–72

Rational emotive, 44, 60–61
Reciprocal inhibition, 49–50
Reddy, W. B., 38, 301
Redl, F., 28, 234
Reformatories, 251–252
Regression fantasies, 141
Reincarnation techniques, 219–220
Reinforcement, 49, 132
Reinforcer, 120, 122, 125, 132–133
Relatives, 237–238, 266
Reports, 276, 279–283
Research, 276, 287–296
Resistance, 46
Restrictive solutions, 56
Rogers, C. R., 6, 28, 35, 38, 50, 52, 117, 137, 138, 277
Role playing, 101, 225–229
Role reversals, 101, 227–228
Rosenbaum, M., 38, 76, 157–158, 159, 160
Ruitenbeek, 15, 22, 23, 274

Safety precautions, 145–149
Scheidlinger, S., 38
Schilder, P., 27, 28, 276
Schizophrenics, 238, 257–260, 290

Schools, 233
Schutz, W., 35, 38, 67, 140, 191
Schwartz, E. K., 30, 38
Screening, 74–79, 144, 146, 235, 259, 299
Secrecy, 147
Self actualization, 40, 41, 291
Self as subject, 51
Self disclosure, 131–132
Self knowledge, 136–137
Sensory awareness, 101
Sex, 233, 260–263
Sex offenders, 260
Sexual problems, 261–263
Shapiro, J. L., 4, 13, 38–39, 120, 158, 221, 226, 251, 253, 288, 295, 298, 301, 302–305
Silence, 83–85, 86–87
Size, 146
Slavson, S. R., 5, 29, 134–135, 266–267, 274
Smoking, 245, 250
Somatic conditions, 235–238
Spotnitz, H., 29, 115, 137
Stabilization, 53
Statistics, 276, 286–287
Statuing, 212–214
Steiner, E., 39, 52
Stock, D. S., 29, 288, 297
Stoller, F., 39, 305
Stroke patients, 236
Structural analysis, 53
Subjective experience, 51
Suicidal, 273
Supervised practice, 150
Synanon, 7, 244, 269
Systematic desensitization, 49–50, 221, 245, 263

Tavistock, 25
Teachers, 272
Techniques, 187–229
Termination, 68, 97, 106–113
Termination exercises, 223–225
Test anxiety, 241–242
Test of appropriateness, 192
Test of consent, 192
Test of theory, 192–193
Test of timeliness, 192
Testimonials, 276–279
T-Group, 289–290, 292, 297
Theory, 41–45, 153, 168–169; de-limiting function, 41, 42; descriptive function, 41, 42–44; generative, 41, 42; integrative, 41, 42

Therapist characteristics, 133–138
Therapy phase, 69, 97–106
Therapy vs. encounter, 11–12
There and then, 84, 85–86, 90
Tillich, Paul, 35
Tillich, R. S., 16, 18
Timing, 101, 136, 189
Tinker toys, 206–207, 208
Training, 7, 140, 142, 149–157, 233, 271–273, 305
Training schools, 249–251
Transactional analysis, 6, 52–55, 60–61
Transexuals, 263
Transfer of training, 106–107, 108–111
Transference, 46
Treatment (techniques), 189, 196–206
Truax, C., 39, 133, 248, 292
Trust, 108
Trust exercises, 198–206
Truth pillow, 205–206
Tuberculosis, 235

Ulcers, 238, 239
Underachievers, 270, 271
Unfinished business, 48, 107–108

Venereal disease, 236
Verny, 190, 191
Videotape/audiotape, 154–155, 303
Vocational problems, 271
Voluntary nature of group techniques, 187, 188

Warmth, 134, 136
Watts, A., 35
Whitaker, C. A., 30, 158
Whitaker, D. S., 29, 55
Wolf, A., 30, 39
Women, 273

Yalom, 4, 5, 37, 39, 67–68, 76, 151, 152, 158–159, 190, 259, 273, 286, 301

THE BOOK MANUFACTURE

Methods of Group Psychotherapy and Encounter: A Tradition of Innovation was text-designed by Herbert Pinzke Design, Inc. The cover was designed by Harvey Retzloff. Typesetting was Weimer Typesetting Company, Inc., Indianapolis. Printing and binding was by The Parthenon Press, Nashville. The typeface is Times Roman with Helvetica display. The cover material is Kevtone C.